A CELEBRATION OF POETS

GREAT LAKES
GRADES 4-6
FALL 2008

creativeCOMMUNICATION
A CELEBRATION OF TODAY'S WRITERS

A Celebration of Poets
Great Lakes
Grades 4-6
Fall 2008

An anthology compiled by Creative Communication, Inc.

Published by:

creativeCOMMUNICATION

A CELEBRATION OF TODAY'S WRITERS

1488 NORTH 200 WEST • LOGAN, UTAH 84341
TEL. 435-713-4411 • WWW.POETICPOWER.COM

Copyright © 2009 by Creative Communication, Inc.
Printed in the United States of America

ISBN: 978-1-60050-235-4

FOREWORD

When Charles Dickens wrote, "It was the best of times, it was the worst of times," he was describing a period of history that occurred over one hundred years ago. Dickens' words could easily describe many periods of history. They seem to be especially applicable today. If you listen to the media, we have much to fear: terrorism, crime, the economy. These are all messages that bombard us through newspapers, radio and television. However, in reading the poems inside this anthology, these student writers reflect a much different world. These poets reflect their world in a fresh voice. This book is not filled with pessimism and fear. Instead, they provide an optimistic hope. The "best of times" is still with us.

We hope you enjoy this book as much as we enjoyed reading each poem. There were thousands of poets who entered our writing contest and were not chosen to be published. I congratulate all the poets who entered. They each took the time to share a bit of themselves with us. This book is dedicated to them and to those that helped inspire and guide their words.

Thomas Worthen, Ph.D.
Editor
Creative Communication

WRITING CONTESTS!

Enter our next POETRY contest!
Enter our next ESSAY contest!

Why should I enter?

Win prizes and get published! Each year thousands of dollars in prizes are awarded in each region and tens of thousands of dollars in prizes are awarded throughout North America. The top writers in each division receive a monetary award and a free book that includes their published poem or essay. Entries of merit are also selected to be published in our anthology.

Who may enter?

There are four divisions in the poetry contest. The poetry divisions are grades K-3, 4-6, 7-9, and 10-12. There are three divisions in the essay contest. The essay divisions are grades 3-6, 7-9, and 10-12.

What is needed to enter the contest?

To enter the poetry contest send in one original poem, 21 lines or less. To enter the essay contest send in one original essay, 250 words or less, on any topic. Each entry must include the student's name, grade, address, city, state, and zip code, and the student's school name and school address. Students who include their teacher's name may help their teacher qualify for a free copy of the anthology. Contest changes and updates are listed at www.poeticpower.com.

How do I enter?

Enter a poem online at:
www.poeticpower.com

or

Mail your poem to:
    Poetry Contest
    1488 North 200 West
    Logan, UT 84341

Enter an essay online at:
www.studentessaycontest.com

or

Mail your essay to:
    Essay Contest
    1488 North 200 West
    Logan, UT 84341

When is the deadline?

Poetry contest deadlines are August 18th, December 3rd, and April 14th. Essay contest deadlines are July 15th, October 15th, and February 17th. You can enter each contest, however, send only one poem or essay for each contest deadline.

Are there benefits for my school?

Yes. We award $15,000 each year in grants to help with Language Arts programs. Schools qualify to apply for a grant by having a large number of entries of which over fifty percent are accepted for publication. This typically tends to be about 15 accepted entries.

Are there benefits for my teacher?

Yes. Teachers with five or more students accepted to be published receive a free anthology that includes their students' writing.

For more information please go to our website at **www.poeticpower.com**, email us at editor@poeticpower.com or call 435-713-4411.

TABLE OF CONTENTS

STATES INCLUDED IN THIS EDITION:

INDIANA
MICHIGAN
OHIO

Fall 2008
Poetic Achievement
Honor Schools

* Teachers who had fifteen or more poets accepted to be published

The following schools are recognized as receiving a "Poetic Achievement Award." This award is given to schools who have a large number of entries of which over fifty percent are accepted for publication. With hundreds of schools entering our contest, only a small percent of these schools are honored with this award. The purpose of this award is to recognize schools with excellent Language Arts programs. This award qualifies these schools to receive a complimentary copy of this anthology. In addition, these schools are eligible to apply for a Creative Communication Language Arts Grant. Grants of two hundred and fifty dollars each are awarded to further develop writing in our schools.

Abbott Middle School
West Bloomfield, MI
Mrs. K. Bertolini*
Julia Music
Ellen Seiss
Erin Wynn*

Allen J. Warren Elementary School
Highland, IN
Ms. Fleming*
Mrs. Natelborg
Sally Pagorek*
Mrs. Paplomatas

Ann Arbor Christian School
Ann Arbor, MI
Janet Comella Jansen*

Assumption BVM School
Belmont, MI
Hazel Bolin
Katie Leeder

Bailly Elementary School
Chesterton, IN
Crystal Callaway*
Cris Petro*

Barrington Elementary School
Upper Arlington, OH
Clay Bogart*

Beck Centennial Elementary School
Macomb, MI
Mr. Kurmas*
Christine Polson*

Becker Elementary School
Cincinnati, OH
Connie Conrad*

Birchwood School
Cleveland, OH
Helene Debelak*
Jennifer Jackson

Boulan Park Middle School
Troy, MI
Fran Blatnik
Cliff Cyplik
April Reem*

Central Grade School
Traverse City, MI
Jaye Lynn Trapp*
Tracy Westerman

Churubusco Elementary School
Churubusco, IN
Julie Mast*

Cloverdale Middle School
Cloverdale, IN
Judith Allee
Cathy Ames

Corpus Christi Catholic School
Holland, MI
Megan Willems Koster*

Crown Point Christian School
Saint John, IN
Mrs. Broersma*
Mrs. Corder
Larry Koontz

DeKalb Middle School
Waterloo, IN
Kristin Chamberlin*
Ms. Hamman

Detroit Country Day Middle School
Beverly Hills, MI
Julie Bianchi
Carla Chennault
Cheryl Duggan
Charles Duggan
Michael Mencotti
Carol M. Tabaka
Stephanie Trautman

Dobbins Elementary School
Poland, OH
Elaine Morlan*

EH Greene Intermediate School
Cincinnati, OH
Mrs. Anastasi*
Leslie Burklow
Tracy Coleman
Patty Durbin*
Michelle LaCalameto

Eisenhower Middle School
Oregon, OH
Carolyn Hemsoth*

Emmanuel-St Michael Lutheran School
Fort Wayne, IN
Connie Hoyer*

Eugene M Nikkari Elementary School
Saint Louis, MI
Reneé Fabiano*

Floyd Ebeling Elementary School
Macomb, MI
Jacquelyn Barker*
Tracy Bettys*
Lisa Bruce*
Rachel D'Angelo*
Mrs. Edwards*
Mrs. Fisher*
Mrs. Jarzyna
Margaret McIntyre*
Mrs. Pipitone
Mrs. Pizzo*
Mrs. Sandison*
Mrs. VanGilder*
Mrs. Vittiglio*
Melisa Wassel*
Christine Zatell*

Frank H Hammond Elementary School
Munster, IN
Carol Schaap*

Frank Ohl Intermediate School
Youngstown, OH
Mrs. Collings*
Donnamarie Polak
Bernadette Porinchak*

Galesburg-Augusta Middle School
Augusta, MI
Katie Fotis*
Mrs. Weise

Gesu Catholic School
University Heights, OH
Maura Dacey
Josephine A. Jones
Monica Matia
Dottie Rule

Harding Middle School
Lakewood, OH
Ruth Pangrace*
Donna Tomlin*

Harmon Middle School
Pickerington, OH
Mrs. Goldsberry
Terri Smolewski*
Jan Wild*

Helfrich Park Middle School
Evansville, IN
Lynn Alford*

Henryville Elementary School
Henryville, IN
Amanda Biesel
Vanessa Goodknight*

Heritage Intermediate School
Middlebury, IN
Stephen Hamilton*

Holy Angels School
Sidney, OH
Jeanne L. Schlagetter*

Holy Family Middle School
Bay City, MI
Laura Sprywa*

John Simatovich Elementary School
Valparaiso, IN
Paul Hirstein*

Kenowa Hills Intermediate School
Grand Rapids, MI
Mary-Lyn Frost*

Keystone Academy
Belleville, MI
Michele Jones
Amanda Magnuson

Legend Elementary School
Newark, OH
Nancy Schaefer*

Licking Valley Intermediate School
Newark, OH
Mrs. E. Fee*

May V Peck Elementary School
Warren, MI
Yvonne Beauchaine*
Cathie Gresko*

Mayfield Elementary School
Middletown, OH
Cheryl Ames*
Dani Ortega*

Melrose Elementary School
Wooster, OH
Marty Boyle*

Midland Academy of Advanced and Creative
Studies
Midland, MI
Mrs. Brant*

Nancy Hanks Elementary School
Ferdinand, IN
Judy Lindauer
Dave Westrich

Normandy Elementary School
Centerville, OH
Jan Taylor*

North Knox East Elementary/Jr High School
Edwardsport, IN
Kathy Stephens*

Northern Heights Elementary School
Columbia City, IN
Sarah Eames
Michelle Simmons*

Northfield Elementary School
Northfield, OH
Wendy Bailey*
Lisa Bass*
Jennifer Beck*
Sharon Berkley*
Lynn Cutright
Jaime Hoon*
Terri Javorsky*
Patricia Kecskemety*
Ms. Ventre

Norwich Elementary School
Hilliard, OH
Marla Getty
Cathie Maple*
Linda Rock*

Pennfield Middle School
Battle Creek, MI
Christine Jordan
Lois Rae Werner*
Kathy Woodside

Perry Central Elementary School
Leopold, IN
Darlene Davis
Carmen Fischer*
Jamie Guillaume
Becky Hubert*
Angela Shelby*
Francie Wagner*

Pike Delta York Middle School
Delta, OH
Jane Foor*

Pinewood Elementary School
Elkhart, IN
Carol Cantzler*
Beckie Clawson*
Mrs. Corson

Red Cedar School
East Lansing, MI
Alyjah Byrd-Goode*

Riley Upper Elementary School
Livonia, MI
Dona Gossett*

Riverside Elementary School
Constantine, MI
Carolyn S. Niblock
Brenda Potts*

Rocky River Middle School
Rocky River, OH
Amanda M. Liskovec*

Roosevelt Elementary School
McDonald, OH
Debbie Crish*
Patty Gault

Rootstown Elementary School
Rootstown, OH
Teresa Sopko*

Sanderson Elementary School
Lancaster, OH
Melinda Kitsmiller*
Cathy Trimmer*

Spaulding Elementary School
Goshen, OH
Lisa Drees*

St Clement Elementary School
St Bernard, OH
Sr. Carol Louise*

St Gerard School
Lansing, MI
Marie Hickey*
Mrs. Zelenka*

St John the Evangelist School
Saint John, IN
Connie Hass*

St John the Baptist Elementary School
Whiting, IN
    Mrs. Bagull
    Mrs. Chiluski
    Karen Nee
    Frank Vargo

St John Vianney Catholic School
Flint, MI
    Elizabeth Petrides*

St Jude Catholic School
Indianapolis, IN
    Suzanne Halloran*

St Maria Goretti School
Westfield, IN
    Emily Miller*

St Michael School
Brookville, IN
    Krista McKinney
    Carey Weiler*

St Patrick School
Ada, MI
    Suzie Gilbertson*
    Barbara Vezino

Stanley Clark School
South Bend, IN
    Mary Dickerson*
    Doris E. Smith*
    Mr. Walsh*

Stonegate Elementary School
Zionsville, IN
    Muff Biber*
    Mrs. Skura

Tippecanoe Middle School
Tipp City, OH
    Andrea McKinney*

Tremont Elementary School
Upper Arlington, OH
    Pauline Endo
    Julie Fryman*
    Patrick Hurley
    Debra Welch

Tri-West Middle School
Lizton, IN
    Patty Jensen*

Trilby Elementary School
Toledo, OH
    Kathy Chaka*
    Jan Ellenberger*

Union Local Middle School
Belmont, OH
    Leslie Stiles*

University Liggett School
Grosse Pointe Woods, MI
    Kelly Boll*
    Walter Butzu
    Mrs. Ray
    Christine Reif

Veale Elementary School
Washington, IN
    Marcia McClure*

Washington Township Elementary School
Valparaiso, IN
    Beverly Zborowski*

West Washington Elementary School
Campbellsburg, IN
    Mrs. Boling
    Mr. Clements
    Mrs. Stewart

Westview Elementary School
Jackson, OH
    Christina Smith*
    Pam Steele*

Woodward Park Middle School
 Columbus, OH
  Carol Weimer-Morris*

Wooster Christian School
 Wooster, OH
  Karen Masowich*

Language Arts
Grant Recipients
2008-2009

After receiving a "Poetic Achievement Award" schools are encouraged to apply for a Creative Communication Language Arts Grant. The following is a list of schools who received a two hundred and fifty dollar grant for the 2008-2009 school year.

Acushnet Elementary School, Acushnet, MA
Benton Central Jr/Sr High School, Oxford, IN
Bridgeway Christian Academy, Alpharetta, GA
Central Middle School, Grafton, ND
Challenger Middle School, Cape Coral, FL
City Hill Middle School, Naugatuck, CT
Clintonville High School, Clintonville, WI
Coral Springs Middle School, Coral Springs, FL
Covenant Classical School, Concord, NC
Coyote Valley Elementary School, Middletown, CA
Diamond Ranch Academy, Hurricane, UT
E O Young Jr Elementary School, Middleburg, NC
El Monte Elementary School, Concord, CA
Emmanuel-St Michael Lutheran School, Fort Wayne, IN
Ethel M Burke Elementary School, Bellmawr, NJ
Fort Recovery Middle School, Fort Recovery, OH
Gardnertown Fundamental Magnet School, Newburgh, NY
Hancock County High School, Sneedville, TN
Haubstadt Community School, Haubstadt, IN
Headwaters Academy, Bozeman, MT
Holden Elementary School, Chicago, IL
Holliday Middle School, Holliday, TX
Holy Cross High School, Delran, NJ
Homestead Elementary School, Centennial, CO
Joseph M Simas Elementary School, Hanford, CA
Labrae Middle School, Leavittsburg, OH
Lakewood High School, Lakewood, CO
Lee A Tolbert Community Academy, Kansas City, MO
Mary Lynch Elementary School, Kimball, NE
Merritt Secondary School, Merritt, BC
North Star Academy, Redwood City, CA

Language Arts Grant Winners cont.

Old Redford Academy, Detroit, MI
Prairie Lakes School, Willmar, MN
Public School 124Q, South Ozone Park, NY
Rutledge Hall Elementary School, Lincolnwood, IL
Shelley Sr High School, Shelley, ID
Sonoran Science Academy, Tucson, AZ
Spruce Ridge School, Estevan, SK
St Columbkille School, Dubuque, IA
St Francis Middle School, Saint Francis, MN
St Luke the Evangelist School, Glenside, PA
St Matthias/Transfiguration School, Chicago, IL
St Robert Bellarmine School, Chicago, IL
St Sebastian Elementary School, Pittsburgh, PA
The Hillel Academy, Milwaukee, WI
Thomas Edison Charter School - North, North Logan, UT
Trinity Christian Academy, Oxford, AL
United Hebrew Institute, Kingston, PA
Velasquez Elementary School, Richmond, TX
West Frederick Middle School, Frederick, MD

Grades 4-5-6

Top Poem Grades 4-5-6

Let Freedom Ring

"Let freedom ring"
What does this mean?
It is the sacrifice that others made
So that I may live my dream.

It is more than the words
To a song I sing.
I remember the ones who gave up everything
So that we may live in peace and harmony.

I will not take for granted
This country that I love.
The greatest nation on Earth
Is truly blessed from above.

So join with me on this special day
When we honor our heroes in a thoughtful way.
Let us never forget the joy it brings
To be able to sing
"Let freedom ring!"

Claire Barrington, Grade 6
Monroe Elementary School, OH

Top Poem Grades 4-5-6

Being a Child

Us kids feel like we can't do a thing,
We think that adults are like our king,
They tell us what to do,
From what door to open to how to tie our shoe,
The things we are capable to create,
From date to date,
Amaze all our families and friends,
As each day ends,
We tell them a story,
While they think of the glory,
They will have that day,
And that is not all I have to say,
About every one of us,
We are very bright plus,
We make many people happy,
And we are always snappy,
Those are just a few things an adult can't do,
They cannot tell the best stories, I know it is true,
In this world that is so mild,
So that means the best thing to be is a child.

Alison John, Grade 6
Birmingham Covington School, MI

Top Poem Grades 4-5-6

A Perfect World

Having a perfect wonderful world,
With all nations under one flag unfurled,
Would be such a glorious, wonderful sight,
Reaching all goals with strength and might,
No sad times, no hard times, no grief, no strife,
Living a wonderful tremendous life.
So let's come together in one large nation.
Let's be a family in one great location.
It's called the wonderful amazing great Earth.
It will be the beginning, the creation, the birth.
So, let's come together to create this dream,
No matter how difficult that it may seem.

McKade Kennedy, Grade 5
Northern Heights Elementary School, IN

Top Poem Grades 4-5-6

The Fourth of July

The night sky flashes with pale light.
Sparks hang in the dark night,
as emerald flowers bloom in the sky.
Shining rubies and sapphires fall from the heavens.
They dull to the color of diamonds
and float down to the calm surface of the lake.
The motors of pontoon boats throb
heading to see the glorious event in the sky.
The multicolored sparks
seem to play a never-ending game of tag
in the heavens.
As they descend the dark
staircase of the clouds,
I watch in awe.

Bradley Long, Grade 5
Stanley Clark School, IN

Top Poem Grades 4-5-6

Beautiful Sights

As I'm walking I have beautiful sights before my eyes.
Something brushes softly,
lightly against my cheek
like a friend trying to get attention,
like a soft flower rubbing against my face.

I hear chirps, like rain coming down on a pond.
Glittering and glowing I cup some up.

Feel refreshed as I gently splash my face.
Splashes from it coming up like little minnows — jumping.

Colors of red and blue,
I pick up one of the red plants
makes my senses come alive, flattered by the smell.
Colorful creature flies by
butterfly kisses on my cheek.

Sarah Maschino, Grade 4
Midland Academy of Advanced and Creative Studies, MI

Top Poem Grades 4-5-6

One Foggy Fall Day

We were out and about
On this foggy fall day
Happy, ready and wanting to play

Instead of playing
I gave into my needs
I sat down and looked
At these beautiful trees

Looking and seeking autumn's treasure
Wanting and needing this addicting pleasure.

Noelle Perry, Grade 6
University Liggett School, MI

Top Poem Grades 4-5-6

Ordinary Morning

I'm sitting on the front porch
on a dark silver morning
in the sunrise.
As these two seconds tick by,
I sense a sacred moment of my life is happening.
The sun rises
as a perfect orange ball on the horizon,
two perfect seconds
of a perfect orange world.
The whole world holds its breath
waiting for someone or something
to make its move.
I want to swim in this crystal clear pool of orange.
All I can do is gasp in awe
as I go back inside.

Aidan Reilly, Grade 5
Stanley Clark School, IN

Top Poem Grades 4-5-6

Shadows

Roaming in the darkness,
they are hidden from view.
They creep up behind you,
but when you turn around,
they are gone, waiting
for you to turn again
so they can roam once more.

Jack Reynolds, Grade 6
Melrose Elementary School, OH

Top Poem Grades 4-5-6

Seasons

The spring uses pastels,
of light pink, green and blue.
The summer uses crayons,
of deep green, yellow, and purple, too.

The winter uses a pencil,
to outline the streets and trees,
But, fall uses a paintbrush,
with reds, yellows, browns and all between.

Katelyn Vlastaris, Grade 5
Birchwood School, OH

Top Poem Grades 4-5-6

The Great Escape

Sometimes I feel trapped,
like a hamster in a ball.
There's no way to get out,
and no one hears my call.
I want to push the escape key.
I want to get away.
I have to see the sunlight,
but there's no other way…
My eyes can't see the exit;
my hands can't feel the door.
I can't do this any longer.
I can't take this anymore.
Because what if there's no escape key?
What if there's no door?
What if there's no sunlight?
I can never be quite sure…
So I'll just have to take it,
for as long as I can stand.
I'll have to stay in darkness,
unless someone gives me a hand.

Emily Wenzel, Grade 6
Virgil I Grissom Middle School, IN

Lindsey

L ikes going out to play
I like to go on the grass and lay
N ever had to lie at home
D oes go off and roam
S ees snow fall on the ground
E xplores places to be found
Y es I am very shy

A nd I don't lie
N ever break my stuff
N ever will be tough

B eginning to be very strong
E xcited to sing a song
C anned food is not my favorite
K angaroos are my favorite animals

Lindsey Ann Beck, Grade 5
Frank Ohl Intermediate School, OH

Fall

When it comes
I jump for joy
Swirling leaves
Scented pines
I want fall to be mine
In October we see ghosts and ghouls
In November it's all cool
Pretty pumpkins
Colorful leaves
Pumpkin pie
Apple delight

Eva Laser, Grade 4
Stonegate Elementary School, IN

Tree

Tree
Christmas
Holiday glee
Santa's coming soon.
Please, no coal for me!
Cheery sleigh bells ring,
Carolers coming to sing.
Hot cocoa by the fire,
It's the most delicious thing!
Curious packages under the tree,
I hope at least one is just for me!
Colossal dinners fine and tasty,
The packages can wait, don't be hasty!
Last minute shoppers colliding carts,
Looking for gifts to warm others' hearts.
Cold noses touch as two people kiss,
Under mistletoe, mister and miss.
Christmas is wonderful. What is your
Wish?

Rayna Sherbinow, Grade 4
Emerald Elementary School, MI

Silent Night

Winter is a time for fun and excitement.
The cold air blowing at your face, blowing your hair everywhere you go.
The white snow is sticking to your gloves as you're picking it up.
The frozen city silent, not a sound the ear can hear.
The sidewalk is as slippery as soap when you're washing your hands.

Breeanna Davis, Grade 6
Waverly East Intermediate School, MI

Summer Time

Summer is near, finally at last.
Summer is always an awesomely fun blast!
Whether it's playing basketball or swimming in a pool,
There are always enjoyable things, always something to do.
It's a time for relaxation, some family time too.
Summer is so fun that I can't wait, what about you?

I love summer time; it is fun, refreshing, and sometimes quite cool.
The best thing is, it's a break from boring old school.
No more "Be quiet!" and "Here's a ton of work,"
But a lot of fun and not giving much worth.
Before that time happens, I should definitely pay attention.
I might get yet another detention!
I need to be patient, calm, and relaxed.
Who am I kidding? Summer is an awesome time and a really great blast!

Joshua Hahn, Grade 6
Corpus Christi Catholic School, MI

See What's Out, Not In

People may think you're different because you don't have the latest trends.
Fitting in doesn't mean you lie to your new friend
that thinks a guy is cute, even if he's your best guy pal.
Oh, and if she doesn't like a certain girl, well, she's your best friend.
I know it's hard to choose friends because
you want to hang out with the girls that are so pretty,
always gets the guys, and are just so popular.
There's more to life than that.
I hang out with the people I hardly have anything in common with.
The truth is we have so much in common we're all like sisters.
Everybody wants to have a fun year, get good grades, and have a lot of friends.
You don't have to be cool just to have all eyes on you.
Try not to fit in, if you're different,
everybody will want to hang out with you.
Fitting OUT is the way to be COOL.

Marisa Churchill, Grade 6
Woodrow Wilson Middle School, IN

Mercury

M ercury has an extremely hot surface in the day and in the
E vening the temperature gets very cool. Mercury's surface has a
R eally dark gray color. It is also very heavily
C ratered.
U nder the surface, Mercury is made mostly of rocks and metal. No one has ever
R eally found life on Mercury. Viewed from Earth,
Y ou can see that Mercury is very bright.

Liam O'Neill, Grade 6
Pinewood Elementary School, IN

Winter

Winter reminds me of joy.
Joy reminds me of happiness.
Happiness reminds me of presents.
Presents remind me of Christmas.
Christmas reminds me of Jesus.
Jesus reminds me of church.
Church reminds me of Christmas Eve.
Christmas Eve reminds me of Christmas music.
Christmas music reminds me of family.
Family reminds me of love.
Love reminds me of people.
People remind me of giving.
Giving reminds me of smiles.
Smiles remind me of winter.

Collin Germain, Grade 6
Waverly East Intermediate School, MI

I Am

I am athletic and determined
I wonder what I'm going to name my kids
I hear the crowd going wild
I see myself being a mother of five
I want to be a veterinarian
I am athletic and determined

I pretend to be a teacher
I feel competitive when I'm on the soccer field
I touch a soccer ball
I worry about my family
I cried when my grandpa and brother died
I am athletic and determined

I understand life isn't fair sometimes
I say if you believe you can you can
I dream to be a famous soccer player
I try to do my best in soccer every day
I hope I get to be a U.S.A pro soccer player
I am athletic and determined

I am Meagan VerVaecke
Meagan VerVaecke, Grade 4
Floyd Ebeling Elementary School, MI

The Sounds

I hear a butterfly,
As I listen,
A chorus joins in.
One by one I distinguish,
The sounds,
That comprise the pretty music.
The music that makes a bird sing,
The music that makes a grasshopper hop,
The music that I love,
The music of the Earth.

Shreya Menon, Grade 5
Logan Elementary School, MI

Cheyenne Sturgeon

Cheyenne
Nice, Cheetah lover, good writer, likes country songs
Related to Michael, Christy, Genevieve, Delores
Lover of horses, ice cream, drawing
Who feels good, happy, and glad
Who needs my parent's, clothes, and food
Who fears of spiders, getting an F on my homework.
Who gives hugs to my dad
Resident of Bristow
Sturgeon.

Cheyenne Sturgeon, Grade 5
Perry Central Elementary School, IN

Kittens

Four kittens were taking their first steps
as their mother Smokey crept from the room.
They seemed scared at first, but soon overcame
their small fear.
Slowly and clumsily, they stumbled
around the den.
I saw so much in so little time:
They were black fuzz-balls.
They walked like wobbly blobs of fur
with eyes, a nose, a tail, and legs.
I reached out to touch them —
they hissed and ran!
Hiding under Smokey, who recently returned, they cowered,
hissing like snakes.
I reached out again, only to be bitten
by tiny razor teeth.

Garrick Meyers, Grade 5
Stanley Clark School, IN

If I Was in Charge of the World

Lower the price in gas to fifty cents
Make a tunnel that will go through two states
Help the homeless
Fix the roads so the potholes are covered
Save the animals from being extinct
Stop pollution in oceans and in the air
Everyone would have rights
Take warm food to people who are too old to make it
Make oil reusable
Give to the poor
Never let light bulbs lost light
Make weapons harder to buy
Everyone would be nice
Help the economy
A penguin could be a house pet
Animals could not be put down
Time could be reusable
Stop destroying habitat
Pop would not be allowed
Schools would be allowed to have four field trips

Anna Schmidt, Grade 5
Sanderson Elementary School, OH

Baseball

I hit you
I throw you
I give you no respect
I'm sorry, really sorry
You act like you're screaming out
With your tethered seams and leather
I would bet you wish
You were treated better
I'm sorry, really sorry
With your dirt stains and hit marks
Like battle scars and war paint
You envy the ones
Who do not share the same fate
I'm sorry, really sorry
But in the end, you're just a ball
And this is what you were meant for
But I can't help but think
What if I shared your same fate?
I'm sorry, really sorry.

Avery Satayathum, Grade 6
Harding Middle School, OH

Poetry

Poetry is like a windowpane
Giving you a bunch of strain
High and low not knowing where to go
Speaking your wisdom
Thinking your wonder
People shouting
Not understanding why you are pouting
Writing away
Not thinking about what you will say
Ideas coming fast
And always will last
Going nowhere
With a wide blank stare
Coming across but now you are lost
Exhausted for the night
People say I am a fright
But that is all right!

Candace Kitchen, Grade 6
Sashabaw Middle School, MI

The Snake

Past the garden.
Across the river.
Over the hill.
Below the rocks.
Near the fence.
By the pine tree.
Like a worm.
Up the wall.
Down the drain.
Is a snake I see.

Logan Harshman, Grade 5
Churubusco Elementary School, IN

My Friend

Whoosh! Whoosh! Whoosh!
Goes my friend,
As fast as lightning,
Blowing my hair.
Whoosh! Whoosh! Whoosh!
She blows
On a breezy day.
Whoosh! Whoosh! Whoosh!
She's the wind!

Shannon Garrison, Grade 6
Wooster Christian School, OH

Fall Speaks

Fall speaks with every season.
Fall speaks with the moon and stars.
Fall speaks with an open heart.
Fall speaks with every language.
Fall speaks with the wind and rain.
These words involve no sound.
What is the Earth without the sound?
This is fall.
This is how fall speaks.

Elizabeth Foley, Grade 6
Rocky River Middle School, OH

Llama Louie

Llama Louie
Spit a lugey

It went so far
It hit a car

It broke the windshield
So he ran into the field

His mama caught him
And slapped him on the bottom

The car owner sued
And Louie was one mad dude

Now Llama Louie
Is stuck in juevey

Jessica Keck, Grade 6
Trilby Elementary School, OH

Halloween/Christmas

Halloween
Spooky, haunted,
Screaming, trick-or-treat, scaring,
Friends, pumpkins, tree, presents,
Decorating, sledding, snowing,
Cold, colorful,
Christmas

April Kelly, Grade 5
Norwich Elementary School, OH

Christmas Reminds Me Of…

Christmas reminds me of joy.
Joy reminds me of happiness.
Happiness reminds me of feelings.
Feelings remind me of warmth.
Warmth reminds me of fire.
Fire reminds me of water.
Water reminds me of summer.
Summer reminds me of sports.
Sports remind me of new equipment.
New equipment reminds me of presents.
Presents remind me of toys.
Toys remind me of playfulness.
Playfulness reminds me of X-mas trees.
X-mas trees remind me of winter.
Winter reminds me of Christmas.

Tyler Eastman, Grade 6
Waverly East Intermediate School, MI

Winter

Snow falls silently
Tea warm as the fire waits for
The children to come

Sami Blair, Grade 6
Perry Central Elementary School, IN

School

The big yellow bus comes every day
To pick me up, then I'm on my way
We come to a stop!
Right on time, 8:00
We go inside to greet our teachers
We have rooms full of stuffed creatures
Then we start learning, my favorite thing
The next thing I know, I hear a "Ding!"
School's over, too bad,
But I get to come tomorrow…I'm glad!

Emily Murzyn, Grade 6
Abbott Middle School, MI

Flowers

Sitting up on the tall grass,
I look down on the ground
for a friend.
There I see a worm.
It came up on my stem and
tickled me as he crawled up.

The wind blew and I swayed
side to side.
As the wind stopped,
I saw a beautiful butterfly.
It was so colorful.
The butterfly started
to tickle my stem with his hairy feet.

Kayla Kasper, Grade 6
Helfrich Park Middle School, IN

Dreaming

Sleeping through the night, so many hours.
Thoughts running through your head.
Displayed like a movie,
Sometimes sweet.
No one wants to wake up,
Sometimes scary.
You wake up abruptly,
Frightened by your own thoughts.
How do you control your thoughts through the night?
Wish you could make every night peaceful,
But you can't.
Everyone knows dreaming is dreaming,
It is entertainment through the night.

Carina Taylor, Grade 6
Abbott Middle School, MI

I Am a Cat

I am a kitty pet trying to get out of the house.
I wonder if I'll ever get out.
I hear Thunderclan battling and cats
losing their lives.
I see Bluestar hunting for prey and
feasting on it.
I want Firestar to accept me.
I am escaping to the wilderness!
I pretend I'm a Warrior.
I feel my owners pick me up.
I touch the carpet of the house.
I worry I won't be able to join a clan.
I cry "Let me out!"
I understand I'm a lazy kitty pet.
I say I can be brave.
I dream I fight Shadowclan.
I try to sneak out again.
I hope I don't get caught.
I am outside!

Louise Reed, Grade 5
Tremont Elementary School, OH

It's All About…Me

Mikayla
Spunky, active, smart
Sister of Maddox
Lover of shopping, softball, and Aeropostale
Who feels nervous at the first day of school
    and when the power goes out
Who gets excited about summer vacation
    and when I go on vacation
Who needs to ask for an allowance and read more often
Who gives kisses to my baby brother
Who fears heights and my friend's dog
Who would like to be a famous singer
Resident of Austintown, Ohio
Mills

Mikayla Mills, Grade 5
Frank Ohl Intermediate School, OH

I Am

I am funny and cool
I wonder if I will ever see my dad again
I hear myself playing a guitar
I see myself flying
I want a high-tech desk
I am funny and cool

I pretend I can do anything
I feel my hands drawing
I touch soft snow in the winter
I worry about global warming
I cry when someone in my family has died
I am funny and cool

I understand people's feelings
I say that everyone has a different opinion
I dream to be floating on a cloud
I try to do my best
I hope I am rich
I am funny and cool

I am David Garbarino

David J. Garbarino, Grade 4
Floyd Ebeling Elementary School, MI

The Beach Shore

Smoothing rocks by the shore,
The sand in between your toes,
Seeing the colors blend in front of you,
The ocean waters crash on the beach shore,
Hearing seagulls by the water,
Laughing by the sunset,
The smell of sea water,
The beach is a beautiful place

Laura Duggan, Grade 5
May V Peck Elementary School, MI

Let Freedom Ring for All

Freedom rings
For all good things
Soldiers fought
For all that was thought
All that is well
Will go so swell
And even I
Really try
We're all free
For it rings
We're free to walk
And to trot
We're free to sing
For it rings
And freedom rings
For all good things

Shadow Bennett, Grade 6
North Knox East Elementary/Jr High School, IN

Cat

Purring companion,
Lazy calico feline,
Waiting to be fed.
Jake Watkins, Grade 6
Holy Angels School, OH

Winter/Summer

winter
frosted, freezing
snowboarding, skiing, tobogganing
jackets, boots, shades, shorts
swimming, water skiing, golfing
summer
Connor Larson, Grade 5
Floyd Ebeling Elementary School, MI

Hurricanes and Winds

Hurricane
Wet, windy
Devastating, overwhelming, ruining
Storm, nature, strong, fast
Breaking, destroying, changing
Strong, invisible
Winds
Lindsay Deaton, Grade 6
Mayfield Elementary School, OH

Brave Ones

V ery brave
E very day
T he work
E verything, any time
R ed and white
A merica
N ight and day
Lydia Hatten, Grade 4
Westview Elementary School, OH

Winter Fun

In winter
above all that snow
constructing snowmen and war
opening presents on Christmas day
winter fun
Mateo Deda, Grade 5
Floyd Ebeling Elementary School, MI

Fall

Cold, leaves
Changing, freezing, snowing
Chilly, colors, warm, green
Growing, thawing, raining
Radiant, beautiful
Spring
Levi Schmitmeyer, Grade 6
Holy Angels School, OH

A Taliban Soldier's Life

Setting up landmines all through the west,
Then the children touch it and yelp for the Taliban is the best.
Taking away people's families for almost no reason.
The family knows they do it to everyone in every season.
Cutting off hands of those who are innocent.
And they all deserve it those ungrateful peasants!
Chasing young women out of the marketplace,
Yelling if you don't got a man with you get out of here in disgrace.
Its hard work patrolling the streets day and night,
Hunting people around the town when it's time for me to sight.
Going to different cities and killing everybody I see.
Them telling me "Give mercy to my family just kill me" they plea!
Bombing some buildings and killing people all day,
People still live there rebuilding it, no one wants to stay.
Most of the Taliban can't read or write,
But who needs to be educated when they're always right.
I hate it how people are scared of me they never want to talk to me,
I want them to know that I was forced to be in the Taliban you see.
Being a Taliban soldier is exciting but sometimes I wonder,
Why can't the Taliban just go away and surrender?
Alex Powers, Grade 6
Ann Arbor Christian School, MI

Thanksgiving Joy

The joy tastes great yum, yum, yum!!!
Thick, tender turkey.
As I bite, I remember the taste from years past.
The homemade stuffing and cranberry sauce tastes, oh so great
The crisp fall day could only lead to this moment
As I sit in this bright, joy filled room,
The wonderful smells fill my nose.
As the birds chirp we talk of happiness and sadness.
As the starry sky fills the night with beauty,
The music plays a peaceful song.
I ask myself will I stay up late?
Will this day come again?
If so when?
I wish to repeat this happy day.
When I start to eat, smiles and laughter fill the room.
As I think of tomorrow the aroma of the feast rejuvenates my hectic mind.
The joy tastes great, yum, yum, yum!!!
Charlie Supp, Grade 5
EH Greene Intermediate School, OH

A Better Place

If I were in charge of the world...
I would lower the gas prices so that more people can have money for taxes.
I'd give money to homeless people.
I would banish spinach from all of food.
Smoking would be against the law and if you get caught
You would either be arrested or have a large fine.
The Colts would be banished from the NFL.
The Bears would have first pick in the draft every year.
If I was in charge of the world it would be a better place.
Josh Howk, Grade 5
Churubusco Elementary School, IN

Soccer Player

S is for to strike the ball to go into the net.
O is for to own the ball to steal it from the other team.
C is for captain, there is a captain because he is the best player.
C is for controlling your foot to hit correctly.
E is for effort, you use your effort to win the game.
R is for remembering the movement to get past players.

P is for to pass the ball to your teammates.
L is for loyal, you be loyal to your teammates.
A is for always keep your eyes on the ball.
Y is for you, you play the game fairly.
E is for everyone plays in the game.
R is for returning the ball to the other team.

Pauline Paulo, Grade 4
Keystone Academy, MI

Spring Time!

Very pretty
Flowers gleam in the midnight moonlight
Drip!
    Drop!
        Drip!
            Drop!
                Drip!
                    Drop!
                        Drip!
                            Drop!
Rain! Rain! Rain!
FLOWERS GROW!!!

Rachel Stankiewicz, Grade 4
Midland Academy of Advanced and Creative Studies, MI

Rain

Dark clouds roam the sky
Rain pours down among the trees
Pushing leaves far down

Jolie Goldberg, Grade 4
Frank H Hammond Elementary School, IN

Oh, What Could It Be?

Boom, Bang, Crunch!
I hear something on the roof
Oh what could it be? Oh what could it be?
There's a bear whiter than snow
A belly bigger than an elephant
A giant red suit.
Oh what could it be? Oh what could it be?
A silly elf?
Or Santa Claus?
Oh what could it be? Oh what could it be?
Come on and let's see!
It's Santa Claus it's really him!
Hurry up the stairs — like the wind.
Hop in bed and go to sleep.

Sara Zebrak, Grade 4
Midland Academy of Advanced and Creative Studies, MI

Christmas

The wonderful smell of Christmas
The wonderful sound of bells
A tooting train, boots, and a plane
Shorts and dresses, chicken and crescents,
Green and red
Ham and bread
Christmas is wonderful but when the
clock strikes twelve it is over.

Marcus Bennett, Grade 4
Stonegate Elementary School, IN

I Am

I am a girl that loves horses
I wonder if I will ever have a boyfriend
I hear people calling me Doctor Sikes
I see a world without meanness
I want my brother to come home
I am a girl that loves horses

I pretend that I am a rich and famous doctor
I feel that some people hate me
I touch the hand of my brother
I worry that my brother will not come back from Iraq
I cry when people make fun of me
I am a girl that loves horses

I understand that I will die someday
I say "It doesn't matter what is on the outside,
it matters what is in the heart."
I dream that someday I will walk with God
I try to be a good person
I hope that someday I can find a cure for cancer
I am a girl that loves horses

Jessi Sikes, Grade 6
Helfrich Park Middle School, IN

Ohio

Ohio is where I was born.
Ohio is where I live.
Ohio is a magnificent place,
Home of the Great Lake Erie.
Ohio is a sweet place,
Home of the sweetest corn, and vegetables.

Heather Haas, Grade 4
Legend Elementary School, OH

Friends Are Always There

Who gets you in trouble for something they did?
Who laughs for no reason?
Who's over at your house just to talk about nothing?
Who feels the pain of your heart even when it's not broken?
Best friends do all of this
Right now it might not seem true
But as the years go by trust me they do

Leslie Burbank, Grade 5
May V Peck Elementary School, MI

Faces

Sad faces, happy faces, sick faces
crying faces, mad faces, joyful faces
silly faces, masked faces, smiling faces
faces faces every day
what faces will you see today?

Peter Abou Haidar, Grade 5
Birchwood School, OH

Clay Atkins

C lay is my name
L oves video games
A nnoying his big brother
Y oung and handsome

A lways playing games
T ough and mean
K nows what's going on
I don't like school
N eeds less homework
S its and plays video games

Clay Atkins, Grade 5
Perry Central Elementary School, IN

Ryan

R eally tall
Y ells a lot
A lways plays football
N ever gives up

Tyler Maiorana, Grade 4
Northfield Elementary School, OH

Disgusted

Disgusted is a purple color,
It tastes like raw fish,
It smells like trash,
It reminds me of my brother,
It sounds like gagging,
Disgusted makes me feel purple.

Sydney Thomas, Grade 5
Tremont Elementary School, OH

Change

Change is coming
It's on the way
The world will change
Will be seen in a different way
It has already started
History in the making
Obama is coming to save the day
Change is coming
Hip hip hooray!
Change is coming
Get ready for it
Get ready for a new day!

Lyric Harden, Grade 6
Akiva Academy, OH

Whispering Wind

It's like an invisible fan
It's here, there, everywhere
It's sometimes cold
Sometimes warm
You can feel it
But you can't see it
It can cause trouble
Or sometimes be double
What is it?
It's the WIND
The sound of the wind
Moves through the meadow.

Audrey Funwie, Grade 4
Detroit Open School, MI

Night Woods

Cold in the night woods,
The only light is the moon,
Foggy sky — birds fly!

Isabela Nanni, Grade 6
Stanley Clark School, IN

Autumn

A utumn is cool
U ntouched candy
T rees without leaves
U nsolved mysteries
M onsters come at night
N othing scares me!

Alan Teet, Grade 6
Eisenhower Middle School, OH

For Sale

A dog for sale,
A cat for sale,

A hog for sale, too,
Each of which would be perfect for you!

A mammal for sale,
A fish for sale

Won't anyone bid?
Not even a kid?

Come on people,
Won't you bid?

A quarter,
A dime,
Not even a nickel?

I guess I'll keep my lovely animals,
Unless you bid.

Ally Witte, Grade 4
Stonegate Elementary School, IN

Snow

Snow is on the ground.
Snow is on roof tops.
Snow is all around.
Snow is on driveways.
Snow is on decks and porches.
Snow is on cars.
Snow is on trucks.
Snow is on the road.
Snow is falling.
I love snow!

Noah Jenkins, Grade 4
Legend Elementary School, OH

The Veterans' Plight

Fear was common,
Courage was sought.
Bonds were formed
Among those who fought.

Bombs exploded,
Shrapnel flew.
The searing sun
Burned too.

People were injured,
Some never returned.
All dreamed of ceasefire,
Battle was not adjourned.

Fighting on foreign lands,
Home seemed very far.
Safe were the many,
But veterans bore the scars.

Katie Steinberg, Grade 6
EH Greene Intermediate School, OH

My Sour Milk Heart

I sit alone in a big empty house
Eating to my heart's content
Pondering the loss of a loved one
I take a swig, yuck!
Sour milk!
I think to myself,
My soul feels like
Sour milk too.

Sam Borick, Grade 6
Harding Middle School, OH

Christmas

Christmas
Snowy present
Giving, eating, shopping
Sleepy, happy, thankful, joyful
X-mas!

Izabelle Galvin, Grade 4
Bailly Elementary School, IN

Triskaidekaphobia

They say it's an unlucky number,
They say it's bad as bad can be,
But personally, I like this number,
Because it ends in 3.
But what about 14, 15, 16, and 17?
They say seven is a lucky number,
So wouldn't 14 be double the luck?
For 7 is straight in between.
But 13's just 1 down from 14,
So close,
Yet they still insist that it's negative luck.
All full of mist is my brain right now,
So muddled, so muggy, so mixed.
It's my job to clear 13's name,
So I'd like to go and play tug-of-war,
Two teams, 13 and 7, mark the score,
And see who wins the game.

Elena N. Dupen, Grade 5
Northern Heights Elementary School, IN

Veterans

We sob and cry when we see them go,
And jump for joy when they come home,
We know they leave for a good cause,
But fear they'll come back wrapped in gauze.

We're gathered here, on this day,
To honor those for whom we did pray,
They have come back, hip, hip, hurray,
Now I just have one thing to say.

They go to war to do their part,
For their great country and everything in their heart,
When all is peaceful, finally at last,
They come back home to their past.

They are heroes for you and me,
Honored and cheered you see,
We love these men, true patriots indeed,
They helped our country when it was in need.

What they have done is truly a gift,
Hip hip, hurrah,
For God, our country, and all America!

Anthony Popenoe, Grade 6
EH Greene Intermediate School, OH

Saturn

S aturn is a gaseous and
A lso bitterly cold planet.
T o go there we would have to travel past Jupiter. It is
U nrealistic though because it has no hard surface. The
R ing around Saturn is composed of infinite
N umbers of small rings made of ice, dust, and rocks.

Alexandra Anderson, Grade 6
Pinewood Elementary School, IN

Christmas Day

On Christmas Eve, when the candles are lit
Everybody's asking the same question
"What am I going to get?"
Early in the morning of Christmas Day
You hear cries and cheers of Yea!
You can hear the wrapping paper being torn
Because of a special baby that was born
Eating truffles and chocolate of all kinds
Can't wait for some to be mine
You can smell the sticky buns in the oven
That everyone will soon be lovin'
Some people are as happy as if they were there
That very same day in the very year
When Christ was born
This is the happiest time of year
When you hear Christmas songs and feel
The Christmas cheer
Joy, joy, joy!

Sarah Thompson, Grade 5
EH Greene Intermediate School, OH

How an Afghan Lives

The marketplace is always flowing,
men and women are coming and going.
Merchants hoping to sell their wares,
bargaining with people 'til their shelves are bare.

A woman without a man will get a stare.
A woman without a burqa, don't you dare.
Women can't work, that's a rule.
Just like girls can't go to school!

Nan, is chewy, soft, bland-tasting flat bread,
people will use it to get fed.
They eat it with almost every meal.
Using it to scoop soup is very real.

Their homes are sad, simple, small,
very bleak and not very tall.
Houses are made of concrete or mud brick.
The bombed out shells of homes will make you sick.

Many land mines from war are left here.
Never knowing if you'll ever step on one creates fear.
Land mines can be disguised to look like toys.
If you step on one it will make a big noise.

Lindsie Egedy, Grade 6
Ann Arbor Christian School, MI

My Guinea Pig

My guinea pig's eyes are black like flaming ashes!
My guinea pig's hair looks like an orange!
My guinea pig's heart holds love like a red rose!
My guinea pig lives in a pen and eats apples!

Rebecca Hunt, Grade 5
Henryville Elementary School, IN

Winter Time

Winter time is fully of joy,
Winter time is for opening toys.
Winter time is for sledding with friends,
Winter time is tons of spend.
Winter time is a time for sparkling lights,
Winter time is for having snow fights.
Winter time is for Jesus Christ,
And winter time is for sliding on ice.

Jennie Besario, Grade 6
Corpus Christi Elementary School, IN

Fall

Fall
A wonderful season
Green, orange, brown, colorful leaves
Pumpkin seeds,
Turkeys

Jarred Eshenaur, Grade 4
Bailly Elementary School, IN

Veteran's Day

Honor those who served.
Blue for alive,
Gold for the dead.
Red poppies for our veterans.
Purple hearts for the injured,
A medal for the disabled,
Once called Armistice Day.
Honor those who served.

Remember our flag.
Remember our country.
Remember the disabled.
Remember our veterans.
Remember Veteran's Day.

Andrew Comstock, Grade 4
Dobbins Elementary School, OH

My Home in a Winter Wonderland

Snow is falling,
Santa's calling,
My home in a Winter Wonderland,
Shoveling snow,
Our master calling "Ho Ho Ho,"
My home in a Winter Wonderland,
Having fun
Without a sun,
My home in a Winter Wonderland,
Call the reindeer,
Christmas is here,
My home in a Winter Wonderland,
On his way,
With a filled up sleigh,
My home in a Winter Wonderland!

Lauren J. Liles, Grade 5
May V Peck Elementary School, MI

Myself

Ben
Fast, athletic, short
Brother of Amanda, Emily, Sarah, Jacob
Lover of football, Ohio State Buckeyes, Cleveland Browns
Feels nervous when it's the last 2 minutes of a Browns game when losing by 3 points
Gets excited about an Ohio State versus Michigan football game.
Needs to get neater.
Gives kisses to my dog.
Fears tornadoes
Would like to play in the NFL for a job as a Cleveland Brown
Resident of Austintown, Ohio
Rouan

Ben Rouan, Grade 5
Frank Ohl Intermediate School, OH

Winter

Chilly winds are blowing,
outside it is snowing.

White snowflakes swirling around and around,
falling slowly to the snowy ground.

Bright evergreen trees are everywhere,
steaming hot chocolate warms the chilly air.

Red holly bushels are in the halls,
all the trees decorated with ornaments, candy, and popcorn balls.

Lamp lights cast an icy glow,
Santa sings jollily, "Ho, ho, ho!"

On Christmas morning I unwrap the gifts he left under the tree,
and if I really like them, I dance and dance with glee.

Brenna Wyffels, Grade 5
Browning Elementary School, MI

My Best Friend

A best friend is someone to tell secrets to in the dark.
I tell her shhh! Be quiet don't be a nark.
She's with me through the best and worst of times.
She is the person to whom I sing my rhymes.
She always has a hand to lend.
I know she will be with me until the very end.
Her name is Sarah Pointdexter and she's my best friend!

Tracy Parker, Grade 6
Kesling Middle School, IN

The Fall Season

Fall is a colorful season.
The leaves turn yellow-green.
There are lots of orange pumpkins in the patch.
There are also lots of yummy pumpkin seeds to eat.
As I rake the leaves, they make a crunching sound under my feet.
I love the fall season!

Courtney Pike, Grade 6
Holy Family Middle School, MI

Summer into Fall
Summer
Hiking, swimming
Playing, vacation, fun
Biking, steaming hot, leaves, warm colors
School, homework, assignments
Friends, Halloween
Fall

Kaitlin Wells, Grade 4
Norwich Elementary School, OH

Roses
I am red, sharp, and pointy.
I am a beautiful little flower
but do not touch me
for your hand will bleed.
I am a rose.
Please do not fear me.

Addison Housand, Grade 6
Michiana Christian Montessori School, IN

Our Heroes
They fought for freedom and for peace,
In jungles, sand and shores.
Some lost their legs, some lost their lives,
In long and vicious wars.

They left their family and their friends,
And risked their lives to help our country.
They fought all day, they fought all night,
Just so we could be free.

They bravely fought through the winter,
They fearlessly fought through the spring,
They waited for that vital word,
To let freedom ring.

Some of them were drafted,
Others chose it on their own.
They all fought for our nation,
But many are still unknown.

These are the veterans of our land.
We owe so much to each of them.
They never gave up throughout the years.
These are our heroes, all the women and men.

Atiya Dosani, Grade 6
EH Greene Intermediate School, OH

Venus
V is very hot. No signs of
E xtraterrestial life on Venus have been
N oticed. Venus is
U sually referred to as Earth's
S ister planet because they are close in size.

Matt Lyon, Grade 6
Pinewood Elementary School, IN

Nature
N ever stops growing like you and me
A lways there for us to see
T ruly an amazing thing it can be
U nimaginable like the clouds in the sky
R eaches out to greet the eye
E njoys everything that goes by watching us in silence

Ali Snare, Grade 6
Harmon Middle School, OH

Walter Payton
Walter Payton was a Chicago Bear,
He had really curly black hair.
Football was his favorite game,
Sweetness was his nickname.

Austen Porzel, Grade 5
Washington Township Elementary School, IN

I Am
I am optimistic and athletic.
I wonder how computers actually work.
I hear an empty folder crying.
I see my imaginary friend
playing poker with another imaginary friend.
I want a 42-inch plasma TV.
I am optimistic and athletic.
I pretend to play the guitar.
I feel jealous because
my imaginary friend won the lottery.
I touch a pink tiger.
I worry about what will happen in my future.
I cry because I never met my grandma.
I am optimistic and athletic.
I understand that we are fortunate to be free.
I say everyone should have a chance
to make his or her dreams come true.
I dream about becoming a pilot.
I try to do my best in sports.
I hope I have a good future.
I am optimistic and athletic.

J.J. Penix, Grade 6
Galesburg-Augusta Middle School, MI

Friends
Who is someone you can trust when you are sad?
Who can you trust when you are mad?
They comfort you and they cheer you up.
Oh how wonderful it is to have friends.
They will be there for you and they will stay with you,
And they will make a wish for you.
And you will make a wish too.
So when you need help,
Trust in your friends and don't struggle
Because you'll fall into a puddle.
But your friend will be there for you.

Jennifer Lopez, Grade 5
Auburn Hills Christian School, MI

Big Dog

Big dog
Running, playing
Playing Frisbee all day
Big brown patches all over it
Cute dog

Brelyn Kunz, Grade 4
Riverside Elementary School, MI

Kittens

Kittens
Soft and silky
Have playful attitude
Need rest

Mallory Potter, Grade 4
Warren Central Elementary School, IN

Popcorn

Popcorn
Popping in heat
Yum! Delightful! It's great.
Butter fills the air with delight.
Popped corn.

Mariah Bement, Grade 4
Bailly Elementary School, IN

Love!

Love is to love
Love is to be locked in your heart
Love is to give
Love is to have
Love is for every person
Love is to be serious
Love is to kiss
Love is to hug
Love is to keep each other safe
Love is to be responsible
Love is to keep your heart open
Love is not to judge
Love is to be special
Love is to be in love

Kaylah Talley, Grade 5
May V Peck Elementary School, MI

Basketball

B askets
A rt
S kills
K obe Bryant
E ntertaining
T eaching
B alls
A erobics
L aughing
L earning to play.

Jeff Kempf, Grade 4
Mayfield Elementary School, OH

About Me

C ute
A wesome
I ntrusting
T ruthful
L oud
Y outhful
N osy

L oving
E xcellent
W onderful
I ntelligent
S uper

Caitlyn Lewis, Grade 5
St Jude Catholic School, IN

Sorrowful

S weet taste of blood.
O utrageous mauling from Spirit Bear.
R ed on the grass sweeps down.
R egret overcomes him.
O n the verge of death.
W ay over his head.
F ear of pushing up daisies.
U rgent need of food.
L osing life's source.

Kasey Holter, Grade 6
Harmon Middle School, OH

Triple Play

Bases loaded.
Crowd silent.
Last inning.
Ball thrown.
Ball hit.
Crowd gasps.
Ball caught at third, first out.
Third base tagged, second out.
Crowd screaming.
Yelling,
Hollering.
Base runner runs back.
Third base man on his heels.
Runner tagged, third out.
Game Won!
Crowd cheered, untamed.

Liam T. Cowen, Grade 6
Assumption BVM School, MI

Zebra

Zebra
Runs in the field
Grazes in a field of flowers
A wildfire

Zackary Bradley, Grade 4
Riverside Elementary School, MI

What I Don't See

I see the sky, dark and gloomy.
I see the grass, wet and soggy.
I see the raindrops pelting the ground,
Like little jumping beans.

I see the trees, sad and droopy,
But what I don't see is the sun.
I don't see the sun trying to brighten
Somebody's day.

The only thing I see is negativity.

Kristen Stevens, Grade 6
Greencastle Middle School, IN

Autumn Leaves

Autumn leaves are falling
Falling from the sky
Red, orange, and yellow
They look like they will fly

Flying to the ground
They move fast, soft, and quiet
Please don't break the silence

There are so many on the ground now
We'll rake them up
And jump in them all
Oh how I love fall!

Autumn is over
It's starting to snow
I'll have to wait 'til
Next year
When the autumn leaves
Glow

Shelby Joslin, Grade 5
Heritage Intermediate School, IN

One

One letter can start a word.
One word can start a sentence.
One sentence can start a book.
One person can start an army.
One army can start a war.
One person can end world hunger.
One person can end hatred.
One person can end poverty.
One person can start world peace.
One cloud can start a storm.
One strong wind can start a tornado.
One piece of wood can start a house.
One house can start a city.
One city can start a state.
One state can start a country.

Brendan Caporale, Grade 6
St Gerard School, MI

Four Little Sunday School Girls

Four little Sunday school girls,
With all their hair in pretty curls.
Making their lessons all in a line,
They didn't know this would be their last time.
The safest pace on earth to be,
Suddenly turned into a place of misery.
The explosion was ear shatteringly loud,
A terrified gasp went through the crowd.
How could people want to injure others,
Even if they are of different colors.
We are all different, but all the same,
But some people just want to cause others pain
Some people believe that his was right,
While others didn't want to cause a fight.
All people deserve love and care,
The world is for all to share.
Four little Sunday school girls,
With all their hair in pretty curls.
Their lives were taken without a fight,
But now most people know what is right.

Monica Lee, Grade 6
Detroit Country Day Middle School, MI

All About Me

S ometimes I like to play baseball
A s I feel the crowd cheering
M y parents always root for me
U sed to feeling pumped
E yes are always on me
L ifting my bat, I swing

E very time I reach first base quickly
A s the crowd cheers, I know I am safe
R eady to run to the next base or score a homerun
L eader on the team, my coaches say

B ook in the bag project expert
U nderstands the food web
N eeds to eat breakfast every morning
D oes my best at Language Arts
Y es I have improved with Dibbles

J oyful when I return home from school
R eady to see the world

Samuel Earl Bundy Jr., Grade 5
Frank Ohl Intermediate School, OH

My Enemy…Homework

I find my homework really boring.
Sometimes I wake myself up with my snoring.
I don't understand the point of homework at all.
It makes me want to bang my head against the wall.
I can't wait for the summer to start.
No homework during summer vacation…now that is SMART.

Jack Kelly, Grade 6
Rocky River Middle School, OH

What Moves Me

What moves me is when I go to Myrtle Beach.
The ocean splashes all around me.
I surf, I swim and I boogie board.
I play and I play but I never got bored.

Brody Garitson, Grade 4
Creekview Elementary School, OH

It

It slowly slithers.
The thing rattles its tail.
In the country it hides in hay.
Watch as it snaps at its prey.
They are the desert's beast.
It camouflages better than the Iraq soldiers.
Stare long enough it might do a trick.
The rattle snake.

Tanner Garrett, Grade 6
Woodward Park Middle School, OH

Thanksgiving

T he knife cutting the turkey for everyone to eat
H aving people playing football with you in the front yard
A lways playing in the leaves no matter what happens
N ever knowing who will show up
K ind people being with you on a special day
S erving me this delicious food
G iving me a chance to be with these wonderful relatives
I nviting my whole family to have a good time
V iew the beautiful horn-of-plenty
I 'll help my mom and dad prepare
N ature here and nature there is what I love
G iving everyone a bite of Mom's turkey, made just right

Sarah Spires, Grade 5
Perry Central Elementary School, IN

I Am

I am competitive and cool.
I wonder which way to hang the toilet paper.
I hear a door ringing.
I see 8 crocodiles in the desert.
I want a big car!
I am competitive and cool.
I pretend that I know everything.
I feel happy that my dog earned 3 medals for talking.
I touch a cloud.
I worry that I will never see my dad.
I cry about dogs that die of starvation.
I am competitive and cool.
I understand why my friends are mad.
I say to stay strong.
I dream about meeting my dad.
I try to be optimistic.
I hope to be a veterinarian.
I am competitive and cool.

Shannon Willever, Grade 6
Galesburg-Augusta Middle School, MI

Snow

When snow falls
I think it's really beautiful
Watching it fall
From the sky to
the ground.
Kids building snowman
and kids making snow angels.
Now winter is gone
Now it's spring
All the snow melted away.
I will see it next year.
Snow, I love it!
Ashley Sikora, Grade 5
May V Peck Elementary School, MI

Thanksgiving

Thanksgiving
The happiness joy
Comes on thanksgiving and we
Celebrate because we
Enjoy
Arielle Hurt, Grade 4
Bailly Elementary School, IN

My Favorite Holiday

On Christmas Day,
Comes Santa and his sleigh,
Down from the rooftop,
He fills our stockings with joy,
And presents we enjoy.

Wake up in the morning,
To presents and songs,
Everyone is singing,
And dancing along.

Tearing and ripping,
Uncovering my toy,
My eyes get wider,
As I jump with joy.

Feasting is now,
Family time at the table,
Blessing our food,
Remember Jesus in the stable.
Trevor Waite, Grade 6
Tri-West Middle School, IN

Jesus

Jesus
Died for our sins
He did that on the cross
Loves us more than we love ourselves
Savior
Amy Long, Grade 5
Calvin Christian Elementary School, MI

Christmas Reminds Me Of…

Christmas reminds me of snow.
Snow reminds me of the trees that have snow on them.
The trees that have snow on them remind me of Christmas trees.
Christmas trees remind me of ornaments like bells.
Ornaments like bells remind me of the bells on Santa's sleigh.
Santa's sleigh reminds me of the big red bag in his sleigh.
The big red bag in his sleigh reminds me of toys and presents.
Toys and presents remind me of fun.
Fun reminds me of my family.
My family reminds me of great memories.
Great memories remind me of Christmas parties.
Christmas parties remind me of fun games.
Fun games remind me of happiness.
Happiness reminds me of life.
Life reminds me of Christmas.
Ana-Teresa Moreno, Grade 6
Waverly East Intermediate School, MI

An Ode to Papa Mike

He's the best grandpa in the world.
he was there when I first hurled.
He always played with me.
He always said not to mess with thee.
He would always cheer me on when I play baseball or basketball.
He would always catch me when I fall.
We would always curl up on the couch and watch the three stooges on tv.
No matter what he was always there for me.
My papa was the biggest White Sox fan.
It's hard to strive for but when I'm older I want to be a better man.
It hurts so bad I miss him so much.
I would give anything if we could just touch.
He would always give me piggy back rides
and the way he would look at me was with pride.
He would always let me ride in his boat
He would always make sure that I could float.
My papa was a teacher that worked in a workshop.
He would always drink gingerale pop.
He was with me when I caught the biggest fish.
For him to be here is my biggest wish.
Joshua Almazan, Grade 5
Allen J. Warren Elementary School, IN

Winter

Winter is fun.
You get to play in the snow.
You get to build snowmen.
You get to go skiing.
You get to go sledding, too.

Winter is fun.
You get to drink hot cocoa.
It is fun playing with friends in the snow.
You get to go to the Christmas tree farm and pick out a tree.
You get to decorate the tree, and Santa will put presents underneath it.
Alec Shrode, Grade 6
Corpus Christi Catholic School, MI

Trooper

T rooper loves me
R estless little guy
O ak nuts he thinks are small bouncy balls
O ver excited little guys
P layful and fun
E xcited and 1 out of 2 of my favorite dogs
R eady for anything!

Noah Brown, Grade 6
Mayfield Elementary School, OH

Spiders

Major role is to eat insects
Have been on Earth for millions of years
More than 30,000 different kinds are known
Have exoskeletons like insects
No wings, no antennae
Molt their outer covering during growth
Live about one year
Don't chew food
Spiders.

Zach Bindler, Grade 4
Dobbins Elementary School, OH

The Stars

The moon was looking for Mars but ran in to the stars
The fun began while they ran with the moon
But soon they noticed it was the afternoon
Then the moon whispered to the stars goodbye
See you tonight.

Adam Davis, Grade 6
Woodward Park Middle School, OH

Grandpa

I miss you, you don't know how much.
Grandpa, do you know how much you mean to me?
You were there when I needed you.
Guess what grandpa?
You were perfect,
You were sweet,
You were kind,
You were loving too.
Grandpa I miss you,
I miss your hugs. They were good as gold.
Grandpa,
You will always be in my heart.
I miss you, I hope you miss me too,
Because now I see,
The deepest love held inside of me is you,
Only you, grandpa,
I can't wait to see you again,
I will dream about you,
Now grandpa,
You will see how much you mean to me,
I miss you grandpa.

Sarah Terry, Grade 5
Perry Central Elementary School, IN

Lady Hornets

Run shout
I'm open
Get the ball
Run to the court with sneakers squeaking
You hear kneecaps crack and snap
Bleachers squeaking
Crowds cheering
We won!
Crowds screaming
We won!

Sarah Johnson, Grade 5
Henryville Elementary School, IN

Mars

M ars has 95% carbon dioxide, 3% nitrogen, 1.6%
A rgon, oxygen, and water. It's covered in
R ed dust, white polar caps, and craters. It has
S oil, organic molecules, and rocks on its surface.

Taylor Axsom, Grade 6
Pinewood Elementary School, IN

Volleyball

Volleyball is very fun.
We love to play with everyone.
We bump, set, spike, and serve.
We also have practice.
That's the only way we can learn.

Andriana Howard, Grade 6
St John the Baptist Elementary School, IN

My Savior

Who is my Savior?
My Savior, the one who watches out for me.
Makes sure I'm safe, every moment.
I feel my guardian protecting me.
That is my Savior.

Before I was born, He knew who I was.
When I was born, He said,
"That is my precious child."
Every time I fall, He helps me up.
And with the wind He whispered,
"You are now ok my child."
That is my Savior.

He sent an angel down from heaven
To write every good and bad I have done.
The birds sing like thousands of angels praising the Lord.
That is my Savior.

When I'm with my friends and having a good time,
I know He can say, "I've sent good parents for you."
And also can say, "I've done a good job."
The one and all powerful God is my SAVIOR.

Johely Martin, Grade 6
Woodward Park Middle School, OH

The Timid Kitten

I am a timid kitten
Lying fearfully on the porch
Resting on a cozy blanket
But still as cold as ever!
I'm shaking as the wind blows
I am a timid kitten,
In need of a reassuring hug.

Ciera Miller, Grade 5
Westview Elementary School, OH

Class Time

Class time is not play time
nor time for jokes or games.
Class time is time for books
and teachers and learning
and other kids to be quiet
and being trapped inside…
Class time has one part that
will be very happy for you
and it's lunch and recess
and you're free from class
for one hour and then
you're trapped again!

Shawna Brinley, Grade 5
Henryville Elementary School, IN

Music

Move to the music, feel the beat,
Use your head and use your feet.
Play a guitar, bass and bongo,
Flute, trumpet, and piano.
People really love to sing
Use some bells and make a ring.
Music is the holy king,
Oh, YES, music is my thing!
Rock and roll, and hip and hop,
You will never want to stop.
Please don't play until you get sick
Just praise and love the world's music.

Scott Hevel, Grade 5
Central College Christian Academy, OH

My Dog's Day

Out of my room
down the stairs
into the living room
on the couch
off the couch
through the kitchen
down the hallway
past the door
in the family room
on the couch
into a deep sleep

Hannah Shirey, Grade 5
Rootstown Elementary School, OH

A Cold Winter Day

Rushing down the hill,
your hair blowing in the wind.

You burst into a smile,
from all of the excitement.

You feel very hot,
from all of your clothing.

You touch the snow,
and feel the coldness.

When you're just getting
to enjoy your ride…
PLOP!

You hit the end.
A dead end.

Amanda Boschman, Grade 5
Browning Elementary School, MI

My Super Fun Neighborhood

My neighborhood is a fun place,
here is where it begins.

A lake with people swimming.
A forest growing near my house.
Kids playing baseball outside.
Cars zooming past my house.
Birds chirping in the tree.
People playing by their house.
Kids running for ice cream.
Dogs barking across the street.

See, I told you it is a fun place!

Alex Massey, Grade 5
Allen J. Warren Elementary School, IN

Moon

The moon hangs up at night
The moon looks at us with
her coldness and brightness
Seeing her shadow is
Amazing!

Stephanie Marshment, Grade 5
May V Peck Elementary School, MI

Beanbag

I am a beanbag
Sitting in the corner
Smelling dirty rear ends all day
People squishing me flat…
My stuffing's coming out…
People, go sit somewhere else!

Samantha Comer, Grade 5
Westview Elementary School, OH

Super Spiderlings

S pinning webs, waiting
P erfect prey to eat
I 'm very deadly to my mate!
D angerous, yes I am!
E ating flies as I dine, dine, dine
R un, run, catch that dinner.
L et me hang on to Mom's legs
I t will be fun to eat lunch.
N ets I spin, so fine
G raceful little spinners
S o extremely interesting!

Sarah Swogger, Grade 4
Dobbins Elementary School, OH

Jeremy

Brother
little, annoying
playing, learning, loving
makes everyone smile
Jeremy

Jessica Walland, Grade 6
Tippecanoe Middle School, OH

Indians

The man ran outside
He called out for his people.
There it was. Bison.

Jack Le Boeuf, Grade 6
Barrington Elementary School, OH

The Wobbly Wall

I glance up the wall.
Its swaying and steepness make
it fierce. I'm ready!

Mario Manta, Grade 6
Stanley Clark School, IN

Fall

fall colors, red, orange, brown,
don't forget the yellow,
the fall colors are a beautiful thing,
it has all the apples,
Halloween, with all the candy,
and the costumes
they are scary and pretty
and the Jack-o'-lanterns
oh, how they are scary.

Gwen Winer, Grade 4
Norwich Elementary School, OH

Spinning

Dizzy, dizzy up
Spin around and stop, stop, stop
Walk forward, turn, drop.

Eric Blickensderfer, Grade 6
Stanley Clark School, IN

I Am

I am joyful and friendly
I wonder if I will be a singer
I hear waves call my name
I see music notes everywhere
I want to set a good example for my brothers
I am joyful and friendly

I pretend I am in my own world
I feel the sun shine down on me
I touch the moon with my hands
I worry about my friends and family
I cry when I am sad
I am joyful and friendly

I understand that I cannot get what I want
I say God is real
I dream about everything
I try to get all good grades
I hope my life will be great
I am Hannah Ayar

Hannah Ayar, Grade 4
Floyd Ebeling Elementary School, MI

My Favorite Sunset

My favorite sunset is only once a year,
With beautiful colors right by the pier.
I'd sit there and watch the sunrise
While the scenery had stolen my eyes.

Emily Musenbrock, Grade 5
Washington Township Elementary School, IN

Sun

Flaming, firing ball of gas,
I look upon you
and all I can imagine is a large, magical sphere.
You go away from me at dusk
then at dawn, you rise again.
When I sneak a glance at you,
I see the ultimate answer to everything.
I see everything that once was and is still to become.
I can't think of how such an amber-colored beauty
could be nothing more than a ball of gas.

Sarah Sanford, Grade 6
Melrose Elementary School, OH

When It All Went Down

The air begins to chill
As the sun begins to hide and the sky goes gloom
I feel the pitter-patter of rain of my face
But as they fall,
They dance for they are free
As I feel so wet and damp
I remember that summer's day
When it all went down into the gloomy rain

Jasmine Caldwell, Grade 6
Woodward Park Middle School, OH

The Watch Dog

My owner calls me the guard dog
I sleep in my doghouse by a garage
I will bark at someone I don't know
Someone that I do not know I will lunge at them with my teeth
Then they will move back really fast
They will be afraid of me
Sometime if they move slowly toward me
I am on a long chain so I don't run away
I am a dangerous dog
I can be very fast
I am nice to kids
I am nice dog with my owner

Anthony Clark, Grade 6
North Knox East Elementary/Jr High School, IN

All About Me

Mark
Athletic, friendly, funny, smart
Brother of Grace
Likes video games, pizza, basketball
Who feels happiness
Who needs TV
Who gives kindness
Who fears tornadoes
Who would like to see the Great Wall of China
Lives in Indianapolis, Indiana, United States of America
Silver

Mark Silver, Grade 5
St Jude Catholic School, IN

My Favorite Book

There are many books I know about
only one series I truly love.
The titles are very cool,
there is mystery too.
There are many books like it,
but none are the same.
The author is known for his books
because they are so scary.
You would all have nightmares
just look at the cover!
Goosebumps series.
Beware!
You are in for a scare!

Shawn Zebrak, Grade 4
Midland Academy of Advanced and Creative Studies, MI

Scared

Scared is red,
It tastes like burnt mush.
It smells like a fire in our neighbor's backyard.
It reminds me of no power.
It sounds like firecrackers.
Scared makes me feel red.

Ashley Carter, Grade 5
Tremont Elementary School, OH

Eagle

E ven though the constellation is called eagle, the Greek man was named
A quila. He was a servant of Zeus. He
G ave up his job to be turned into an eagle to punish Prometheus. Aquila ate Prometheus's
L iver until Zeus made him a constellation. The
E agle still shines today.

Dan Kreider, Grade 6
Pinewood Elementary School, IN

St. Patrick's Day

St. Patrick's Day, full of screaming and dreaming and excitement.
There are crisp leaves crunching and people bunching together for this marvelous holiday.
When the flowers start to bloom, everyone sees March's true beauty with their very eyes.

There are glamorous streamers flashing green and gold; the party has almost begun
And the food looks mouth waterin' good.
But when the people have seen what we have done to the place one thing only will drop…
Their mouths.
We have clothed ourselves with clovers and stars,
And downstairs is neat (which at our house is a treat).

There's screaming, whispering, laughing, gossiping,
And most important, party talk.
But today we must pray that no one goes away,
At our spectacular holiday party.

But there are still a few questions I really must know:

Who's staying?
Who's leaving?
Who's eating?
Who's watching TV?
And most importantly, how long until this great war of fun happens again, again, again?

Kevin Fitzgerald, Grade 5
EH Greene Intermediate School, OH

There Is a Jellyfish in My Sister

There is a jellyfish in my sister with tentacles like a force field and a body like a bowl of jello.
It moves like a snail.
It strikes like a bolt of lightning.
It lives in my sister's head and makes her grumpy.
It makes me take cover when she comes into my room for I never know when she'll strike.

Daniel Sanders, Grade 6
St Maria Goretti School, IN

The Hidden Place

As I move the vines, they look like curtains.
Then I see the waterfall flowing down to the beautiful lake.
When I set up birdhouses and bird feeders, all the birds fly in like jets.
The bushes were as soft as pillows.
The sky was as blue as the ocean. The clouds look like folded blankets.
The tree's bark was as hard as concrete.
When I took off my flip-flops, while I was walking on the barefoot soft green grass, it felt like silk.
The tree's leaves chattered in the wind like maracas.
As I sat down on the stump, I looked at my beautiful hidden place that was all mine.

Kylie Morgan, Grade 6
Cloverdale Middle School, IN

Christmas Time

Christmas time is a blast
Even though it comes really fast.

Christmas is a time of giving
And I'm glad that this Christmas I'm living.

We decorate the tree
And sing songs merrily.

We think of our Lord Jesus who was born
As we wake up this Christmas morn.

Lindsey Hansen, Grade 5
Immanuel Christian School, MI

Fall

Fall means leaves changing beautiful colors and
    falling from trees.

Fall brings yummy pumpkin seeds,
    as the smell sweetens my nose.

Windy weather whipping
    through the trees as they helplessly stand!

As the trees stand cold and bare
    their limbs reach up as if arms to worship God.

Thanksgiving brings yummy turkey,
    as we smell the sweet savoring smell of fresh baked turkey.

As the leaves tumble down,
                down,
                        down,
    they cover the ground, holding it like a blanket.

Ali Bourcier, Grade 6
Holy Family Middle School, MI

Mom

Mom
sweet, crabby
caring, encouraging, loving
she really loves me
Parent

Paige Ruesch, Grade 5
Washington Township Elementary School, IN

Jesus Christ

Jesus enters your soul like a wonderful breeze in the wind.
He teaches us the requirements for life.
He's like a car, rolling down its path.
This car has a destination.
Jesus will soon stop and call you home.
That means you have gone through the most wonderful thing…
Life.

Seth Diller, Grade 5
Washington Township Elementary School, IN

Waiting for Winter

Fall has been here, just look around.
The leaves have fallen on the ground.
The sun sets early, the air is cold.
The moon is shining bright and bold.
But where is winter?
Where can it be?
There is no snow as you can see.
I want to make a snowman, and sled down a hill.
I want to drink hot cocoa to take off the chill.
I want to make igloos and angels in the snow.
I want to do it all, don't you know?
But I'll have to wait, it's not time yet.
It's only raining and I don't want to get wet!

Casey Olah, Grade 5
Allen J. Warren Elementary School, IN

All Me All the Time

Courtney
Cool, funny, sporty
Sister of Emily
Lover of basketball, soccer, and Chinese food.
Who feels nervous when I get in trouble
    and on some really BIG roller coasters.
Who gets excited about new clothes
    and basketball practice.
Who needs to read more biography books
    and needs to practice flute for band more.
Who gives kisses to my wonderful mom and cute cat.
Who fears many bugs and the school's principals.
Who would like to play soccer in a stadium
    with David Beckham and Mia Hamm.
Resident of Austintown, Ohio
Macphee

Courtney Macphee, Grade 5
Frank Ohl Intermediate School, OH

Thanksgiving Day

Thanksgiving Day is coming
We all say hooray
Mashed potatoes to eat
Creamy or clumpy
Turkey to eat
A wishbone to find
Make a wish
Hope it comes true
Pies you like
Pies you don't like
Pumpkin, pecan
Apple and many more
Gravy so creamy
Just like soup
To pour on turkey and more
But after this
Comes Christmas, Kwanzaa, and Hanukah

Unyime Usip, Grade 6
Akiva Academy, OH

Apples
Apples
Bumpy, juicy
Juggling, throwing, eating
I feel happy about apples
Apples
Lacy Leffler, Grade 4
Westview Elementary School, OH

Can You Imagine
A printer without paper
A computer without a screen

A yard without grass
A drink without a glass

A bike without a wheel
A foot without a heel

Lunch without food
Fire without wood

A star without a luster
A hot-dog without mustard

School without a book
An eye that can't look

Halloween without a BOO!
A day without you!
Linnea Benson, Grade 4
Stonegate Elementary School, IN

Campfire
Blazing hot ruby sparks burst in the air
Awakening all creatures of the night
Shattering the cold away
Destroying the midnight darkness
Glowing coals burning the wood
Bursting in the air with smoke
Heating the frost on the ground.
Ben Derrenkamp, Grade 6
St Clement Elementary School, OH

My Favorite Things About Christmas
I like playing in the snow
And drinking hot cocoa.
I like baking cookies
And making cards.
I like to trim the tree
And have presents given to me.
I like to shop for presents to wrap,
And maybe even sit on Santa's lap.
I like to see the nativity
And the twinkling lights before me.
Sabrina Barnett, Grade 5
Monroe Elementary School, OH

In a Trash Can...
Inside this trash can there are many smelly things,
Scraps, bad grades, things you don't need anymore,
Food, broken toys, drawings that aren't good, soda cans
Things not meant to be in a trash can.
So many secrets crumbled up
That certain people weren't supposed to see,
So many lost things just thrown away
Because no one claimed them
This trash can holds every last thing people didn't care for.
Inside it are poems, short stories that authors are famous for today.
Now all this stuff is in a square at a dump.
Michael Fleck, Grade 6
St Maria Goretti School, IN

Pick Poppy!
Hi I'm Poppy, the pumpkin, that's me,
Waiting in a pumpkin patch to be chosen,
Uncle Tim is gone,
So is Aunt Edna,
Mom, dad and Sally too,

Here come the kids,
I hope I look my best,
Here comes a girl,
She plucks me from my light green skinny vine,

I am set on paper filled with tragedies, excitement and more,
I feel a sharp pain in my head,
My stomach, heart and brain are plucked one by one from my body,
Soon I'm nothing inside,
In a split second there are two eyebrows where my eyes are,
Two eyes on my nose,
A nose on my mouth,
And a mouth on my chin,
One shimmering candle is placed and rests inside me,
I'm officially a jack-o'-lantern!!!
Alyssa Sanderson, Grade 5
Beck Centennial Elementary School, MI

Winter Images
Winter is full of wonderful things to see such as beautiful white snow,
And brown white tailed deer coming out of the woods.

There are many sounds such as wolves howling at the bright winter moon,
Or bears snoring when they are asleep for the winter.

And you can feel many things such as cold snow on the earth,
Fuzzy warm sweaters, and furry boots I wear to keep me warm.

And what I taste is hot chocolate, and Christmas dinner.
And things I smell are ham, turkey, and stuffing my family cooks.

What I love most of all is my family and I together
And giving to all the people we love and care for.
Cierra New, Grade 6
Erie Elementary School, OH

I Am

I am athletic.
I wonder what is going on in the world.
I hear a lot of people talking.
I see candy land.
I want all the rock candy in the world.
I am athletic.

I pretend I'm playing in a rock band.
I feel happy when I'm drawing.
I touch my brother's DS game.
I worry that I will never learn how to read.
I cry when my family is sick.
I am athletic.

I understand our economy is not good.
I say I believe in God.
I dream I was playing with monkeys.
I try to learn how to read.
I hope to get a lap top.
I am athletic.

Kyle Campbell, Grade 4
Floyd Ebeling Elementary School, MI

What Moves Me

S occer moves me when I kick the ball up in the field
O r when I dribble the ball up the field
C rying mom when I make a goal
C heering parents when I get the ball
E xciting games until it stops
R acing up the field for the ball

Davey Young, Grade 5
Central Academy, OH

Love

Love can be easy
Love can be hard
Love is tricky
Love is how you sign a card
Love heals horrible pain
Love lights a dark lane
Love is a single flower
Love is such a great power
Love helps me and you
Love can renew
Love is what I feel
Love is positive
Love is cool
Love is like a rule
Love is how I solve problems
Love is a promise
Love is grand
Love is one touch of a hand
Love is your mom giving you a funny hairdo
I can feel it how about you?

Caroline Piecuch, Grade 6
St Gerard School, MI

Getting the Christmas Tree Ready

I go into the large green wood
To find the perfect Christmas tree.
I find it, I cut it down,
Then carry it back with glee.

I stare at my tree again
And know that it is great.
I get out a box of ornaments
Then I start to decorate.

I love to use colored lights
So the tree doesn't look plain.
I wrap them around the tree
And they look like stripes on a candy cane.

Now that the tree is done
I just have to wait for Santa.
This is going to be the best Christmas ever,
A Christmas extravaganza.

Jared Roth, Grade 5
Central Grade School, MI

Dad

D ads buy you things
A dad is good to you and protects you
D ads take you places like four-wheeler riding

Dustin Cassidy, Grade 5
Perry Central Elementary School, IN

Halloween

F airies laughing with moms by their sides
A nnoying kids up and down the street
L aughing Batmen from house to house
L ittle things that make Halloween.

Diana Whitten, Grade 6
Eisenhower Middle School, OH

Snow at Night

I walk through the glimmering rainbow, as the sun sets,
The air bites at my breath colder and colder,
I run, run through the light, and through the dark,
No reason to stop,
The trees seem to follow me through the snow,
The cold warms my hair, wet with thoughts,
I love this time of year,
I run past frozen lakes and the horizon,
Falling into the crystal flakes face first.
I laugh and look out across the stars,
The moon renews my energy,
Who needs the sun? Who needs the day?
The night is so brisk, and wonderful,
The snow falls with shapes of sparkling flowers,
Each more complex than the other.
The stars sure shine this time of year.

Teagan Storch, Grade 6
Black River Education Center, OH

My Little Fur Ball

My little kitten's name is Chloe.
Chloe is a big ball of fur,
like her mom.
Chloe and me play in the leaves.
Chloe and me watch TV.
I made Chloe a bed
but she jumps in bed with me anyway.
Chloe runs at me when I open the door.
I love Chloe so much.
It will be sad when I have to move.
I will miss her so much.
I love Chloe so much.

Morgan Bentley, Grade 4
Licking Valley Intermediate School, OH

Race Cars

Machines
Loud, exciting
Speeding, passing, crashing
Going until they see the flag
Winning

Daniel Becker, Grade 4
Riverside Elementary School, MI

Kathleen Keck

K ind
A thletic
T ruthful
H elpful
L ovable
E nergetic
E ncouraging
N ever gives up

K ind of silly
E xcellent at math
C aring
K atie is my nickname

Kathleen Keck, Grade 4
Sts Joseph and John School, OH

Christmas

Christmas is a joy,
Full of love and happiness,
Friends and family!

Gabriella Saputo, Grade 5
May V Peck Elementary School, MI

Winter

Winter
freezing, cold
cooking, ice fishing, sledding
snowing, beautiful, white, flakes
Winter

Benjamin Dubois, Grade 5
Floyd Ebeling Elementary School, MI

Winter

The snowflakes cold touch on my skin,
The beauty of the different shapes and designs of each unique one.
A snowman sits outside in the cold winter chill,
Dreading the day summer would come.
Snowballs whiz through the air,
The sparkling laughs of many ecstatic children fill the air.
The season when hot chocolate is famous,
The time when snow cones and icy delights are retired.
When sledding and skiing,
Are just the beginning.
Through blizzards through snowstorms,
Winter brings joy to many people.

Hope Chen, Grade 6
Boulan Park Middle School, MI

Christmas Time Is Here!

I sit around the Christmas tree, with festive ornaments and luminous lights,
This night is like no other, restless in bed, thoughts racing through my head.
Christmas Time is here!
I smell Santa Claus' crisp chocolaty cookies baking; I wonder if I can have one?
Everyone makes me speculate what my presents are; a toy, a game, is it joyful or lame?
Christmas Time is here!
Christmas music is a beautiful sound, laughter and children running around.
Snow from outside shines white light into the room,
There's not a fright in the world, everyone's as joyful as a puppy.
Christmas Time is here!

Shea Cronin, Grade 5
EH Greene Intermediate School, OH

Here in Afghanistan…

Because of the Taliban, I must wear a chador,
To cover my head and my face, when I go out the door.
Mother must wear a long, dress-like burqa when not at home,
Like every other Afghani woman wherever they roam.

Because of the Taliban, every man must grow a beard,
They're long, and they're itchy, and may never be sheared.
We women and girls can't be pretty from the use of nail polish.
There are so many things we enjoyed the cruel Taliban abolished!

Because of the Taliban, our beloved music is gone,
Not from voice, not from radio, not a single song.
Because they could give us hope, no more televisions are in sight.
We need help, we are miserable, this is our plight.

Because of the Taliban, life is horrible; it used to be fun.
We flew kites, had school, played games, and got to just run.
Our faces were free, and we had food in plenty,
But those were the old days, now bombs fall in twenties!

Because of the Taliban, if you steal or break a rule,
You'll be jailed, beat, killed, or lose a limb — not cool!
I hate the Taliban; they make me angry and depressed,
The Talibs just make life bad, we are so oppressed.

Sophia Bryson, Grade 6
Ann Arbor Christian School, MI

Fall
Leaves twirl all around
Trees start to go to sleep now
The weather has changed
Alyssa DeJoan, Grade 4
Frank H Hammond Elementary School, IN

One
One word can save a life —
One feeling can say a lot.
One life is all we have —
One wish is all we get.
One season can make you smile —
One art collage can be magnificent.
One glance is all it takes —
One thing can be gone in a breath.
One act of kindness can make a difference —
One pencil can start a book.
One animal can start a zoo —
One idea can shape the future.
One person can show you the way —
One scrape can cause tears.
One dream can lead to adventure —
One butterfly can brighten any day.
One prayer can change everything —
So you see, it's all up to me.

Olivia Akerly, Grade 6
St. Gerard School, MI

Sand, Oh Sand
As you walk on the beach,
and feel the breeze
you remember the good ol' days
out at the sea.

The sand running through your toes,
as you walk step by step
the memories embraced,
is what you call this.
Sand, oh sand.
Madison B. Nichols, Grade 6
Emmanuel-St Michael Lutheran School, IN

Cake!
MMM!! Mommy baked a cake today,
Luscious, scrumptious cake!

With butter cream filling and ice cream on top,
I'm drooling at the very thought!

I tried to get some frosting, but all I got was a frown!

Mommy said, "No cake for you!
Aunty gets some first and then Uncle Lou,
George and Tom come all before you!"
Samantha Kane, Grade 6
St Patrick School, MI

I Am
I am awesome and sporty
I wonder if I'll be a MLB player
I hear screaming fans
I see myself playing baseball with Magillo Ordonez
I want a trillion dollars
I am awesome and sporty

I pretend I hit home runs every time I bat
I feel happy at 3:15
I touch the bat and glove
I worry about bad weather
I cry when I get hurt
I am awesome and sporty

I understand that my whole family likes Spartans
I say I'm awesome
I dream of being a motor cross expert
I try to do my best
I hope that I get *Guitar Hero World Tour* for my birthday
I am awesome and sporty

I am Aaron Ferdinande
Aaron Ferdinande, Grade 4
Floyd Ebeling Elementary School, MI

Kayla
K ind
A lways fun to be around
Y oung
L ively
A nimals she loves
Courtney Nice, Grade 5
West Washington Elementary School, IN

If I Ruled the World
Nobody would be poor
Everyone would have a home
No more wars
Lower gas prices
Make a lot of things free
Everyone should be treated fair
Don't destroy animals' habitat
Do the 3 R's, reduce, reuse, recycle
Everyone should have a good education
Try to protect animals that are becoming extinct
There will always be world peace
No summer schools, but! Let there be punishment
Make sure people have their basic needs
Every person is healthy and has food and shelter
Respect everyone as they would respect you
Cut down school hours
Have more classes about Spelling
Wish everyone had a friend
Change the world from BAD to GOOD!
Olivia Hubbard, Grade 5
Sanderson Elementary School, OH

John McCain
Honest
War soldier
I wish he won
Senator of Arizona
He cares
Jack Holman, Grade 5
Tremont Elementary School, OH

Gymnastics
Awesome, sporty
Exciting, amazing, entertaining
Always enjoyed — never boring
Interesting, working, helping
Fun, enjoyable
Me
Kelly Hines, Grade 5
St Jude Catholic School, IN

Nature
The wind wandering through the trees,
Gardeners cutting weeds,
Nature is the way of life,
Wake up with the morning light,

Nature will never end,
Animals will never be banned,
Take very good care of the earth,
And earth will take care of you,

Nature is great,
Nature makes a beautiful day,
Have fun before life ends,
The world is in our hands.
Tristian Siglin, Grade 6
Erie Elementary School, OH

Puppy/Dog
Puppy
Biting, playful
Barking, destroying, chewing
Silly, energetic — calm, peaceful
Bigger, stronger, faster
Lazy, guarding
Dog
Kelsey Jackson, Grade 6
Helfrich Park Middle School, IN

Autumn
A lways falling leaves
U nexpected season
T rick-or-treat season
U ntouched beauty of fall
M uffins and cider
N o hot weather anymore.
Brooke Ruffin, Grade 6
Eisenhower Middle School, OH

A Walk in the Winter
Lights adorn the evergreens,
where birds are nestled snug.

Snowmen with happy smiles,
that warm just like a hug.

The wreaths in windows bows on doors,
bells and mistletoes.

Santa and his reindeer,
can see candles bright.

Follow lanterns and stars,
that shine in the night.

Colorful candy canes,
and skaters hand in hand.

To walk around on Christmas Eve,
is a step to fairyland.
Lauren McLean, Grade 5
Browning Elementary School, MI

Green
Green is the grass.
That we step on all the time.
It disappears during the winter.
Green are vegetables.
Keeping us healthy all the time.
Green is all around us.
Without green we would be dead.
We write on green all the time.
We use green a lot.
It is the most important color in our life.
We buy goods we need and want.
Green is not just a color.
It is our way of life.
Eric Wills, Grade 6
Harding Middle School, OH

Ohio
Ohio is a state.
Ohio has a river, the Ohio River.
Ohio has tall mountains.
Ohio is where lots of people live.
Ohio's state capital is Columbus.
Ohio is a beautiful state.
Ashley McClain, Grade 4
Legend Elementary School, OH

Luscious Waters
Luscious, clear water
Full of amazement and joy
Surprisingly, free.
Dylan Durham, Grade 5
Westview Elementary School, OH

Animals
There are some that are cute
Some get the boot
They are very crazy
There are some that are just lazy
Some hate the cold
Others just don't care they're so old
Some like to hoot
Others like to toot
Many animals are very beautiful
Few animals are crippled
Many are fluffy
Some are just bulky
I love animals yes I do
My favorite animal is a kangaroo
Lexi Carpenter, Grade 6
Mayfield Elementary School, OH

A Fantastic Game
I see the bat hit the ball.
It makes a loud sound.
I taste the dirt.
From diving for the ball.
Yuck!
I smell the fresh cut grass.
I touch the bat when I get ready to hit.
Paul Kirk, Grade 4
Licking Valley Intermediate School, OH

October
Squirrels scamper
around the immense oak tree
collecting nuts to bury
they fluff their fur to keep warm
rabbits put on their winter overcoat
excavate a burrow woodchucks stir
they fatten up for hibernation
the birds soar south and
humans guzzle frigid apple cider
as for me,
I am the owl who hoots and observes.
Joseph Mets, Grade 5
Beck Centennial Elementary School, MI

Morning Dove, O' Morning Dove
Morning Dove, O' Morning Dove,
Gracefully flying overhead.
Dipping and diving unable to catch.
Morning Dove, O' Morning Dove,
So gray as a rock.
But a dove can move.
The lonely rock cannot move or see.
Morning Dove, O' Morning Dove,
Cannot see at night.
The dove is sleeping in a twig nest.
Matt Szczerbinski, Grade 5
Kenowa Hills Intermediate School, MI

Christmas Is Nearing

Gifts are for giving
also receiving
carols I hear them singing
jingle bells are ringing
families gathering
everyone exchanging
gifts we will soon be opening
now it's time to be sleeping
soon children will be waking
happy faces they will be making
for Christmas is exciting
Christmas will be nearing
soon kids will be cheering

Morgan Cox, Grade 5
West Washington Elementary School, IN

What a Day

Oh, what a wonderful day it was
I remember it like it was yesterday
I woke up early to the morning sun
I grabbed my favorite pair of jeans
Grabbed my boots and helmet
Running to the barn with breakfast in hand
Tacking up very quickly
Out of the barn we went
Her golden brown bay coat
Her black mane as dark as the night sky
Loping, not quickly, but fast to me
Riding through the woods we went
The little critters scurrying
Ridding, petting, and loving her
My horse, my very own

Suzanna Postma, Grade 6
Crown Point Christian School, IN

The Beach

The beach. Oh how I love the beach.
The soft and smooth white sand.
It's stunningly beautiful with a large crowd and
now and then an ice cream stand.
I smell the salty ocean. I take in a breath of air.
It's a beautiful day and it's good to see children playing there.
I look out to the ocean and wonder if it's true
that among the fish in the sea there are mermaids watching you.
The sun has gone down. The beach is quiet.
But, I don't mind that there's no riot.
I see the moon and the stars.
I hear no sound but the waves and passing cars.
I get up from the ground
and take a last look around.
I walk down the street
feeling simply beat.
I hate to go.
But, I tell myself, "I'll be back tomorrow."

Mary Devore, Grade 5
Michiana Christian Montessori School, IN

Dreams

Not all dreams happen while you're asleep.
Some dreams happen while you're in a Jeep.
Or a train, or a plane or just standing there.
Some dreams happen while you're combing your hair.

Dreams aren't just for night time, they're for any time of day,
In the classroom, the lunch room, at work or at play.
Dreams are conversations that we have with our self.
Or fantastic discussions with the toys on the shelf.

They're our hopes and our dreams for the future ahead
Our subconscious thoughts that float through our heads
When reason starts to fade and your soul starts to talk
Grab the leash off the wall and take your brain for a walk.

So dream as you will and as much as you want
Take yourself to the world's most magical spot
There's no limit to what we can do
When we dream a great dream and discover something new.

Sadie Simon, Grade 6
Abbott Middle School, MI

Stanaitis, Arthritis, Laryngitis…Who Am I

Following me so closely, like a boa
Getting tighter and tighter
Is the name Stanaitis,
It does not trip me, but makes others stumble;

"Is it a disease,
A virus, an achy pain?"
Or
"Is that even a real name or just a bunch of letters?"

Although Stanaitis travels with me
Wherever I go,
It takes a long time
Until it is spoken with the correct pronunciation.

Though, still I accept my name with pride
No matter how it is spoken,
Because it is unique and special in many ways,
For I am the last Stanaitis.

As I will often tell those who question
That I am not a disease or virus
But from time to time, an achy pain I am.

Kaitlin Stanaitis, Grade 6
Harding Middle School, OH

Sioux and Buffalo

The Sioux tribe ate buffalo.
Their teepees were made of their hide.
Where the buffalo went, they would follow,
The buffalo were always nigh.

Evan Rodgers, Grade 5
Barrington Elementary School, OH

I Hurt My Arm Today

I hurt my arm today
It twisted in a way
that I screamed
I prayed it would heal
but I gave another shrill
I was walking down the hall
when I
f
  e
    l
      l
        and twisted it
Now it's in a sling
At least my arm has a little swing
Aaron Hochstetler, Grade 5
Heritage Intermediate School, IN

Halloween

H owling in the night
A rmloads of candy
L icorice sticks by the dozen
L adies and men handing out treats
"**O** ne at a time" says the ticket taker
W hisper scary stories to friends
E nter the haunted house!
E ntertain your friends with jokes
N ow go home and trade your treats
Molly Crosley, Grade 5
St Jude Catholic School, IN

Fall

Looks like trees and leaves
Sounds like leaves crinkling
Tastes like apples from trees
Feels like wind blowing
Smells like burning wood
Michael Oliver, Grade 5
Northfield Baptist Christian School, OH

Dogs

D ogs are furry creatures
O n a summers day they love to play
G oing to the vet is a threat
S o they get a treat to sit quietly.
Briana J. Lowe, Grade 6
Trilby Elementary School, OH

When Friends Are Together

When friends are together
The angels sing songs of joy
Songs with perfect tunes.
When friends are together
The sun meets the moon.
A perfect time.
Regan Dilley, Grade 4
St. John's Lutheran School, OH

Texting

I got a text from my BFF Sadie.
It said, "LOL my mom is a crazy lady."
"She took my computer and started to yell."
"If I don't finish my chores, she's going to take my cell."

So I texted Evelyn with what Sadie had to say.
She typed back, "OMG R U JK?"
I sent back, "No but BRB"
Because now Katie was texting me.

Katie asked, "Did you hear about Sadie's mom?"
"Sadie told me she went off like a nuclear bomb!"
I replied with, "Yeah and as far as I can tell Sadie might just lose her cell."
Katie wrote back saying, "If Sadie loses her cell, I might just have to yell."

"Oh great now I can't feel either thumb."
"All this texting made them both go numb."
"This is insane, I mean OMG."
"Pick up the phone and just call me!"

Cassandra Leslie, Grade 6
Abbott Middle School, MI

If I Was in Charge of the World

No torturing animals
Make a NW Passageway across the world
Lower gas prices
Make sure everyone has a home
Make cures for cancer
Try to save every animal
Lower some food prices
Make sure everyone has food and water
Give Christmas presents to little kids that don't have much
Make some schools safer
Make sure bad people don't try to hurt other people
For Thanksgiving make sure everyone has a feast to eat
Change in some countries that they can believe in what they want to
Send our soldiers a big meal for Christmas and Thanksgiving
Get rid of drugs and violence
Don't make kindergarten go all day
Make better health care
Make sure everyone in a nursing home is taken good care of
Let kids go on more field trips
Make sure people are respectful to our flag
Jessie Six, Grade 5
Sanderson Elementary School, OH

My Desire for the Mystery Island

Sandy, wet, wavy beaches
Active volcanoes like boiling pots of water
Clickity, clank goes the Sugar Cane train as it chugs through the fields
Sweet, juicy pineapple and sweet, warm bread
make me feel like a hibernating bear
Relaxing days with rainbows in the afternoon
I long to be in Hawaii
Grant Gleason, Grade 6
Holy Angels School, OH

8:00!

Sitting there
Very impatient
Watching the snow fall
Like a bunch of marshmallows
Presents sitting in front of me
Come on clock!!!
8:00!
"WAKE UP! WAKE UP!
IT'S CHRISTMAS!"

Victoria Chambers, Grade 4
Midland Academy of Advanced and Creative Studies, MI

November Is

November is the time when gentle, icy snowflakes fall,
each one has a different pattern,
like us, who have our own unique shape and personality,

November is the moon that glows on us,
like the sun that shines upon us,
the shimmering stars gather 'round,
waiting for a story to be told,
by mother moon's smiling face,

November is steaming hot cocoa, with melting chocolate chips,
giving a swirling, mouth watering scent,
marshmallows floating around like toy boats,
mixing vanilla sprinkles for a colorful finishing touch.

Yasmin Gad, Grade 5
Beck Centennial Elementary School, MI

The Soft Crackle of the Dia

I concentrate as I guide
The rough wooden match through the air
The Dia with its gold and red glitter
Across its green painted body.

As the wick flamed to life with a dancing fire upon it
The room filled with a great feeling
As fast as a hawk dives for its prey
Everyone fills up with the feeling of happiness
In the blink of an eye
In the dim room filled with the glow of the Dia.

Now I ask myself
Does he feel as happy as me?
Is that present mine?
If so what is in it?
Many questions I ask few answered.

But then that feeling swells back up
As I hear the laughter and talking
Of my friends and family.
Wow, what an
Amazing, amazing, amazing feeling.

Animesh Bapat, Grade 5
EH Greene Intermediate School, OH

Ode to Feet

My feet help me walk,
They help me stand up straight.
They take a lot of weight,
Yet they never fail.
Even if they are sore,
They never complain.
I am happy because I am not my feet,
For I alone cannot support more than 45 pounds.
So I thank you my feet,
For helping me stay up to beat.

Susmita Roy, Grade 6
Birchwood School, OH

Sunrise

Every day, I rise up and out of my bed.
I open the blinds to see how good of a day it is.
I see the sun rising out of the cloud,
and in the valley, I see the sunrise above and beyond the valley.
Oh, what glorious light it is and what wonders.
It is the view from the bed.
It's a shame — why not go outside
and be there for real?
So, I get my clothes on
and run outside.
But it has disappeared.
What a gorgeous song of the light
when I see a sunrise.

Sikander Jalhaul, Grade 6
Melrose Elementary School, OH

Gifts

G iving.
I 'll get a gift.
F or you are a gift
T o me.
S o we all get gifts.

Jared Bills, Grade 5
West Washington Elementary School, IN

Dawn Rising

The sky was streaked with colors like a painting
The breeze was as fresh as the first snow in winter
I could hear the crickets speaking to one another
The clouds looked as swift as a silk blanket
I didn't see any animals, none at all
They were as quiet as a pin dropping
I walked on the ground, it felt stiff
The ground felt rough like rocks
I couldn't hear anything but the wind chimes
The music felt quiet, but it was loud
It sounded like a flute
The sun cracked behind the clouds
Like a single candle in a cave
The dawn rising looked as beautiful as heaven

Prathyusha Mahasamudram, Grade 6
Boulan Park Middle School, MI

If a Shark Got Braces

If a shark got braces
How much would it cost

If a shark got braces
How long would it take

If a shark got braces
How bad would it hurt

If a shark got braces
Would they rust — would they break,

If a shark got braces
would it matter what they ate…?
TOO LATE!

Ian Bomberger, Grade 5
Heritage Intermediate School, IN

A True Friend

A true friend is kind.
A true friend can be small.
A true friend can be tall.
A true friend doesn't bully.
A true friend shares ideas.
A true friend shares interests.
A true friend stands up for you.
A true friend helps you.
A true friend can be young.
A true friend can be real.
A true friend can be imaginary.
A true friend hangs out with you.
A true friend won't fight you.
A true friend keeps your secrets.
Anyone can be a friend,
But it takes someone special to be
A true friend.

Matthew Dake, Grade 6
St Gerard School, MI

Pumpkins

Pumpkins
Are great
Delicious pumpkin pie
Chewing, eating, pumpkin pie
Pie

Shawn Conklin, Grade 4
Bailly Elementary School, IN

Christmas Trees

I did the bead chains,
You did the ornaments,
They did the lights,
We turned it on,
It was a great Christmas tree!

Tyler Stoker, Grade 6
Harmon Middle School, OH

Farmer

We feed the pigs well
Our black cows are nice and fat
Horses have long tails.

Jace Perdue, Grade 4
Westview Elementary School, OH

Kittens

Kittens are playful.
Kittens know their way around.
Kittens are cuddly.
Kittens are cute.
Kittens are lovable.
Kittens are soft.
Kittens play with you.
But they are just kittens.
They don't know better.
Kittens are really smart.
I have seven kittens.
I love my kittens so much.

Paige Bailey, Grade 4
Legend Elementary School, OH

Winter

Winter
Winter is the best
You can make a snowman
So get bundled up.

Leanne Smiley, Grade 5
May V Peck Elementary School, MI

Rabbits

Rabbits
Graze in the grass
They jump all around
Fuzzy, bouncing, eating, drinking
Fur balls

Taylor Rodman, Grade 4
Riverside Elementary School, MI

Can You Imagine

A dog without a bark
A match without a spark

A bee without a hive
A diver that won't dive

A cloud without a sky
A heart that will not die

A cat that doesn't meow
An Indian that doesn't say "how"

An ant that's not a bug
A mom without a hug

Jacob Benson, Grade 4
Stonegate Elementary School, IN

Personality of Jacob

J ubilant and happy that's
A lways me, and not
C arefree, I'm a member
O f a team, I love
B aseball and that's part of me

D oes listen to parents
O n a daily basis, I'm
N eplusultra in all my work,
A ll time sports lover, on time
L uckily on the
D ot

D ogs are my favorite animal
O n my scale, I love to
R un around the
B lock and ride my bike
I n the street
S wimming is something I like to do
H ow about you?

Jacob Donald Dorbish, Grade 5
Frank Ohl Intermediate School, OH

Football/Baseball

Football
Push, block
Smashing, tackling, passing
Intercepts, kickoffs, swings, throws
Running, pitching, batting
Hit, tag out
Baseball

Ben Montgomery, Grade 6
Holy Angels School, OH

Karate

I like karate,
I like it a lot.
There are tournaments
And a belt order.
In tournaments,
You can fight, do a routine,
And a self-defense.
But you don't want it to hurt
Because you get intense.
Karate has belts,
Ten to be exact
The belt order is
Hard to extract.
White, yellow, orange,
Green, purple, blue,
Red, brown, black-white,
And black.
Now!
What do you think about that?

Meryl Schor, Grade 6
Akiva Academy, OH

Fall

The colorful leaves
fell from their home
like a rainbow in the sky
as they hit the ground.

The pumpkins
grow big and round.
They look like a bunch of orange dots
as they are ready to be sold.

The cold wind
whistles and turns
through the trees
as it nips at your nose.

As Halloween
sneaks up behind you,
all the children pop out like a bunch of fireflies
because of their neon tape.

Benjamin Christe, Grade 6
Holy Family Middle School, MI

Ten Little Frogs

Ten little frogs walking in a line
one frog swerved and then there were nine.
Nine little frogs went on a date
one kissed a girl and then there were eight.
Eight little frogs were going to heaven
one fried in the sun and then there were seven.
Seven little frogs playing with sticks
one got tripped and then there were six.
Six little frogs went for a dive
one got lost and then there were five.
Five little frogs walk through a door
one tried running and then there were four.
Four little frogs climbing up a tree
one fell off and then there were three.
Three little frogs picking up a screw
one got hit and then there were two.
Two little frogs having some fun
one got too crabby and then there were one.
One little frog was lying in the sun he was burnt
and then there were none.

Victoria Wynsma, Grade 6
Crown Point Christian School, IN

Freedom

F ighting for our rights as a nation
R emembering the veterans that fought in the American wars
E veryone can make a difference
E ncouraging people to vote
D eaths in the middle of the chaos
O ne of the strongest nations in North America
M any parents watching their children go to war

Christopher Voight, Grade 5
Sanderson Elementary School, OH

I Am

I am crazy and athletic
I wonder how I am going to look when I am older
I hear birds chirping
I see a fade of darkness
I want to be a vet
I am crazy and athletic

I pretend I am in a beautiful meadow
I feel wind blowing through my hair
I touch the dark sky
I worry about my reading level
I cry when someone dies
I am crazy and athletic

I understand when I get bad grades
I say God is real
I try so hard to get A's on my work sheets
I hope my sister has nothing wrong with her
I am Hannah Marie Fotion

Hannah Marie Fotion, Grade 4
Floyd Ebeling Elementary School, MI

Water Parks

I love water parks because of all the fun.
When I go on a slide. How we go in a tube.
When it's completely dark. Plunging in the water.
Getting hit by waves. That is what moves me.

Jake Yazell, Grade 5
Miller Ridge Elementary School, OH

The Envies of Summer, Winter, and Spring

A growing country
And a home to many a creation
A silken thread of the purest white
Snares the blessing gifts of trees

Blazing rockets flutter by
Goal is to survive the frost
Fallen stars find thy shelter
And make thou comfortable

Shattered crystal lying still
Often doused in aqua
Eight slender trees fall into line

Their skin sheds so much
You can see their spine
A shining beacon worthy of Midas
Shedding golden wonder

Waving sadness lost and forgotten
Not needed in the evening
A wondrous creation of Arachne
Stretched on a loom of nature

William Bradford Hastie Loner, Grade 6
University Liggett School, MI

Freedom

F reedom that we have because
veterans fought for us
R ed, white, and blue are
America's colors
E very brave soldier fighting
for the people
E veryone should know
the National Anthem
D ay and night soldiers are
protecting us
O ur flag is very important
to our country
M ay we thank all the veterans

Kristen Appleton, Grade 5
Sanderson Elementary School, OH

Snow

The gentle snow is falling,
I hear my mother calling,
I really have to go inside,
The snow and I will have to bide.

From my window,
I see it resting on a tree,
It looks so beautiful,
A wondrous sight to see.

Snow!
Rachel Hogue, Grade 5
Central Grade School, MI

Christmas

Christmas is loving,
time to love your family more,
Christmas is awesome.
Jerry Bennett, Grade 5
May V Peck Elementary School, MI

The Cherry

s
t
e
m
crunch
crunch crunch
red red red red
cherry cherry cherry
red cherry cherry cherry
cherry cherry cherry cherry
cherry Ouch! A pit! cherry
red cherry cherry cherry
red red red red
crunch crunch
crunch
Mackenzie Kirkham, Grade 4
Bailly Elementary School, IN

Darkness

The darkness creeps up around me, like a wolf stalking its prey
A tear rolls down my cheek, as frightful thoughts fill my head
I curl up in a ball and lie down on the floor, as silent as a thought
Darkness
My pupils blacken, and stare into the abyss as if they are frozen
I am scared, like a deer running for its life from a hunter
Noises echo in my head
My eyelids shut, and I fall asleep
As quickly as a mouse scurrying across the floor
Darkness
My eyes snap open
My body jolts
Two vivid glowing eyes stare at me from a distance
They come closer, and closer, and closer
Until they are close enough to touch
Darkness
The eyes vanish
Where did they go?
I try to stand up, but lack the strength
Again, my eyelids shut
But this time…
I sleep peacefully

Mark Elinski, Grade 6
Boulan Park Middle School, MI

I Am

I am cool and funny.
I wonder what my report card will look like.
I hear water burp.
I see the Telly Tubbies in my house.
I want a million dollars.
I am cool and funny.
I pretend to read a book.
I feel mad when my mom takes Santa Claus to dinner and not me.
I touch a talking scarecrow.
I worry when I get bad grades.
I cry when I have to go to scary stuff during Halloween.
I am cool and funny.
I understand I am not smart.
I say Santa is real.
I dream only scary dreams.
I try to do school work.
I hope I get a good job when I grow up.
I am cool and funny.

Kenny Matthews, Grade 6
Galesburg-Augusta Middle School, MI

A Sunset for a Few Seconds

Orange, purple, yellow, and red stripes burst out from every side of the sunset.
All around me I hear the roar of zooming cars going by Notre Dame at dusk.
I'm caught in the last rays that shine on the glistening Golden Dome.
It looks like the only gold coin left in the world.
I freeze for a second and turn slowly into the magical light.
For that split second I feel free.

Amy Diamond, Grade 5
Stanley Clark School, IN

What a Day

What a day!
A white day!
Down I go, ready for snow.
There it is! As white as cotton!
Little lizard, scratching away, ready for a fun day.
What a sight, so colorful;
Needles on the floor,
Everywhere!

Tiny tracks outside;
Light streaming, drapes floating,
Room engulfed in peaceful light, quiet hush.
Quiet music behind me, pancake smell in front of me.
And, oh! What a tree! All of the ornaments in front of me!
Snow crunch, pancake munch;
Sweet, gooey honey

In the snow, ready to go;
Speeding sown the hill, what a thrill!
So bright!
Inside, presents wait, hiding under the tree.
We all gather, ready for joy;
My heart beats *thump, thump, thump!*

Misha Sweeney, Grade 5
EH Greene Intermediate School, OH

Special Memories

There are so many special feelings so often unspoken,
But it seems right to let you know today,
How wonderful it's always been to have you for a friend,
The kind who means so much in every way.

Sarepta Courtney, Grade 5
Perry Central Elementary School, IN

Friendship

Friendship is as loving as a heart
Friendship is the sweet nectar of a flower
Friendship is the warmth of a hug
Friendship is the blow of the kiss
Friendship is more valuable than 50 pounds of gold
Friendship is the sweet smile of a person
Friendship is the bright sunshine in the sky
Friendship opens up a human's mind
Friendship is a colorful horizon
Friendship is helping each other reach goals
Friendship is having a Sleepover
Friendship is as beautiful as a daisy
Friendship tastes as good as a caramel apple
Friendship smells as good as perfume
Friendship sounds like a kid laughing
Friendship feels like the warmth of a campfire
Friendship looks like the waves in the hazardous sea
A friend is greater than inheriting the gold throne
Friendship is the bond between Patrick and SpongeBob

Rishi Kayathi, Grade 5
Indus Center for Academic Excellence, MI

About Me

Chad
Athletic, intelligent, funny, helpful
Brother of Rachel
Likes chocolate, friends, the Colts
Who feels great when the Colts win
Who needs sports
Who gives friendship
Who fears the Patriots winning the Super Bowl
Who would like to see a Yankees game
Lives in Indianapolis, IN, U.S.A.
Ramsey

Chad Ramsey, Grade 5
St Jude Catholic School, IN

The Fall

The leaves crunch beneath my feet.
Autumn arrives like an owl, quick and silent.
The air is cool; the leaves crunch,
And fall is in the air.

The crispy leaves crunch and fall.
The wind whispers like whistling birds.
The birds are a choir, singing on and on.
Their songs are a beautiful melody.

Halloween finally arrives with lots of candy.
All the kids dress up and trick-or-treat.
The costumes are scary and frightening.
Everyone gets a waterfall of candy.

Trevor Ambroziak, Grade 6
Holy Family Middle School, MI

Boats

Riding on boats is so peaceful and so calming.
The water goes back and forth,
That makes the boat move slow as the fish go by in the water.
The wind blows as the boats go by
And it makes your hair fly as the fish jump so high.
As the wind blows the boats go so fast,
And it makes the trees and grass blow so fast.
It's getting dark as the sunset goes by,
Which makes the flowers glow so light.
Now the sun's down and it's so-so dark.
Now all the animals go to sleep!

Ashley Pister, Grade 4
Immanuel Scholars Home School Academy, IN

I Am From...

I am from green, white, and gold.
I am from a big family with many cousins.
I am from an iPod playing music.
I am from a house always loud and busy.
I am from crazy friends and siblings.
I am from the month of happiness and hearts.

Emily Bullard, Grade 6
St Maria Goretti School, IN

Cheyenne

C ute
H umble
E nergetic
Y oung
E verlasting fun
i **N** dependent
N ice
E ntertaining

Atea Taylor, Grade 6
Eastmoor Middle School, OH

Christmas

People in the malls
shopping everywhere.

Christmas trees and decorations
in every house and lawn
presents under the Christmas tree.

Lots of snow on the ground
Snowmen on the lawn
Christmas is finally here.

Julie Wilson, Grade 5
May V Peck Elementary School, MI

My Dog Shelby

S oft and fluffy
H alf Husky half Lab
E ats dog food
L ovable and fun
B ushy tail
Y ellowish brown fur

Jared Seger, Grade 6
Holy Angels School, OH

Palm Trees

palm trees so tall
with long green branches
hanging down so softly
when the gentlest of breeze
touches one of the leaves
and make a rustling sound
oh, how I love the sound of rustling
palm trees

Faith Swieringa, Grade 5
Kenowa Hills Intermediate School, MI

My Father

F aithful
A mazing
T ruthful
H ero
E ncouraging
R esponsible

Jenna Haldeman, Grade 5
St Jude Catholic School, IN

My Crazy Cats

I like to play with my cats,
They look really cute in hats.
We run around the yard,
We play really hard.
We run around and play,
Every single day.
Sometimes my cats are bad,
That makes my dad really mad.
They climb on the screen,
That makes me really mean.
They climb up the trees,
In a really cool breeze.
When I pet them on their fur,
I get to hear them purr.
But if they get too far,
They might get hit by a car.

Brooke Dougan, Grade 4
Chrisney Elementary School, IN

Friday

It's Friday, it's Friday,
There is nothing to do
Except stay at home and
Watch TV 'til 2.

It's Friday, it's Friday,
It's snowing outside.
My brother has gone crazy
He's losing his mind.

It's Friday, it's Friday,
Still nothing to do.
But my dog is outside
Jumping like a kangaroo.

Natalie Lewis, Grade 5
Spaulding Elementary School, OH

Seeds to Food

Popcorn
Crunchy, salty
Popping, munching, sharing
Kernels, hulls, carving, seeds
Eating, crunching, crackling
Hard, salty

David St. Clair, Grade 4
Norwich Elementary School, OH

Trees

Swaying trees,
Above my head,
Muddy bark,
Crispy, breakable branches,
Happiness
Enters into my heart.

Brennae Asaro, Grade 4
Normandy Elementary School, OH

can you imagine

a human without a brain
a railroad without a train

a cyclist without a bike
a hiker that cannot hike

a picture without a frame
a best friend without a name

a race car without a track
a skeleton that has no back

a dictionary without a word
an open field without a herd

american idol without a singer
a hand without a finger

Max Bohrer, Grade 4
Stonegate Elementary School, IN

An A+

I wrote a paragraph
You checked
They typed
We gave it to the teacher
We got an A+

Taylor Owens, Grade 6
Harmon Middle School, OH

Halloween

Halloween
Fun, exciting,
Eating, laughing, giving
Friends, families, neighbors, candy,
Walking, running, looking,
Happy, lively
Trick-or-treating

Arianne Sherzai, Grade 4
Norwich Elementary School, OH

Amelia's Bell

Every day at 3 p.m.,
A single bell rings.
For this bell is my bell,
Amelia's Bell.
Every day I hear it ring,
While robins sing high in the trees.
Today, I am 12,
And I'm waiting.
I am waiting to hear my bell.
It's 3 p.m. but I can't hear my bell,
And the robins aren't singing
That was when I remembered,
Remembered that I am deaf.

Tess Carroll, Grade 6
Rocky River Middle School, OH

Blackfoot Tribe

As we boil buffalo,
We hear the Rocky Mountains calling our names.
When dawn breaks,
The women pack up the teepee and our belongings.
As we are the strongest tribe,
We believe we can make this move,
Even with the challenges we may face.
Far ahead on our journey, we take a break to eat,
Eat the venison we had packed before.
The cooling fire sits in our teepee as we start a new life.

Claire Moody, Grade 5
Barrington Elementary School, OH

Wet/Dry

Wet
damp, moist
raining, snowing, sleeting
dew, frost, desert, Antarctica
evaporating, withering, dying
arid, barren
Dry

Andrew Yarber, Grade 5
Washington Township Elementary School, IN

My Brother's Portrait

My brother's eyes are like little tree stumps
My brother's hair is like the ocean's waves themselves
My brother's heart is full of laughter like a white star
My brother lives in Lego world and eats all the bad guys
My brother Kevin

Emily Hollis, Grade 5
Henryville Elementary School, IN

I Am

I am fun and athletic
I wonder what I am going to do today
I hear my class talking
I see dreams when I sleep
I want to be a professional soccer player one day
I am fun and athletic

I pretend that I am the best soccer player in the world
I feel the power of two magnets repelling
I touch food and water
I worry that there will be a tornado warning
I cry if I get hurt real bad
I am fun and athletic

I understand how to do work in school
I say God is real
I dream to score six goals in a soccer game
I try to be real good at sports
I hope I will get straight A's
I am Joey Albus

Joseph Albus, Grade 4
Floyd Ebeling Elementary School, MI

Taurus

T aurus in Greek mythology is
A beautiful bull with mother of pearl horns.
U ranus's grandson Zeus took the form of the bull.
R unning out of nowhere came the bull
U nexpectedly. Europa was scared but then
S he realized the bull was friendly.
The bull took her to Crete to rule as queen.

Mason Harger LaPorte, Grade 6
Pinewood Elementary School, IN

Mountain Lion

I look around I see the big gray mountains.
I hear hunters all around.
I see my herd I lead.
I taste the weeds and meat I hunt.
I feel stones that have fallen off the cliff.
I am a mountain lion.

Bridget Brocksmith, Grade 5
North Knox East Elementary/Jr High School, IN

What-if*

Just last night, while I lay in bed
Some What-ifs popped right into my head
And they scampered and scurried all around
They sure did make a lot of sound.
What-if my best friend turns on me?
What-if my mom gets stung by a bee?
What-if a rumor goes around about me at school?
What-if I forget to follow the rules?
What-if a family member dies?
What-if everybody sees me cry?
What-if I die before the next day?
What-if a drunk driver crashes into me and I have to pay?
What-if my parents get into a fight?
What-if I can't get to sleep tonight?
Everything looks good, and then
The What-ifs pop into my head again.

Dannica Culler, Grade 6
Pike Delta York Middle School, OH
*Based on Shel Silverstein's poem "What-if"

Deer

I love those deer.
What's to fear?
With their black noses,
And their poses.
The bucks rub their racks against trees,
Bark splitting like cheese.
The does are taking care of their young.
They are giving them baths with their tongue.
The grasses that they eat,
Are really sweet.
Now it's time to sleep.
They won't make a peep.

Meg Carrie, Grade 5
North Knox East Elementary/Jr High School, IN

Sun

Big, yellow
Shining, burning, growing
Bright, star, night, white
Turning, changing, moving
Big, circle
Moon
Kaede Fukada, Grade 6
Tippecanoe Middle School, OH

Swimming

Up the ladder
I jump into the icy water
underneath the water I feel relaxed
around me the water is sizzling
off I go out of the water
but I want to keep swimming
Matthew Goodyear, Grade 5
Rootstown Elementary School, OH

Bruce

Even though I didn't cry
I still knew that in my heart
The tears were building up.

I didn't get to hug you
I didn't get to see you
All I got to do is say goodbye.

All I see
All I do
I will always love you

My family that you loved is still here
Waiting to see you again.
We hope you are happy where you are.

The world that you knew
Is still here missing you too
You hold our dreams and hopes.

All they see
All they do
They will always love you.
Cristen Lea Curtland, Grade 6
Trilby Elementary School, OH

Air Craft

Airplanes
Aerodynamic, sleek
Speeding, zooming, swaying
Majestic birds flying around.
Rolling, diving, rising
Magnificent, airborne
Airliner
Gregory Fritts, Grade 5
Wooster Christian School, OH

My Life as a Pumpkin Pie

If I were a pumpkin pie, I would taste like the pumpkin spice you like.
I would be full of spicy, sweet goodness.
I would like to be eaten with your family.
I'd want to be decorated with whipped topping.
If I were a pumpkin pie, I would be overjoyed to be shared.
I would wish to be filled with sensational taste.
I would love to be eaten at a slow pace.
I would listen for stories your family tells.
I would say goodbye after Thanksgiving night.

Lauren Cooper, Grade 5
Reed Middle School, OH

Writing Relief

Oh this is so hard,
I mean they tell you to write a poem,
It's like 3, 2, 1, GO!
WRITE! WRITE! WRITE!
10 more minutes!
It seems like 2 minutes later…
Your teacher's telling you to wrap it up and come on over to share,
Breathing Deeply,
Making up the rest of your writing as other people share,
Uh oh, they're good,
I feel like an idiot sitting here,
My turn to share,
There goes my reputation!
They say GOOD JOB!
Wow, they liked it
Phew. Pressure off.

Kaitlin Cole, Grade 6
Batesville Middle School, IN

Colors

Red is the color of my heart. Blue is the color of the sea.
Yellow is the color of the hot beaming sun. Green is the color of the nice cut grass.
Orange is the color of the sun when it sets.
What's your favorite color?
Alex Cunningham, Grade 4
Northfield Elementary School, OH

Neighborhood

Follow me to 44th Street
Where you can see my neighborhood.

As you can see, my big yellow house and my big backyard are really peaceful.
In the morning I hear chirping coming from the birds.
There are many children playing or riding their bikes around the neighborhood.
There are many colorful houses and cars.
People are power walking around the block and people are riding bikes too.
Outside I see my neighbor smiling at me.
I wave hello.

As you see, all is true.
Thank you for riding with me in my neighborhood.
Abigail Cortez, Grade 5
Allen J. Warren Elementary School, IN

Fall

Fall is when leaves
Change their color.
Fall is when the
Leaves look like gems in the sky,
Beautiful and gold.
Halloween is in the fall.
You get lots of
Yummy, chocolatey,
Delicious candy.
In the pumpkin patch,
Pumpkins grow big and tall, long and short.
Some are orange or even green
And some are colors in between.
Corn grows really high,
Almost as if it
Could touch the sky.
Corn is crunchy,
Sweet, and good.
Fall is when nature
Goes to sleep, ready
To wake when God beckons.

Elisabeth Carr, Grade 6
Holy Family Middle School, MI

Rain vs Maracas

In the night the rain falls down.
It is maracas.
Pitter patter or softly loud.
So pretty and calm.
Love to be around.

As you hurry through the city street.
The rain down pouring.
You hear something familiar.
It's just the same musical beat, beneath your feet.

Kaitlyn Sullivan, Grade 6
Harding Middle School, OH

Free

Life is a flower,
Dusted with powder,
With petals of green,
Here comes spring!

We go to the park, take a swing
And listen to the sweet hummingbirds sing.
We turn on the sprinkler
And spin around,
Until we get dizzy
And hit the ground.
The sun on our face,
The wind in our hair,
As free as a bird
Without a care.

Jacqueline Brown, Grade 5
Spaulding Elementary School, OH

I Am Death

I am Death.
You know me for pain.
I creep among families,
young and old, kind and mean, right and wrong.
I poison men, women and children.
I kill mercilessly. I feed on pain.
I drink over sorrow.
My job is horrid, but all must die.
I create Sorrow and Death.
For these things
keep Earth in balance.
My foe is Life, for it takes over.
Without me chaos would reign.
My friend is hope.
The world needs balance,
Death and life, courage and fear,
Fire and water, cool and hot.
Fear not, there is more.
But Death comes to everyone,
no one can escape him.
So remember thy name…Death.

Kevin G. Schascheck, Grade 6
Kesling Middle School, IN

Paul Revere

Once there was a man named Paul Revere,
He warned the village the British were near.
He's famous for the line, "One if by land, two if by sea."
When the village heard him they came out to see.

Noah Masson, Grade 5
Washington Township Elementary School, IN

Seasons

Fall
Crisp and cool
Leaves falling in a multitude of
Colors of the world fading from the occasional frost

Winter
Cold and icy
Everything covered in white, snowy,
Blankets wrapped 'round every chilled body.

Spring
Sudden break of warmness
Flowers popping up in
Meadows and lawns returning to color
From the very frigid cold of winter

Summer
School's out!
Many splashes of kids in many different
Pools of water from rain
Refurbishing the land

Jillian Krebs, Grade 6
Rocky River Middle School, OH

The Peacefulness of Nature
Ah how I love the peacefulness of nature.
Flowers are as blue as the sky.
As leaves the colors of the rainbow, fall down to the graceful grass.

I lay on hills as high as a mountaintop.
I swim through the wondrous water.

As I sit here in a clover patch I pick beautiful purple flowers.
I'm picking purple flowers because they remind me of my mother.
My mother is a graceful woman as her long blonde hair flows in the wind
For my father is gone with it, but my brother is way different, he is Tarzan #2.

My dog is like a cheetah so stunningly fast. Her speed can go from 10-30 mph in one minute.
But I'm more different than my family, for I'm always sitting here in this bed of flowers,
Waiting all day and all night for something new.

Tatiana Raney, Grade 6
Cloverdale Middle School, IN

Burns Are Love, But Me and Him as Difference
As our love burns, my heart pumps until it sends our love to heaven, and an angel comes to me and calls her name far and far hence. But at last I love him but shall I tell him or never let him notice me. Or even row-call, but never speak of his name or him as smart, cute, and handsome as the hot intensity of a thousand suns burning so bright. But people call me ugly and him as cool, but let me be free to be a smart girl on my own, or fall into his arms as I fall from the heavens to him like a soft little snowflake from the white, puffy cloud. Or hide under a shell forever and ever as I fall into pieces like a jigsaw puzzle and lie so I don't be seen in public forever and ever hence, but let me go and don't ever notice me for shall I go and tell but never not it's me, cause I'll be back to say I love you so, but I have to be happy ever hence. "But two roads diverge in a yellow wood and I — I took the one less traveled by. And that has made all the difference."*

*From the *Road Not Taken* by Robert Frost.

Shelby Brockman, Grade 5
Churubusco Elementary School, IN

Fall
The first reddish orange leaf of autumn drifts to the ground, swaying back and forth as if listening to a lullaby. The cool autumn breeze flows through the trees knocking the loose leaves to the ground. The bright orange pumpkins are ripe and ready to carve. The nights are getting cooler, I can almost see my breath in the evening air. The days are getting shorter, there is a slight chill in the air; telling us that winter will soon be here to greet us. As I step outside, I hear Canadian geese honking as they fly south for the winter. Everything is changing right in front of my light blue eyes. The forest is now an autumn blaze filled with powerful colors of red, orange and yellow. The glory of fall has arrived!

Holly Masters, Grade 6
Badger Middle School, OH

Baseball
It is the bottom of the 9th, bases loaded and your team is down by three runs. The coach says, "You are up to bat." The pressure is on you. If you get a hit, you will, if not, well, we all know what will happen. That pitch comes in and you are set and ready to hit the ball. The ball comes in and you swing and miss. "Strike one!" yells the umpire. You are so mad at yourself because you missed such a good pitch. The next pitch comes. You are ready and you let it by you and the umpire yells, "Strike two!" Now it all comes down to this. The crowd is screaming, your teammates are yelling too. You think in your head, I have to do this. The next pitch is about to come. You grip the bat tightly. Then the pitch goes by you and the umpire yells, "Ball one!" The pitcher gets back into his windup. You grip the bat even tighter. This time the pitch comes in and you swing; you swing with your eyes closed. All of a sudden you hear the bat hit something. You think, "Could it be that I have hit the ball?" You open your eyes. You see the ball flying way back and then you see the ball clear the fence. All of a sudden you feel like a hero to your team and to the fans. You run the bases and once you step on home plate you feel like a million bucks. Believe me it is a good feeling.

Ross Lehman, Grade 6
Miller City-New Cleveland School, OH

Winter Reminds Me Of…

Winter reminds me of white cold snow.
Snow reminds me of sledding with friends.
Friends remind me of laughter.
Laughter reminds me of happiness.
Happiness reminds me of family.
Family reminds me of love.
Love reminds me of joy.
Joy reminds me of Christmas.
Christmas reminds me of coldness.
Coldness reminds me of hot cocoa.
Hot cocoa reminds me of warmth.
Warmth reminds me of sitting in my house during the cold.
Cold reminds me of having snowball fights
Snowball fights remind me of fun.
Fun reminds me of winter.

Mollie Tuthill, Grade 6
Waverly East Intermediate School, MI

Something About You

There's something about you,
That makes me smile,
Even when you're doing something wrong.
There's something about you
That makes me laugh,
Even when you're not even talking.
But there's something about you,
That I can't quite explain,
But it's absolutely amazing.

Fabiola Belaen, Grade 6
Abbott Middle School, MI

Seasons Passing

The leaves fall from the trees
As they blow in the wind.
I run outside and jump into the leaves,
and you hear the crunching
like a nice crisp autumn apple.

The wind is cold and brisk.
I bundle up like an Eskimo in an igloo.
The cold wind is on my face,
but cannot penetrate my armor.

Halloween is here!
All the children going from doorstep to doorstep
collecting candy as they trick or treat.
They all make chills run down my back.
The children are like ghosts and goblins
popping out and scaring each other.

Well, fall is passing and winter is arriving.
We all get ready for the next season.
Christmas is right around the corner too.
Thanks for coming fall, "See ya, next year!"

Benjamin Szczypka, Grade 6
Holy Family Middle School, MI

Saturn

S aturn is a planet with an
A tmosphere composed of hydrogen and helium. While
T he neighboring planet,
U ranus, rotates on its side, Saturn
R otates on its slightly tilted axis. Saturn's surface is
N early all gas.

Kathryn Kiefer, Grade 6
Pinewood Elementary School, IN

Dogs I Love

They're so cute and cuddly,
They come in every shape and size,
If you teach them just right,
They'll be number one.
They like to play like you and me,
They like to mess around,
They're just fun to have around.
Even though they may not be the cleanest,
They sure are the bestest.

Sanjana Roy, Grade 6
Birchwood School, OH

Caspian

C ocks his head.
A lways loves me.
S its on my lap.
P lays with me.
I s so cute.
A lways comforting.
N ever wants to be mean.

Jordan Dotson, Grade 6
GATE Program Mayfield Elementary School, OH

The Moon

The moon, the moon
The moon is a big light in the sky
The moon, the moon
The moon is like the sun, it's high
The moon, the moon
I like the moon, it is a big light
The moon, the moon
It is big all through the night
The moon, the moon
It is our light, like God
The moon, the moon

Roy Williams, Grade 6
Granville T Woods Community School, OH

Old Chevy Pick-Up

I'm an old, red Chevy pick-up truck
With my tires spinning
My engine fluid running low,
My tailgate and doors rusting…
I just want to park in my driveway to rest.

Hayley McCormick, Grade 5
Westview Elementary School, OH

Friends

F riends are the best
R espect each other
I nteresting conversations
E asygoing
N ice, caring, loyal, lovable
D epend on each other
S pecial memories

Margo Baker, Grade 6
Holy Angels School, OH

Home

Home is a good place
You can even read about outer space!
You can play and dance
You can even prance
Watching TV is what you can do
Even play Clue
Try to play and have some fun
Pick up dad who weighs a ton
Home is the place I love best
Even though cleaning up is a pest!!!

Alex Neville, Grade 4
Chrisney Elementary School, IN

Fall Colors

White fluffs whisking by
Blue blanket as far as I can see
Red hands waving from the trees
Brown squirrel chattering on a branch
Gold bales of hay stretching across fields
Yellow sun setting in the horizon
Black cats hissing on Halloween
Orange pumpkins glowing in the night
Fall colors gracefully turning
Fall colors quickly vanishing.

Ashley Burket, Grade 6
Tri-West Middle School, IN

Depressed

Depressed is purple,
It tastes like flat root beer,
It smells like outside on a rainy day,
It reminds me of a rainy day,
It sounds like an organ,
Depressed makes me feel purple.

Eric Colombo, Grade 5
Tremont Elementary School, OH

Mom

Mom, mom, mom
Funny mom
Respectful, learning, gentle mom
Patient, peaceful likable mom
Last of all best of all, my mom

Briar Montezuma, Grade 5
Perry Central Elementary School, IN

Fall Is a Ball

fall is playing with a ball
not time to be dull
raking leaves or playing with me
so don't you see
fall is a wonderful thing

Kent Hummell, Grade 4
Norwich Elementary School, OH

Baby Sister

Being a baby sister
Is like being
The smallest
Lion cub

Everyone is trying to protect you
And sometimes it gets annoying

I am going to be last to do
EVERYTHING
Even though I get clothes
I was last to start school
Last to graduate fifth grade
And last to start middle school
Both sisters are in high school

And I am going to be
A vet with my own practice
But I will be last to get a job
No one after you just before you

But I am ok with it
I guess it is ok to be the littlest
Everyone looking out for you

Jenna Kohut, Grade 6
Harding Middle School, OH

Fall

Fall, oh glorious fall,
Come all.
I need strength to hold me back,
Go get a snack.
Go outside and play in the leaves,
Go and believe.
I like to play tag,
But don't brag.
Fall, you are the best season,
You are a good reason.

Sarah Bender, Grade 4
Chrisney Elementary School, IN

Warm Water

I can see the water.
The water is very warm.
The fun is starting.

Marshall Dungy, Grade 6
Stanley Clark School, IN

Winter Is Awesome

W onderful winter
I ndependent snow
N ice holiday
T rees in the meadow
E xciting little kids
R eally great

Natasha Mayes, Grade 5
May V Peck Elementary School, MI

Veteran's Day

Important, tragic
Suffering, cherishing, battling
Disastrous, commemorate
An important day!!!

Savannah Rae Jones, Grade 5
Cloverdale Middle School, IN

Short

We run onto the court
Our server is up
Waiting,
Watching,
Hoping,
Caring,
The whistle blows like a mad bird
She takes a single breath
Serves
We watch intently
It goes up
Comes down
Disappointment
It was short
We move on

Mary Fix, Grade 6
Assumption BVM School, MI

Past

Summer is past
Winter is here
It's snowing outside
Let's all give a cheer.
With all little children
All snug in their beds
They know Santa's coming
They've nothing to dread.

Karisa Schock, Grade 5
Spaulding Elementary School, OH

Shooting Hoops

Down my street
At my house
Between the mailboxes and my house
In my driveway
Is me shooting hoops

Landon Pence, Grade 5
Churubusco Elementary School, IN

Dirtbike

Here I am stuck in this shed all alone,
but when my owner gets home from school,
it's time to ride.
Next year he will race me,
and whatever happens on that track
will be one thing to remember.

Trever Kincaide, Grade 6
Helfrich Park Middle School, IN

My Dog Lilly

My dog Lilly is a furry ball of fun
When I get home she runs to me,
Sometimes I am mad at her,
But we still love each other.

Jessica Fisher, Grade 5
Washington Township Elementary School, IN

Fall

In the fall there are all kinds of leaves.
They are red, orange, brown.
Fall is a time for a little fun, when
You can jump in piles of beautiful leaves.
A time when it's okay if you get your hair messed up.
Fall is warm or cold or even hot.

When we gather in celebration for Thanksgiving
All my cousins come over.
Everybody cooking, baking all that wonderful food!
We eat sweet potato pie
It's so, so good!
We eat turkey with dressing, macaroni,
Deviled eggs and cornbread.
Yum!
Fall is also a delicious time.

Zaire Battle-Holmes, Grade 4
Matthew Duvall Elementary School, OH

Silence

It's golden; it's precious, like a baby child,
It's awkward and strange and can also be wild!
It's so fragile that when you say its name,
It shatters to millions of shards!
It will NEVER be at a party,
With dancing and people playing cards!
A whining child may never know what it's like.
A city won't know, with cars and kids on bikes!
It's wanted by mothers with a screaming kid.
It's like this after a farewell is bid!
It's a wonderful thing that CAN be broken —
But won't if nothing is done or spoken.
Be careful…be quiet…it'll come when ready…
Sometimes it's random…sometime it's steady…
But no more worries! Have no fear!
At the moment it's not here…

Maryssa Small, Grade 6
Northwood Elementary School, IN

Video Games

My eyes are frying
My brain is dying
My hands are numb
I have a sore bum
I must be playing video games.

Jonathan E. Fix, Grade 5
Northern Heights Elementary School, IN

The Trip

I sit on a damp ship floor waiting
Waiting to be sold, waiting for my life to end

The other slaves weep, and some lay in agony
Awaiting torture and disease, I wish I were

Them because they will die and dying is
Better than what is awaiting me in the strange land

I wish that I were with my family, at least
With them I could find comfort

Comfort from being punished when I do wrong
Comfort when I'm in the cotton fields

We arrive with more than half of us dead
We arrive without hope of rescue we arrive

With tears in our eyes, even I weep knowing
That I will never see my family again.

Kayla Jones, Grade 6
Mayfield Elementary School, OH

Autumn

Leaves fall far from home.
Wind whistles wildly through the trees.
Rain roaring, ripping through the air.
Colorful, creative, crunchy leaves pile up.

Fall, a time of change.

Big Black Bass took the bait.
Temperatures turn terrible during the season.
Football fumbles far from the fast player.
Hunting hearing hustling deer.

Leaves, trees and nature.

Kids create costumes for Halloween.
People put pumpkins outside for decorations.
People give chocolaty, crunchy candy to kids.
There are dark decorations during this season.

Activities and sports all create
Impressions during the season.

Mitchell Samborn, Grade 6
Holy Family Middle School, MI

Savannah

Savannah
Pretty, smart
Chilling, relaxing, caring
Funny, stylish
Savannah is my friend for life.
Lauren Rae Patterson, Grade 5
Cloverdale Middle School, IN

Pugs

Today I saw two pugs
They were rolling in the snow
They seemed to be good friends
Their names were Bruce and Bo.

The snow began to fall
As they ran around the park
Bruce found an orange
And he called to Bo with a bark.

They hit it here
They hit it there
In the snow the orange went everywhere.

Neither one wanted to lose
But now it was time to snooze!!
Allyson Shinaver, Grade 6
Eisenhower Middle School, OH

Sadness

Sadness is blue
It smells like a skunk
It looks like no life
It tastes sour
It sounds like the blues
Sadness feels like a butterfly
With no flowers around.
Brandon Payeff, Grade 6
Eisenhower Middle School, OH

My Friends and Enemies

Friends
helping, caring,
trusting, giving, amazing,
awesome, loving, mean, thoughtless,
rude, selfish, careless,
awful, horrible,
Enemies
Alexis Broomes, Grade 6
Harmon Middle School, OH

Leaves

Leaves, leaves are falling off the trees.
Down, down red, yellow, and brown.
Leaves, leaves are falling down.
Riley Canfield, Grade 5
Cloverdale Middle School, IN

Dog

If I were a dog I would roam the house like a scavenger looking for food.
I would beg my owner to rub my belly.
I would bark at the UPS truck.
If I were a dog I would chase the mailman.
I would sleep anywhere I would like to.
I would run around like a freight train.
If I were a dog I would have the life of Riley.
I would run the house.
I would do dog kind of things.
You know…chase my tail, run around in circles, play fetch, things like that.
I am a dog.
Matt Stauder, Grade 6
St Maria Goretti School, IN

The Monster

The buttery smell of cooked walleye and pike
rose with the fire into the clean Canada air.
On the shore I took my second cast and got that jerk bait deep.
I set the hook on a heavy fish.
Line shot from the reel like a gun as the fish took on a run.
I slowly turned the fish around and started pulling him in.
The big form of a nice northern pike appeared about five feet away.
The rock point got shallow and sharp,
so he was having trouble getting another run in.
But that didn't stop his acrobatics.
He was tail-walking and jumping like crazy.
After about seven minutes of battling, I brought the big pike to shore.
My dad tried to net him, but he was too big for the net.
Our guide started yelling, "Stop!"
He ran over and grabbed the fish by the gills so he would stop thrashing.
When he lifted the monster up, I got excited.
It weighed over 20 pounds. He was a fatty.
We brought him over to the boat and measured him. He was thirty-six inches long,
A trophy fish!
Ben Martin, Grade 5
Stanley Clark School, IN

All About the Life of Alexandra Franken

Alexandra
Funny, creative, active
Sister of Amanda, Randy, Melissa, Paul, and LeeAnna
Lover of softball, my dog, and reading
Who feels nervous when I go to the doctor
    and when my room isn't clean
    because then I have to clean it
Who gets excited about getting a good grade on a test
    and when I get a hit in softball
Who needs to not have so many temper tantrums at home
    and to study for tests more.
Who gives kisses to my dog Dot.
Who fears my basement at night and my closet when I'm going to sleep
Who would like to become a famous author like Beverly Cleary
Resident of Austintown, Ohio
Franken
Alexandra Franken, Grade 5
Frank Ohl Intermediate School, OH

The Key

The key is a strange little thing.
People say it is not a plaything.
The sound of it is a little ding-a-ling.
It's almost as if it could sing.
Some people hang it on a bit of string.
It would be funny if you used it as an earring.
Some people hide it under the porch swing.
I say that is the weirdest thing.
People could find it ding ding ding.
True or not people say it shines like a diamond ring.

Emma Hanebutt, Grade 4
Chrisney Elementary School, IN

Squirrels

Squirrels climbing up trees, laughing gloriously.
Laughing! Laughing!
Chubby cheeks storing beige colored nuts.
Laughing! Laughing!
Rubbing backs against trees, shedding fur.
Laughing! Laughing!
Playing tag gracefully, swiftly.
Climbing in circles around the tree.
Laughing! Laughing!

Dalon Vura, Grade 6
Wooster Christian School, OH

Someday…

Someday I will be a billionaire.
Someday I will go to Hollywood.
Someday I will have twelve motorcycles.
Someday I will have a Lamborgini.
Someday I will have two maids.
Someday I will make a movie.
Someday I will have a movie theater in my house.
Someday I will have my own business.

Tyrell Packer, Grade 5
Becker Elementary School, OH

Fall

Fall, leaves change and die,
colors falling out and fading.
Crinkle, crunch, and cascade to the ground
grasping the spectacles as they fall.

Fall brings Halloween to the scene.
Jack-o'-lanterns shining at night.
Children dressing up pretending to be
someone they're not.
Tasting the sweetness of the treats,
Hershey's, Skittles, and Caramel.

Back to school in the fall,
now and forever until next year,
then winter comes and fall ends.

Logan Wenz, Grade 6
Holy Family Middle School, MI

Once Upon a Bedtime Story

Once upon a bedtime story,
A girl lay in bed.
All tucked in and wide awake.
"A bedtime tale?" she asked.

"Once upon a time," she said,
"Was a little golden fish.
He lived alone in a pond
With his little friend the frog.

They played each day and night
With little thought of danger.
Though one day when a stranger came by,
They were scared and knew little to do.

They saw its scales and big sharp teeth,
"It's an alligator," they cried.
The fish was scared when the frog went to fight.

He took one peek and saw at once
That his friend was victorious at last."
"What a wonderful story," said mother
"Now it's time for bed."

Casey Mazza, Grade 6
University Liggett School, MI

Nicholas Etienne

N aughty, I am not.
I ntelligent, inquisitive, and insightful some say.
C areful, cunning, and courageous on the football field.
H ard working in the classroom.
O pen-minded in many subjects.
L ucky, I am.
A ctive in football games.
S hh, shy my mom says.

E very vacation we get lost in Atlanta, Georgia.
T ired when my parents get me up in the morning.
I ntroverted around most adults outside my family.
E ager to get good grades.
N ice to many people.
N ever failing in class.
E nvious of millionaires.

Nicholas Etienne, Grade 5
Perry Central Elementary School, IN

I'm Sorry

I'm sorry I lost your dog.
It looked like it needed a walk.
I forgot the leash
so it ran away.

P.S. I'm not giving you another dog
because I probably will lose that one too.

Madeline Stewart, Grade 5
Tremont Elementary School, OH

Churubusco

C ome in to my house.
H ow are you doing?
U can have some hot cocoa.
R un to the store.
U can have some apple juice.
B usy day at work.
U seem so sleepy.
S ee my artwork.
C an you play with me?
O uch, my foot hurts!

Autumn Marie Gray, Grade 4
Churubusco Elementary School, IN

Christmas Tree

Christmas tree is so tall
I hope I hope it never falls.
It also smells like pine
It looks so fine.
Do you like Christmas tree?
I do can't you see.

Jared Ward, Grade 5
May V Peck Elementary School, MI

Seasons

Bike tires crunch leaves,
Summer winds blow on southward.
Now the spring winds blow.

Sarah Nowack, Grade 5
Kenowa Hills Intermediate School, MI

The World's Quilt

We each have our own face,
And our own mind,
Our skin color is not the same,
And we all have different opinions.

We are a sea of different people,
But we learn to tolerate each other,
Like siblings.
And we all come together,
Helping, holding, and harmony,
To make one big quilt,
The world's quilt.

Kaitlyn Hathaway, Grade 6
Harding Middle School, OH

The Ride

Katie
I love to ride.
By the beach's tide.
As the sun seems to die.
Because it seems to play
A relaxing trick on me.
When I ride.

Katie Rasche, Grade 5
Nancy Hanks Elementary School, IN

Slavery

S orrow all over the place.
L ocked up by mean people.
A ttacked by unfair men.
V ery hungry nobody ate.
E verybody's face looks very sad.
R un away for a change of life.
Y ou will never regret to be free.

Kylee Brewer, Grade 4
Mayfield Elementary School, OH

What Moves Me

W ild weather
H orses
A ttitude for dancing
T he sunset

M y dog
O ur family
V ery giving people
E veryone around me
S eeing new places

M y friends
E very animal around me

Jayna Thompson, Grade 4
Miller Ridge Elementary School, OH

Fall

All the birds are flying,
And my mom is buying.
The leaves are falling,
I am crawling.
I am raking,
My mom is baking.
My sister is singing,
I am swinging.
My dad is cooking,
My grandpa is looking.
The weeds are bending,
The day is ending.

Matthew Graham, Grade 4
Chrisney Elementary School, IN

Lost at the Observatory

Fear mixes with calm,
Breeze ruffles a quiet lake —
Lost, as the sun sets

Elizabeth Bays, Grade 6
Stanley Clark School, IN

Sand Pit

Running in hot sand,
Trying not to slip and burn,
Falling in the pit!

Daniel Goodman, Grade 6
Stanley Clark School, IN

Nighttime Fires

Crackling upon the coal
Sparkling colors in the night
Withering away at the wood
Burning the midnight oil
Wreaking havoc in the darkness
Heating the cold creatures as they sleep
Turning the wood to ashes
Glowing like the sun in the day
Making all the chills go away
Melting away at the break of day

Ryan Barnes, Grade 6
St Clement Elementary School, OH

Books

They suck you in…
They stuff you up…
They capture you in other lands.

They show you faces…
They show you looks…
They teach you feelings…
They are books!

Grant Jones, Grade 5
Tremont Elementary School, OH

Interception

The score was 0-21
We're down
They hiked the ball
It's thrown
Up up up
I got it I got it!
Interception!
The crowd roars like lions
Running out of real estate
We scored
Our first
Or only
Touchdown of the season
The crowd does the wave
The final score 6-21
Steve…
Voted V.I.P. of the season

Patrick Truskowski, Grade 6
Assumption BVM School, MI

Water/Fire

Water
Cool, clear
Still refreshing, rain
Wet, soaked — dry, burning
Blaze, red, hot
Steaming, roasting
Fire

Katie Schnautz, Grade 6
Helfrich Park Middle School, IN

I Am

I am strong and athletic
I wonder if the Lions win the Super Bowl
I hear the crowds roaring in the stands
I see a meteor falling from space
I want to be a football player
I am strong and athletic

I pretend I am a professional football player
I feel someone tackling me onto soft grass
I touch a shooting star
I worry about my grandparents
I cry when I am grounded from football
I am strong and athletic

I understand I will get in trouble for talking
I say football is fun
I dream I am the strongest man alive
I try to get better at football
I hope I become a football player
I am Joshua Bartold

Joshua Bartold, Grade 4
Floyd Ebeling Elementary School, MI

Me

My smile is like the sun rising in the morning sky
My eyes are like beautiful crystals.
My ears are like a hawk.
My hair is wavy.
My heart holds a lot of love that is pink as the morning sky.
I live in a small Indiana town.
I eat all of my bad thoughts away.

Cassidy Mull, Grade 5
Henryville Elementary School, IN

That Special Light

I was created
Up in Heaven above
He gave me that special light
Because He loves me so.

The Lord sent the stork
For me to be born
I see that special light
It hurts my precious eyes.

I had my children
And while they were born
They could be just like me
Because they saw that special light.

I am on my deathbed
All my family is there
I think I am going to die
I can see that special light.

Christine Wright, Grade 6
Emmanuel-St Michael Lutheran School, IN

The Tremendously Terrible Taliban

Afghans consider the Taliban horribly mean.
They don't care when doing one bad scheme.
The extraordinary rules that the Afghans do,
Banned images, movies, girls from school too.

1996 the Taliban took control of Afghanistan.
Mazar-e-sharif, Kabul, not too close to Pakistan.
The Taliban cause a terribly bad living condition.
No one can do anything to help the situation.

See the Afghans rejoice on September 2001.
The Taliban are gone so we can have our fun.
It seems awhile but we have freedom at last.
But the Taliban may gain control once again fast.

A miserable thing happens five years later.
Taliban come back and are like invaders.
After the Afghan freedom for so many years.
Afghans want to weep and shed their tears.

No more freedom in Afghanistan I guess.
Freedom for Afghans growing less and less.
Some things in life just won't ever change.
The Taliban disposed is far from range.

Josiah Kim, Grade 6
Ann Arbor Christian School, MI

Stephanie Mazon

Stephanie
Kind caring and serious
Sister of Sophia
Lover of soccer, animals and the Steelers
Who feels nervous when I do a test
    and when someone yells at me
Who gets excited about going on vacation
    and getting a good grade
Who needs to study hard to get better grades
Who gives kisses to my mom, dad and sister
Who fears snakes and spiders
Who would like to be a policewoman when I grow up
Resident of Austintown, Ohio
Mazon

Stephanie Mazón, Grade 5
Frank Ohl Intermediate School, OH

Blue

Blue is the feeling of freedom.
Blue is the sound of fire popping.
Blue is the taste of a big lollipop.
Blue is the sound of birds chirping.
Blue is the taste of cotton candy.
Blue is the color of a massive, summer sky.
Blue is the feeling of rolling in tall grass.
Blue is jubilant and relaxed.

Colin Reed, Grade 6
Wooster Christian School, OH

Poems

P oets write them
O de (a type of poem)
E ndless choices
M any kinds to choose from
S uper fun to write

Alexandra DiPaolo, Grade 4
Sts Joseph and John School, OH

Awesome Autumn

Choppy wind
Gusts
In the morning,
Crackling leaves
On the sidewalk
Crimson,
Gold yellow,
Great green.
The smell of
The wind
The sight of the trees
The feel of
The breeze
Blowing across
My face
Awesome autumn
Is here.

Alex Scicluna, Grade 5
Riley Upper Elementary School, MI

Useless Things

A person without a heart
A dart game without a dart
A jail cell without bars
A night without stars

A car without a wheel
A robber that does not steal
A frog that cannot leap
A person that cannot sleep

United States without a president
Apartments without one resident
A school without teachers
A game without bleachers

Soup without a bowl
A train without any coal
A piano without keys
A hive without bees

A book without a cover
A kid without a mother
Skies that aren't blue
I can't live without you

Tyler Harmon, Grade 4
Stonegate Elementary School, IN

I Am

I am a smart and fun guy
I wonder if I'll ever have kids of my own
I hear lions roaring in Africa
I see two orangutans partying in the next room
I want to be able to see the world like no other can
I am a smart and fun guy

I pretend to have the greatest ancient army ever seen
I feel the pain of my friends' hurt souls
I touch the heavens far above the clouds
I worry mankind will destroy itself
I cry when I see many starving people in third world countries
I am a smart and fun guy

I understand I will not live forever
I say there is nothing wrong with crying
I dream of world peace finally happening
I try to discourage violence
I hope one day the world will finally have some common sense and stop polluting
I am a smart and fun guy

Elijah Orth, Grade 6
Helfrich Park Middle School, IN

The Riverside

Away from any people,
I sit alone,
among the enormous shimmering boulders,
listening to the symphony of birds like an orchestra,
next to the roar of the sparkling waterfalls that look like crystal.
The soothing smell of pine cones dangling from the towering pine trees fills the air,
and the wind sings and whistles a sweet tune like a gentle flute.

Jason Jaworski, Grade 5
Stanley Clark School, IN

Wonderful Summer

Walking along the rocky shore, I see water and sun, meeting on the horizon.
Beside me, I see rocks climb out of the endless waving water.
I can almost taste the saltwater on my lips.
I hear the seagulls cawing. Above me, they circle, sparkling white.
The water is strikingly blue today.
Looking down, I see pebbles and water.
The rocks are grey and some of them are brown.
My feet get stuck in the grey-black mud;
The seaweed in the water is red-orange, and in it I see
little daddy crabs and mommy crabs,
and I see maybe some tiny baby crabs.
I touch the rough rocks.
I now walk into the waves,
Ah! The icy cold of the water…my teeth chatter.
I look down in the water to see some glowing green and bronze sea glass.
Maybe, on this lucky day,
I could find some rare blue sea glass, or even rarer clear glass.
Where am I?
I am at the best place on Earth, Allen's Cove Beach, Brooklin, Maine.

Emily Vetne, Grade 5
Stanley Clark School, IN

Kit

I have a cat named Kit,
She sometimes throws a fit.
She chases the mice,
Which is not nice,
I wish she would just sit.

Lauren Kleist, Grade 5
Washington Township Elementary School, IN

I Am

I am caring and kind.
I wonder why the sky is blue.
I hear chocolate flowers when they sing.
I see the disco ball picking bumblebees.
I want someone who likes me for me.
I am caring and kind.
I pretend I am a star.
I feel sad when kittens yell.
I touch puffy clouds in the sky.
I worry about my friends sometimes.
I cry when bad thoughts race through my mind.
I am caring and kind.
I understand that life is a roller coaster.
I say everyone should live in peace.
I dream for a good future.
I try to get good grades in school.
I hope some day I'll get a pool.
I am caring and kind.

Kasey Eckelbecker, Grade 6
Galesburg-Augusta Middle School, MI

What Do I See?

I see what you see
The stars, the moon, the sun, the sky
but I see more than what you do

I see the sun tell stories of the Volcano Stone,
the stone that is made of fire
I see the stars dance across the sky
a sight that inspires me so

I see the moon's dreams
that glisten around with beauty
I see the sky so beautiful
that takes me on a journey

Now I know what you see
and you know what I see
If you believe, you can see
the stars, the moon, the sun, the sky

Maybe you'll see what I am
I'm the sea that spreads very wide
Though people pollute me, I will not hide
My beauty will shine through in time

Ayana Logan, Grade 6
Woodward Park Middle School, OH

I Am

I am understanding and nice!
I wonder, what is it like on the moon?
I hear the girl on the cover of my book singing.
I see the girl on my book dancing.
I want to grow up strong!
I am understanding and nice!
I pretend that I am an astronaut!
I feel surprised that my pet eraser just got married.
I touch the skin of an alien.
I worry that someday I will die.
I cry that my guinea pig just died.
I am understanding and nice!
I understand that we are all humans!
I say that you can always make mistakes.
I dream that one day I might be president!
I try to be a good student!
I hope that one day I will get married.
I am understanding and nice!

Genna DeHart, Grade 6
Galesburg-Augusta Middle School, MI

Autumn

Winning prizes at the fair
Asking my parents for more money
Smelling delicious fair food
Riding Zero Gravity over and over
This makes autumn.

Candy falling into bags
Kids saying "Trick-or-treat"
Feet smacking on the pavement
Chocolate crunching in my mouth
This makes autumn.

Smoke billowing from the chimney
Wood and leaves crackling in a fire
Brown hot dogs in my mouth
My dad and I getting firewood
This makes autumn.

Scooping out pumpkin goo
Carving out creepy scary faces
Tasting delicious pumpkin seeds
Seeing your pumpkin on Halloween night
This makes autumn.

Harrison Gilmore, Grade 5
Sanderson Elementary School, OH

Horses

Horses
beautiful, graceful,
loving, caring, running,
gliding fast among the plains
Pony

Jude Connelly, Grade 5
Washington Township Elementary School, IN

Poetry

P oetry is peaceful
O k, or great
E motional
T reacherous too
R ead it with me
Y ou can read it too

Sonnie Sauvinsky, Grade 5
Rootstown Elementary School, OH

The Rock Wall

I face the rock wall.
I'm climbing higher, higher.
I'm above the world!

Sarah Hosinski, Grade 6
Stanley Clark School, IN

Diving Play

Pressure rising,
Immense attention,
Two outs on the board,
Opponent batting,
Strike one,
Strike two,
SMACK!
Ball flies like a bullet,
I dive,
I fall,
Crowd stands as curious as a cat,
Ball captured in glove,
He's out!

Alec Ockaskis, Grade 6
Assumption BVM School, MI

Bench in the Sun

Sitting here: lake's smell,
Towel's warmth, wood bench's cool.
Sun's here, with no clouds.

Erin Luck, Grade 6
Stanley Clark School, IN

Music

M any people love it
U se it to be happy
S ee it and hear it
I love it and enjoy it
C reate and listen

Cameron Mathis, Grade 6
Mayfield Elementary School, OH

Leaves

Yellow and red
Falling, twirling
I love to rake
Leaves

Joey Kiss, Grade 6
Eisenhower Middle School, OH

Music and Me

Flowing through my instrument,
Music speaks to me,
Feeling the rhythm of the beat,
Music becomes a part of me.
Surging through me, here it comes,
Music from my flute and me.
Flying fingers over the keys,
Music is an expression of me.
Sharing with audiences,
Music becomes a gift from me.

Kasey Cross, Grade 6
Tri-West Middle School, IN

Small But Powerful

I am a small animal
Ready to fight!
But right now
I appear to be a lazy cat!
But next time
I'll be waiting for my rival…
That dog!
My claws are sharp and ready
I am a small, powerful animal.

Collin Massie, Grade 5
Westview Elementary School, OH

Rachel

R eally nice
A wesome
C ool
H appy
E xcellent
L izard

Alyssa Colombo, Grade 4
Northfield Elementary School, OH

Monster

There was a monster under my bed
He was big, furry, and cherry red

He came to see me every night
But never came out when it was light

I never saw him anymore
After I turned four

Katie McCarthy, Grade 5
St Jude Catholic School, IN

He Was an Old Hammer

Always fixing gadgets
Taking machines apart
Hitting nails and wood
But never being thanked
I wish I had legs to run away

Austin Baker, Grade 5
Westview Elementary School, OH

Fall Is Here

Time for raking leaves
Squirrels putting away food
Darkness comes early
A cold chill swallows the night
Nature tells me fall is here!

Shaw Newsom, Grade 5
Westview Elementary School, OH

Sisters and Brothers

Sisters
helpful, careful
adventuring, caring, respecting
wise, successful, rude, unthankful
creating, wondering, traveling
different, honest
Brothers

Samantha Mason, Grade 6
Harmon Middle School, OH

Red White and Blue

I am true
To red, white, and blue
I would fight
To keep the flag in flight
The flag stands for freedom
From all other kingdoms
Oh how it is so true
I love the red, white, and blue

Bradley Singer, Grade 5
St Michael School, IN

A Bird's Feather

Beautiful, little and bright.
Slow as a cloud
In a breeze.
It sparkles to the stars.
The little feather
Lands on a windy day.
And the little feather
Floats like a boat
Again, back and forth,
Back and forth.
White as a snowflake
Flying through the air.
Again, and again.

Savannah DeBoard, Grade 4
Legend Elementary School, OH

Cookies

Sounds like a beep from the oven,
Smells like chocolate on Christmas day,
Looks like stars, angels and trees,
Feels like a warm melted marshmallow,
Tastes like a sweet, sugar candy land.

Courtney Dudley, Grade 5
Northfield Baptist Christian School, OH

Gummy Bears

Sweet and sour wrapping our skin together
Red and green volunteer to go first
Slowly oozing their insides out
All begging for mercy not wanting to go next
All scatter on the floor
A long pink and brown tongue picks them up and…
Down
Down
Down
They all go

Anna Perez, Grade 6
St Maria Goretti School, IN

Down Under

Cool, still waters,
Drowning in blue,
To dive in and swim,
Is what I'm longing to do,
In the depths, concealed are fish,
To float with them is what I wish.

Leah Mills, Grade 5
Northern Heights Elementary School, IN

Sports

Basketball
Swoosh, bank shot
Fast break, passing, dribbling
Dunks, 3 pointers, alley oop, finger roll
Team

Baseball
Hitting, catching
Single, double, triple
Fans, cheering, smack, home run
Skills

Football
Hitting, tackling
Quarterback, running back, receiver
Touchdown, score, linebackers, Super Bowl
Bruises

Track
Fast, running
Jumping, stretching, goal
Seconds, minutes, inches, winning
Gold

Gavin Schaefer, Grade 6
Nancy Hanks Elementary School, IN

Winter

Falling winter snow!
Icicles, freezing, snowballs!
Snowmen, igloos, Brrr!

Ethan Pell, Grade 4
Eugene M Nikkari Elementary School, MI

Halloween

Leaves flutter to the ground full of crimson and gold,
Scarecrows are about, defiant and bold,
Brave children wiggle the haunted gate latch,
While other kids swarm through the pumpkin patch,

Children all run for Halloween sweets,
Walking up to each door with a loud, "Trick-or-Treat!"
Some look for spooks, though their search is in vain,
Haunts can't be caught as they rattle their chains,

Old houses creak with all their might,
While witches fly into the dark, starry night,
They cackle mercilessly as they streak across the moon,
"We'll be gone for now but we'll be back soon!"

Vampires search for something to bite,
No light can penetrate the oncoming night,
No one knows what the darkness holds,
The danger of night has increased by tenfold,

Then the creatures disappear, all of them are gone,
Halloween has left too, with the next breaking dawn.

Monica McDonough, Grade 6
Rocky River Middle School, OH

Dominant Hurricanes

Hurricanes come in with a blare.
When powerful winds come they damage homes.
If water is nearby, lakes will flood from heavy rains.

Hurricanes are like packs of wild horses
Trampling on the ground.
Hurricanes leave like cats
Creeping up on mice.

Ashley Musil, Grade 6
Wooster Christian School, OH

Writing Poems

I cannot write this poem
My ideas just ran out
I will never get this finished
I think I'm going to shout
My mother thinks it's easy
My teacher thinks it too
But I just can't write this poem
I don't know what to do
My brain is flipping inside out
My thoughts just won't connect
I wish this poem would write itself
My train of thought just wrecked
But what is that you say?
I just wrote a rhyme?
Phew, I'm glad that's over
And just in the nick of time

Bailey Goff, Grade 6
North Knox East Elementary/Jr High School, IN

Jumping Off Coop's Tower

Thirty feet up high
Standing over dark water
I jump up, off — SPLASH!
Conner Correira, Grade 6
Stanley Clark School, IN

Coops Tower — High Dive

I'm getting goose bumps.
Below, my friends cheer me on!
I jump off the top.
Maggie Lowenhar, Grade 6
Stanley Clark School, IN

Waterfalls

waterfalls howling
quickly down a steep mountain
as fast as can be
Christian Smith, Grade 6
Roosevelt Elementary School, OH

The Summer Sky

I sit and watch the clouds go by
Across the orange summer sky
I make out pictures with my eyes
As I sit and watch the summer sky

The sun will soon go down tonight
Turning daylight into night
The moon and stars are shining bright
Changing darkness into light

I peek through my telescope just to spy
I love looking at the summer sky
Kellyn Vale, Grade 6
St John the Evangelist School, IN

Halloween

Spooky, scary
Creepy, fun, weird
Spectacular, costumes
Holiday
Kylie Koors, Grade 5
St Jude Catholic School, IN

Falling

Raking leaves into a pile.
Raking, raking, raking.
Run, jump, land, thump.
Leaves falling everywhere.
Whoosh,
Fall,
Bump,
Thump,
Land.
Thomas Gillotti, Grade 4
Norwich Elementary School, OH

I Am

I am smart and a Colts fan
I wonder what I will be like once I get older
I hear people screaming my name as I walk out on the Colt's field
I see the Colts win the Super Bowl
I want an Escalade when I get older
I am smart and a Colts fan

I pretend that I am a fashion designer
I feet great when someone compliments me
I touch my dad's heart when I make signs for him while he runs
I worry how my day will go
I cry when I think of my grandparents
I am smart and a Colts fan

I understand that everyone has bad days
I say that everyone is the same
I dream that everyone will be treated equal
I try to help everyone get along
I hope I am rich one day
I am smart and a Colts fan

Morganne Geiser, Grade 6
Helfrich Park Middle School, IN

My Soul Is a Metaphor

My soul is an artist painting the world
Making a masterpiece in my mind of my own
The brush is my creativity in my ideas and thoughts
When the paper is blank, it is finding the knowledge to paint
And when the paper is colorful and the masterpiece is completed,
It is my brainwork gently brushed onto a panel
The colors are the different lessons on a subject
The painting, when I am done, is all the education I have learned
Cathleen Huang, Grade 5
Meadowbrook Elementary School, MI

My Terrible Day

Beep, beep, beep my alarm clock rang,
My skateboard was on the floor and I slipped on it and made a big bang.
She said stop fooling around and come eat,
But first clean your sheets.
I packed my books for school and my favorite book about the night,
My mom dropped me off at school and I was late,
We were in a hurry I hardly had ate.
I ran to class but a teacher said you know the rule,
No running in school.
I said to myself you know what is not cool,
About that school's rule.
I went home and took a nap,
But I was awakened by a loud tap.
You're in trouble!
All I could hear was bees,
And I yelled out where are my keys.
My sister said you have detention,
All I did was not pay attention.
Christian Araniva, Grade 5
Auburn Hills Christian School, MI

Tucson, Arizona

Nowhere but in the West
Are the mountains purple, orange, green and blue
Where the day bakes and the night chills

My grandparents' winter adobe
Has a lemon tree, and fernlike cacti.
We wake up as early as a cactus wren
And pick the delicious lemons.
The saguaro and its countless arms,
The javelina eating the prickly pear, make it heart-shaped,
The hawks and wrens,
These all coexist in the Sonoran Desert.

Sabino Canyon's abundance of wildlife is unimaginable for a place so arid
Coyotes, deer, and mountain lions.
Once Ethan, two friends, and I had our picture taken by a "Beware of Mountain Lions" sign
Shaped like a diamond.

Noah Sandweiss, Grade 6
Binford Elementary School, IN

Christmas Day

I come downstairs with excitement growing inside me. I race to the family room like I'm on fire. The stockings are filled to the brim and the presents are stacked up high underneath the tree. I scream happily as I begin to rip open my presents.

I look outside and the sun is just coming up. The lights on the tree are twinkling like the stars on a clear night while the fire is burning like the sun on a warm summer day.

While everybody is ripping open their presents I stop and listen. I listen to the Christmas music. I hear the shrill of joy and lots of laughing. The sound of crinkling wrapping paper is like a violin playing a beautiful song.

I have so many questions. How did you know? Where did you get this? Does this day have to end?
The snowflakes are dancing angels and the tree is alive. I feel like I'm soaring a mile high. I feel happier than I ever have before.

I know it is
    Christmas
    Christmas
    Christmas

Caroline Janssen, Grade 5
EH Greene Intermediate School, OH

Madison Bieker

Caring to everyone I know, outgoing, freckles covering my body, and singing is so cool
Sister of Tyler Bieker
Lover of my family because they care for me so much, my pets because they are so fuzzy and friendly,
    and my friends because they care for me just like my family
Who feels homework is not bad, my brother is mean to me sometimes,
    and weekends and vacations are so much fun
Who needs someone to love and someone to love me, to have the best life ever, and to give love to my family
Who gives food to my pets when my parents say to,
    does not give an attitude with my parents, and respect to my family
Who fears getting scared by my sibling and his friends,
    lightning because it feels like it will hit me, and moving because I have to make new friends
Who would like to go shopping because it is fun, go to Hawaii because I can go to the beach,
    and go to school because Mrs. Trimmer makes it fun

Madison Bieker, Grade 5
Sanderson Elementary School, OH

The Mouse

What if
The mouse
Could scurry faster?

Then when the people
Would try to catch him
All they'd get
Would be a bit of plaster!

Phillip Hedayatnia, Grade 5
Birchwood School, OH

For the Vets

For all the vets,
Who hope and pray,
That trouble and harm,
Will not come their way.

For the vets who died bravely,
And those who survived,
Who are burdened with sorrow,
The rest of their lives.

For all the vets,
Who fought for you and me,
And even more so,
To defend liberty.

For all the vets,
Who flew just like birds,
The friends that they've lost,
And the screams that they've heard.

For all those who fought,
On land, air, or sea,
We give big thanks,
From the Land of the Free.

Mark Hancher, Grade 6
EH Greene Intermediate School, OH

United States

Historical sites everywhere.
How many states?
Fifty states, fifty large states.
Every state has a civilization
Big beautiful mountain ranges,
Grasslands and rivers.
Large lakes in the Midwest.
Tons of large cities.
What are some?
Detroit, Los Angeles, and Seattle.
Sport teams in almost every state.
The best natural resources, everyone
Looks to us.
Great place to be, America.

Nathaniel Hornyak, Grade 5
May V Peck Elementary School, MI

The Wind Can Be Very Tricky

The wind is nice.
The wind is cool.
It shakes the trees outside of school.
Sometimes I'm so cold I feel I could cry.
The wind could blow all day and night.
The wind could even give me a fright.

In the summer the wind is your friend.
So enjoy it while it may last.
Because winter comes fast.

Christina Rivera, Grade 6
Trilby Elementary School, OH

Fall's Here So Look Around You

Fall is brewing
Look around you
Apple orchards are opening
Pumpkins are growing
So look around you
Fall is here

Kelsey Berry, Grade 5
Kenowa Hills Intermediate School, MI

The Snake

Snake
Green, white
Slithering, hissing, striking
Strikes then swallows
Snake

Andrew Long, Grade 5
Rootstown Elementary School, OH

Teenagers

T hink they are cool
E ntering where they should not be
E ighteen and up are bullies
N ight falls and they are gone
A t night they go to parties
G oing and doing anything
E very night doing new things
R eliving their lives every night
S omewhere they are found

Cierra Gifford, Grade 6
Mayfield Elementary School, OH

We Won

He's down, He's down
He's been tackled to the ground.
We cheer, we cheer,
As the offense takes the field.
We score, we score,
Leave the audience wanting more.
We won, we won,
Winning touchdown at the gun.

Nathan King, Grade 5
Spaulding Elementary School, OH

My Dog

Plain, brownish, black
Running, barking, hyper
Kind, loving, mean, active,
Large pup

Lane Nusbaum, Grade 4
Riverside Elementary School, MI

The Season of Change

Flocks of birds fly overhead,
Away from the lake.
The ground is buried in fallen leaves,
Brilliant colors take place,
Instead of the usual bland concrete.
The air is as cool as an ocean wave.
I can see my breath,
Like steam in the frozen air.
I am hugged by many layers of warmth.
Winter is near, but there's still time,
To enjoy autumn, the season of change.

Sydney Alibeckoff, Grade 6
Rocky River Middle School, OH

If I Were a Turkey

If I were a turkey,
I would taste juicy.
I would be full of stuffing.
I would like not to be killed and stuffed.
I'd want to live.
If I were a turkey,
I would gobble all day long.
I would wish I could fly.
I would love for no Thanksgiving dinner.
I would listen for the hunters.
I would have tons of freedom.

Jachob Shaffer, Grade 5
Reed Middle School, OH

Lonely Snowman

I am a lonely snowman
Hit with snowballs
I freeze overnight
I have no family in sight
I am a snowman living my way…
Alone and cold.

Keanu Jordan, Grade 5
Westview Elementary School, OH

Winter

Snow flakes falling on your tongue
Ice crisp on pine trees
Birds flying south
Wearing toasty coats
Drinking hot cocoa
Throwing snow balls.

Chelsea Lancaster, Grade 5
May V Peck Elementary School, MI

My Dog, Petey

My dog, Petey, is a great little sweetie.
He will always make a big bark
At my friend Mark.
He always makes a high whine
When we are at dine.
He likes to play with my brother, Bradley.
Sometimes he cries very sadly.
Later he will have fun in the snow;
I just totally know.

Brendan Stephens, Grade 5
Rochester Hills Christian School, MI

Countdown

Everyone's gathered in one place,
Fireworks are ready to blast,
Some are writing resolutions,
Soon this will all be the past.

The sky's black, it's almost midnight,
Yet on inside are all the lights.

Counting down to zero,
Lively people sound,
Getting louder every second,
Inside them hearts do pound.

Why do people watch fireworks pop?
Why do others watch the grand ball drop?

Outside, what looks like cotton that flies,
Is only snow falling from the skies.
This holiday is like the Fourth of July,
You get to see fireworks up high.

Happy New Year!
Happy New Year!
Happy New Year!

Sabrina Kaul, Grade 5
EH Greene Intermediate School, OH

Solar System

S tars are everywhere
O ur Earth is in the solar system
L ife has not been found on Mars
A stronauts go into space
R ings around Saturn are made of
 ice crystals, rocks, and dust

S cientists study the planets
Y oung astronauts train to go into space
S aturn is the seventh planet in the solar system
T ravelers are astronauts
E arth is one of our eight planets
M oon is called Luna in Mexico.

Maddie Munn, Grade 4
Westview Elementary School, OH

Halloween

Pumpkins are orange, plump, and round
Faces glowing through the spooky and dark night
Carving fun all through the day
Smiling or frowning they are all still pumpkins
Ghosts, witches, and goblins
All trying to scare you 'til you can't take it
Costumes scary or funny
All get candy from all kinds of houses
Witches flying on brooms
Ghosts hovering through walls
Goblins trying to haunt everyone
Candy everywhere you go
Lollipops, candies and tootsie rolls
All in one spectacular night!

Zachary Johnson, Grade 5
Washington Township Elementary School, IN

Love

why would you give yourself up…
just for love?
I don't think I'll ever get it
unless it happens to me

love we write about it
we say we feel it what is it
that makes us want someone there
is it just human nature

no…it's not
love…
it's everything to everybody
when you don't have somebody love alone is there

love is alive
why aren't we celebrating
it's sad we know it's there and we can just let it go

why…ask yourself why
why…love
why…now
why…me

Brenna Gates, Grade 6
Logan Hocking Middle School, OH

November

November is the standing trees
Stretching their branches out far and wide
Like a skeleton's creepy-crawly bones
November is the clanking on the empty plates
ready to eat all of the food on the Thanksgiving table
so hungry that their stomach is growling
like a monster comin' out of the cold
Witches and ghosts go back to their ghastly caves
waiting to haunt Halloween lovers again and again!

Brianna Zajac, Grade 5
Beck Centennial Elementary School, MI

Party Stuff

Party
Happy, cheerful,
Singing, eating, playing
My tenth birthday party
Perfect

Frank Young, Grade 4
Floyd Ebeling Elementary School, MI

Homework

Homework
Work due tomorrow
Something that brings great sorrow
Luckily, my dog ate it
Are you sure you want it back?

Lillian Richards, Grade 6
Abbott Middle School, MI

Dragonfly

Dragonfly
Beautiful, light
Drifting, soaring, swaying
Painted mystique
Dragon's kiss

Paige Krommes, Grade 6
Melrose Elementary School, OH

My Dad

Father
Handsome, worker.
Tries his best every day.
He is very loving, joyful.
Loves me.

Rachel Stallard, Grade 6
Wooster Christian School, OH

Life and Death

Life
bright, cheerful
running, jumping, skipping
joyful, happy, sad, mournful
lying, rotting, decomposing
dark, gloomy
Death

Josh Ward, Grade 5
Perry Central Elementary School, IN

Winter

Winter
Cold, windy
Snowing, sledding, shoveling
Freezing, frostbite, fun, climbing
Running, biking, tricycling
Hot, sunny
Summer

Quinton Anderson, Grade 5
May V Peck Elementary School, MI

The Jolly Christmas

On the morning of Christmas, I can smell the scent of cinnamon in places.
I hear laughter, and see smiling faces.
The morning light suddenly blazes,
As if grinning and we go through ice skating mazes,
Tumbling in the snow.
I hear laugher and joy, while mothers are yelling to the naughty children no, no, no.
The children hear echoes of Santa's jolly ho, ho, ho.
Is my present small?
Could we ever catch Santa? Have I been naughty at all?
The children stare in awe as their older siblings perform amazing tricks,
And they try to imitate, doing a mix of ballet and gymnastics.
We are having much fun on this Christmas Day,
Everyone smiling, as they play.
We don't mind getting messy, no, no, no.
But everybody has one thing on their mind: The jolly echo of Santa's

Ho,
Ho,
Ho.

Kristine Kim, Grade 5
EH Greene Intermediate School, OH

Hug

Hug.
Always there for me.
Before school, after school, and at night; you are always there.
You have never missed a day and you never will, I can rely on that!
Whenever I need you, you are there;
When I'm fortunate or gloomy, anytime.
Smiling at me, waiting to embrace me in a long, cozy squeeze.
Maybe for others, you sneak away quietly with a giggle.
Not for me, I can count on you, hug.

Hanna Szentkiralyi, Grade 6
Harding Middle School, OH

Ways to Amuse Yourself After School

Make a small fire with no adult supervision
Play outside with friends when it is bright outside
Watch your favorite television show
Play computer games when you should be doing homework
Read a book when your mom told you to clean your room
Walk your dog if you are bored and have nothing to do
Play a bored game with your family
Go to volleyball practice and learn some new skills
Ride your bike and get some extra exercise
Play badminton with your brother or sister
Go shopping and buy some cute, new clothes
Ride your scooter and glide down the street
Play around with your dog
Fight with your siblings if you are in the mood
Talk on the phone until your mom says that you are wasting minutes
Play Wii with your parents and do not tell them how bad they are
Have a sleepover on the weekend if you do not have anything to do in the morning
Eat ice cream if you have some in the freezer
Throw a huge party if your parents are not home

Mackenzie Cohen, Grade 5
Sanderson Elementary School, OH

Class Run

Let's go! Let's go! Let's hurry up!
We are almost out of luck.
We've got to move! We've got to go!
Let's move! Let's move! Let's move along!
We cannot get this answer wrong!
We've got to go very fast.
Because it's almost time for class!

McKena Boos, Grade 5
Kenowa Hills Intermediate School, MI

Christmas Reminds Me Of…

Christmas reminds me of presents.
Presents remind me of happiness.
Happiness reminds me of friends and family.
Friends and family remind me of love.
Love reminds me of hearts.
Hearts remind me of holidays.
Holidays remind me of joy.
Joy reminds me of Santa.
Santa reminds me of workshops.
Workshops remind me of elves.
Elves remind me of snow globes.
Snow globes remind me of snow.
Snow reminds me of ice.
Ice reminds me of winter.
Winter reminds me of Christmas.

Jacara Moore, Grade 6
Waverly East Intermediate School, MI

If Kids Took Over School

If kids took over school,
There would be
No more homework,
And no more tests!
If kids ruled the school,
There would be
More recess,
And more time to rest.
There would be no science or social studies,
And we would get to talk with all our buddies.
No more homework!
No more rules!

Lajayeda Ocasio, Grade 4
Legend Elementary School, OH

Roller Coasters

Roller coasters
Roller coasters are fun they have loops
Roller coasters
When they go fast people scream.
The best ones are the Maverick, Millennium Force
Also Dragster, Raptor, Mantis, and the Snakefalls River
Roller coasters can go 121 mph
But the scariest of all is the Dragster.

Trey Mayer, Grade 4
Churubusco Elementary School, IN

Baseball

Baseball is a time to make good friends
Sometimes we fight but we make amends
Whenever we gather on the field to play
The time just seems to fade away
When we get a double play
The whole team will shout hurray
When I get up to bat
The pitcher sulks inside his hat
When the ump makes a bad call
We will all begin to brawl
Now that you know the game
You will never be the same

Zackery Charles Duff, Grade 6
Emmanuel-St Michael Lutheran School, IN

Clouds

The cloud takes me up and away
Below I see the people at the bay
Carry me away, away, away
As the wind blows the cloud dances to the beat
It makes me want to get up and move my feet
Carry me away, away, away
The cloud pulls me up above the stars
From here I can still see the stars
Carry me away, away, away
It's night and it's time for me to go home
The clouds are fluffy they start to look like foam
Carry me away, away, away

Makayla Warren, Grade 6
Woodward Park Middle School, OH

I Am

I am athletic and funny
I wonder if I will play for the Texas Longhorns football team
I hear fish jumping out of the water when I fish
I see a big largemouth bass on my fishing line
I want my art to come alive
I am athletic and funny

I pretend I'm Tony Stewart winning the Daytona 500
I feel so excited on Christmas morning
I touch my PS2 controller
I worry about breaking a bone
I cry when I get hurt
I am athletic and funny

I understand you have to work for what you want
I say Utica rocks
I dream of being a pro Supercross racer
I try to get better at fishing
I hope I will meet Kevin Vandam and Tony Stewart
I am athletic and funny

I am Clay Holmes

Clay Holmes, Grade 4
Floyd Ebeling Elementary School, MI

I Am From…
I am from the "corn" state people call Indiana.
I am from a family of five with a dramatic sister and a spontaneous brother.
I am from friends doing basketball, friends doing Tae Kwon Do, and friends doing cheerleading.
I am from a catholic school with class clowns and friends.
I am from a family with love.

Olivia Stuart, Grade 6
St Maria Goretti School, IN

Friends
Friends are kind. Friends go out at recess together. Make sure hat your friend is right for you. Friends tell jokes. Friends are friends who comment about each other. Friends are people who care about each other. I love friends they are very kind and generous.

Casey Radford, Grade 4
Veale Elementary School, IN

Winter
Days darkening,
Cold creeping through your bones.
Slush slowing everyone's day
Blankets of ice slipping under your feet,
And snow,
Begging for your attention like a puppy begging for food, but needing to be shoveled anyway.

But when you get past the pestering,
And walk through the door to be greeted by family,
Smiles and laughter,
Bright light and decorations,
And beautiful holiday music playing washes away the bad memories and the stress,
Only to keep you going one more day of
Winter

Patrick McMahon, Grade 6
Harding Middle School, OH

The Arikara Indians
In the morning, dawn crept up the horizon. During growing season we worship corn like we would worship a god. My tribe travels in canoes across the wide highway of the Missouri River. In the late 1700's the strong Sioux sadly defeated the Arikara Indians in a battle. The Arikara Indians are like buffalo because they travel in groups, such as their brave migration from the Missouri River to North Dakota. They are very strong.

Isabelle Peters, Grade 5
Barrington Elementary School, OH

My Life
My life is…sports. Dribble. Shoot. Kick. Save. Goal. Basket. Point. Bump.
Set. Spike. Serve. Catch. Pitch. Throw. Win. Lose.
My life is…school. Run. Tardy. Pass. Fail. Pop quiz. Notes. A+. D-.
My life is…music. Rest. Play. Practice. Memorize. Recital. Concert.
My life is…friends. Laugh. Live. Shop. Hang out. Talk. Ask. Faithful. Fun.
My life is…family. I love you. You're grounded. Get out of my room! What do you think you are doing? Laugh. Together.
My life is…God. Prayer. Chapel. Faith. Comfort. Love. Protection. Eternal life.

My life is…crowded, busy, tight, fun, pressed, exciting. Me…fun-loving, competitive, happy, talkative, weird, interesting, smart
100% Samantha Jo Brown,
athlete, scholar, friend, musician, daughter, sister, catholic.
That's me, pure me. My life.

Samantha Brown, Grade 6
Corpus Christi Catholic School, MI

I Am

I am athletic and blonde.
I wonder where unicorns live.
I hear my unicorn sing.
I see my unicorn working.
I want to go to Tennessee State for softball.
I am athletic and blonde.
I pretend I'm Spiderman.
I feel jealous when my unicorn gets a cookie.
I touch my unicorn's soft fur.
I worry about my family's health.
I cry when my animals die.
I am athletic and blonde.
I understand that I'm not perfect.
I say that I have lots of friends.
I dream that I'm a nurse that types really fast.
I try to pitch faster.
I hope that my hitting gets better.
I am athletic and blonde.

Whitney French, Grade 6
Galesburg-Augusta Middle School, MI

All About Me

C ool person to be around
H e hates brussel sprouts
R esident of Austintown, Ohio
I s a right-handed person
S erious about school
T akes martial arts at Northeast Martial Arts
O pinions in school
P atient person
H as good grades in school
E xcellent in school
R adiant person

R aymond is my grandfather's name
A ttends Frank Ohl
Y oungest in household

D rug free student
R eally nice friend
O utstanding at martial arts
E nthusiastic person for trends
G reat friend to people
E asygoing

Christopher Ray Droege, Grade 5
Frank Ohl Intermediate School, OH

Anger Is Red

Anger is red,
It tastes like bad tacos,
It smells like smoke from a house on fire.
It reminds me of revenge on someone,
It sounds like rage and fists,
Anger makes me feel red.

Can Bekcioglu, Grade 5
Tremont Elementary School, OH

I Am From

I am from my achievements and my mistakes
I am from my birthdays with big awesome cakes
I am from my brother with whom I fight
I am from the pets I have loved with all my might
The friends that are there when I am down
I am from the treasures I have found
From the day I was born to the day I die
I am from what I hear, touch, feel, and see

Coleson Sharp, Grade 6
Northwood Elementary School, IN

I Am

I am sporty and competitive
I wonder how technology will change
I hear a video game blasting away
I see a real live pokemon standing in front of me
I want to have a holographic video game
I am sporty and competitive

I pretend I like school
I feel happy on Christmas morning
I touch a real live breathing pokemon
I worry about a thief stealing my pokemon stuff
I cried when my dog Marley died

I understand why my dog Marley died
I say that I miss my dog Marley
I dream that my pokemon were alive
I try to get stronger
I hope I become a video game master
I am sporty and competitive

I am Nathan Hebel

Nathan Hebel, Grade 4
Floyd Ebeling Elementary School, MI

My Amazing Neighborhood

My neighborhood is no walk in the park.

On my way home I see
Birds chirping and dogs howling.
Kids are playing tag.
Some run as fast as cheetahs.
Most adults are yawning or snoring.
Lots of people are slamming their car doors.
I hear a train pass by.
Some kids are playing basketball.
I see a fish jump out of the lake.
I'm home.
Before I go inside I look to the right
And see my neighbor waving.
I wave and go inside.

That's my walk home.

Amanda De Jesus, Grade 5
Allen J. Warren Elementary School, IN

Tiger

I am a very fierce tiger.
Ready to attack
Any creature that threatens me.
I will stand for myself.
Running toward dreams like prey.
Ready to take on the world.
I am a very fierce tiger.

Adrianna Carver, Grade 5
Westview Elementary School, OH

Fall Festival

F un
A pple cider
L ots of food
L emonade

F amily time
E ating
S now cones
T all trees
I ce cream
V anilla
A wesome time
L ots of rides

I ces
N ight

O ctober
H amburgers
I ndian corn
O ver stuffed

U nder the stars
S ticky buns
A ttractions

Brandon Solomon, Grade 5
Akiva Academy, OH

Scarflight

Scarflight is like
A secret on the mind
Waiting to be
Reveled to the
World.
Scarflight is
A leader
A fighter
A strong-willed mind
A cat with some personality
A role model to many
A teacher
A hunter
This is Scarflight.

Meg Morris, Grade 6
Woodward Park Middle School, OH

I Am

I am pretty and curious.
I wonder if bumblebees have birthday parties.
I hear a flower crying.
I see candy laughing.
I want to be a professional actress.
I am pretty and curious.
I pretend to be a super hero.
I feel happy because I found out that I can walk on water.
I touch a fuzzy radio.
I worry about breaking my leg.
I cry about knowing that some children in other countries are starving.
I am pretty and curious.
I understand that the population around the world is growing.
I say that ghosts are real.
I dream about falling from buildings.
I try to improve on getting my left splits.
I hope that someday there will be world peace all over the world.
I am pretty and curious.

Calli Ragotzy, Grade 6
Galesburg-Augusta Middle School, MI

Happiness Is Like…

Happiness is yellow like a sun on a hot and bright sunny day.
And also like God's light guiding the way to heaven.
It flows through my mind like a beautiful yellow bird soaring through the sky.
It reminds me of when I was playing with others and I had a terrific time.
It makes me feel refreshed and pure.
It makes me want to share my happiness with others.

Christina Taylor, Grade 6
St Maria Goretti School, IN

My Angel, My Best Friend*

I see her face everywhere I go,
She's here with me and this I know.
She was more to me than just a sister,
And right now, I wish with all of my heart that I could be with her.
She changed my life in so many ways,
I'll never forget her in all of my days.
I miss her, I want her right here with me,
I'll run around the world,
I'll cast out to sea,
But will I find her?
No.
She is something much bigger now,
My angel standing out in the crowd.
In my heart she has beautiful wings,
She stands above the clouds and sings.
And one of those songs, she sings for me.
And she cries.
Tears of joy stream down her face,
While she's living in amazing grace.
She lives, she breathes,
Forever.

Hallie Kile, Grade 6
St Michael School, IN
*In loving memory of my sister and best friend, Jessie Kile

The Sioux Indians

As the morning says hello,
I set off to fish in the cool, clear lake.
I watch the fire as it does its morning dance,
It's red-orange glow blazing brightly,
As the cotton ball clouds hang high above my head.

I smile and think about the wonderful feast
Our people had last night and how lucky I am
To be a Sioux Indian.

Emma Ortquist, Grade 5
Barrington Elementary School, OH

The Underworld

The underworld is a crazy place,
There are dangerous creatures and an ugly race,
There's goblins, witches, poisonous snakes,
Bubbling cauldrons and lava lakes.

Devilish laughter through the cave,
You cannot run you cannot save,
Skeletons roam the ghostly trails,
And ghostly trains run stone cold rails.

But once a mighty hero had risen,
And freed most from this ugly prison,
For he was told to be brave and bold,
And showered with gifts of gems and gold.

The underworld is a crazy place,
There are dangerous creatures and an ugly race,
There's goblins, witches, poisonous snakes,
Bubbling cauldrons and lava lakes.

Kazzi Ervin, Grade 4
Springfield Local Elementary School, OH

Summer

Summer is a great time of year.
Summer is a warm, gentle breeze.
Summer is spending time with your family at the lake.
Summer is feeling the water at the lake get warmer.
Summer is long weekends and no homework.
Summer is having friends over for the day.
Summer is feeling lazy and relaxing.
Summer is visiting with relatives.
Summer is catching up with friends.
Summer is a fun pool day.
Summer is watching the sunset.
Summer is not caring what time the sun sets.
Summer is letting the sun wake you.
Summer is rolling over and sleeping longer.
Summer is long runs with my mom.
Summer is bike rides with my family.
Summer is picnics at the park.
Summer is the best time of the year!

Teddy Terzian, Grade 6
St Gerard School, MI

Pillows Rock

Pillows are for your bed
They are to rest your head
They are for when you are down
They allow you to frown
They are comforting when you cry
They hold your head up high
You can squeeze them tight as you sigh
A cushion for your head as you gaze for stars
And muffle the sound of the cars
As you see, pillows rock
They are there for you around the clock
So whether they are for sleeping, snuggling, drying your tears,
You can have a pillow for many years.

Emily Rooks, Grade 6
Abbott Middle School, MI

Christmas Time

Christmas is my favorite time.
I like to hear the bells chime.
I went in the living room to see if Santa had come,
Under the tree was still bare so I was glum.
The Christmas tree looked so pretty,
Some ornaments were little bitty.
The tree was so big,
I saw only one little twig.
Christmas time is here,
It is my favorite time of the year!

Brittany Waters, Grade 4
Chrisney Elementary School, IN

The Falcon

A dark, gray shape soars through the sky,
With magnificent wing and piercing eye,
Floats calmly through the bright-blue dome,
With ferocity that bleeds straight to the bone.
Then darting to the old stone quarry,
Awaiting food and powerful glory,
To do battle with the sinister serpent,
Who has caused him almost endless torment.

The evil snake knows of this great beast,
And prepares himself for the vile feast,
With poisonous fangs and whipping tail;
The young, vain creature thinks he will not fail.
Fang meets beak, and tail meets talon,
The snake's foul mouth in a hideous grin,
The falcon's beak tight with hate,
Sealing what was the serpent's fate.

The savage snake knew his inevitable fate,
Seeing the dark underworld gate,
With his last strength he bit his foe,
Then departed to where all the evil ones go,
Finishing the hunter's final task.

Patrick Evans, Grade 6
Stanley Clark School, IN

Barack

Barack
Obama won
He is the first black man
To be president. McCain lost
It all.

Jack Campise, Grade 5
Tremont Elementary School, OH

Cows and Calves

Cows are fun
When the sun goes down
In the summer
It is scorching in the milk parlor
In the winter
It is frigid fr- fr- eezing
Cows are a pain
Because they consume too much grain
Calves are cute
When they don't need the vet's bute
Cows are calm
Because their sore udder needs balm
Calves are cute
But p-u — they sure can pollute
Calves usually get covered in muck
But they like the clean bottle they suck
So can't you see?
Don't you agree with me?
Cows are fun
When the sun goes down!

Luke Hilgenhold, Grade 5
Perry Central Elementary School, IN

Ocean

Cracking of the beautiful shells
Swimming of the colorful fish
Eating of the gray sharks
Softness of the tan sand
Splashing of the jade waters
Grossness of the green algae
Chirping of the beautiful seagulls

Emily Meirose, Grade 6
St Clement Elementary School, OH

Respect

Respect means many things
Let me listen them for you.

R is for responsibility
E is for everything you do
S is for self control
P is for people that care
E is for everyone around you
C is for confidence we have
T is for together we care

Tatum Manos, Grade 4
John Simatovich Elementary School, IN

Snowflakes

My exquisite shapes and designs
are perfectly formed
as I swiftly and slowly glide
down, down, down
to the Earth below.

My brothers and sisters alike
cover the calm surface
with a sheet of white.

Jessica Budz, Grade 5
Central Grade School, MI

Peanut Butter

P eanutbutter
E asily
A ccessed
N ear the crust
U pon
T he

B read
U ltimate
T aste
T o the
E nd of
R avingly

Jakob Mangus, Grade 6
Erie Elementary School, OH

Grocery List

Beets that are red,
Bacon that is crispy.
Bread that is wonderful,
Bubblegum that goes pop!
Blueberries, the sweeter the better.

Lexi Aders, Grade 6
Perry Central Elementary School, IN

River

As the river flows
A log races without slow
And a barge horn blows

Margaret Doster, Grade 6
Harmon Middle School, OH

Fall

The butterflies flying
as the flowers sway
the animals are getting
a cool, cool breeze
the birds are singing
the wind is slightly blowing
now summer is asleep
and fall is awake.

Kyla Tramper, Grade 5
Kenowa Hills Intermediate School, MI

Football

Football is my life.
Football is awesome,
You get to sack the quarterback,
You can create a fumble.
You can bolt away with the ball,
And score a TD to win the game.
Football is my life.

Zach Rogier, Grade 5
Perry Central Elementary School, IN

Fall

Watch the fall leaves drop,
Fluttering down from treetops
Harvest time arrives,
Hurry, squirrels, find your nuts,
Before winter blankets us.

Daniel Watts, Grade 5
Westview Elementary School, OH

Daniel

Daniel
Happy, caring
Loving, talking, working
A loving happy person
Daddy

Daniella Battani, Grade 4
Floyd Ebeling Elementary School, MI

Dad

Dad
Amazing, awesome,
Loving, helping, guiding
My dad
Father

Mark Jones, Grade 5
St Jude Catholic School, IN

Hyper

I
was dancing, weee
in my house
in the middle of the bright night
because I was so hyper.

Anthany Bemis, Grade 6
Perry Central Elementary School, IN

Snow/Rain

Snow
Cold, white
Freezing, snowing, playing
White snow, cold rain
Dripping, drizzling, raining
Clear, wet
Rain

Emily Nicole Davis, Grade 6
Perry Central Elementary School, IN

I Am

I am funny and smart.
I wonder if there is another world in another universe
exactly like ours with the same people and things.
I hear my shoes singing.
I see magical unicorns.
I want a furry Chihuahua.
I am funny and smart.
I pretend I can fly.
I feel disappointed I don't have a green cat.
I touch purple trees.
I worry the world's going to end.
I cry during Oprah.
I am funny and smart.
I understand school is important.
I say nothing is impossible except impossibility itself.
I dream life is a dream, and when you die
it's like you're waking up into a whole new life.
I try to take good care of my animals.
I hope to be successful when I grow up.
I am funny and smart.

Logan Sondgerath, Grade 6
Galesburg-Augusta Middle School, MI

My Father Was Wrong/Right

I went on a hike.
Now I'm on my bike.
I felt myself lift high, high, high.
Into the sky as I said good bye.
I say my father is wrong.
As I was singing a song.
I flew a little more.
And then I let out a roar.
Cause I flew into a tree.
I whispered oh, oh, me.
You stumbled over a rock
As I barely could hear my mom talk.
I guess my father was right.
That was not a pretty sight.

Madison Meurer, Grade 5
North Knox East Elementary/Jr High School, IN

Fall

It is time for fall to come,
Hands will be numb.
Leaves are falling, it is time to rake,
I may see a snake.
I have to rake,
Jake has to bake a great cake.
Abbey has to take the leaves out of the pool,
Because the weather is turning cool.
Apples are falling,
Someone is calling.
Fall is awesome,
Now, you won't see a blossom.

Bailey Stahl, Grade 4
Chrisney Elementary School, IN

Slave Pen

It is so dark and lonely in here,
As I look around and shake with fear.
Strange as it is I miss watching the crops,
All day long 'till the farmer says to stop.
No one wants to look or play with me,
Sadly one week ago I lost my family.
I just sit in the corner all alone and sad,
While others look happy when they know they're mad.
I wish I could be outside feeding the hens,
But instead I'm stuck in this dumb slave pen.

Nina Stewart, Grade 4
Mayfield Elementary School, OH

Reading a Good Book

Reading a good book is such a thriller!
Just trying to figure out the killer!
Mysteries are my favorite kind,
But nonfiction gives me a confusing mind.

Science fiction is such a bore!
But historical, give me some more!

Scary stories are not for me,
And reading boring mythology, help me!
I would rather be stung by a bee!

My opinion decides what books are for me.
Yours can tell you too, if you just look and see!

Jana Schroeder, Grade 6
Miller City-New Cleveland School, OH

I Am

I am intelligent and curious
I wonder if I'll be a scientist
I hear bubbling chemicals
I see test tubes and chemicals
I want to do experiments
I am intelligent and curious

I pretend I like doing chores
I feel gloves on my hands and goggles on my face
I touch the test tubes and sponges
I worry if my dog will die soon
I cry when my hamsters die
I am intelligent and curious

I understand if someone dies
I say if you hold on to a dream it will always come true
I dream of being a scientist
I try to do my best at school
I hope I will become a scientist
I am intelligent and curious

I am Caden Witte

Caden Witte, Grade 4
Floyd Ebeling Elementary School, MI

Weather

Oh, out in the sun,
So bold and bright,
Just shining on me
Every day and night.

Watching the sun
Go up and down,
Just so pretty
Like a lovely gown.

I go outside;
I play around
Hey, it's raining —
I think I could drown.

That's it — go inside
And watch some flicks.
I am sad — that's okay.
Maybe I'll do some tricks.

Morgan Bright, Grade 6
Melrose Elementary School, OH

Swimming

Wet, liquid
Swimming, water ski, volleyball
Fun to play in
Olympics

Carly Jean Jarboe, Grade 6
Perry Central Elementary School, IN

Feline Hunter

I am a feline hunter
Looking for a mouse
Climbing a tree
Running through the grass
Pouncing on the victim
I will eat well tonight!

Jerrit Crosier, Grade 5
Westview Elementary School, OH

On the Ship

Aboard the ship
Across the sea
Without any food
Near the shore
Till we land
On the island

Jacob Klicman, Grade 5
Rootstown Elementary School, OH

Three Meter Jump

I gain my courage.
Greenish-blue water waiting.
Water smacks my feet!

Evan Todd, Grade 6
Stanley Clark School, IN

I Am

I am athletic and joyful
I wonder if I will be rich in the future
I hear wind in my head
I see waves in my head
I want my future to be the best ever
I am athletic and joyful

I pretend to be a pro soccer player
I feel the power of the Earth in my hands
I touch the snow in the winter morning
I worry that there might be a tornado
I cry when I get hurt really bad
I am athletic and joyful

I understand that no one will always get what they want all the time
I say that my soccer team is good
I dream that my soccer team is good and they will win the soccer game
I try to do my best in soccer
I hope that I get A's in the future
I am Vito Palazzolo

Vito Palazzolo, Grade 4
Floyd Ebeling Elementary School, MI

Wheelbarrow Moment*

Plip, plop goes the rain like a leaky drain pipe.
A red wheelbarrow gets speckled with dewy drops.
I am in the damp garage of my house
looking at the red wheelbarrow that I use
to transport sand bags to my dam of soil outside to stop the flood.
I have been doing this for two days now.
It is another cold, damp, and rainy morning.
The rain makes the day colder;
I want to go in to a nice warm fire.
So much depends on the red wheelbarrow.
The chickens are safely tucked
away in their cage upstairs

Luke Burke, Grade 5
Stanley Clark School, IN
Dedicated to William Carlos Williams

Family Reunion in the Woods

I wander away from Cabin #9, my home.
The darkness creeps around me,
the moon shining silver and bright.
The wolves howl in the distance.
These are the last seconds of pure peace.

BAM! The sun shoots up bright orange!
Just then my cousins drive into the clearing:
Aunt Marilyn, Uncle Jeff, and cousins Austin, Brittany, and Johnna.
They jump out of my uncle's Jeep, laughing and joking.
The quiet peace is gone, but I am happy and joyful;
My family is here enjoying the bright, great sunshine.
This is the best time of my life.

Vincent Belkiewitz, Grade 5
Stanley Clark School, IN

One

One shot can win a game.
One vote can choose the president.
One rain can save a crop.
One meal can save a life.
One song can encourage a person.
One teacher can change a student.
One flower can show love.
One letter can make someone's day.
One smile can be contagious.
One bird can sing a beautiful song.
One tree can provide shelter for many birds.
One ocean can hold many boats.
One drink can quench thirst.
One donation can help the poor.
One life can make a difference.
One church can offer faith.

Ben Respecki, Grade 6
St Gerard School, MI

I Am

I am funny and caring.
I wonder if they will ever build a flying car.
I hear my eraser burning as I erase.
I see my socks running from my feet.
I want one million dollars.
I am funny and caring.
I pretend to be good.
I feel mad when my pencil bites my fingers when I write.
I touch the burning flames of the sun.
I worry about my grandma who's in the hospital.
I cry when someone in my family dies.
I am funny and caring.
I understand 8th grade math (sort of.)
I say I hope I will go to heaven.
I dream I will do good.
I try to do my best.
I hope that I will be successful.
I am funny and caring.

Nick Bradstreet, Grade 6
Galesburg-Augusta Middle School, MI

The Beauty of Autumn

The leaves change in this beautiful season,
Yet we do not think of how, but why perhaps.
The leaves change for beauty, or for your soul,
To give it a chance for you to see that
Just about anything, even a tree, can brighten up your day.

Ian Langevin, Grade 4
Stonegate Elementary School, IN

Fall

trees are changing colors
dropping leaves before winter
now endless raking

Hannah Manson, Grade 5
Washington Township Elementary School, IN

Race Horse

I feel my rider on my back.
He says, "Go on, girl, go to the track."
I hear voices and cars go by.
When I'm in the racing pen.
I hear horses snorting and ready to run.
Then I hear the horn
I hear the horn!

It's time to run!
I hear the people yell, "Go, Lightning, go!"

I see the finish line
I feel no other horses around me.
I make a fast move.
I win! I win!
I am so happy!
So is my owner!

Kay Bland, Grade 5
North Knox East Elementary/Jr High School, IN

The Pawnee on the Prairie

The Pawnee roamed the earth like sun and rain,
hunting buffalo and wild game.
Sometimes the prairie grass was just so soft
that the Pawnee tribe would take their moccasins off.
The bow and arrow the Pawnee used,
just like every scrap of food.
When men hunt and children play
the woman will pick berries and bake all day.
We want to protect the Pawnee tribe
so every generation will keep their heritage alive.

Olivia Kompa, Grade 5
Barrington Elementary School, OH

Look Out It's the Diving Tuxedo

What does a penguin know?
Leaping and diving.
Steel, solid bones,
All the ocean's colors and tones.
Shimmering, short, soft, shiny
Fur.
Freezing, frost places,
Burr!
Warm water and whistling wind,
Black and white tuxedo type skin.
Swimming not soaring,
Playful not boring.
Football shaped body,
Webbed feet and wobbly.
Ice and sunlight,
Short, stiff wings,
Propel through the water with 15 miles of speed.
Thousands of feathers, so short and so small,
This is an animal that is stout and not tall.

Meghan Knorp, Grade 5
Riley Upper Elementary School, MI

The Amazing Day

I watch TV
Play a board game
Work with Grandpa
He calls me Scrappy, Shortstuff, GRANT
Ahh!!
Help Grandma in the house
Eat them out of the house
I love Grandma's no-bake cookies
I can see Grandpa working
They help me when I need it
THEY ARE THE BEST.

Grant McHugh, Grade 4
Licking Valley Intermediate School, OH

What Moves Me

B is for best.
A is for awesome.
B is for baby.
Y is for you.

S is for sweet.
I is for sometimes intelligent.
S is for silly.
T is for tough.
E is for entertaining.
R is for rough.

Chandler Grace McGraw, Grade 4
Creekview Elementary School, OH

Red and Gray

Red and gray,
Ohio State.
Touchdown!
For Ohio State!
Gliding down the field,
Tackling, fighting,
For the ball.
Each player's special red,
All together we're one!
T-E-A-M,
Team!

Ayden Felix, Grade 4
Legend Elementary School, OH

Veterans

Being free
Fighting for us
On the eleventh hour
Of the eleventh month
On the eleventh day
Giving lives
For our freedom
it's Veteran's Day!
Show respect to all who served.

Peter Koulianos, Grade 4
Dobbins Elementary School, OH

Starlight

Twinkling lights in the sky —
they never move very far.
You always want to know
what goes on up there.
You never know what you'll
see up in the sky.
Only if you dream.

Anna Pyers, Grade 6
Melrose Elementary School, OH

Super Knockdown

Defense breaks out of huddle,
I go to safety position,
Offense hikes the ball,
I see the receiver,
I spring to him,
He stops,
Waiting,
Looking,
See the ball,
The receiver,
I jump,
I hit the ball,
Knockdown,
Crowd cheers like 100 howler monkeys,
Coach asks,
"How does that feel?"
"Good," I say.

Alex Markules, Grade 6
Assumption BVM School, MI

The Season of Fall

Fall is the season of change.
There are many fun memories.
Lasting images that leave impressions.

As I look at that yummy caramel apple,
I touch the coating of the nuts.
There is a very sticky feeling.

The leaves are very colorful.
Red, green, tan and orange.
The texture is very stiff and crinkly.
They make a crackly sound,
The last breath dies out,

Apple cider, pumpkin bread
All are very tasty.
Halloween, I love the candy,
Sugary sweetness melts in your mouth.

Fall is the season of change.
There are many fun memories.
Lasting images that leave impressions.

Catherine Rochelle, Grade 6
Holy Family Middle School, MI

Flowers

Flowers
Smell beautiful
Swaying with the warm breeze.
It feels like a soft spring meadow
Bouquet

Grant Vawter-Walton, Grade 4
Bailly Elementary School, IN

All About Me

K ind.
E verybody is nice to her.
Y ells.
L ikes kind people
E veryone knows her.
E ven likes the color blue.

Keylee Tow, Grade 4
Shoals Elementary School, IN

Creek

An ocean
With fields
Of rushing water,
Slithering creatures
On its floor,
With fish
Darting about.

Sydney Fowler, Grade 4
Normandy Elementary School, OH

Snowy Sky

Freezing,
Wind blowing.
Spreading its cold
Snowflakes on the ground,
Wintertime.

Kaaliyah Tapscott, Grade 6
Harmon Middle School, OH

Christmas

My family is near,
Children laugh with cheer.
My favorite time is here,
It's Christmas!
Icy streets and sidewalks,
Only ten more days,
The parents always say.
It's Christmas!

Alaina Taylor, Grade 5
Auburn Hills Christian School, MI

Fall

Breezy burning fire
Falling leaves come from the sky
Sounds ring of autumn

Taylor Barhorst, Grade 6
Tippecanoe Middle School, OH

The Land of Tears and Fears

In my house is where I stay throughout the night and day.
I'm a girl who just turned ten; my boy twin gets our pay.
A chador mostly covers my face if a stranger nears where I play.
A shalwar kameez (baggy pants/shirt) I wear here or away.
Land mine "toys" killed my friends, is what people say.

Daily, I work in the busy market, for naan and tea to pour.
My sister is my twin, but she has to stay indoors.
I wear a pakol (cap), and a shalwar kameez that I tore.
To get money I sell things; gum, cigarettes, and more,
And I am a tea-boy that sells store-to-store.

I stay inside but when I go out, a burqa is what I wear.
In my burqa, I feel enclosed indoors, though I'm not there.
I wear a shalwar kameez all day even if I don't feel fair.
I miss hearing kids, miss teaching children without cares.
Will I be killed along with the others? They wouldn't dare.

Our family's torn, living in bombed homes across the sand.
When women go out, a related man takes their hand.
Taliban outlaw school — it's "the Muslim way" in this land.
Money's hard to earn so we're hungry — like food is banned.
Our husband, father is lost forever, dead by the Taliban.

Joanna Vuylsteke, Grade 6
Ann Arbor Christian School, MI

Halloween

H owling ghosts, ghouls, and goblins
A ll are coming out on this night
L et them come out
L et them be free
O ut in the open
W e better run and hide
E very ghost will be out to get us
E veryone beware
N ever let one get you, or you're gone for good

Lindsey Davenport, Grade 5
Washington Township Elementary School, IN

Gifts

G iving to others,
I t's wonderful to have,
F un to open around the house,
T ree limbs hanging over top of them,
S anta brings them on Christmas Eve.

Racheal McCarty, Grade 5
West Washington Elementary School, IN

Squirrels/Rodent

Squirrels
Burnt chestnut
Jumping through trees
Joyfully scurrying through fields
Rodent

David Green, Grade 4
Frank H Hammond Elementary School, IN

Fall Leaves

Red leaf, yellow leaf, orange, and brown,
None of them at all will ever give me a frown.
They're colorful, beautiful, and part of nature's life
To me they look like a golden sight.
But when winter comes, and fall fades away
It starts to get colder, and new fun is on the way.

Mary VanSuch, Grade 4
Dobbins Elementary School, OH

Gifts

G ive is what you do.
I s that what they want?
F amily and friends gather around.
T ime to open your gifts.
S omething is always nice.

Tristin Kirby, Grade 5
West Washington Elementary School, IN

That Horse

I love that horse!
She ran the race course
as fast as she could —
like the wind.

Smells like a rose —
with a pink nose.
Feels fluffy
she never got disciplined.

Big and white like a polar bear
soft like a cuddly, teddy bear
with a pinned ribbon
in her beautiful hair.

Kristina Jonas, Grade 4
Midland Academy of Advanced and Creative Studies, MI

Thanksgiving Day

On Thanksgiving day, we cook the food.
Then we decorate the house.
My friends and I play outside.
When my family gets here, we bake turkey,
Sometimes ham.
Then when we're done, I can help bake the dessert.
And sometimes we take a journey to the woods.
November is a fun month, and
A fun journey for me!
Every year I learn many things;
We gather fruits and vegetables,
Then we have a celebration
Called Thanksgiving.
It is so much fun,
To do the stuff we do
Happy Thanksgiving,
Everybody!

Anitra Mason, Grade 4
Matthew Duvall Elementary School, OH

Dancing

Dancing is the best.
I'll never stop to take a rest.
Some people say it's the worst.
Whoever does will be cursed.
I'll be done in six more hours.
If you need me, I'll be in the shower
Dancing.

Carlee Jones, Grade 5
West Elkton Elementary School, OH

The Beauty of the Night

Before the morning's dawn,
After the day's dusk,
At night's long darkness,
Beside the eternal stars,
Above the tides of the ocean,
Under the universe's watch,
Along the galaxy's planets,
Around outer space's chill,
Within its eternal darkness.

Noah Stucker, Grade 5
Churubusco Elementary School, IN

Summer

I can stay up late
And sleep until noon.
I can lie in the grass
And stare at the moon.

There are bonfires and bugs;
Birds fly and sing.
My best friend comes over
And we don't do a thing.

We splash through the pool;
We toss balls in the air.
We laugh all day long
Not knowing a care.

The fun that we have
Gives us a reason
To feel that summer
Is the greatest season.

Isaac Peterson, Grade 5
Immanuel Christian School, MI

Spring

Can you tell it's spring?
The birds are singing like 100 violins
Can you tell it's spring?
The flowers are blooming
Can you tell it's spring?
The new life cycle is starting again
Now can you tell it's spring?

Samantha James, Grade 5
May V Peck Elementary School, MI

Sleep

Sleep, you mock us
You make us weary, or reenergize us, like a new battery, you fill us with energy
Time and time again, you tease us in the car, at school, at work
You are merely a state of mind
Nevertheless, without you we cannot say conscious
Invisible, but so real
Unfathomable, yet so genuinely there

You sit by my bed each night and whisper, "goodnight"
As consciousness drifts away, you are there seated next to me

With a tiara in your golden hair
You change every night
Tonight you are my dream of feathery white snow

You wear a smooth dress and a choker made of snowflakes
You are my snowy field in my dream, tonight

You gaze at me with ancient eyes as I gaze back, the world disappears
And my mind goes behind my eyelids

Then off to another bedside to award one more person with slumber
A present to humanity

Callan Foran, Grade 6
Harding Middle School, OH

4th of July Magic

The sky after a long day of activities is like a world of opposites.
The dark, dark, sky, the colorful vivid fireworks flying around.
They are the only sources of light.
The thundering and booming of a thousand horses spreads all over the place.
The older kids do the camp cheer, the little ones stumble along.
I can faintly hear the music but it feels closer than it sounds.

Why are fireworks so meaningful?
It brings that true summer feeling to mind and screams to me,
"Yeah, I'm really here right now doing the thing I've been waiting to do."

Black canvas sky being decorated by an exploding paintbrush,
And then slowly disappearing and coming back again.
Real happiness is painted in my heart.

The magical feeling of America is calling me — but in beautiful patterns above.
Summertime, lemonade — boom;
Summertime, pool parties — bam;
Summertime, magical feeling of America — bang!
Now I know — the magical feeling of America is real.

Claire Lefton, Grade 5
EH Greene Intermediate School, OH

In a Guitar

Inside a guitar are the unknown tunes ready to be played.
From the simpleness of one note to the complexity of a whole composition.
A creative mind, nimble fingers, and a single guitar can change almost anything.

Conner Howell, Grade 6
St Maria Goretti School, IN

Leaves

Leaves
They hang out by the oak tree trying to get a tan,
But some of them get sunburned.

Leaves
They slide off the slippery branches.

Leaves
They bounce off the diving board into the pond of grass.

Leaves
When the wind blows, they race across the road.

Leaves
They're worried when it rains,
And they shiver when the rain hits hard.

Amanda Glorio-Riley, Grade 6
Boulan Park Middle School, MI

Mom

M y mom loves me
O h how sweet she will always be
M y mom always tells me how I
will see that someday I will be
as nice, sweet, and caring as her
and then she says be happy we are free.

Hope Baylis, Grade 4
Shoals Elementary School, IN

Puppies

Look into these little puppies' eyes
And what do you see?
Sweet, innocent, balls of fluff
Staring straight at me.
No!

Some might say they are cuddly and fun
But, when you see them
They'll make you want to run!
When no one is home these curious pups chew pillows,
Go through garbage, and even rip up toys!
These pups have been very bad girls and boys!

However, at the end of the day
When they no longer have the energy to play,
I'll kiss them and give lots of hugs
And thank God they're all snug as a bug!

Stephanie Schuller, Grade 6
Eisenhower Middle School, OH

Leaves

Leaves swaying to land
Ruby, chestnut, and olive
Crunching under our feet

Anthony Niemiec, Grade 4
Frank H Hammond Elementary School, IN

Fall

leaves all around me — red, yellow, green
crunching and raking — jumping into leaves
sweaters and coats and getting dirty
getting forced to take showers
grasshoppers moving
in the leaves

BJ Cosgray, Grade 4
Norwich Elementary School, OH

Gifts

G etting gifts is so much fun
I n the wrapping paper is something to be
F un times is always good you see
T rees oh trees all around me
S haring presents playing them too,
always gives you something to do

Catherine Cardwell, Grade 5
West Washington Elementary School, IN

Veteran's Day

It's Veteran's Day indeed,
Where we celebrate a soldier's good deed.
He fought so fiercely,
For freedom we love.

He stepped in without fear
Even as the foe would leer and jeer.
Some might think it very queer
That he will fight so fiercely.

As he marched in,
The foe would pay for their sin!
Under that great flag of ours,
Our wonderful soldier marched with power.
His foes seemed to be devoured
By the might of our great Veteran.

Yes, it's Veteran's Day,
Where the Veterans take a rest,
Because Veterans are the best!

Joseph Vaz, Grade 6
EH Greene Intermediate School, OH

Christmas

There are present wrapped in red and green
And many colors in between
Pine trees get ready
And are put in homes nice and steady
We are ready to bake
So we can make cookies for Santa to take
Presents are underneath a tree
Ready for many faces to see
Christmas time is here today
So let us celebrate and say hooray

Breana Kloski, Grade 6
Corpus Christi Elementary School, IN

Night and Day

A star is a very bright sight
With the moon in the night

The sun is as light as fire in blue sky
Oh so high

In the sunlight I like to play
In the night I like to lay

Wesley Shelton, Grade 4
Veale Elementary School, IN

Wonderful Colors

Red is as bright as a rose.
Green is like the green grass.
Blue is a bunch of blueberries.
Orange is like pumpkin pie.
Purple is like a ripe plum.
Yellow is like a sunflower.
White is as bright as snow.
I love colors they're so beautiful!

Gina Varner, Grade 4
Northfield Elementary School, OH

Hockey

H itting
O minous refs
C up
K illing penalties
E quipment
Y elling

Luke Friss, Grade 4
Northfield Elementary School, OH

Wishes

Video games
TV for my room
Christmas comes soon!
New Gameboy games
Wish it snows!
I make some new friends
Hope I drink a lot of hot chocolate!
Give me some money!
MY WISHES!!

Nathan Johnson, Grade 5
St Joseph Parish School, OH

Trojans

T rojans is our name.
R ough is how we play.
O utstanding is what we are.
J ostle is what we do.
A nd
N obody can beat us,
S o don't even try!

Morgan McKinney, Grade 5
St Michael School, IN

Stars

Piercing the sky with their every gleam
Some will fall and some will rise
Dancing the midnight ball
Hiding in the day appearing in the night
Giving off a strange glow
Some are far far away
Some are planets wanderers of the night
Strange figures of the night.

Spencer Strotman, Grade 6
St Clement Elementary School, OH

Today

We have the power,
To change this world,
It's our day,
It's our turn,
To take charge,
Of what we have made,
For the better of tomorrow,
And for today,
Change the perspective of everyone,
the outcome,
This battle we will have won,
The selfish things,
We spend so much time on,
But the real problem,
The light on that has gone,
Now the want for a new day showers,
The world is yours,
No,
The world is ours :]

Ashley Zimmer, Grade 6
Waynesville Middle School, OH

Music

It flows through me
Like the river and the sea.
The vibrations flowing
The temp growing.

I can feel the beat
I can feel it in my feet
I can feel it in my soul.
It's the soothing rock-n-roll.

Cars go beep beep
Birds chirp cheep cheep
It incorporates itself in everything I do
I can hear it, can't you?

Every time I sing
Every time I pluck a string
On my amazing guitar
With the music, I'm a star.

Keiland Cooper, Grade 6
Tri-West Middle School, IN

That Summer Day

I was laying by the bay.
Seeing sharks and
Dolphins jump out of the water.
The wind blowing.
Seagulls talking to one another.
The sun going down.
Seeing little and big crabs come
Out of the sand.
On that great summer day.

Alec Meunier, Grade 5
Nancy Hanks Elementary School, IN

Fall Fun

Pumpkin
Orange, round
Eating, glowing, picking
Pies, jack-o-lantern, costumes, sweets
Dressing, trick or treating, walking
Exciting, tasty
Halloween

Rachel McManamon, Grade 4
Norwich Elementary School, OH

The Three Little Penguins

Slide splish,
Slide splosh,
Slide pop,
Swim swim swim!
They waddle around
Waddle up and slide down,

Slide splash,
Slide pop,
Slide splosh,
Swim swim swim!
Now they waddle
To the top
And do it again
On the icy banks.

Cassidy Poe, Grade 4
St Joseph Montessori School, OH

Wavy Lake

Beyond my house
Through the grassy yard
Across the road
Past my neighbors house
Below the hill
Past the flag pole and flag
Around the pier I walk
Up over my knees the water runs
Over my toes the sand sits
With the water around me
The lake waves fascinate me.

Shyenne M. Greve, Grade 5
Churubusco Elementary School, IN

The Seasons

In the winter time frosty winds
howl at the barren trees
leaves no longer drape the hillside in color;
monotony day after day
In the winter time

In the spring time tentative crocuses
peek through the snow and
tender green buds bring
bright new life to the world
In the spring time

In the summer time delicate
blossoms shroud orchards in
a pink and white cloak and
the sound of laughter fills the air
In the summer time

In the autumn time fiery colors
burst all at once from every limb and
twig and the world is still and
in awe at the panoply nature presents
In autumn time

Maria Luciani, Grade 5
Central Grade School, MI

Listen to the Stars

The stars are brilliant.
The stars tell very good stories.
The stars will tell you the secret of life.
The stars guide you to make good choices.
There are many types of stars.
Stars will tell you about the past.
Stars are good friends.
So hush, get comfortable and listen to the stars.

Joshua Jefferson, Grade 6
Woodward Park Middle School, OH

One Person

One person can start many things,
One person can start a family,
One family can start a neighborhood,
One neighborhood can start a town,
One town can start a county,
One town can start a city,
One city can start a state,
One state can start a region,
One region can start a country,
One country can start a nation,
One nation can start a continent,
One continent can start a world,
One world can start a solar system,
One solar system can start a galaxy,
One galaxy can bring infinite possibilities.

Jayson Osika, Grade 6
St Gerard School, MI

Carrot Cake

Hello, will you eat me sir,
My name is carrot cake,
I was cooked with tender love and care,
And took an hour to bake,
I promise I won't let you down,
I'm scrumptious and I'm yummy,
Trust me, you will like me, sir,
I will fill your tummy,
He quickly took a bite of me,
I said, "Drat, I've forgotten,"
He quickly spat me out as I groaned,
"Sir, I am half rotten!"

Aubrey Stoll, Grade 6
North Knox East Elementary/Jr High School, IN

Does It Bother Me?

Does it bother me when people have bad manners?
If they are slurping,
If they are burping,
Does it bother me?
If they giggle till milk squirts out of their nose,
If they pick dirty things from between their toes,
Does it bother me?
If they do all that, Yes, it bothers me!

Sadie Bauserman, Grade 4
OHDELA Academy, OH

If I Could Write an Awesome Poem

I'd write the best poem ever this century.
I'd be the new Shel Silverstein.
I know I can do a nice poem.
But soon I will write an awesome poem.
Then it will be great.
Man do I wish I could write a good poem.
Oh what do you know!
I just made my dreams come true.
I like…everything about my poem.
I'd change…nothing about my poem.

David L. Knezevich, Grade 4
Churubusco Elementary School, IN

Fall

In the fall I have a ball.
The leaves fall.
I like to play football,
Sometimes in the fall I get a phone call.
I wish I could swim in the pool,
But the only problem is school.
I'm real cool.
I'm glad I don't go to Saturday school.
I'm glad soccer ball is in the fall.
I have had a handball before in soccer ball.
I wish I had a wake up call.
That way if there was a big snowfall I could wake up on call!

Ben Waninger, Grade 4
Chrisney Elementary School, IN

Cheerful Flamingo

Tall, plump, graceful
Wading
Slowly, slowly, slowly.
Angela D. Trimble, Grade 5
Cloverdale Middle School, IN

Jell-O

Jelly Jell-o
jigglily, wigglily
green, yellow, red, and
blue too! Jiggle
Wiggle Jell-o
Wahoo!!
Lexi Pede, Grade 4
Bailly Elementary School, IN

Veterans

V aliant
E ffective
T actics
E lite
R espected
A drenaline
N oteworthy
S oldier.
Clay Billman, Grade 4
Legend Elementary School, OH

Veterans Day

V eterans Day!
E leventh day
T oday we honor you
E verything you've done
R ed, white, and blue
A rmy
N ever quit!
Shayla Cales, Grade 4
Westview Elementary School, OH

Sarah and Ben

Oh, my brother and sis,
Will you please quit your fighting.
For my ears deserve quiet,
And the sounds are not inviting!

I'm tired of waking to loud noises.
Can't your mouths be shut for an hour?
Let's get a movie to start playing.
Oh, no! We have no power!

So stop all these fights —
You'd better watch out.
'Cause if you don't stop soon,
You'll get whacked on the butt!
Hannah Otto, Grade 6
Melrose Elementary School, OH

Spiders

Sneaky little crawly critters, they make me go eeekk!
They crawl up and down your walls spying on you week by week.
Making webs through the night
By day they give you such a fright!
Tessa Carelli, Grade 6
Rocky River Middle School, OH

I Am

I am a silly girl who loves volleyball.
I wonder what I'm going to be when I grow up.
I hear the crowd cheering for me.
I see other players lifting themselves up for warming up.
I want to win a scholarship.
I am a silly girl who loves volleyball.

I pretend I'm the greatest volleyball player ever.
I feel the balls hitting my face when I fail.
I touch the sun and moon when they rise.
I worry the world is going to fade away into dust.
I cry when my brother leaves me to go back to Washington.
I am a silly girl who loves volleyball.

I understand that some people really do not like animals.
I say no matter what happens God will always love us
I dream that I can someday have children and hopefully still be a volleyball star.
I try to get good grades for college.
I hope the poor and homeless will live their dreams.
I am a silly girl who loves volleyball.
Savannah Mosby, Grade 6
Helfrich Park Middle School, IN

Merry Christmas

I am sitting in the dark. Silence.
I turned on my TV and watched Christmas specials.
When I got tired, I turned off my TV.
Now complete silence in my room.
All I see is my room.
Also I see the snow falling outside.

Now. The middle of the night.
Sleep. Fast asleep.
Dreaming. Dreaming, and thinking about Christmas day.
Dreaming…dreaming. Beep, beep, beep
The sound of my alarm clock.
My little brother comes in my room.
"Wake up" he says. Christmas day.

Mom tells me to go downstairs. Christmas music playing.
Christmas lights on the Christmas tree are on.
Six-thirty a.m. Opening presents, and showing Mom what I have.
Taking pictures of my brother's presents.
Ten o' clock a.m. Christmas parade is on.
Calling people on the phone saying:
Merry Christmas!
Mikayla Shepherd, Grade 6
Erie Elementary School, OH

Sea

Splashing onto rocks
Spraying everything in its path
Sometimes calm, sometimes fierce
Waves pounding strong
Calmly rippling in a never-ending blanket of blue
Katelyn Benson, Grade 4
Stonegate Elementary School, IN

Cheese

Can I have some cheese?
Pretty, pretty please.
I am a big fan.
Of the cheese called American.
It is so very good.
And it is popular in my neighborhood.
When I am in the mood.
I eat it like any other food.
Jordan Meurer, Grade 6
North Knox East Elementary/Jr High School, IN

Christmas

C andy canes were on the gifts.
H ave a holly jolly Christmas.
R ain and snow was in the air.
I s it Christmas time?
S anta Claus is coming to town.
T ime for Christmas.
M P3 players rock.
A lways have joy.
S nowmen are in the yards.
Emily Lee, Grade 5
West Washington Elementary School, IN

Fall

Leaves fall to the ground
Making a colorful mound.
Brown, yellow, orange, red,
Making a colorful bed.

Orange smiles looking at me,
What could they be?
Carved and glowing
It's a jack-o-lantern that is what is showing!

Next is Thanksgiving,
It is when we all feast.
It is when we celebrate when the pilgrims came over
And thought the Indians were beasts.

It is time for fall to end
And winter to come,
Good-bye colorful leaves and jack-o-lanterns
Now there is a white blanket of snow
Scattered on the trees.
Claire Coyne, Grade 6
Rocky River Middle School, OH

Departure

A single strike, attack or fight.
A conflict knowing that some
Will never come home again.
With both sides having loved ones
That they may never see again.
Combating in the darkness,
They may never see light again.
Fighting for what they believe in.
They may never breathe again.
Praying for their dear ones,
They may never pray again.
Dreaming for a victory,
They may never wake up again.
Warring for a country
Which they may never arrive in again.
Living through cloudy skies with the hope
That the sun will shine again.
Pavan Nimmagadda, Grade 6
EH Greene Intermediate School, OH

Colts

Blue and white playing the lights
People screaming Colts rule
Man I wish I could be with you
People screaming touchdown touchdown
Colts saying let's go Colts we are not stopping now
And yelling Colts win!!!!!!!
Jarren M. D. Geiger, Grade 4
Churubusco Elementary School, IN

Two Darling Dogs

Somewhere over the rainbow, way up in the sky
My dear old dog Macy breathes a silent sigh.
This dog that I loved, meant so much
Her white, curly fur was soft to the touch.

"They can't fix her," my dad said.
I was only eight, I didn't understand.
Dear old Macy, why must you be dead?
So as I write this stanza I am trying not to cry,
I wish dear old Macy didn't have to die.

One year later what a wonderful surprise,
To see a new puppy with clear, brown eyes.
It was my birthday and I didn't expect,
A wiggling ball of fur, as my best gift yet.

I named him Barkley and he did bark,
When he wagged his tail, it left a little mark.
Through these years I've had two pets both of which I loved
One is black and brown the other white as a dove.

One has passed, the other alive
They have changed my family's lives.
Alysha Marie Szczublewski, Grade 6
Trilby Elementary School, OH

Princess

Princess is my dog.
My sister calls her bed hog.
She barks and plays.
She laughs all day;
She is fun.
At the end of the day
I say, "We're done."
I take her on walks.
People really talk;
They say she's cute.
I say, "Thank you."
She plays tug-a-war,
I play hug-a-war.

Kayla Mullins, Grade 5
Rochester Hills Christian School, MI

The Sun

Helps flowers grow well
Shining over the great earth
Rays smiling at you.

Marissa Latcheran, Grade 6
Roosevelt Elementary School, OH

The Sea

The sea pulls me away from the world.
It listens to me.
It reminds me that I am one with it.
The sky sings while the sea dances
back and forth, back and forth.
The moon calms the sea.
Telling it stories about the stars.

The sea is like a child.
It is growing every day.
This is the sea.
This is part of me.
The sea calms me.
While I sit on the beach.
The warm sun warming the sand.
I can feel it on my feet.
This is the sea.
This is part of me.!

Sara Carr, Grade 6
Woodward Park Middle School, OH

Steelers

S weat
T ough
E xcellent
E xciting
L oud
E ntertaining
R eal
S uper

Elijah Turner, Grade 4
Northfield Elementary School, OH

Football

F urious hits
O nside
O ffside
T ouchdowns
B alls
A ction
L inemen
L inebackers

Josh West, Grade 6
Holy Angels School, OH

What Moves Me

I -tunes is what moves me.
T he fun of dancing to it.
U nreal sounds of music.
N ew music all the time.
E very day I listen to it.
S ound is very cool.

Josh Senft, Grade 6
Stephen Vail Middle School, OH

Exploring

Through the murky cave,
Over the strenuous crag,
Down the steep valley side,
Under the bottomless ocean,
Out of the deadly rising waves,
Across the ancient bridge,
Inside the colossal pyramid,
Into the endless darkest,
Between the intimidating traps,
Past the vivid rainbow,
By the insane leprechaun,
With the golden treasure,
I explore.

James Johnson, Grade 6
Harmon Middle School, OH

Him

On the stage
With a microphone
Beyond the cheering fans he sings
During the night
Inside the stadium
Stands the cute boy
Joe Jonas at a concert

Alex Sutton, Grade 5
Churubusco Elementary School, IN

The Forest Whispers

An immense forest will scream!
But a small forest will murmur.
When the breeze passes through
The tiny forest whispers.

Jared Campbell, Grade 5
Wooster Christian School, OH

I Miss You

Petey Weety, I miss you.
Don't you cry, 'cause I'll cry too.
You are high up in the sky
And I know why.
I miss you a lot
With your pretty spot.
I will always be thinking of you
It's because I miss you.

Brandi Benson, Grade 5
Spaulding Elementary School, OH

Tions

If you want to know about something,
That's information
If you multiply two times two,
That's multiplication
If you talk on the phone,
That's communication
If you brag about everything you do,
That's exaggeration
If you ride in a car,
That's transportation
If you make something new,
That's an invention
If you do something bad at school
And you go to the principals office,
That's detention.

Alexis Penny, Grade 5
Frank Ohl Intermediate School, OH

Winter Fun

In winter,
a snowman was built.
Then he dashed away, what fun!
"Snag that snowman," kids say.
They adore winter fun!

Connor Daugherty, Grade 5
Floyd Ebeling Elementary School, MI

If I Was a Billionaire

If I was a billionaire…
I would buy a limousine for my family.
Let people come in,
Let people drive it.

If I was a billionaire…
I would care for the poor more.
Build them houses,
Give them money.

If I was a billionaire…
I would buy a jet,
Pick up my friend,
Go to Atlanta.

Andrew Steele, Grade 5
Becker Elementary School, OH

Neptune

N eptune is seventeen times the mass of
E arth. It is the eighth
P lanet from the sun. Neptune was
T he Roman god of the sea. Its twin is
U ranus. Even being twins, Uranus is smaller than
N eptune. This planet looks pale blue
E xternally.

Braden Sherwood, Grade 6
Pinewood Elementary School, IN

Tide the Friendly Sea

I stretch out,
My legs heat up in the evening sun.
The waves are loud as they attack the shore.
They are pulling all my troubles out to sea,
Till they hit the crevasse and,
Poof.
At night I watch a creature,
Down deeper,
Than any living thing,
Come alive,
And lay down on his bed of sand,
Turning on his lighthouse nightlight.
He reaches with his arms,
Upon the beach to grab his blanket of sand.
He cleans off the toys and shells and then lightly,
Tide,
Drifts off to sleep till tomorrow.

Julianna Jackson, Grade 6
Abbott Middle School, MI

Indoor Amusement Park

It was my 10th birthday,
so my family and I went to Shipshewana,
to an indoor water park, Big Splash.
But when I opened the lobby door,
the place was as quiet as a church mouse.
Then we found the arcade.
The machines glowed bright colors, like green,
but it was dark, like black.
My family was so excited.
We mostly rode on a roller coaster;
We could smell smoothies.
They smelled like strawberry.
I can hear our screams and laughter.
That day was the best time of my life.

Mia Washington, Grade 5
Stanley Clark School, IN

Ts

Three tired tires
tumbled toward town
to take the tables to Toronto
to try to tumble them too.

Sarah Lindholm, Grade 6
Michiana Christian Montessori School, IN

Good Apple vs Bad Apple

Good apple:
Inside a good apple there is juiciness and crunchiness.
There is also delight and content.
Like a person that everybody wants to be around.
Bad apple:
Inside a bad apple there is mold and a little green worm.
There is also hatred and depression
Like a person that nobody wants to be around
If it were up to me, I'd rather be a good apple.

Bailie Pelletier, Grade 6
St Maria Goretti School, IN

What Kind of World Do You Want?

What kind of world do you want?
One with violence, teases, and taunts,
Or one with lots of love and little wants
What kind of world do you want?
One with fuels and gasoline burning,
Or one with teachers teaching and kids learning
What kind of world do you want?
One with sorrow, poverty, and loss,
Or one with happiness and not a person that is cross
So that leaves you with one little question,
What kind of world do you want?

Anna Russo, Grade 6
Allen J. Warren Elementary School, IN

Deer Hunting List

870 Remington 20 gauge, make it black
A box of 20 gauge slugs
Camo clothes, the warmer the better
Those big camo blinds, make sure they're water proof
A grunt call
A doe decoy to attract my buck
And a camera to show my big buck off to my buddies

Lance Elmer, Grade 6
Perry Central Elementary School, IN

PB + J

PB + J
Oh, a *heavenly* creation
With peanut butter, thick and chewy
And jelly so sticky and gooey.

Ham and cheese that's boring to me
Bologna and ketchup what a yawn as you see
BLT that's overrated
You need something more updated.

The peanut butter, the jam
No need for deli ham
PB + J is just better, so go for the classic
The all time favorite, no need for new
Wouldn't you like to try some too?

Paige Brown, Grade 6
St Patrick School, MI

Dots

Do dots come in all different designs? Yes! You can make all different designs and pictures of things. Here are some examples:
Some are humongous some are teensy-weensy.
You can make squares, triangles, and maybe, if you are good, (which you are!) you can make anything that you can think.
Some are humongous some are teensy-weensy.
You can make dogs, cats, and other vertebrates.
Some are humongous some are teensy-weensy.
You can make cars, bikes, and other types of transportation.
Some are humongous some are teensy-weensy.
You can make a house, a school, and other buildings.
Some are humongous some are teensy-weensy.
You can make babies, children, and people of other ages.
Some are humongous some are teensy-weensy.
You can make pens, pencils, and other writing utensils.
Some are humongous some are teensy-weensy.
You can make sharks, whales, and other underwater animals.
Some are humongous some are teensy-weensy.

Gabe Lamer, Grade 5
Calvin Christian Elementary School, MI

Ryan Morgan

Ryan
Outgoing for karate classes, determined to succeed, fond of most Legos, and likes to draw comics
Little brother to Katie
Lover of my dog, Maggie, my two black cats, and my family
Who feels we should protect the environment, study hard in school, and end the war and stay neutral
Who needs a pet to love when I am bored, a friend to play with when I am outside, and books to get information
Who gives my sister money when needed, a smile to everyone I see, and a joke to everybody
Who fears air pollution will get too dense, too many trees will get cut down, and that Maggie will not live forever
Who would like to visit Hawaii for the sun, receive every Lego set in the world, and go to the Air Force to bring the war to an end
Resident of Lancaster
Morgan

Ryan Morgan, Grade 5
Sanderson Elementary School, OH

A Salute for Today and Forever

Sometimes I sit and wonder, about Veteran's Day,
when all the Marines, Army men and Air Force pilots who have retired get a day.
To ponder their sacrifice in the heat and the cold,
for their work, they have all earned a piece of gold.

Some people have perished, lost limbs, or have lifelong aches and pains that they have never craved,
but the hardships and worry of their last day alive that they have braved.
But for those who have lived to tell the tale,
are lucky to have survived a violent gale.

They have always been in danger especially at times of furious chase,
and many a brave have gone missing without a trace.
"Am I going to be alive tomorrow?" That they would have thought,
they have chosen the hardest occupation in the world, when another job that they could have sought.

We should appreciate them for their valor,
even as enemy strikes a deathly pallor.
And as they come marching home, we salute them as they parade,
and we cheer them on, as if it were a brigade.

Naveen Viswanath, Grade 6
EH Greene Intermediate School, OH

After the Taliban Take Over

Dirty and destroyed, Afghanistan life is hard.
In 1996 the Taliban came and the land was scarred.

Women and girls must wear burqas and chadors.
The clothing, no school, and no jobs aren't adored.

As a girl I can't go outside without a relative man.
That's my complicated life in Afghanistan.

My brother was forced into being a Taliban.
He arrested my father and told me to scram.

I haven't seen either of them in a year.
My father, my brother his heart is gone, I fear.

I am now recruited into being a Taliban.
I hear little children say, "Mom, look at that man."

My leader told me to cut a man's hand off.
That's something that even I could not scoff.

Every single day I hear people yell and cry.
I hear explosions sometimes, and I ask myself, why?

The Talibs walk around thousands of people who are dead.
I hear nothing, and see people who bled.

The leader told us to spread disguised land minds out,
I am sad for the people who will be out and about.

Leanne DeVries, Grade 6
Ann Arbor Christian School, MI

My Horse

My horse has the sun captured
in her beautiful buckskin coat.
Her jet black mane and tail
glow like the night sky lit with stars.
When she jumps, for those few short seconds
I fly,
and feel the wind in my hair
and her power beneath me.
Then she lands and we go on,
preparing, jumping, flying.
We rush around the arena, time and time again
I feel the air —
I love it.
We're up to the wall now,
I hope she can make it.
We jump,
and we're over, almost to the end.
Two more jumps,
and we're finished,
we have the fastest time.
My horse and I, together, have won.

Stephanie Rietveld, Grade 6
Crown Point Christian School, IN

Christmas Time

The snow rests gently on the trees
There's a feeling of Christmas in the breeze
The boys and girls start counting down
Till the day of Christmas comes around

On Christmas Eve they sit in bed
With thoughts of Santa Claus in their head
When they wake up they look under the tree
Then open their presents full of glee

The boys and girls play all day outside
Then listen to carolers singing with pride

Grant Ellison, Grade 5
Central Grade School, MI

The Storm

When I awoke from my slumber
I saw a flash and heard the crackle of thunder.
Rain was pounding the windows with no end in sight,
I just hoped for the comfort of daylight.

Like a crumbling wall, my confidence did not last
The rain was so hard and the wind was so fast.
My fear increased because the house was tipping
I could hear trees falling and concrete ripping.

Just when my terrible fate was sealed,
The truth was finally revealed.
In a split second, everything was back to what it seemed.
All of the terror was just a dream!

Amit Mizrahi, Grade 6
Abbott Middle School, MI

Halloween Night

I could smell the fire in the middle of the court
I was getting tired
Dancing as a whoopee cushion
And handing out candy

The light came from fires, candles, and street lights
My shadow was long and sometimes disappeared
When I hid, waiting to scare

The sounds of jolly people by the fire
And on the street
Filled my ears

What were they talking about
I don't know

The candy was as good as subs
The fun of walking and people giving you candy
Is like going to Wal-Mart and getting free cards
The candy was yum, yum, yum

Matthew Vaughn, Grade 5
EH Greene Intermediate School, OH

Flight

Birds fly in the sky
I spy a stunning eagle
As it lands on trees.

Keith Hill, Grade 5
Westview Elementary School, OH

School Is Cool

S chool teaches you things
C heat and get into trouble
H oping not to miss many on the tests
O MG, I made a really cool new friend
O utside recess, inside class
L ittle kids, big kids

I love school
S o many students here

C oming to class every day
O ut for the weekends
O ut for the snow
L ovely year we have

Ariel James, Grade 5
Perry Central Elementary School, IN

Buddies

Friends
Fun, nice
Laughing, playing, running
To have a good time with
Buddies

Emma Kremer, Grade 6
Tippecanoe Middle School, OH

Summer

Summer is a fun and hot season.
Summer brings these things:
Fun with water,
Spraying people with a water hose,
Drinking lemonade,
Playing football,
Eating ice cream,
Going fishing,
Playing on beaches,
Going to water parks,
Riding bikes around the lake,
Grilling out with my dad,
Going camping,
Vacation,
No school during summer,
Staying up late,
In with shorts, out with pants,
Playing outside more,
Allergies get worse,
Spending more time with family.

Alec Hacker, Grade 5
West Elkton Elementary School, OH

The Lord Lay Quiet

The Lord lay quiet in a pile of hay He did not cry when the horses neigh.
Even on a cold winter day, the Lord lay quiet in a pile of hay
The Lord sleep sweetly He may, the Lord is born this day the angels say.
On a cold winter day the Lord lay quiet in a pile of hay.

Casey Barner, Grade 5
St Joseph Parish School, OH

On the First Night of Chanukah

On the first day of Chanukah night
As we sat around the crackling firelight
Inside it was so cozy and warm,
But outside Mother Nature was brewing up a storm
My family played dreidel and I got Shin,
But whoever gets Gimmel is surely to win
After a long time of dreidel we were done
And this is where it starts to get fun
I wasn't sure what I would get this year
But I was sure it would bring me cheer
We ripped open the paper and were so excited
The expressions on our faces were very delighted
The latkes are like a mixture between potatoes and fries
As you smell them in the kitchen you'll get a mouthwatering vibe
The latkes are like a mint melting on your tongue
Out of all the Chanukah foods latkes are number one
All of the kids were laughing so hard
It was like a wish upon a star
Everyone was having a good night
All was calm and all was nice
Good times, good times, good times

Cameron Foy, Grade 5
EH Greene Intermediate School, OH

Believe

Barack Obama is now our President
The very first of African descent
He inspires us to believe in the power of change as we should
And to believe in the possibilities of all things good
in Barack Obama I see a little piece of me,
But I also see those in far and distant lands than we
He showed us all that Martin Luther King's dream is still alive
In spite of a world that would lead one to believe that it was only jive!
On inauguration day, Obama! Obama! Everyone will yell,
During that time, I'm certain many an eye will swell
Swell with tears of joy and pain
Boy oh boy, I hope on that day it doesn't rain!
Even if it does, the sun still shines
Will shine on states like mine
Michigan, Michigan beaten down by a bad economy
And just when it seemed that nobody but us in Michigan could see,
Along comes Barack Obama, inspiring us all to believe what could be,
Change we can believe in, change we'll see,
That Michigan and the entire country will be on its way to economic recovery
Yes, change can be good
As Barack Obama inspires me in many ways that it could.

Tierra Riddick, Grade 6
Abbott Middle School, MI

Black and White Keys

I play an instrument that has black and white keys
With the tempo I move my knees
While I play my hands move like bees
There are 88 keys
Remember they are black and white
Sometimes I make my hands so light
And other times I have to make my hands fight
I play with all my might
Sometimes I play all day and night

Diba Ossareh, Grade 6
Abbott Middle School, MI

The Road Is Always Rough

Land mines kill, and people fight,
When will the future be in sight?
Most of the buildings are bombed to bits,
Our babies cry and always give fits.

Refugees' bombed out homes always haunt,
To them all the Taliban does is taunt.
When I hear missiles flying through the sky,
It always reminds me of my father's goodbye.

Sheds for houses with windows painted black,
Why can't we have the old government back?
Having a good paying job, "Yeah right,"
Feeding your family can often be tight.

A woman in a burqa rarely ever sees,
A male relative escorts her in his shalwar kameez.
Scenes in the market aren't always good sights,
Why won't the Taliban give us some rights?

Yet our symbol of pride you may have seen,
Our wonderful flag colored black, red, and green.
We believe in Allah and seek him through prayers,
Even when it's rough we know that he cares.

David Conzelmann, Grade 6
Ann Arbor Christian School, MI

School Is Great!

I love school
Isn't it cool
With the books
And the looks
Of the teachers every day
Especially when they say
"Today is a great day"
Friends are there
Almost everywhere
To help you
And to be beside you like a crew
And kids should have fun
All the time no matter what.

Kassandra Barraza, Grade 6
St John the Baptist Elementary School, IN

Florida

Warm, breezy
Middle of summer
Late at night
People talking, seagulls squawking
Ocean, people eating, buried people in sand
Boogie boarding, swimming
Next July
Excited, ready

Kory Florence, Grade 6
Tippecanoe Middle School, OH

Ghost Path

Past the dark, misty forest.
Over the soft, spongy moss.
On the ancient, worn dust path.
Near an old, scruffy owl.
Through the small, gurgling creek.
Under a festering, fallen tree.
Past the gray, spherical boulder.
Across the elongated, cobblestone bridge.
Behind the familiar, sweet-smelling apple tree.
Into the silent, shadowed wood.
To the deep, frozen lake.
Returning to her final resting place
Drifts the ghost.

Daniel P. Lyons, Grade 6
Harmon Middle School, OH

Leaves

Saffron, olive, gold
Gracefully swirling around
The most peaceful time

Perima Shah, Grade 4
Frank H Hammond Elementary School, IN

Horses

Horses are very special!
They can drive cattle.
Horses are big and small!
But have a huge population in all.
Horses can be Bay, Palomino, or Dun!
They can mean serious work or can be playful.
Horses are strong and weak!
They might be able to speak.
Horses can be ugly or pretty!
They can love or hate a kitty.
Horses may have originated from a different place!
For shows, you can decorate your horse with lace.
Horses can be wild or tame!
They can be cool or lame.
Horses can be happy or tired!
It can be snappy and admired.
You can name your horse whatever.
And keep it forever!

Alexandria Warnimont, Grade 6
Miller City-New Cleveland School, OH

DaWan

D is for dominance
A is for achieving
W is for working hard
A is for awesome
N is for never give up

DaWan Smith, Grade 6
Pennfield Middle School, MI

My Baby Cat

I just got a newborn animal —
Everyone loves my cat.
Even though lots of people say
That he looks just like a rat.

I think that is just mean
And I'll still love my cat.
I know he eats a lot,
But I don't want him to get fat.

My kitty cat eats all the time —
He loves to eat tuna fish.
Mom got mad one time when
He licked our family dish.

I still didn't figure out his name.
My friends say he's fat like a rat.
So I wonder if that should be his name?
But that's why I'm calling him Frat.

René Campailla, Grade 6
Melrose Elementary School, OH

Bowling

B owling is an
O utstanding sport
W hile playing, you can talk to friends
L ike other sports, bowling has a ball
I love cosmic bowling
N o one should miss the bowling alley
G o there! It's awesome!

Cal Barrett, Grade 4
Keystone Academy, MI

Flowers

Flowers, flowers,
Flowers blowing in the wind,
Bowing their head.
Flowers, flowers,
Giving to God a sweet scent.
Flowers, flowers,
Love the color.
Flowers, flowers,
Pick another.
Red, white, blue
They're all new!

Elijah McAtee, Grade 6
Wooster Christian School, OH

Snow

Snow, snow, falling down.
Piling up, on the ground.
Pile, Pile, pile up high.
Will it ever reach the sky?

Playing 'round
In the snow.
It's really cold,
As you know.

Snowman, snowman, with a hat,
Finding snow prints from a cat.
Hot, hot chocolate, very good.
Getting warm,
As fast as you could.

Noah Billingsley, Grade 5
Spaulding Elementary School, OH

Energy Drinks Rock!!!

Energy drinks are awesome.
They can make you awesome.
They are good.
Very good.
There are different kinds.
Here they are.
Red Bull.
Amp.
Red Jak
Monster.
Rockstar.
Nos.
Red Bull is the best.
Don't forget Nos.
Or Monster,
Amp is good.
Rockstar rocks.
I like energy drinks!!!!
I ROCK!!!

Grant Shumaker, Grade 4
Licking Valley Intermediate School, OH

Chocolate

Chocolate brownies, chocolate cupcakes,
Chocolate bars, and chocolate milk!
They are all good to me,
But my favorite of all chocolates
Is the chocolate chip cookie.

Jake Traxler, Grade 5
Rochester Hills Christian School, MI

Tucker

Searching for rabbits
Barking as loud as can be
A dog named Tucker

Daniel Alvey, Grade 6
Perry Central Elementary School, IN

Veterans

V eterans,
E xperience,
T rust,
E xtreme,
R ifle,
A rmy,
N avy,
S ervice.

Levi Cole, Grade 4
Legend Elementary School, OH

Poetry

I'm not saying anything good or bad
I'm not doing anything you have to find
I'm not saying anything that is sad
The one thing I had in mind
The one thing I like the most
Can this one only be
The one thing you don't need to boast
Poetry

Shannon Gray, Grade 5
Northfield Baptist Christian School, OH

I Am

I am beautiful and an angel
I wonder what my future will be like
I hear laughter from my friends
I see myself under beautiful fireworks
I want my uncle to come back from war
I am beautiful and an angel

I pretend to play school with my friends
I feel happy to have pets
I touch softness off my hamster's back
I worry about my uncle
I cry when my pets cry
I am beautiful and an angel

I understand why school is made
I say Salena and Natalie are great friends
I dream to fly so far up into the sky
I try to do my best at my work
I hope fourth grade will be my best year
I am Sawyer Steelman

Sawyer Steelman, Grade 4
Floyd Ebeling Elementary School, MI

Green

Disgusted is green,
It tastes like rotten garbage,
It smells like chewed up fish,
It reminds me of sour pus
It sounds like revolting squirmy worms,
Disgusted makes me feel green.

Nicholas Tatakis, Grade 5
Tremont Elementary School, OH

Ode to Daddy Dearest

Oh daddy dearest
  You're the strongest, smartest guy.
  To me you're the greatest champion of all time.

Oh daddy dearest,
  With your cool stylish looks
  You're always close in my mind.

Oh daddy dearest,
  With your luminous sporty personality
  And rocking guitar skills.

You'd make any person jealous and
Maybe even start to cry.

Because they know very truly that
They don't have a dad as cool as mine.

Katie Shelton, Grade 5
Allen J. Warren Elementary School, IN

I Am

I am curious and smart
I wonder when we are going to use the laptops
I hear the pencil sharpener raging with anger
I see a fairy
I want a sirius satellite radio
I am curious and smart
I pretend to fly an airplane
I feel sad that my brother sat on my imaginary friend
I touch air
I worry about my grandpa
I cry about my grandpa
I am curious and smart
I understand 2 + 2 = 4
I say Freddy Krueger is real
I dream that I will go to MIT
I try to do good in school
I hope my grandpa gets better
I am curious and smart

Tyler Walker, Grade 6
Galesburg-Augusta Middle School, MI

Bailey

Bailey
Barking from excitement
As I enter the house
As I walk into his area
He jumps with delight
I crouch down slightly
And rub his soft, clean fur
I get a thorough face licking
Then I throw his slobber tug covered in drool
We snuggle up on our warm, soft couch
And drift into a deep sleep

Kelsi Clark, Grade 5
Washington Township Elementary School, IN

October Is When!

Mice scamper across the forest floor in search of food
Football starts and players get anxious
Coats come out of spooky dark closets and boxes
Plump pumpkins get picked off their skinny little vines
Pumpkins are transformed into spooky jack-o'-lanterns
Hay is spread across fields of shredded corn
October is a very busy month.

Matthew Malinchak, Grade 5
Beck Centennial Elementary School, MI

Winter

W aking up to icy foggy windows
I cicles hanging from the trees
N ever ending fallings of snow
T ired after a full day of playing outside
E njoying hot cocoa Mom makes
R unning from the snowballs in the snow wars

Ricky Entzian, Grade 6
Corpus Christi Elementary School, IN

Christmas Morning

I sit with the carpet in my toes
That aroma of pine makes you not want to go
The morning light of seven a.m.
Illuminates the joy that wanders within
All the excitement and mystery
Is the next present mine?
Did I get what I wanted?
Will I remember throughout time
The next present presented?
On our tree are the lights
Gleaming blue, green, and red,
All the colors you can't get out of your head.
You approach the next present
Filled with excitement but dread
Is this the big present?
Or just another hat
To wear on your head
You open it up
"My gosh…"
Christmas
Just joy and wonder, joy and wonder

Jack Good, Grade 5
EH Greene Intermediate School, OH

Fall

Fall is when I'm playing football,
Fall is when I see the mall.
Fall is when I have study hall,
Fall is when I hear the phone call.
Fall is when my brother threw a spitball,
Fall is when my sister thinks she is a know it all.
Fall was when I played with a Barbie doll,
Fall is when we chew a gumball.

Anna Autry, Grade 4
Chrisney Elementary School, IN

Emotions

All destruct
One can build
Love and hate
Never the same
Merely alike
When the ache fades
The masquerade to hide the emotion
Goes too.

Each is followed by another
They flow like seasons —
One to another
Seasons change
Like these feelings —
One is missed
The others barely known
When love appears again
Numbing and healing
Emotion.

Ileane McGettigan, Grade 6
Abbott Middle School, MI

Riding a Bike

I ride my bike everywhere
I ride it to Chicago,
To Chris' house,
To New York,
And just about any other place,
I also like to ride my bike to restaurants,
Like Dairy Queen,
To Long Horn Steak House,
To Coldstone,
To Don Pabloes,
And Unos Pizza.
I also ride my bike in the forest,
The farm lands,
The bad lands,
And even a dirt track.

Ryan Barnes, Grade 6
Crown Point Christian School, IN

Dogs

Doggies
Fun, floppy ears
Barking, chasing, growling
Smallish, cute, funny animals,
Puppies

Austin Benjamin, Grade 5
Perry Central Elementary School, IN

Canoeing

I smell fresh water,
Brown branches soar above me;
I hear birds chirping.

Audrey Dixon, Grade 6
Stanley Clark School, IN

Jealousy

Jealousy poisons your personality,
Jealousy is a bad reflection of someone else.
Jealousy will sicken your mind,
Jealousy will stop you from living your life.
Jealousy can affect your friends,
Jealousy can affect your surroundings.
Jealousy makes you mad,
Jealousy makes others sad.
Jealousy is a mean grin from the soul,
Jealousy is the unkind word from your brain.
Jealousy can be the mental ability not seen in you but in other people,
Jealousy can by the physical ability seen not in you but in other people.
Jealousy can be painful like a needle in your side,
Jealousy is a part of thought that makes us feel smaller and hidden inside.
Jealousy must not be spoken for it is poison.

Erica Statly, Grade 6
St Gerard School, MI

Spirit Bear

A large bear with shiny, black eyes
In the woods, looking at something.
But what?
He is looking at a distrusted boy.
A rebel of Minneapolis, beaten daily by his drunken father,
Causing a gap from all others.
He meets this boy many times,
One of them, almost killing him,
The last, to earn and harvest the trust of this lost soul,
Letting the boy touch him, and run away with a clump of the bear's own hair,
While looking at him with deep, trusting eyes.
Allowing, not only the boy, but the bear as well to be trusted.

Kerry Connor, Grade 6
Harmon Middle School, OH

What Am I?

If I were a shoe I would smell all different smells from foods to the bathroom floors.
I'd taste gum, foods from all over, and the leftovers.
I'd visit everywhere all over the world.
I'd be grumpy by being hit in the face all the time.
I'd go as fast as a cheetah or as slow as a snail.
I'd be gooey from all the bugs and gum.
I AM A SHOE!

Will Hall, Grade 6
St Maria Goretti School, IN

Love

Love is like my heart pumping faster and faster until I stop running
and like Gracie's bright red water bottle.
It oozes through my heart
like when you squeeze a tube of toothpaste and put it on your toothbrush.
It reminds me of the time when my mom and dad just hugged me so tightly,
that I thought blood would ooze out of me.
It makes me feel radiant like when the sun is shining brightly on us.
It makes me want to shout to the world all my innermost secrets.

Jennifer Allemeier, Grade 6
St Maria Goretti School, IN

Christmas Time

Chipmunks cheer for all the toys this year
Santa hustles and bustles on this very day
It's Rudolph's time to shine
On this beautifully magnificent night.

Andrew Skidmore, Grade 6
Bellefontaine Middle School, OH

New Years Day

5-4-3-2-1
It's a new year!
New goals to set,
There's no need to sweat.
It's a huge crowd
Gathered around Times Square
The crowd roars loud,
As the ball hits the ground
The laughter, the cheer
In my home right here
Is enough for a lifetime
Let alone just one year
The ball inching closer
We all just can't wait
Time to let go
Time to celebrate!
It's a new year!
Come on, let's cheer!
It's a great feeling,
Of all of our troubles from the year before,
Just simply disappearing, disappearing, disappearing.

Caroline Gao, Grade 5
EH Greene Intermediate School, OH

Winter Vacation

Winter vacation
It's so much fun.
Playing in the snow and having a gay time.
Riding my four wheeler.
Going to sled.
Sometimes I fall.
But I always get up.
Parents don't like it.
It's always too cold.
Slipping and sliding.
Driving in a car.
We get in a wreck and call 911.
Flying in a plane.
One the way to somewhere warm.
Going to dinner.
Not wearing a coat.
Thinking in my mind.
Wow, I wish I could stay.
When we go back home where there were plow trucks.
Driving to school, the plow truck passes.
It hits snow, head on, and pushes it to the side.

Nick Tamarkin, Grade 6
Akiva Academy, OH

All About Me

B rother of Blake Andrew Jeffries
E nergetic and fun
A stounding at playing sports
U nique and talented

J ester and playful
A nnoying to brother
M y cousins are like my best friends
E asy going with everybody
S uper good at reading

J ovial and fun loving
E van is my best friend
F rike is my nickname
F rake is my brother's nickname
R unning back is my favorite football position
I am sonorous when I pound the drums
E PSN is my favorite TV channel
S our apples are my favorite fruit

Beau James Jeffries, Grade 5
Frank Ohl Intermediate School, OH

The Winter

Every day I wake up with a start,
I touch the glass on my window,
And see a mountain of snow outside.
Then make my first snowball.

The turkey in the oven
Eating cookies by the fire,
The aromas are crawling across my nose.
And then there are the tastes of sweetness.

Little kids with glowing faces,
Lighting up Christmas Eve.
Waiting for the tip tap of Santa's feet,
And the jingle of his sleigh.

The weather is getting colder,
My nose starts to get numb.
I bundle up in warm clothes,
It's finally winter.

Sean Weddell, Grade 6
Harding Middle School, OH

Miley

I have a puppy named Miley.
She is always so grouchy.
In the middle of the day,
She always wants to play with the neighbor's dog.
When she smells the eggs cooking, she'll whine and cry.
She doesn't always win,
And when she doesn't, she'll keep jumping on you.
Then, we sigh, and say, "Ok, here."

Abbey Evans, Grade 5
Washington Township Elementary School, IN

Volleyball

Bump, set, spike the ball
Then hit it over the net
And the score goes up.
Lexy Sangalang, Grade 5
St Jude Catholic School, IN

Dance

The leaves dance with the breeze
I dance with ease
I dance to the wind's beat
And I make it look good
I like to groove
And the leaves love to move
I do the splits and shake my hips
They move around so you don't miss
Esther Otasanya, Grade 6
Woodward Park Middle School, OH

America/Mexico

America
simple, patriotic
sledding, spending, skiing
snow, English, Español, mariachi
learning, dancing, confusing
different, new
Mexico
Brittany Misencik, Grade 5
Northfield Baptist Christian School, OH

The Three Dogs' Day

Three little dogs
They all look the same
They love to play soccer
That is their game.

They love each other
As they sit on a swing
They all love each other
As they all sing.

They have black heads
And cute little noses
They have pointy ears
And cute little toes.

They went to school
All together in a line
They all came home
Just pretty and fine.

They got some food
As happy as can be
They went to bed
And they all fell asleep.
Morgan Connor, Grade 6
Eisenhower Middle School, OH

My Friend Emily

A Friend
Awesome, Sporty
Playing, Considering, Encouraging
A Friend I can count on
Emily
Audrea Davis, Grade 5
Perry Central Elementary School, IN

Useless Things

Christmas with no presents,
A kingdom without peasants.

An asylum with no one insane,
A window without a pane.

A mansion without a maid,
A guest who's never stayed.

Einstein without a brain,
A puddle but no rain.

A map without a place,
A mystery but no case.

Cheese-It's with no cheese,
Thank you's without please.

A train with no coal,
A heart but no soul.

A lemon that's not tart,
A friend without a heart.
Abigail Mangus, Grade 4
Stonegate Elementary School, IN

Chores

Chores are fun,
And sometimes boring;
If you're doing your chores,
Is it fun or boring?
I would think boring,
Sometimes I would like to be snoring;
Instead of doing chores,
How big is your house,
If it is really big you should get a maid;
I really mean it too,
If you don't have a maid;
It must take hours to clean your house,
Does your dad make you clean,
My mom makes me,
And to me or you,
I think they're very boring,
But if you think they're fun;
Good Luck!
Meagan Dankert, Grade 6
Immanuel Christian School, MI

The Bird's Song

The bird sings a sorrow song,
A song of hate,
And a song of chaos.
But yet the bird sings of joy and cheer,
And love and tears.
And the bird sings of all we desire
And all we admire.
Not too far away the rock tells of war,
And the wind whispers the truth.
The turtle tells a tale of all he has seen,
And the ox cries out with mercy.
But what do we tell of?
And the ocean claps for victory
As the waves hit the shore.
As the bird sings a song.
Trevor Gambill, Grade 6
Woodward Park Middle School, OH

Happiness!

H aving a day off from school.
A nother day of football practice.
P laying in hockey tournaments.
P lanning our next vacation.
I love going out to eat after practice.
N ever going to bed early.
E xercise makes me happy.
S taying at a friend's house.
S leeping in on Sundays.
Kyle Beemiller, Grade 6
Harmon Middle School, OH

Calming Water

While I lay in bed,
I'm full of dread!

But then, I hear the rain!
And I feel no pain.

I feel…calm,
Like when I touch my nephew's palm.

The storms come, and the storms go,
I wish life went with that flow.
Steven A. Salinas, Grade 6
St Patrick School, MI

Volcano

Rumbles inside
Bursts up
Explodes scarlet and orange colors
Throws fire up and down
Burns the air
Paints the surface of the Earth
Settles down and turns into rock
Jack Hausfeld, Grade 6
St Clement Elementary School, OH

I Am

I am awesome and sweet.
I wonder why people want to write books that go on forever.
I hear SpongeBob with his annoying little laugh in my head.
I see a panda bear dressing up like a penguin.
I want 5,000 dollars or more.
I am awesome and sweet.
I pretend that I am in Hawaii.
I feel sad because SpongeBob just screamed at Patrick.
I touch the sky.
I worry about my family.
I cry when I get mad (sometimes).
I am awesome and sweet.
I understand that school has to be 8 hours long.
I say some people deserve to be happy.
I dream that I could be in a cartoon.
I try to get good grades.
I hope to be a vet and get rich.
I am awesome and sweet.

Lilly Ellison, Grade 6
Galesburg-Augusta Middle School, MI

Sports

When you hit a homerun
You feel the heat from the sun.

Shooting from far, far away
Thinking of making it a great day.

While blocking the goal in your uniform
You hope that the big, dark clouds won't make a storm.

As your hoping to make a hole in one
Jumping up and down having fun.

Throwing the ball to the other team
Other girls are on the beam.

Chelsie Cox, Grade 5
Mayfield Elementary School, OH

A Bird of Prey

Bird
Unique, quiet
Flapping, gliding, swooping
Flying silently through darkness
Owl

Evan Goodell, Grade 4
Eugene M Nikkari Elementary School, MI

Run Out

Inside my imagination are millions of thoughts run out
It's like a pen ran out of ink and has nothing left to say
It's like a beautiful day with nothing to do.
Inside my imagination it's starting to rain and there's
Nothing to say.

Jourdan Corbett, Grade 6
St Maria Goretti School, IN

Fall

The leaves are falling down,
Green, orange, yellow and brown.
Here comes one colored red,
It landed on my head!

The leaves are changing.
Jeans and coats are waiting.
I can't wait until the little kids come to the door,
And say trick or treat, give me more!

Halloween is here!
All the trees are cleared,
Look what's at my door,
Goblins, witches and more…

Allison Ramirez, Grade 6
Holy Family Middle School, MI

Picture Past

"Click"
Then this simple movement saved a memory
You think it's purposeless
But it's much more
Because the movement
Lead to memory
Then memory lead to purpose
The purpose of this simple movement is to
Look at the past
To remember…
To remember what you forgot
Through all those years
And you're maybe even proud
Because you remember your hopes, dreams
And much more, more than you or anyone else would think

Olivia Slagle, Grade 6
Holy Angels School, OH

Sad

Sad is red,
It tastes like food my grandfather used to cook,
It smells like a wilting flower,
It reminds me of my brother crying,
It sounds like my mother calling me,
Sad makes me feel red.

Sabrina (Amiin) Abubakar, Grade 5
Tremont Elementary School, OH

March

March comes on the feet of a lamb,
Softly and steadily,
Creeping in after February, on its tip toes,
Bringing joy, laughter, and spring
With its lilies, roses, and forest green leaves.
Then she runs on her legs as a cheetah,
Sprinting into spring.

Sarah Patching, Grade 6
Wooster Christian School, OH

It's All About Me

If I were in charge of the world…
I'd make it rain ice cream
I'd be the queen
I would not do my homework
I'd make me a millionaire
I'd have my driving license when I'm ten
I'd drive on the wrong side of the road
I'd be on the news
I'd eat steak any time I wanted to
It would be great for me but…
It would be a disaster for you.

Lindsey Standridge, Grade 4
Churubusco Elementary School, IN

Thin and Bone

See upon a hill
A cemetery where
Bones will live
White and thin
But a crack
With a rat
But…
When you open
The gate

Creeeeek

You will hear
This is the night
The bones
Come alive again

Jesse Gard, Grade 5
Heritage Intermediate School, IN

Santa

Santa
Red, white, jolly
Delivers great presents
Grateful, happy, love in heart full
Saint Nick

Naomi Draus, Grade 4
Bailly Elementary School, IN

Softball

Sit on the bench
Above the ground
At the park
Across the gate
After batting
Beside Cassidy
With Gatorade
Outside with dirt
I play softball
And I love it.

Alyssa Anderson, Grade 5
Churubusco Elementary School, IN

Bombings in Birmingham — 1963

Boom! I heard the loud explosion
And to my chagrin, I knew who was inside that church in Birmingham.
On a hot summer day, a bomb went off
And folks all over town were crying and shouting and fighting.
This is not right, I think to myself — a wave of anger washes over me,
Why? Why did this happen I ask, even though I know the answer.
Sadness and anger run through me and fear rips up my insides
For I know what it's like to almost lose somebody.
One day in summer my cousins and Aunt,
Were all at church enjoying a performance
When, suddenly a man with a gun comes in and shoots innocent people.
Why? I ask again — this is not right! This time I don't know the answer.
Anger, hate, and fear tear through my body like a bulldozer
Though they are safe, some people are mourning.
And my mind goes back to the four girls in Birmingham
And my heart breaks in two.

Elizabeth Estes, Grade 6
Detroit Country Day Middle School, MI

Love of the World

Parents are as mighty as a tree, standing tall and proud.
They take care of us like mother birds.
If parents weren't here life would be a disaster as we know it.
Parents make the world go round, if they weren't here the world would stop spinning.
Parents will go to the end of the world for their precious children.

Marissa Kaminski, Grade 6
University Liggett School, MI

Mars

M ars is named after the Roman god of war. It is also referred to
A s the "Red Planet" because of its red glow.
    Three spacecrafts that are orbiting Mars are the Mars
R econnaissance Orbiter, Mars Odyssey, and Mars Express.
S pirit and Opportunity are the names of two Mars exploration Rovers
    currently residing there.

Truth Hensley, Grade 6
Pinewood Elementary School, IN

Mr. Koontz

Mr. Koontz is my favorite teacher.
He has a daughter named Cassidy.
Mr. Koontz is my Bible teacher.
Whenever you ask to get a drink,
He says, "Yes, but from the sink."
And when you ask to get a book,
He says, "Yes, I will wait here."
He is my favorite because he is nice, funny, and gives no homework.
His daughter Cassidy is one of my best friends.
She is a lot like her dad, very sweet and kind.
I cannot wait until next year,
When he will be my homeroom teacher.
For some reason he always puts me and Cassidy by each other.
Well, that is why I love him so much.
I love Mr. Koontz!

Danae Mollema, Grade 6
Crown Point Christian School, IN

Something's Calling

It whispers my name day and night,
I listen but try to remember
what is calling me.
It brings us joy, and looks heavenly
like a dark night sky.
Who is calling me?
It's far and high, bringing
us to dreamland where
we stand lovingly.
Where is the call coming from?
I wonder, what is on my mind
I can't get it out! It would ruin everything.
My hard work gone!
When would it stop?
But I can't resist, I take a bite
Then…

Huyen My Truong, Grade 6
Woodward Park Middle School, OH

Imagination

Sometimes it's good to
let your imagination soar.

You can travel to many far away places.
You could be famous,
or become a princess
or just be yourself.

When you imagine
you can be powerful,
or just an ordinary kid.

But when you're done visiting your imaginary world,
you come back to Earth,
knowing there's a special place
just for you!

Kristina Curtiss, Grade 5
Central Grade School, MI

Fall

The trees look like rainbows; they're so bright.
The vibrant leaves are an assortment of colors.
Browns, reds, yellows, and oranges.
They are as beautiful as can be.

The birds are migrating getting ready for winter.
They fly in great giant flocks.
All I can hear is their chirp, chirp, chirp.
Preparing for the monstrous cold that will come.

Halloween will be here soon
and the air will be full of laughter.
The children will come and go from house to house
hoping to get something sweet to eat.

Jacquelyn Gasta, Grade 6
Holy Family Middle School, MI

Wolves

Wolves are gray.
Wolves hunt today.
Wolves stalk and kill their prey.
Wolves are bright.
Wolves always fight.
They watch everything in sight.
Wolves howl at the moon.
They can kill a raccoon.
The wolves will be there soon.
Wolves can see clearly in the night.
Wolves look everywhere even left and right.
To me wolves rule the night.

Jeffrey Jacobs, Grade 4
Chrisney Elementary School, IN

Writing Magic

Everybody else is far ahead of me in our writing assignment.
What will they think of me?

I can't think of a single word to say.
Will anybody help me?

I start to think I won't have anything but
doodles on my paper when it's time to share.
What will I do?

Boom, scribble, poof!
I looked at my paper.
It was filled,
with my handwriting.
It was like magic.
Were the rest of my papers filled with writing too?

I looked in my folder;
my papers were filled
with my handwriting.
Now, what will they think of me?

Taylor Keppel, Grade 5
Calvin Christian Elementary School, MI

Autumn

A ll the leaves are falling
U nder the leaves I make a fort
T rees are looking bare and the wind is getting colder
U nusual colors are on the leaves that fall
M other bakes apple pies all day long
N ow the season is over, goodbye autumn and hello winter!

Rebecca Glesser, Grade 6
Eisenhower Middle School, OH

Pandas

they are black and white
with taste buds that like bamboo
delightful pandas

Cierra Wheeler, Grade 5
Washington Township Elementary School, IN

My School
School
Great, spectacular
Learning, teaching, writing
My school is great
Ebeling
Jeff Tan, Grade 4
Floyd Ebeling Elementary School, MI

Fantastic Fall
Freezing fruit
Lasting leaves
Horrible houses
Daring decorations
Creative costumes
Kids saying TRICK OR TREAT
Creepy costumes
Constant candy
Pumpkin faces all over
Getting candy at every door
Pumpkin guts bleeding out
Wagons rolling up and down streets
The funniest costumes I have ever seen.
What a fantastic fall.
Keith Yermak, Grade 5
Riley Upper Elementary School, MI

Hamster/My Pet
Hamster
Smells good, gray eyes.
Likes to play with his ball.
I like him because he is fun.
My pet
Stacey Garcia, Grade 4
Riverside Elementary School, MI

Spring
Spring smells sweet and nice
Animals wake up from sleep
Baby robins hatch
Aaron Lutgring, Grade 5
Perry Central Elementary School, IN

Football
Punt and catch
Run and fetch

Out on the line
I'm doing just fine

See me tackle
Hear gear crackle

Victory here I come
'Cause we are number one
Greg Spearman, Grade 6
Holy Angels School, OH

A Month to Remember
December creeps in like a tiger,
Going to get what it wants.
It washes away the heat
And pours in the cold.
Then darts away like a hunted animal!
Savannah Chaffee, Grade 6
Wooster Christian School, OH

My Room
My room is messy yes it is
I spilt a drink like doctor fizz.

I find a hairy, fairy, ox
In my big blue box.

I told you stuff about my room
I don't know why I use a broom.

I don't know why I wear,
My stinky, dirty underwear.

My mom thinks I'm a brat
Because I have a smelly old rat.

If you leave I will give you a bun
So now the day is done.
Zane Gayer, Grade 5
Perry Central Elementary School, IN

Gentle Spring
Green bamboo trees sway
In the gentle breeze of spring
As bright birds tweet-tweet.
Emily Jewell, Grade 5
Westview Elementary School, OH

Candy to Apple Pie
Candy
chewy, sticky,
unwrapping, exciting, sharing,
gooey, good, sweet soft,
chewing, making, inviting,
yummy, crunchy,
Apple pie.
Darian Sapp, Grade 5
Norwich Elementary School, OH

Disgusted
Disgusted is green,
It tastes like sour lime juice,
It smells like squashed road kill,
It reminds me of green slime,
It sounds like smashing pumpkins,
Disgusted makes me feel green.
Joe Levitt, Grade 5
Tremont Elementary School, OH

Pets
My pets are fun and they jump around.
But I hate when they fall down.

My pets like to play with toys.
But I like to hang out with boys.

Pets are awesome I can't resist.
It makes me want to hug and kiss.
Brittani Smith, Grade 5
St Jude Catholic School, IN

I Am
I am a talented Steelers fan
I wonder if I'll ever break a bone
I hear the crunching of helmets
I see the scoreboard
I want to get a touchdown
I am a talented Steelers fan

I pretend I play at Reitz
I feel football is great
I touch the numbers on jerseys
I worry I'll hurt my knee
I cry that my football season is over
I am a talented Steelers fan

I understand I can't live forever
I say we shouldn't pollute
I dream I am a pro football player
I try to be the best I can
I hope to go to college
I am a talented Steelers fan
Zane Golike, Grade 6
Helfrich Park Middle School, IN

Reality
Through the window, it seems so free,
Out there in the world, in reality
Trees going past,
Cars zooming fast
Road as far as you can see,
Out there in the world, in reality
But you're stuck in the car,
And you won't go far,
Because you're scared to be,
Out in reality
No one there with you,
Nothing to do
You have no company,
Out there in reality
You're going back home,
To your safe little dome,
Because you no longer want to be
Out there in reality
Erin Turner, Grade 6
Harding Middle School, OH

The Leaf's Journey

The leaf falls from the tree
Like a skydiver just opening his parachute.
Then it waits for winter
To fall asleep in a blanket of snow.
In spring, the leaf jumps up and shakes off the snow
As the wind carries it far from its home.
The leaf falls slowly to the ground
Feeling sad to be so far away from home.
The leaf dreams of being on the tree again.

Olivia Braun, Grade 6
Boulan Park Middle School, MI

Veteran's Day

Veteran's day is for heroic people defending our country.
We honor you for risking your life.
Thank you for our country to have peace.

Veterans are soldiers who fight for our country.
Veterans are not just people, they're heroes.
Thank you for fighting in the wars we had.

Veteran's Day is on this day
November 11
because World War I ended
on the 11th hour of the 11th day of the 11th month.
Veteran's Day is an important day
of the year because some veterans died
and some survived.

Christopher Manquen, Grade 5
Beck Centennial Elementary School, MI

November Is

Leaves scattered on a lawn like sprinkles on a cake,
Wood burning bonfires fill the air with smoke,
A clear white snowfall like a blanket on a bed,
Windy cold days as cold as a freezer with ice cubes,
Paw print tracks in the snow leads a path through the trees,
As a pencil races across the paper as fast as a race car
Kids write wish lists for Christmas
November is here,
Can't you tell?

Brenna Irwin, Grade 5
Beck Centennial Elementary School, MI

The Moonlight

The moonlight
glows in the middle of the night.
It shines in my room
almost every night.
It comes in different shapes, different times of the year.
The harvest moon
shines oh so bright with a reddish orange color like a balloon
I really do love
The moon!

Taven Jenkins, Grade 6
Granville T Woods Community School, OH

My Savior

He knows what you have done past, present, and future
What risks you have taken
Which roads you have traveled on
He knows everything
He is in total control
He accompanies you through good times
He carries you in His hands and guides you through trouble
Night and day He is by your side
Ready to help you in any way possible
He knows every person on earth
Every star in the sky
Every ounce of dirt in the ground
Like the palm of His hand
Just ask Him anything through prayer
And if you have faith
You can do anything through Him
I trust and love Him
My God, Jesus Christ is my Lord and Savior

Bethany M. Hart, Grade 6
North Knox East Elementary/Jr High School, IN

Mysteries: Solved

I'll go investigate the Yeti in the Himalayas
And the monster of Loch Ness Lake.
I'll try to find proof of the Jersey Devil
To prove that they're all fakes. (Aren't they?)
I'll take a risk at the Bermuda Triangle
Even if I don't get back for awhile.
Oh, no! I've fallen off the ship!
Looks like I'm going to take a dip!
A sea monster rises right before my eyes!
50 ft. tall and 20 ft. wide!
It plunges at me and — Beep! Beep! Beep!
My alarm clock goes off and I wake with a leap!
"It's all over now," I try to look at my shelf.
Instead I see killer spiders all over myself!

Connor Starks, Grade 4
University Elementary School, IN

October Is...

The taste of the scrumptious juicy caramel apples
The blissful purrs of the black cats
The leaves change to vibrant colors
There is a plethora of orange pumpkins
I feel the breeze sending chills up my spine

Warm apple cider tingles my tongue
Frightening decorations always have delicious candy
The anticipation of Halloween night
The steamy pumpkin pies with whipped cream

I cautiously walk up to the haunted houses
Halloween brings happy faces to children of all ages
Children scampering up to every doorstep

Alexandra Spanopoulos, Grade 5
Beck Centennial Elementary School, MI

Brianna

B right
R aces
I ncredibly cool
A thletic
N ice
N eat
A wesome

Brianna Gottman, Grade 4
Veale Elementary School, IN

I Don't Understand

I don't understand…
Why there is night and day
Why time goes so fast
Why new things become old.

But most of all…
Why people have to die
Why people fear so much
Why people are happy and sad.

What I understand the most is…
Why we go to school
Why we get jobs
Why we need love.

Taviance Maxberry, Grade 5
Becker Elementary School, OH

Apples

Apples
Bumpy, green
Feed the deer
I feel happy!
Apples

Hannah Phipps, Grade 4
Westview Elementary School, OH

Hurricane

A hurricane comes charging in
Like a herd of bison stampeding.
It frightens people
By causing floods and destroying homes
Off by the coast by the sea.
It leaves quietly, back to the ocean
Leaving the destruction it caused.

Zachary Fritts, Grade 5
Wooster Christian School, OH

Stars

S tars are beautiful.
T hey are very shiny.
A shooting star.
R emember they are up in the sky.
S tars! Stars! Stars!

Briawna Thompson, Grade 4
Westview Elementary School, OH

Winter Wonderland

The snowflakes danced down to the ground like reindeer.
None the same as another like in a classroom full of children.
Some children were rolling in the snow making snow angels that were soft as silk.
Big kids were throwing snowballs like massive bombs.
My eyes sparkled like crystals as I watched the spectacular event.
Others laughed like hyenas in the true winter wonderland.

Jack Percy, Grade 6
Boulan Park Middle School, MI

Thanksgiving

Thanksgiving, as we sit at the crowded table and wait for the turkey to be carved
all the family and friends at the table are starved.
We wait by the many candles dancing and flickering light that floods our eyes.
Giggling, knocking, and clacking meets the ear as everybody is in good cheer.
I feel thankful, overcome with joy
I wonder if this is what the first Thanksgiving felt like;
I think of Thanksgiving as the song of a glorious mockingbird,
gorgeous and sweet while it lasts but over far too soon.
Give Thanks
Give Thanks
Give Thanks

Elizabeth Walden, Grade 5
EH Greene Intermediate School, OH

A Cool Outfit

Shirt, you are my favorite.
I love your darkness and long sleeves.
You keep me warm like fur on my dog.
You make me stand out like the sun shines on the moon.
You keep me comfy like my sister's pillow comforts her little head.
You make me pretty like my eyes make me cute.

Skirt, you match my shirt perfectly.
You let my eyes stand out and my smile, too.
You twirl and swirl like a washing machine.
You sparkle like stars in the night sky.
You bring out the best in me.

Leggings, you go under my skirt to keep me warm.
You match with my plaid skirt but you don't make me mad.
You are the best.
I love this lovely outfit.
Thanks for being mine.

Miranda Menzyk, Grade 5
Allen J. Warren Elementary School, IN

I Am From

I am from an enormous farmland with lots of odorous cows
I am from dogs and cats and fish together all day long; in peace
I am from a crazy man who goes biking at 5 a.m. in winter
I am from olive skin and Mary's roses in winter
I am from a surfer; soon to return to its home, the beach, for it has moved away.
Did you get the hint?
I am from a little girl that is moving away from her home, family, and friends forever.

Ellie Jones, Grade 6
St Maria Goretti School, IN

Life

The trees on this earth are a blessing
But in a flash can be gone
You can hear the cutting of wood
As they disappear one by one
The forests are bright with color and light
The beautiful life can be taken away
When man is careless with fire and such
The effects on wildlife can be harsh
With one small spark
A forest fire can begin
But in the blackness
A new life begins
Through the dark ashes and soot
Plant life and such can begin
We don't always think why
We just move on with our lives
Will you help save our world?
By planting a tree on Arbor Day

Abigail Jean Else, Grade 6
Emmanuel-St Michael Lutheran School, IN

I Am

I am sporty and funny
I wonder what kind of house I'll live in
I hear ice skates gliding on ice
I see me on the Red Wings winning the Stanley Cup
I want an Xbox 360 with *NHL 09*
I am sporty and funny

I pretend I'm in the NHL
I feel I can score when I'm by the net
I touch the laces of my ice skates
I worry about safety
I cry when I think of my kitten dying
I am sporty and funny

I understand that I can't get a Nike Bauer XXI
I say I believe in God
I dream of being in the NHL one day
I try to be the best at hockey
I hope I get good grades
I am sporty and funny

I am James Nichols

James Nichols, Grade 4
Floyd Ebeling Elementary School, MI

Winter

W ind is blustering
I stay inside with a book
Buildi **N** g a replica of Frosty
T rees covered in snow
E verlasting snowfall
R esting after an intense snowball fight

Allyson Schmidt, Grade 6
Holy Angels School, OH

Fear

Fear is like a closet with a shut door
And also petrifying
Like the Grim Reaper about to kill you.
It pulses through my blood!
It reminds me of the time I was so scared
That I almost peed my pants!
It makes me feel like I am going to have a heart attack
It makes me want to hide in a closet
And never come out…

Brett Sullivan, Grade 6
St Maria Goretti School, IN

I Am

I am funny and athletic
I wonder if I will be the last man on earth
I hear cheering from the bleachers
I see me in the Hockey Town Hall of Fame
I want a million dollars
I am funny and athletic

I pretend I am the last man on earth
I feel smart like an A+ student
I touch my hockey stick
I worry about fires
I cry when I'm drawing my old cat
I am funny and athletic

I understand why I can't have a million dollars
I say I can have it all
I dream I can fly
I try to fly
I hope I can have a million dollars
I am funny and athletic

I am Eric Ross

Eric Ross, Grade 4
Floyd Ebeling Elementary School, MI

November

November is when Thanksgiving arrives.
Thanksgiving is when we bake turkey and
see some snow flurries!
In November we wear winter coats that
are as scalding as a cup of hot chocolate!
Hot chocolate is our beverage
as we stare at the TV to see football.
When we watch football,
fireplaces are on making me warm.
If we are outside, it's a bonfire.
The bonfire is as scalding
as the sun in the summer!
It's a bummer that leaves are off trees
because now I have to rake!
So remember, that's November!

Chase Walper, Grade 5
Beck Centennial Elementary School, MI

I Am

I am funny and outgoing.
I wonder what we're having for dinner.
I hear people talking in Heaven.
I see people in Heaven.
I want more Wii games.
I am funny and outgoing.
I pretend to be in the Civil War.
I feel happy because I have
little people doing my homework.
I touch people in Heaven.
I worry about my brother getting hurt.
I cry because I can't see my dad.
I am funny and outgoing.
I understand my name is Caleb.
I say my brother's name is Hayden.
I dream to become an architect.
I try to become an architect.
I hope I get to go trick-or-treating.
I am funny and outgoing.

Caleb Stenberg, Grade 6
Galesburg-Augusta Middle School, MI

Summer Play

Basketball and uniforms
Jumps, turns, and hops
Sweating for 2 points
Sneakers instead of flip flops
Traveling Indiana
Hoosier Hoops
Cut to the open wing
2-point shot, alley-oops!

Austin Brown, Grade 6
Tri-West Middle School, IN

Halloween

Halloween Halloween
Trick-or-treating
Candy eating
Scary!
Costumes
Bucket loads of candy
Cavities
Dentist
What more could there be?

Eli Sapp, Grade 5
Norwich Elementary School, OH

Happiness

Happiness is yellow
It smells like cookies baking
It looks like a sunny day
It tastes like a birthday cake
It sounds like a roller coaster
Happiness feels like a birthday party!

Ryann Cox, Grade 6
Eisenhower Middle School, OH

Kittens/I Love

Kittens
Are sweet and nice
So cute and cuddly
They are round balls of fluffy fir
I love

Kimberley Rowe, Grade 4
Warren Central Elementary School, IN

The Goal!

The face off.
You win the face off.
You take control of the puck.
You skate past the blue line.
Next you pass it back to me.

After I get the pass
I do something amazing.
I take my stick and wind up.
I aim.
BOOM! I take a slap shot.
It is really fast.

Finally it hits the goalie.
There is a player standing there.
It bounces off the goalie's pads.
The player in front of the net
Turns around and slams it in.
That's how you score a goal.

Cole Helgemo, Grade 6
Abbott Middle School, MI

Animals

I love animals so much
Just the feeling of each of their touch
Each color and shape,
The sound they can make,
With all their features,

Bird or fish,
There's one for every dish,
Dog or bat,
Even if they're fat,
Oh the beautiful creatures

Ashley Pacelli, Grade 6
Corpus Christi Catholic School, MI

Fire vs Water

Fire
hot, dangerous
blazing, burning, smoking
flame, inferno, sparkle, clear
splashing, dripping, drinking
expandable, wet
water

Christopher Egolf, Grade 4
Norwich Elementary School, OH

The Pug and the Bee

There was a Pug
Standing next to a tree
He was looking up
He was watching a bee.

Look little Pug
Look, see what I see
Way up in the tree
There is another bee.

The Pug found a honeycomb
That fell from the tree
It stuck on his nose
Watch out! There's a bee!

Ceara Edwards, Grade 6
Eisenhower Middle School, OH

Birds

Graceful,
Beautiful, winged
Creatures.
Unique songs,
Tweeting softly,
Fluttering,
Under clouds,
Spreading happiness.

Claire Anderson, Grade 4
Normandy Elementary School, OH

Thanksgiving

Thanksgiving is about
Thanks and giving.
Thanks for our family
Giving to others.
Not about what you eat.
It's about fun and love
That's all it can be.

Jake Wallace, Grade 5
Spaulding Elementary School, OH

Winter

Snow is falling,
Snowflake by snowflake.
Kids are playing,
Sledding and snowball fighting.
Cocoa is being poured,
Mug by mug.
Animals are sleeping,
Bears and squirrels.
Birds are flying south and
Roads are being plowed.
These are some reasons
We love winter!

Lyndsay Johnson, Grade 6
Akiva Academy, OH

A Place Called Home

As you drive around my neighborhood
You will find many things:

A bright yellow sign flashing "NO OUTLET"
is what you will first meet.
A sidewalk jutting from the grass
lined with trees so small and neat.
Street lights glowing in the night
will help you find your way.
People lazily trudging out
to throw their trash away.
Neighbors continuing with their daily routine
are welcoming and kind, not harsh and mean.
Children are biking up and down the street
laughing as they play and ride around me.
Motorcycles zooming
around and round the block
Apartments looming
way up high above the walk.

Stay a little longer and you will see,
Just how much this neighborhood means to me!

Hayley Kim, Grade 5
Allen J. Warren Elementary School, IN

My Summer Fun

Hot, sun shining down.
Splashing! Soaking! Diving down.
Having fun! Beach time.

Kodi O'Boyle, Grade 4
Eugene M Nikkari Elementary School, MI

My Baby Sister

She is fun to entertain
Much cuter than you
She sleeps more than anything
You can always tell when she has gone poo!
Sometimes I am jealous
Because she looks so warm
After a long day of peek-a-boo
She lies in her cradle a minute or two
Then
Shh!
The baby is sleeping

Ethan Dolphin, Grade 4
Licking Valley Intermediate School, OH

Mist

Mist comes in peacefully
Like a rabbit hopping softly on the dewy grass.
It whispers softly to the sun
By spreading farther through the sky.
Mist roams around from town to town
And leaves quite so peacefully.

Grace Murray, Grade 5
Wooster Christian School, OH

Sea Turtles

Sea Turtles are large air-breathing reptiles.
They live in tropical and subtropical seas.
Have large flippers.
Have a leather back.
Can come in many shapes and sizes.
Can weigh over 650 to 1,300 pounds.
Can live over 100 years old.
These graceful species swim through seas around the world.
Once in the millions, now close to being endangered.

Myriah Greulich, Grade 6
Nancy Hanks Elementary School, IN

Getting My First Warriors Book

I walk into Barnes and Noble.
I hear the blur of many voices around me.
I smell the sweet foods in the café next to me.
I am with my dad, and he tells me I can get a book!
In the children's section, I browse aisles and aisles of books.
Then I find an aisle with series books in it.
A serious looking, bright orange cat catches my eye.
The title is *Warriors: Into the Wild*.
I stroke its smooth laminated cover.
I must buy it!

Emily Axelberg, Grade 5
Stanley Clark School, IN

Gifts

G iving is fun.
I love gifts.
F amily and friends
T ill the end.
S o you love giving too?

Annie Barger, Grade 5
West Washington Elementary School, IN

I Am

I am smart and fun.
I wonder if people who commit suicide go to heaven.
I see bugs make a heart.
I am smart and fun.

I pretend I'm a dragon with my friend.
I feel sad when I get hurt.
I touch the ghost of my past.
I worry about my brother's surgery.
I cry when I think of my friend of the past.
I am smart and fun.

I understand why we moved.
I say the war should stop.
I dream of going to my old home.
I try to get better at softball.
I hope my friends are o.k.
I am smart and fun.

Laura Schlachter, Grade 6
Helfrich Park Middle School, IN

Sunset

The sunset,
So delicate and its rays beam throughout the skies,
With its salmon colored shade,
Shining over us like a spotlight from the heavens.

Sunset,
Will your heat ever depart from our grasp, and leave us stranded in the cold murky night?
Why must you last only your minute moment?
Where do you go after the shadows engulf the skies?
How do you produce such a beautiful scene while warming our hearts at the same time?

The sunset,
So many questions we cannot answer,
So much beauty we cannot understand,
Yet we are blessed with the pure presence of it.

It isn't if we *can* understand the beauty of it,
Or is we *can* answer all the questions,
Then we can fully appreciate it,
But it is if you can wonder,
And think,
Then you can truly appreciate,
The sunset.

Kyle Wagner, Grade 6
Harding Middle School, OH

Autumn

Autumn is a beautiful painting waiting to be discovered.
The warm vibrant colors remind me of an artist's palette.
The stunning colorful autumn leaves blowing in the wind is a sign that autumn is coming.
Whoosh!
Goes the wind.
Crunch!
Go the leaves.
Autumn reminds me of a new beginning coming again.

Samantha Hall, Grade 6
Harding Middle School, OH

Andrew Sohrenssen

Drew
Small in size but quick on the field, friend to any animal found, and gives his best effort in school
Son of Mike and Amy Sohrenssen
Lover of baseball because it is fun to watch players blast homeruns into the crowd, any Guitar Hero game because the guitar is an awesome instrument, and my family because they love me no matter what
Who feels that riding a bike is a good way to exercise, scoring a goal is better than eating ice cream, and that badminton is a good way to spend time with my friends
Who needs food all the time, friends to play with constantly, and to be tucked in two times a night
Who gives my parents a hard time, love to my whole family, and help to others who need it
Who fears tornadoes for some unknown reason, the dark because it's impossible to see what is going on in my house, and losing my family because it would be very hurtful
Who would like to have my Grandpa Balyo alive again because I never really knew him, become a major league baseball player, and go to Florida again to swim at the beach
Resident of Lancaster
Sohrenssen

Andrew Sohrenssen, Grade 5
Sanderson Elementary School, OH

Guinea Pig/Hamster

Guinea pig
noisy, squeal
bugging, irritating, wiggling,
soft, furry, short, skinny,
tiring, chewing, biting
fast, patient,
Hamster

Breanna Darnell, Grade 5
Washington Township Elementary School, IN

Christmas

Hello Mr. Snowman under the tree,
It's time for Christmas presents for you and me,
'Cuz Christmas gifts are such a delight,
They make my heart become a shining light.

Kyle Szymanowski, Grade 6
Corpus Christi Elementary School, IN

The Important Thing About Me

The important thing about me is that I'm a kid
I love the color blue
I want to learn Kung-Fu
I love making cake
I like eating steak
I don't get stomach aches
For goodness sake, I'm just great!
But the important thing about me is that I'm a kid

Aaron Crawford, Grade 4
Cooper Elementary School, MI

The Fight Between Nature

The sun remembers
when the mountain poked her.
So the sun melted the mountain
the mountain melted into the sea.

The sea showed the sky who's boss
the sky pushed the moon.
The moon cried until dawn
dawn shut him up.

The stars used profane language at dawn
then they slapped the stone.
Stone listens to the fighting
she is very disappointed.

Stone told Mother Nature
she goes to the sun, moon, stars, sky, sea, and mountain
she puts a cloud over the sun
she turns the moon into a floating rock
she turns the sea into a lake
she turns the mountain into a rock
she turns the stars into sky
but she turns the stone into a mountain.

Danielle Davis, Grade 6
Woodward Park Middle School, OH

I Am

I am honest and a dreamer!
I wonder what I will be like in 40 years!
I hear the books yelling my name!
I see a griffin flying by!
I want to live a long and happy life with my family!
I am honest and a dreamer!
I pretend I can soar with the birds!
I feel bashful when the unicorn comes my way!
I touch the gumdrops of the rain!
I worry that someone will harm my family and me.
I cry when I think about my grandpa.
I am honest and a dreamer!
I understand my family is going to be there when I fall!
I say God is everywhere!
I dream of having a healthy family when I am older!
I try to be a beautiful dancer!
I hope I will be a successful leader!
I am honest and a dreamer!

Jessi Charon, Grade 6
Galesburg-Augusta Middle School, MI

Christmas Bells

Christmas is my favorite time of year.
I like the nicely wrapped presents
And the warm cookie crescents,
The pretty white snow
And the festive holiday shows.
But Christmas bells are my favorite thing,
With their warm and welcoming ring.
Bells make me feel aglow,
I hear them everywhere I go.
Sleigh bells and church bells and bells that chime,
Large bells and small bells and bells that sparkle and shine.
There are bells on my Christmas tree and one on my door
Bells on street lights and many more.
They make homes and cities cheery and bright,
And fill our hearts with Christmas delight.
So whenever I hear those marvelous bells
The joy of Christmas inside me swells.
For love and happiness and hope they tell
The jolly, joyous jingling of the
Bells, bells, bells

Astrid Cabello, Grade 5
EH Greene Intermediate School, OH

Christmas

Presents and candy and sweet treats galore.
I can see presents in all kinds of stores.
Santa Claus comes with a Ho-Ho-Ho.
What would it be without the snow?
And then the lights that shine so bright.
Christmas would be dull without them in sight.
Christmas is the best time for happiness and cheer.
I hope you have a good Christmas this year.

Nicole Nemeth, Grade 6
Corpus Christi Elementary School, IN

The Falls

Waterfalls are big
Waterfalls are beautiful
Niagara Falls rocks!

Ryan Exline, Grade 4
Westview Elementary School, OH

Creek

A wet path,
Filled with minnows,
Rocks,
With hidden,
sliding water snakes.
A hiding pool
too many!

Jared Beach, Grade 4
Normandy Elementary School, OH

Halloween/Thanksgiving

Halloween
Fun, outside
Playing, scaring, running
Candy, treats, pumpkins, turkey
Harvesting, thanking, giving
Together, happy
Thanksgiving

Anna Swift, Grade 4
Norwich Elementary School, OH

Ode to the Window

It is a shame that the pane of glass
feels warmth and cold all at once.
It feels the bitter patter and bite of rain.
How can it stand the pain?
It sits there idle but not when it storms.
It shakes and quakes just like the door,
when someone wants to be let in.
It has a wonderful view of the snow,
but also can see my sister's nose
when it is pressed up against it.
Why does it stay and not leave?
How can it feel all that at once?
I cannot see how.

Hannah Yahraus, Grade 6
Birchwood School, OH

The Forest

All the animals are running around,
The birds are making pretty sounds.
The children are playing in the trees,
Trying to avoid the busy bees.
They are all playing in the sun,
Having lots of fun.
Nature is beautiful,
And never fearful.

Alina Rachford, Grade 4
Stonegate Elementary School, IN

Leo

L eo is a constellation in the shape of a lion.
E urystheus ordered Hercules to kill the lion.
O f all the constellations Leo has one of the brightest stars in the sky.

Alexandra Downs, Grade 6
Pinewood Elementary School, IN

Snow

I looked outside to see the snow,
and noticed that it had a certain glow.
I couldn't resist but to go and sled.
I ran into the snow, it was like a bed.
I made a snowman handsome and white,
and hoped he wouldn't disappear throughout the warm and cozy night.
I smiled brightly the next day,
when I saw my snowman had not melted away.

Meghan Magee, Grade 6
Corpus Christi Elementary School, IN

Tree

I am a tree as bright as the sun.
Rocks glitter under me as if they were gold.
When animals walk past me I get as happy as a tornado in a trailer park.
Flowers grow around me like a ring.
I feel as sad as a dog without a bone when my fellow trees get cut to stumps.
I hate it when people litter around me.
It is like I'm a trash can.
Wood surrounds me like a kitten's mom when a storm is going on.
The clouds that hang over me are as dark as the midnight sky.
When I am happy, the sky turns as blue as the oceans.
Sticks come off my trunk as if they were arms and legs.
Dirt surrounds me like a puddle of mud.
The flowers that lay near me look like a beautiful rainbow.

Rylan Mattocks, Grade 6
Cloverdale Middle School, IN

Winter

Grounds turn to white
As I stare out the window
Sugar being shaken from the sky
I pull on a sweater or two, button up my coat, and zip up my boots
Run outside to play today.

The perfect snow, hard, but yet has a softness to it
Crunching beneath my feet with every step
Pack the snow together into one tight sphere, the snowballs flying through the air.
A friend is needed; why not construct him out of snow?
Stovepipe hat, button nose, two eyes made out of coal.

"SPLAT!" Freezing cold ice slides down my back, I've been hit.

We retreat inside for warmth
The hot chocolaty mixture slides down my throat.

WINTER

Tess Jones, Grade 6
Harding Middle School, OH

Saint Nicholas

S anta in a big red suit
A fun special holiday
I cy roads don't slip
N ice little boys and girls get really big presents
T rees light up the big blue sky

N ew Year Eve on December 31st
I cicles sticking to everything
C andy canes so yummy to eat
H o! Ho! Ho! Here comes Santa and the reindeers
O rnaments hanging on the trees
L ights shining like a star in the sky
A jolly holly Christmas
S kating in the cold of a great Christmas

Sofia Palazzolo, Grade 5
Browning Elementary School, MI

Christmas Snapshot

Clustered around the table
Tying up each other's aprons
We search for a bowl, a mixing spoon
Clinking and clanking

Kneading and mixing
Flour, butter, sugar, milk
All dumped into one big bowl
A splash of lime, a dash of cherry
Everything splattered with bursts of bright color

Laid out neatly on a sheet
Into the oven, and we wait
For our masterpiece

Grandma,
In your kitchen
We made more than yummy chocolates
We were mixing up memories

Renee Klann, Grade 6
Harding Middle School, OH

Cousins

This person that I know,
This person I love so.

This person can sometimes not be lovable enough,
This person can sometimes be rough,
This person is tough.

This person is toying with my brain,
This person is driving me insane,
This person is causing me so much pain.

This person I love believe me it's true,
This person I love even when she makes me blue.

Amanda Kathryn Beabout, Grade 6
Trilby Elementary School, OH

My Cat

My cat's eyes are like an ocean
My cat's hair is soft and fluffy
My cat's heart holds love and playfulness
My cat lives with us and sleeps at the end or beside my bed
Its name is…Precious

Matt Sanchez, Grade 5
Henryville Elementary School, IN

My Cat

My cat is very funny like a clown.
My cat has hair like a raccoon.
My cat is mean as a shark.
My cat is crazy like a monkey.
My cat lives like a queen and eats like a pig.
My cat is cool as ice.

Mason Edwards, Grade 5
Henryville Elementary School, IN

A Miracle Flower

A tiny seed, deep in the ground.
It grows and grows, till it is found!
A tiny gem it finally opens.
A bright ruby red jewel,
In a neon green world!

Anja Jaeger, Grade 6
Emanuel Redeemer Lutheran School, MI

Thanksgiving

Turkey, turkey, gobble, gobble, gobble.
Put it in the oven and let it cook.
Turkey, turkey, yum, yum, yum.
Take it out of the oven and eat it all up.
Turkey, turkey, very, very, tasty.
When you are done you're going to be happy.
If you are wondering why, that's
Because it is time for some yummy pie.
Pie, pie, take your pick,
Apple, or pumpkin, or any other kind.
Grandma's are the best in baking
My pie and turkey, too.
Now it's time to go,
I'm so sorry to say.
Give your hugs and kisses
And have a very nice day.

Emily Bruinius, Grade 6
Crown Point Christian School, IN

Dogs

Dogs are soft, kind, they can also hunt.
Dogs are smart, intelligent they can also play.
Dogs are cute, fast they can also run.
Dogs are safe, can keep your house safe, also they can walk,
Dogs are able to smell very far away, can also sleep next to you.
Dogs are soft, kind, and cute.

Anthony LaRosa, Grade 6
Abbott Middle School, MI

Being Responsible

Helping my brother when he needs me
Cleaning the table off after dinner
Helping my mom with my baby brother
Helping my dad find his phone
Bringing down my laundry basket
Clearing my plate off the table
I'm responsible.

Jessica Miller, Grade 4
Dobbins Elementary School, OH

Dog

Dog, dog, dog
Playful dog
Happy, cute, shy dog
Last of all, best of all
My dog
Minnie

Joey Allen, Grade 5
St Jude Catholic School, IN

I Am

I am funny and cool.
I wonder how my dad is doing.
I hear my hands talking to me.
I see dollups in my hand.
I want a million dollars.
I am funny and cool.
I pretend to be in the army.
I feel sad about my friend Silly dying.
I touch my friend Bobo.
I worry that Kayla doesn't like me.
I cry when someone breaks up with me.
I am funny and cool.
I understand I rock.
I say god is real.
I dream that I'll be in the army.
I try to keep my grades up.
I hope my grandma lives.
I am funny and cool.

Jacob Devereaux, Grade 6
Galesburg-Augusta Middle School, MI

What Moves Me

G ets you in shape
Y ou never give up
M y favorite sport
N ever do dangerous
   things without a teacher
A lways try new things
S o much stretching
T umbling and flipping
I love doing gymnastics
C ool outfits you have to wear
S o many things to do

Brooke Shafer, Grade 5
Central Academy, OH

In Tennis I Learned…

In tennis I learned…to keep my eye on the ball until your racket connects.
Front hand, back hand, up close to the net.
Serve it high, serve it low,
Follow the ball where ever it goes.

In tennis I learned…follow through like a golf club,
High ball, spike it, low ball too.
make sure you get up before the ball comes back to you.
Run this way, that way too.
Make sure the ball doesn't hit the ground twice,
For if it does, too bad for you.

In tennis I learned…volley here, volley there,
Don't hit the ball too hard, don't you dare.
For if you do it's out of bounds,
And you will not win the golden crown.
Your opponent will say "Oh, thank you, dear."
But your partner will be in crocodile tears.
All these things I have learned on this here court.
Now I'm in competitions, wish me good luck and good wishes.
Throw me flowers, please no dishes.
In tennis I learned to absorb what I see and just be me.

Mikayla Smith, Grade 6
Abbott Middle School, MI

Gracie

energetic, intelligent, athletic
daughter of Scott and Tina
who loves animals, her friends, and her family
who feels great around nature
who needs more girls in her development, more pets, and a laptop
who gives love, care, and appreciation to her friends and family
who fears nothing
who'd like to meet Miley Cyrus
who dreams of being on TV
a student of S.J.J. school
nickname: Peppers

Gracie Horvath, Grade 4
Sts Joseph and John School, OH

All About Myself

Lauren
Energetic, caring, and hardworking
Sister of Sara
Lover of video games, animals, and vanilla ice cream
Who feels nervous when getting into trouble, getting bad grades,
   and getting shots
Who gets excited about holidays, birthday parties, and water parks
Who needs to play more sports, get better grades, and earn more money
Who gives kisses to my mom and dad at bedtime
Who fears big spiders, scorpions, and robbers
Who would like to live in Florida
Resident of Austintown, Ohio
Wolfe

Lauren Wolfe, Grade 5
Frank Ohl Intermediate School, OH

Potato Soup

Potato soup? Is it true?
I will eat some, but only for you!

Potato soup is my delight
I grab my spoon and take a bite.
It's warm and creamy, yet crunchy too.
I will eat some, but only for you!

Every bite I want to extend,
I really hope that this moment won't end!

Annie Kittendorf, Grade 5
Central Grade School, MI

Eli Thomas Jeng

E xcellent in being mischievous.
L oves to act funny.
I s only two years old, but my favorite brother.

T he very best trickster.
H e's the best baby.
O utstanding boy.
M agnificent brother.
A mazing to understand.
S uper smart.

J umps in every direction.
E nergetic all the time.
N aughty in a funny way.
G ets in trouble a lot!

Sarah Jeng, Grade 4
Keystone Academy, MI

A Nice Christmas

It's Christmas morning
Time for gifts,
It won't be boring.
But it's too early
2:00 a.m.
Those gifts wrapped with bows that are curly
I can't wait,
I need to know
It's like bait
The warm sun is rising
My brother won't be sleeping
I get him up to take a peek
And sure enough he's not asleep
We run down the hall
Having fun
We open our gifts
How'd Christmas come to be so great?
Now I'm cheering with glee
Because I just got a new PSP
And my brother and I
Are laughing, laughing, laughing.

Stone Beyersdorfer, Grade 5
EH Greene Intermediate School, OH

Mars

M ars is red.
A fter Mars on a list of planets would be Jupiter.
R ed dust on Mars is in the atmosphere, too.
S ince Mars has no oxygen a human could not live there.

Channing Hicks, Grade 6
Pinewood Elementary School, IN

Worry

Worry is white like the pale face of a mother
when she hears her child is missing,
and also like a frightened deer
who is running from a hungry wolf.
It creeps up my throat like a spider
that is sneaking up on me.
It reminds me of the time when my dog
went missing and I was crying like a baby.
It makes me feel sick to my stomach.
It makes me want to slam my door in worry's face.

Megan Grady, Grade 6
St Maria Goretti School, IN

Shining Stars

When shining stars go by
it sometimes makes us cry.

Oh the glory my, my, my
what a beautiful sky it can be.

The colors of the night
can be yellow stars and black night.

In the day there is no shining stars.
There are only shining stars in the night.

You will find the most greatest thing tonight.
Go outside and watch the stars at 8:30 tonight.

Olivia Bingle, Grade 4
Bright Elementary School, IN

Softball

I play softball all day and night.
But most of all I love to play under the big lights.
When the game is tight.
I step up to the plate and hit a homerun out of sight.
For I'm the pitcher on the team.
When I throw the last strike my whole team screams.
We have this softball cheer.
That we sing all year.
When I strike out I don't like it because I pout.
But I like it when I strike them out.
Softball is fun.
Especially when we're under the sun.
Go, go, get'em, get'em, go, get'em, go.
Xcel you know!

Mallory Marsicek, Grade 5
St Jude Catholic School, IN

Sabertooth Tiger
S trong
A crobatic
B east
Ov **E** rpowering
R ocks
T ame
O ptimistic
O versized teeth
T rack
H unt

T ear
I nstincts
G ore
E at
R are

Troy Morgan, Grade 6
Tippecanoe Middle School, OH

City Tree
The scintillates are
Twinkling,
And different tinges
Are everywhere

You can peer.
The sparkling lights
Brighten the city up,
And while the lights are flashing
On and off
The cars
Zoom by.

The star is the light of the night.
Leia Sneed, Grade 6
Harding Middle School, OH

Midnight My Cat
M y cat
I s 1 1/2 years old
D aring and a little crazy too
N aughty and nice at the same time
I still love her
G etting into trouble all the time
H itting at her toys
T earing up everything

M ight just be going nuts at times
Y ou don't want to pick her up

C rashes into things at night
A lso cuddly and cute
T he one who messes up the house
Anna Crova, Grade 4
Keystone Academy, MI

My First Game
In the locker room
Getting a pep talk
Finally, we're hitting the floor
My first game

The cheering of the crowds
The squeak of my shoes
Finally, the moment I've been waiting for

Fake right, go left, shoot, swish
Pass, foul, pick, roll
Run,
Run,
Run,
Three…two…one…
Brrrrrrrrrr

Yeah! We won!
Coach is happy; we are done.
Anthony Huls, Grade 6
Crown Point Christian School, IN

Summer/Beach
Summer
Sun, vacation
Swinging, swimming, playing
Enjoying the hot sun.
Beach
Amber Grady, Grade 5
Becker Elementary School, OH

My Pet Dog
I like to pick him up,
Because he is a pup
He licks from cups,
And then has to hiccup.
He acts like he is a nice dog,
He likes to sit and he has seen a log.
My dog is lazy,
He drives me crazy.
He likes to go to school with us,
Sometimes he meets us at the bus.
I named him Jake,
And he loves our lake.
Jordan Dugas, Grade 4
Chrisney Elementary School, IN

Friends
I am a girl
You are a boy,
They are best friends,
We are inseparable,
It is wonderful.
Melissa Schlake, Grade 6
Harmon Middle School, OH

Fall
As summer fades away,
Fall shows more every day.
People harvest their crops,
And wear warmer tops.
People close up their pools,
As the temperature cools.
The colors of leaves
Change on the trees.
I like fall,
And so should you all!
Brooklyn Hubbard, Grade 5
West Elkton Elementary School, OH

Fall/Christmas
Fall
Breezy, crunchy
Falling, crumbling, tumbling
Color, joy, family, presents
Singing, celebrating, praising
Chilly, bright
Christmas
Jenna Walker, Grade 4
Norwich Elementary School, OH

Football
Passing, running, scoring
Even when pouring
Scarlet and gray
Guess the team
Ohio State
The other team will be cream
On a rate from 1-8
I choose 8, Ohio State the best
From the north, south, east, and west!
Go Ohio State!
Nick Thornton, Grade 6
St Joseph Parish School, OH

Aches
As I walk to the field
My body aches
Ever since I got that snakebite
It hurts like a paralyzed body
I've never gotten any medicine
They just let me sit there
Aching in the corner
Wyatt Turner, Grade 5
Mayfield Elementary School, OH

Wet
Alone on the beach,
My pants, socks, and shoes are soaked.
Uncomfortable.
Lev Kendrick, Grade 6
Stanley Clark School, IN

Music!

One sweet sound, with some sour notes. For young or old, If you are dancing down the aisle, there is music somewhere. Dance party or classical. Old school or new school. Find your style.

It can inspire you or make you desire something. Slow or turbo. It is great. On sad days making you full of joy. Oh so cool.

Where did this start you say. Long ago before. When I play this magic instrument that produces this sound you said "Hooray!" Where did this come from? This "thing" we all know. Music is my friend, from a long time ago.

Sabrina Somers, Grade 6
Abbott Middle School, MI

Morgan Kiernan

Morgan
Who is caring, funny and nice.
Who wishes to get As all year long.
Who loves my dog Ozzy, my 2 cats Meagan and Twinkle, my sister Madison and Mom and Dad.
Who dreams of becoming an actress.
Who wonders if the world is really going to end in 2015.
Who fears spiders and my cousin Timmy.
Who likes to play football and having gym.
Who believes in God and Jesus.
Who plans to live in Miami.
Who is a resident of Summit County.
Kiernan

Morgan Kiernan, Grade 4
Northfield Elementary School, OH

Imagination

Imagination is many things. Imagination is everywhere. How would we live without it? What would the world be like? A pile of dust in the middle of nowhere? You decide. Imagination is in your brain. Imagination is on TV. Imagination can be mean or nice if you use it right. Imagination can be a pig with wings, a bunny with three heads, or a ferret that sings. But whatever the reason you think up these things you have to remember that they are just a figment of your Imagination.

Cora Saggars, Grade 5
Northern Heights Elementary School, IN

Jumping Dreams

My sister Camilla, cousins Nicole and Jordan, and I pedaled bikes along a country road.
The four of us were breathing in the warm, crisp air.
The day was shining bright, the sun in our eyes.
It was a fantastic summer day.
We turned down a rocky road. There were no cars at all!
We had our cameras with us, and the sun
was pouring right down the deserted road.
We snapped pictures. I felt like a photographer!
The colors of the sun seemed like a rainbow: Pink, yellow, orange, and more.

We rode a little father down, taking more pictures of waterfalls and trees.
We chatted about Indiana and how pretty it is!
We whispered to each other what we thought about those wonders.
We overheard the birds as they chirped and soared free above us.
We all snapped pictures of ourselves jumping as high as the sky.

As we pedaled back home,
I was thinking how life would be without all those
Birds, trees, blue skies, stars, sun, grass, water, the whole world!
We rarely think about those things that help out our world so much.
I can't live without nature!

Serena Alway, Grade 5
Stanley Clark School, IN

The Great Day

Parents buy them,
Kids open them
Presents
I like that stuff

You see family
You open presents
Christmas
I like that stuff

They hang on
Christmas trees
Their shaped
Like a cane
Candy canes
I like that stuff

Aapri Bellard, Grade 5
May V Peck Elementary School, MI

Christmas

Christmas
Yay! Presents!
Jesus is born!
Happy! Joyous! Proud! Cheerful!
Holiday

Nate Scheerer, Grade 4
Bailly Elementary School, IN

Lazy Cat!

Oh that lazy cat,
that sometimes sleeps on my back!
I love her so
but sometimes I don't know.
She won't play with yarn.
She sleeps out in the barn!
She's afraid of my brother's bat.
Oh that lazy cat!

Shae Humphrey, Grade 6
Woodward Park Middle School, OH

Day on the Ocean

Still moving ocean
nothing in sight but the light
calm as a feather

Ian Turner, Grade 6
Tippecanoe Middle School, OH

In School

Trapped inside
nowhere to hide!
Using tools,
old torn stools…
meeting new friends
I can't wait until the school day ends!

Gokul Srinivasan, Grade 4
Stonegate Elementary School, IN

Love

Love is like a sacred journey.
Love starts relationships and families.
Love warms and heals our hearts.
Love shows people that we care.
Love shows us unity and respect.
Love shines us down paths we choose to go or take.
Love brings us closer together.
Love takes away pain and grief.
Love can brighten any day, any place, and at any time.
Love leads to smiles and cheerful faces.
Love is an important virtue.
Love is a special way of sharing.
Love is a way of helping and listening to others.
Love is for all people we know or don't know.
Love is a great gift from God.
Love is unknown, we don't really know what it is or why we have it.
Love is where we follow our hearts while it guides us on our way.

Madison Hinds, Grade 6
St Gerard School, MI

I Am

I am outgoing and kind.
I wonder what my dog Hope is thinking about.
I hear the walls of the room calling my name.
I see everything closing in on me so I have nowhere to go.
I want a real father.
I am outgoing and kind.
I pretend to be Grandma Hickembottom.
I feel glad when my dragon Rascal comes to see me in my dreams.
I touch the scales of Rascal as we ride off into the night.
I worry that my dog won't be there when I get home.
I cry when I am lonely.
I am outgoing and kind.
I understand that I cannot have an elephant.
I say I believe in Jesus.
I dream of winning a tetherball game.
I try to get good grades.
I hope my dog will like her Christmas gift.
I am outgoing and kind.

Veronica Town, Grade 6
Galesburg-Augusta Middle School, MI

Brandon

Brandon
Hostile, Athletic, a fighter, intelligent, lazy (like Garfield)
Relative — Lauren, Angie, and Bret
Lover of — Yu Gi Oh, family, and girls
Feels — Friends, Playstation 3, candy, and soda
Needs healthy food, TV, girlfriend
Scared of Jason, Michael Myers, and Blarye
Gives friendship, respect, niceness
I would like to see Disney World, Kenny Chesney, Johnny Depp, and Wichita, Kansas
Resident of Indiana
Underhill

Brandon Underhill, Grade 5
Perry Central Elementary School, IN

Winter Magic

Time slips away from the hands of Lady Spring,
bouncing along the hectic road until scooped up
in the hands of Jack Frost.

The wind itself shivers as Jack Frost sneezes,
sending a cascade of winter snow and ice.

The snow brings snowballs and snowmen,
skating and ice carvings.
It also brings happiness and memories.

Christmas and Thanksgiving, Winter holidays,
do not have that special feeling hidden inside
without snow falling past the window.

Therefore, when Jack Frost knocks upon your door,
remember this
without him, there is no magic.
Shoo him not, but bring him in.

Melissa Bush, Grade 5
Central Grade School, MI

November Is...

Fireplaces beam
as if the hot chambers are relieved
to finally glow again, crackling a soft tune,
loud voices trying to be heard
over a roar of others
at a Thanksgiving get-together,
that sounds like an engine starting up,
the sound of clanking silverware
against sizzling food covered plates
fills the dining room,
steam from your breath
gets impossible to see as it reaches past
the clouds, gleaming moon,
and into the heavens,
leaves gently sway off of trees
as the wind blows and feels like a cold sheet,
wrapping you tight,
you whip your head back and forth,
trying to find out where
a spine chilling wolf's howl
came from.

Mary Newfer, Grade 5
Beck Centennial Elementary School, MI

Volcano

Red rocks bursting out in flares like a campfire for the Earth
Runs down the dark smoky surface
Paints the bright yellow sky into a black dark cloud
Burns all of Earth's beauties
Sparks of black confetti burst out
Green grass turns into a black garden of rocks.

John Byrd, Grade 6
St Clement Elementary School, OH

Christmas

C hristmas lights light up in the dark.
H olidays are fun.
R ed stockings hang up high in my house.
I t's a holly jolly day.
S nowmen in everyone's yard.
T rees are up in everybody's houses.
M om and dad hide our presents from us.
A in't it a good holiday.
S weaters are what everybody's wearing.

Adrianna Roberts, Grade 5
West Washington Elementary School, IN

Seasons

October, October
This month it gets colder.
Holidays are coming and snow is almost falling.
November, November
Two months past September.
Vote, vote for a new president.
December, December
It's almost 2009.
A new year will be here.
January, January
It's time for snowball fights.
Let's also make forts.
February, February
Presidents' birthdays.
Valentine's day is here with red and pink hearts.
March, March
It's getting warmer.
And then there's St. Patrick's Day.
April, April
There is the Fool's Day.
Gotcha!

Elle Hendricks, Grade 5
Akiva Academy, OH

Tion

If your teacher tells you to focus,
That's concentration.
If you ask a question and you get an answer,
That's information.
If you write a sentence and put a mark at the end,
That's punctuation. !.?
If you don't do what you're told in school,
That's called detention.
If you tell about something,
That's explanation.
If you can't wait to get out of school,
That's anticipation.
If the teacher is stressed out, tell her,
"That's relaxation."
If your school is empty and you are there,
That's a vacation!

Sydney Precurato, Grade 5
Frank Ohl Intermediate School, OH

Wonderful Pie

Feels hot when fresh from the oven.
Smells so delicious,
great and tremendous.
Grandma's homemade pumpkin pie.
I'm a lovin'.
Tasty and tremendously sweet.
What a great after school treat!
Jacob Clark, Grade 4
Licking Valley Intermediate School, OH

Snow

Snow
Frozen, water
Falling, piling, white
I love snow a lot
Winter
Tamio Marshall Yamamoto, Grade 5
May V Peck Elementary School, MI

Spooky Halloween

H aunted houses
A fraid at night
L ight the jack-o'-lantern
L isten to howls
O wls watching you
W atch the spooks
E erie screams
E ating candy
N ightmares that get you
Patrick Connors, Grade 6
Rocky River Middle School, OH

My Mom's Portrait

My mom is caring like the sun
My mom is joyful like the moon
My mom is sad like rainy days
My mom is happy like sunny days
Cameron Tanner, Grade 5
Henryville Elementary School, IN

I'm Sorry…

I'm so sorry I colored on
All of your books

They just looked so dull
And empty
I thought you would like them more
If they were bright and colorful

But at least now
I know the difference between
Coloring books
And reading books
Mia Smith, Grade 5
Tremont Elementary School, OH

The Wonders of Nature

Yellow leaves and yellow flowers gleam
Like the afternoon sunlight.

Sticks and stones lay in the grass
Like a small sorted array.

Woods, water, and wild wheat,
As calming as a cool summer breeze.

Caterpillars munch on little,
Lively leaves like babies.

Birds soar gracefully
Through the sky like jets.

They rest in their nests in the shade,
As peaceful as a sanctuary.

To me, these are truly
Wonders of nature.
Charlotte Muns, Grade 6
Cloverdale Middle School, IN

Shadow by the River

Leaves rustling in my ear,
For some reason I'm filled with fear.
Seeing the eerie, murky shadow,
Lying by the river.
It gave me a shiver.
Who is this lying before me?
Me.
Who am I?
Grace Williams, Grade 4
Stonegate Elementary School, IN

I Am

I am funny and smart.
I wonder about global warming.
I hear a mouse crying.
I see a monsoon.
I want a laptop.
I am funny and smart.
I pretend to drive.
I feel sad because my pet wolf died.
I touch a mocoon.
I worry about my dad.
I cry when I think of my dad.
I am funny and smart.
I understand that the earth spins.
I say we should not have homework.
I dream that I will be the president.
I hope that I get a laptop for Christmas.
I am funny and smart.
Missy Vickery, Grade 6
Galesburg-Augusta Middle School, MI

Monkeys

Monkeys are silly
Funny, too.
When they get around people
It sounds like a zoo.
Oh monkeys, oh monkeys
How funny they can be.
They never look alike
Or like you and me.
Emily Stanley, Grade 5
Spaulding Elementary School, OH

Westfield Mall

I like the mall a lot,
The clothes are very hot

I shop here and there,
At Hollister and Claire's

I eat at the café
They have a Chick-Fil-A

Their movie cinema is nice,
I've been there more than twice

The mall is a great place,
It puts a smile on my face.
Sierra L. Hawkins, Grade 6
Trilby Elementary School, OH

Running

Along a never-ending road,
Among the enormous trees,
Under the thick white clouds,
Over a sparkling stream,
Up the high mountains,
Past a deserted cabin,
Through the thick woods,
On sandy white beaches,
Through countless neighborhoods,
I run.
Lauren Johnson, Grade 6
Harmon Middle School, OH

Friends

Friends
Friends are my favorite!
Friends are the ones that I love.
Friends
We're never a part
Well maybe by miles
But
Never by heart!!
Friends.
Ashley Robb, Grade 5
May V Peck Elementary School, MI

October

Pumpkins are ripe, pick some
When you get home you sculpt them into scary faces
Then drop a candle in it
Watch your jack-o'-lanterns glimmer in the
Creepy darkness of Halloween night

During fall squirrels scamper around for nuts
Then conceal them in a slit
And scurry off to find extra

When you enter a corn maze
You vanish
You see all that corn you just want to gobble up
You're probably saying look at all that appetizing corn
Then you finally find your way out.

Brent Kuczaj, Grade 5
Beck Centennial Elementary School, MI

Nights in Season

Nights in winter are so cold they make you want to
Curl up by the fireplace and read a good book.

Nights in summer are so hot they make you want to
Sprawl out on something frigid and slumber the night away

Nights in spring are not too fiery and not too chilly
But just perfect and you fall into a drowse right away.

Nights in fall are so beautiful they make you want to
Curl up on the couch and watch a good movie.

And those are the nights of the seasons!

Alexis Hochstetler, Grade 5
Heritage Intermediate School, IN

I Am

I am Loud and Crazy.
I wonder what my sister is doing.
I hear Fairies singing softly in the distance.
I see dead people.
I want to meet Nick Jonas.
I am Loud and Crazy.
I pretend that I'm a famous person.
I feel entertained by very boring stuff.
I touch the blue Fairies' delicate wings.
I worry that my friends talk badly about me.
I cry when somebody dies.
I am Loud and Crazy.
I understand that people think I'm weird.
I say dreams do come true.
I dream I'll become a professional at soccer.
I try to pull pranks on my sister.
I hope I'll become good at soccer.
I am Loud and Crazy.

Katelyn Post, Grade 6
Galesburg-Augusta Middle School, MI

Elliana

I am so happy:
    In the hospital,
which smells of freshly dried laundry.

    My family surrounds me:
My mother in bed,
    My new baby sister in my arms.

The room is secluded:
    quiet and calm,
like a church on Monday in the morning.

        This moment is perfect.
        It's peaceful and good.

Ian H. Havens, Grade 5
Stanley Clark School, IN

Morgan

Morgan
Nice, cool, smart, funny
Sister of Emily
Who likes drawing, sleeping, and playing outside
Who feels courageous
Who needs candy corn
Who gives trouble
Who fears snakes
Who wants to see the Great Sphinx
Who lives in Indianapolis, Indiana U.S.A.
Sells

Morgan Sells, Grade 5
St Jude Catholic School, IN

The Basketball Game

18-17, we were down. The play was set.
It was something we never tried before.
I was guard, Lindsey was point.
The ref's whistle sounds through the gym.
I was impatient.
    Waiting
        Wanting
            NERVOUS
We clear out, the guard is far out
I go to set a screen. A player gets in the way
9, 8
It's open again
7, 6
She dribbles toward the basket,
5, 4
She shoots
3, 2
It misses!
Disappointment overwhelms us
The boys tell us "good try."
We retreat to the team room…for now.

Diana Dinkel, Grade 6
Assumption BVM School, MI

Can You Imagine?

Leaves without trees,
Blind people who can see
Kids without a dream,
Water without a stream

Dessert without ice cream,
Gymnastics without a beam
A floor without a mat,
A back that can't take a pat

A school without teachers,
People who aren't believers
Cars without wheels
Babies without squeals

Garbage without trash,
A light without a flash
A cook without a tong,
Kids without a Mom

A century without a fad,
A kid without a Dad
A day with the flu,
A day without you

Nicole Lisch, Grade 4
Stonegate Elementary School, IN

School

The bell has run.
The school doors have opened.
You hear kids' feet.
You get all your papers done.
You hear the teacher's voice.
You hear pages flipping.
There are faces all around you.
You might be nervous,
But you can't do anything!
It's SCHOOL!

Bailey Coffman, Grade 5
Henryville Elementary School, IN

Puppies

Small pup
Arrowhead nose
Chases tail and running
Chases squirrels and shakes them up
Cute pup

Dawson Ott, Grade 4
Riverside Elementary School, MI

Babe Ruth

He is a good player.
Babe Ruth is the home run king.
Loves to play baseball.

Michael Kent, Grade 4
Westview Elementary School, OH

It's All About Me, Myself, and I

Ally
Loving, active and athletic
Sister of Johnny and Nick
Lover of softball, swimming and basketball
Who feels nervous when I get up in class on the first day of school
Who gets excited about going to a water park and going bowling
Who need to play softball and needs to play outside
Who gives kisses to my mom
Who fears heights and scary stories
Who would like to be a pro softball player
Resident of Austintown, Ohio
Pence

Ally Pence, Grade 5
Frank Ohl Intermediate School, OH

Millie's Tale

We went to the pound to find a new hound.
At the front desk we were told to go on in and have a look around.
When we opened the door,
there on the floor were cages and cages
full of many different ages.
We walked through the aisles,
saw several smiles.
There in a cage
was a pup just the right age.
She was fuzzy and sweet,
and sat at my feet.
I found the one with God's grace.
I picked her up and she licked my face.
We took her home and named her Millie.
She's a great dog but at times she can be quiet silly.

Riley McGrath, Grade 6
St. John the Evangelist School, IN

The Dependable Typewriter

I am your old typewriter,
Passed on some generations to you,
Old, unused, dusty, not cared for,
I wait on a table as the years pass by.
When you look for a computer as dependable
You don't realize I am,
You finally choose one,
An expensive, powered by electricity, easy to use one,
That you think will get the job done.
Then comes a rainy day,
With a bolt of lightning,
The power goes out.
What are you going to do?
You come to me, finally realizing my importance.
We work together, long ours, while I am happy to do the job,
You sell the computer and work every day, happily using me.
A long time later when many years pass by,
And though you are sad to give up such a dependable old friend,
You pass me on to the next generation.

Hanna Kawoosa, Grade 6
Abbott Middle School, MI

I Am

I am friendly and funny.
I wonder how much King-Kong weighs.
I hear a magnet that's yelling.
I see a star-patterned dog.
I want a farm.
I am friendly and funny.
I pretend that I am on top of the world.
I feel happy that chihuahuas aren't guard dogs.
I touch my polka-dotted goat.
I worry that my brother will mess up my room.
I cry because my sisters aren't my age.
I am friendly and funny.
I understand that my brother is too young for a great dane.
I say that J.K. Rowling is the best author.
I dream that I am a detective.
I try to get all A's in school.
I hope for the nicest big dog there is.
I am friendly and funny.

Beth Washburn, Grade 6
Galesburg-Augusta Middle School, MI

Mi Catherine Totterdale

M y eyes are greenish-blue
I love my dog Honey, it's true

C autious is definitely not the word for me,
A lthough I am fun and very carefree
T alkative, without a doubt
H aving fun while learning about;
E verything! Science, reading, math
R eally good at making you laugh
I ce cream is my favorite treat, I
N eed it every day to eat!
E ast, south, north, west,

T aking a treacherous social studies test :~ (
O utstandingly flexible (I can literally bend in half!)
T rying to make holiday crafts
T ickling my brother,
E asily surprising my mother
R eading books is really fun
D aydreaming that I'm number one!
A lways playing soccer, my favorite sport
L ove to go to ski resorts
E nding my poem, of the acrostic sort!!

Maia Catherine Totterdale, Grade 5
Frank Ohl Intermediate School, OH

The U.S.A.

The U.S.A. is where I live.
The U.S.A. is really big.
There's lots of people and places to go.
I really like it here at home.
There is a lot of stuff to do.

Gabriel Lindholm, Grade 5
Michiana Christian Montessori School, IN

Grapes/Fruit

Grapes
Purple, round
Eating, glazing, slipping
Purple fun, refreshing to eat
Fruit

Katie Wood, Grade 5
Washington Township Elementary School, IN

In the Refrigerator

I open the refrigerator
And what do I see?
A tangle of things.
Staring right back at me.
The tomatoes are squishy.
The pot roast is green.
The bread box is empty.
There's a great string bean

There's mold on this thing!
On the inside and out.
This place is a wreck!
Will someone clean it out?
This place even needs mopping.
Not to mention all the shopping
For all anyone knows, there may be a mouse!
I think I'll go eat at my friend Tammy's house.

Emily LaPorte, Grade 6
Corpus Christi Catholic School, MI

Thanksgiving Day

In November Thanksgiving comes
Where we are thankful for the food
That is set on the table
Like corn, beans, turkey, cornbread,
Mashed potatoes, and cake.
Yum, yum-m-m!
What a lovely meal that would be.

The family members that will be cooking will be
Aunt Dee Dee, Mom, Dad, Grandpap, and Grandmom.
What such a lovely family will cook for each other!

Kyla Camp, Grade 4
Matthew Duvall Elementary School, OH

It's All About Me

If I were in charge of the world
I'd stay up to 12:00 a.m.
I'd drive a Mustang and a convertible and a Viper.
I'd own and live in a mansion.
I'll play in the NFL for 7 years or more.
I'll play for the Colts or Jets NFL team.
I'll live on a farm.
I'll have all of the video games,
I'll have all of the video game machines.

Luke Foote, Grade 4
Churubusco Elementary School, IN

Snow

I see snow falling
I will quickly grab my hat
And play with my friends
Sydney Wade, Grade 5
St Jude Catholic School, IN

Skipper and Peyton

Skipper
Lazy, shaggy,
Sleeping, running, saving,
Puppy, cheerful, old, grumpy,
Growling, running, eating,
Cute, selfish,
Peyton
Mariah G. Huge, Grade 5
Cloverdale Middle School, IN

Ode to the Cedar Trees

Oh cedar tree, oh cedar tree
how can you keep amazing me?
Oh cedar tree
how should you weep.
Because we reap
those of your kind.
Though we do love
your lovely look.
We use your wood
in many ways.
I hope your kind stays;
we should give back.

How lovely the world
would be if there
were a tree
on every property.

We should conserve thee
for thou
art a noble tree.
Michael Miller, Grade 6
New Haven Elementary School, OH

The Seminole

We start our work
At the crack of dawn
Like nocturnal animals
Preparing for our day
Lots of things to do
Threats from Andrew Jackson
Are coming this way.
Wait, aim, fire!
The war will take our lives
But our traditions still stand!
Sam Buckley, Grade 5
Barrington Elementary School, OH

Free Throw

I was standing there
Waiting
"Foul" the ref calls
It was silent
Someone fouled me
My chance to shine!
It was like being deaf
All sound was blocked out
I was alone
No one else there
Behind the little blue line
The ref blows the whistle
Knees bent, arms up, jump
The ball flies like a bird
It touches the rim
It goes around
Around
Around
Around
And in
My teammates yell with excitement
Madison Telder, Grade 6
Assumption BVM School, MI

September

The wind and the leaves
Are falling down on my head
Fall in September.
Corey Teaford, Grade 5
Nancy Hanks Elementary School, IN

Oh Deer!

If I could be a pro hunter
I'd have a record for the biggest rack
just because I can
I'd get a deer that weighed 500 pounds
I mean I got the biggest field
I'd build a shooting range
so kids can shoot a gun
Then help needy kids shoot a deer
cause they can't get in a tree
Carson M. Gatton, Grade 4
Churubusco Elementary School, IN

Bird

from the egg
on the nest
in the tree
under the clouds
with their babies
into the sky
about to swallow a worm
from the nest
Jarrod Dolin, Grade 5
Rootstown Elementary School, OH

Run Like the Wind

Waiting for the starting gun to go off,
I'm running as fast as can go,
It was the last lap,
My family said in exciting voices.

RUN

RUN

RUN

Like the wind, Jeffrey.
With a jittery boost.
I finished in fourth place.
Jeffrey Harmon, Grade 6
Assumption BVM School, MI

Spring Break

Celebration, jubilation
No school
Madeira Beach
Family and friends
Parasailing and water splashing
Vacation extravaganza
Claire Johnson, Grade 6
Tri-West Middle School, IN

My Toes

Piggle-wiggle toes
How I love you so.
Count them up to ten,
Standing in a row.

Polished Wooster blue,
Flipping through the sand
Looking for a wave —
They crash and then they land.
Stephanie Walton, Grade 6
Melrose Elementary School, OH

Snow

Snow is white
Like vanilla ice cream
A marshmallow
And white poodles
Sebastian Deak, Grade 5
Birchwood School, OH

Flowers

Leafy, colorful,
Wonderful creations.
Shapes and sizes,
All over nature,
Twirling and gazing,
As I watch.
Karissa Hodge, Grade 4
Normandy Elementary School, OH

I Am

I am an athletic boy who plays football.
I wonder what it would be like in 2040.
I hear ghosts howling at night.
I see cows jumping over the moon.
I want world peace.
I am an athletic boy who plays football.

I pretend I am a NFL football player.
I feel the weight of 500 pounds on my shoulders.
I touch the stars.
I worry that my dad will die.
I cry because my dad smokes.
I am an athletic boy who plays football.

I understand the frustration of hard homework.
I say we are all the same.
I dream of going snowboarding.
I try to be good.
I hope they will outlaw guns.
I am an athletic boy who plays football.

P.J. Johnson, Grade 6
Helfrich Park Middle School, IN

The Kitten That Never Got a Hug!

I am a kitten
With my hair up
I'm just wasting time
I could be relaxing in my bed
Instead, I'm waiting for someone to hug me
Come on people — get with the program!

Talona Jenkins, Grade 5
Westview Elementary School, OH

If I Was in Charge of the World

No animals would go extinct
all people would be free
all animals could be tamed for pets
people could live on all planets
people would have all the food they need
the world would never come to an end
nobody would be poor
there wouldn't be any burglars
people could have whatever job they want
there would be no age limit on voting
every pet would have a home
every day would be winter
strawberries would be included in every meal
I would play sports all day
I would see Mt. Rushmore
all thrill rides would have elevators instead of stairs
there would be a cure to every cancer problem
there would be no global warming
I would go swimming indoors each day
all countries would have a democracy

John Hartig, Grade 5
Sanderson Elementary School, OH

I Am

I am sweet and funny
I wonder if I am going to be living in California
I hear paintbrushes painting
I see me helping animals
I want to dance every day of my life
I am sweet and funny

I pretend I am famous on TV
I feel soft sand
I touch wrapping paper on Christmas
I worry about college
I cry when animals get hurt
I am sweet and funny

I understand everybody is not perfect
I say Santa's real
I dream funny dreams
I try to get good grades
I hope to live as long as life
I am sweet and funny

I am Nicole Kitsch

Nicole Kitsch, Grade 4
Floyd Ebeling Elementary School, MI

I Don't Like…

I don't like wars and soldiers dying
I don't like mothers and fathers crying
I don't like flags flying at half mast
I don't like poverty in our world
I don't like homeless people living on the streets
I don't like people having nothing to eat
I don't like concrete serving as a bed
I don't like people getting drunk
I don't like reckless driving on the roads
I don't like the senseless taking of lives
I don't like discrimination
I don't like how it sets all apart
I don't like that it judges people unfairly
I don't like vandalism
I don't like that it violates us
I don't like people destroying what is not theirs
I don't like our upside down world
Peace and Equality is what I LIKE.

Maria Gonzalez, Grade 6
St Gerard School, MI

Homework

Homework is so lame
I think it's such a shame
Those teachers assign it every day
I'd rather go outside and play
It takes hours and hours to do
I don't even have time to tie my shoe!

Morgan Bales, Grade 4
Northern Heights Elementary School, IN

Apples

Apples are tasty
They grow outside in the sun
Colors, red and green
Lizzy Ruminski, Grade 6
Roosevelt Elementary School, OH

Homework

Homework, homework I hate you so
I wish you would shred into a rainbow
come on homework please blow up
or else I will make a robot
the robot will do my chores
even wipe butter off floors
come on homework please blow up
I give up you win you mutt
but I'll be back
that is so true
homework, homework
will you please shut up!
Denilson Reyes Mazariegos, Grade 5
Kenowa Hills Intermediate School, MI

I'm Sorry

Why must I have this curse desire?
I'm deeply sorry that I had destroyed
your Wii

It just got me so mad when it said
the name "Suzzie."
My name is not Suzzie,
it's Bill,
then I remembered that
your name was Suzzie.
My bad.

I'm also sorry
I attacked you
when you came in.
Now I regret everything
I did
because you will buy
a new Wii
and I
will *never* play it.
Elvia Suli, Grade 5
Tremont Elementary School, OH

Autumn

A pples dipped in caramel
U nusual candy
T rick or treating
U nexpected scares
M aybe it won't be so scary,
N ovember's around the corner.
Andrew Howard, Grade 6
Eisenhower Middle School, OH

I Am From

I am from the town known for its orange huskies.
I am from white-haired men and women.
I am from big feet.
I am from rules that went unbroken for a whole two seconds.
I am from uniform skirts that are the worst color of red and blue.
I am from Tennessee accents.
Shelby Martino, Grade 6
St Maria Goretti School, IN

Hanukkah

Latkes sizzling on the stove
People talking and saying prayers
Sitting in chairs feeling thankful and happy
I smell candles burning on the menorah
The latkes taste so good
Spinning driedles and eating delicious gelt
The house is dark from the outside
The moon is hidden behind the trees
Inside the house is very bright
All the lights are turned on twinkling brightly
People are talking happy voices
As we gather around the menorah for prayers
I hear my cousins laughing as we spin the driedle
I hear wrapping paper being ripped and people saying thank you for gifts
I wonder if they had menorahs in the past to light on Hanukkah?
Will it still burn for eight days?
Why do we win gelt playing driedle?
Hanukkah is like a birthday with candles, chocolate, and gifts
Eating latkes and gelt is like drinking hot chocolate after playing in the snow
All over the house in every room my family is feeling
Happiness, happiness, happiness
Rebecca Kuhr, Grade 5
EH Greene Intermediate School, OH

I Am

I am calm and quiet.
I wonder what makes people have different personalities.
I hear my eraser yell with pain.
I see my pencil dance gracefully while writing this poem.
I want to be who I really am with no fear of judgment.
I am calm and quiet.
I pretend to be a warrior when I play video games.
I feel happy when I see a raven fly to the heavens and back again.
I touch people's buttons using quick-witted conversation.
I worry about the safety of others.
I cry when people die.
I am calm and quiet.
I understand life is hard.
I say you should live 20 years happy
chasing your dreams, then 100 miserable.
I dream about a perfect life.
I try to be good in band class.
I hope to succeed and go to a good college.
I am calm and quiet.
Brandon Brown, Grade 6
Galesburg-Augusta Middle School, MI

I Am

I am athletic and funny.
I wonder if there is a puma and a tiger mix.
I hear my hair crack like a branch as I cut it.
I see a huge dragon.
I want an iPod.
I am athletic and funny.
I pretend I'm in the NFL.
I feel surprised about how many tricks King Kong can do.
I touch a ghost.
I worry that my life will be over soon.
I cry when I watch the New England Patriots lose a game.
I am athletic and funny.
I understand I'm only a kid.
I say that football is the best sport.
I dream that I am a billionaire.
I try to beat a level on my Xbox 360.
I hope I will get at least 100 dollars for my birthday.
I am athletic and funny.

Zach Wortinger, Grade 6
Galesburg-Augusta Middle School, MI

It's All About Me

If I were in charge of the world
I would put sea animals on the great plains.
And I would cancel school forever.
And I would make everyone work at McDonald's.
And I would drive a Viper all over the world.
And my house would be the White House.
That would be me.

Jacob Eyer, Grade 4
Churubusco Elementary School, IN

Alexis Mikayla Hudson

A challenge is what I'm up for
L ove to see my parents' face when I walk through the door
E ven strangers think I'm kind
X -tra chores is something I don't mind
I am caring and that I will always be
S mart is one word to describe me

M y favorite sport is basketball
I love to shop at the Eastwood Mall
K im is my aunt's name
A nd Clue is our favorite game
Y esterday I got an A on my test
L earning makes me the best
A nd in my eyes, I'm better than the rest

H umble is what I want to be
U sing my strengths works best for me
D aydreaming leaves me in a fog
S asha is the name of my dog
O bstacles can't get in my way
N othing can make me have a bad day

Alexis Mikayla Hudson, Grade 5
Frank Ohl Intermediate School, OH

I Am

I am an athletic guy and love baseball
I wonder if I will be alive in one year
I hear the baseball flying by my face
I see birds chirping in the morning
I want everybody to stop polluting the air
I am an athletic guy and love baseball

I pretend I am a professional baseball player
I feel pain when I get hit in football
I touch the sky when I look at the stars
I worry that the world might end any day
I cry for my uncle that is in Iraq
I am an athletic guy and love baseball

I understand that it's hard when someone passes
I say always have second chances
I dream of going to college to play baseball
I try to do my best in everything
I hope the world will last forever
I am an athletic guy and love baseball

Devan Hostettler, Grade 6
Helfrich Park Middle School, IN

Leaves/Plant

Leaves
Bright, colorful
Twirling and swirling
Happily watching others fall
Plant

Tessa Bales, Grade 4
Frank H Hammond Elementary School, IN

Football

The kickoff is underway,
Hearing the shoulder pads clash like a tornado,
Making the huge hit,
Catching my breath before the huddle,
Giving it your all for the tackle,
Scooping up a fumble recovery with hustle,
Getting the extra yard for the first down,
Passing right to the target,
And making the game saving catch,
Blocking for the heroic touchdown,
There goes the whistle,
We had won the game!

Nick Sprecher, Grade 6
Tri-West Middle School, IN

This Time of Year

The year is almost past,
And it's getting colder fast.

Kids will be sledding down hills,
And with Christmas cheer everyone will fill.

Aidan Muth, Grade 6
Perry Central Elementary School, IN

Winter

Winter,
Every year you arrive, announcing your arrival with howling winds, blankets of snow, and bone chilling cold.
You pile up snow and block garages, cause schools to shut down, and accumulate snow on buildings causing them to cave in.
Winter, winter, this is winter.
Winter,
You let people enjoy life, with your giving of skiing, snowboarding, and sledding opportunities.
You show your wonder with drifts, icicles, and mounds of fluffy white snow
Bringing lots of happiness and excitement to everyone.
Winter, winter, this is winter.
Winter,
The trees appear to be leafless, when I wake up in the morning and step outside my door,
Endless white appears before me, like there was nothing more.
Your beauty surrounds me as it seems the world is peopleless, and when I look upon the horizon,
I see your beauty about to be destroyed by a howling winter storm. Like you will be swept up like plant into a dust pan.
Winter, winter, this is winter.
Winter,
You attacked us with howling winds, endless blankets of snow, and bone chilling cold.
Now it seems you are retreating like a bear to its den, it's like you are afraid that something will hurt you.
Your snow is melting, trees are blooming, and plants are springing with life out of the Earth,
As we all know you'll come next year bringing howling wind, blankets of snow, and bone chilling cold.
Winter, winter, this is winter.

Paul Sangree, Grade 6
Harding Middle School, OH

Fall

Apples, pumpkins and trees. Oh! How I love those colorful leaves.
The raking sounds of the leaves on the ground, into piles that are very round.
The kids are becoming so excited and live, Zion shouted hurry! So that we can dive…
Into the leaves it will be so much fun, kids go line up hurry…run.
The kids lined up with smiles on their faces as I sat and watched wishing I could be other places.
I like the fall season here in Michigan but Florida sounds better, there I go wishing again
About the sunshine and heat that we just had, I want it back now! Oh, so very bad.
I like the sunshine and the heat, maybe it's so that I can ride my bike up and down the street.
Well, I guess that's over now I have to believe it is, so let me get back over here to watch these kids,
Dive into the leaves having so much fun, I guess I'll join them…watch out kids here I come, run!
They all began to scatter around looking at me as I slid to the ground,
Laughing and playing with the kids on the street made me forget about the summer heat.

Aniah Jordan, Grade 6
Abbott Middle School, MI

Lauren Strope

Lauren
Short compared to my classmates, new to Sanderson Elementary this year, hair and eyes are the color of brown sugar,
and has one winking dimple when smiling
Daughter of Dan and Jennifer Strope
Lover of fast, physical athletics, shopping for just the right outfit, and reading realistic fiction
Who feels wonderful and warm when the kitty is curled up in my lap, angry when my brother teases me, and triumphant
when my soccer team wins
Who needs friends so I do not get bored, to get all my work right, and my time alone to calm down
Who gives love back to my family, my best work I can possibly do for everyone, and a headache from my chatting to my parents
Who fears being trapped somewhere, being laughed at, and breaking her headband
Who would like to get a house on Buckeye Lake, win a shopping spree, and go to Italy
Resident of Lancaster
Strope

Lauren Strope, Grade 5
Sanderson Elementary School, OH

The Spell

Once a witch cast a spell
And now that spell has a tale to tell
There was a man that was foolish
People feared him because he was ghoulish
And the witch loved him
But he did not love her
This angered the witch
And she decided his life would be full of danger
With the flick of her wand
And a few magic words
The man was cursed
Every time he talked to people it got worse and worse
He locked himself in his house and never came out.

Mikayla Twarog, Grade 6
Union Local Middle School, OH

The Whirling Tornado

Tornadoes touch the ground with the sound of a train
Destroying houses and precious memories
By whipping around and screaming like a black hole.
They happen everywhere except mountain ranges
And vanish with trees and houses existing no more.

Nick Runyan, Grade 6
Wooster Christian School, OH

Winter in My Eyes

Snowflakes fall in front of me,
snow glittering is a pretty sight to see.

The aroma of hot chocolate filters the air,
Christmas lights let off a glare.

Presents rest under the tree,
wrapped so beautifully.

Children dream of snow days to come,
I walk outside and my hands become numb.

The cold breeze chills my spine,
people can't wait until Christmas time.

Wrapping paper surrounds my floor,
Christmas carolers outside my door.

Kayla Blackburn, Grade 5
Browning Elementary School, MI

The Silent Beach

On the crisp sand I lay.
The glimmering sun beating down on my skin.
The rippling water sways in front of me.
The sunset is lowering on the beautiful horizon.
Every surrounding is settled.
The moans of waves are gone.
On the silent beach I lay.

Tommy Hoops, Grade 4
Stonegate Elementary School, IN

The Aquarium

We went to the aquarium today.
Through the door we saw dozens of fish,
As colorful as a rainbow.
They were in tanks as clear as crystal.
We passed by tanks full of sharks,
That were as menacing as monsters.
With rays that swam through the water like birds in the sky.
Tanks filled with jellyfish as strange as aliens.
A tank with dolphins as acrobatic as gymnasts.
And a tank with a jet black and white killer whale
As fast and speedy as lightning.
We went to the aquarium today.

Isabelle Huang, Grade 6
Boulan Park Middle School, MI

Autumn

A shower of leaves dance down to the ground.
Turning gracefully round and round.
They fall to the ground lightly along with the others.
They crunch under my feet crunch, crunch, crunch.

Furry, scruffy squirrels scamper around
gathering nuts in their big cheeks.
They bury nuts in the ground
and build nests high in the lofty trees.

Bright orange pumpkins waiting to be sold
are piled up at the farmer's market.
So many pumpkins to choose from, big or small.
Inside the pumpkin it feels gooey and soft.

The wind whistles through the trees.
It stirs the leaves from their resting spot.
It whispers fall, fall, fall.
But I already know that fall is here.

Madeline Reyes, Grade 6
Holy Family Middle School, MI

All About My Awesome Life

Miranda
Athletic, artistic, spunky
Sister of Franki and Freddy
Lover of softball, dogs, and Aeropostale
Who feels nervous when I am in front of a big crowd
    for a choir concert and when I am at my first
    softball game of the season
Who gets excited about getting new clothes from Aeropostale
    and new shoes from a cool store
Who needs to talk less in school and pay attention
Who gives kisses to my doggy Jewel
Who fears spiders and my room in the dark
Who would like to be a figure skater
Resident of Austintown, Ohio
Noday

Miranda Noday, Grade 5
Frank Ohl Intermediate School, OH

What Moves Me

My birthday with everybody around me
Opening presents
Playing with my cousin
Video games
Outside playing in the sun
Eating my ice cream cake
It was a wonderful birthday.

Matthew Rose, Grade 4
Mayfield Elementary School, OH

Log Flavored Jam at the Top

Log flavored jam is great
it sounds awful but it ain't
Have you ever tasted a log?
That's what I thought
Well I tried a bite after I tried this jam
Logs are magnificent, even ask Sam
It's like eating a crisp piece of heaven
Or a rich piece of golden Aspen

Carra Gilson, Grade 6
Pike Delta York Middle School, OH

Softball

Adrenaline rush
Two outs, last inning
Down by two
Players on third and second
Big expectations
Aim for the glove
Control the pitch
Let it fly
Softball pitcher

Allyson Booth, Grade 6
Tri-West Middle School, IN

Cardinal

Graceful, cardinal
Rare, elegant, smart
Flying
Soaring, red, beautiful.

Nicholas A. Zimmerman, Grade 5
Cloverdale Middle School, IN

Oil Crisis

O il is needed to make gasoline
I t is needed almost everywhere
L ots of people use it

C hina is buying most of it
R unning out of it
I t is becoming scarce
S omeone needs to find a solution
I t is an oil crisis
S TOP THE MADNESS!

Kyle King, Grade 6
Abbott Middle School, MI

In Memory

My childhood world was shattered like ice
Then melted to a puddle of despair.
When the thunder on a sunny day
Reverberated through the ground,
Snared my sixth sense like a deer in headlights, unable to escape.
My insides fell down a deep black pit, my heart skipped a couple of beats.
It climbed into my throat when Mom said my sister was missing.
I clawed my way to church, the picture of innocence crumbling down.
She can't be *gone*? No it was a joke!
Inside the ruins, a cloud had come to prestidigitate.
Things appeared, and then were veiled,
The dust curling in snakes.
I stumbled over a solid block and bent to pick it up.
My sister's Bible, with ragged cover, pages yellowing.
A tear of remorse rolled down my cheek and fell into the book.
Slightly magnified by the drop
The word death.
So many things I should've done,
So many things to say, frozen on my lips.
She was too young to leave. I was so close to her,
But now so hopelessly far.

Madeline Bourget, Grade 6
Detroit Country Day Middle School, MI

Run for Freedom

Horses run wild and free across the land.
Thundering their hooves on the ground.
Their tails whipping behind them in the wind.
Shaking and trembling as they pass.
Their hooves pounding the dirt under their feet.
Their beauty and grace are like angels flying in the heavens.
Horses run wild and free across the west.
You may cage, hold, or pin them in a barn.
But there's one thing you can't take from them…
And that's their will to run to run with freedom
Like the mustang, to run wild and free across the wild west

Brenna Butler, Grade 5
Heritage Intermediate School, IN

If I Were Inside a Telephone…

I'd be very up to date on the latest gossip.
I'd be filled with wires and cords instead of organs and intestines.
I'd wake people up in the middle of their beauty sleep,
only to be disappointed by a wrong number.
I'd be the second most germy thing in the house —
that just shows how much people love me!

Amelia Kramer, Grade 6
St Maria Goretti School, IN

The Zunis

Z unis carried handmade bowls of water on their very steady heads.
U nbeatable in Indian wars.
N ames are given from plants, animals, and elements.
I ndians of the Southwest

Amy McMahon, Grade 6
Barrington Elementary School, OH

Wrigley Field

It was a very hot day at Wrigley Field,
or as I call it, the "Unfriendly Confines."
I was with Dad
and my friend Nathan and his dad.
We sat on the third base line, ten rows up.
The Cubs were playing the Sox, their cross-town enemy.
The atmosphere was great:
It smelled like peanuts and freshly cut green grass.

To the left of us were some very old Cubs fans,
who were screaming, "Go, Cubs, go!"
In front of us was the Sox dugout,
and players were taking batting practice.
The ball sang, Clonk, Clonk, off their bats.
The grounds crew was raking the infield.
It was a perfect day of baseball, but not for long.

The final score was 11 to 6, Cubs.
I was sad, Nathan was happy.
But now my Sox are in the playoffs!

Cole Sandin, Grade 5
Stanley Clark School, IN

Snowman

S nowflakes falling
N o end to snow
O h so many songs will be sung
W ith people shopping
M any kids making snowmen
A nd the sound of laughter
N ow and then you hear the sound of bells

Chantal Goldman, Grade 5
West Washington Elementary School, IN

Life

Life can be a wonderful thing
Life to me is passionate
Life is just a day from morning to night
In the morning you wake-up and look out the window
And say, what will happen in life today
Life teaches you a lot of good and bad things
Life shows you that you can be free
Life shows you that you can get put out of your house
Life is bitter
Life is not as easy as you think

Cherie Cooper, Grade 6
Woodward Park Middle School, OH

The Stars

The stars are gorgeous and radiate light,
Both here and there through the boundless night.
The stars form unique patterns, what a sight!
Though they're sometimes not seen,
The stars are there, all beautiful and bright.

Mitchell Salchak, Grade 6
Massillon Christian School, OH

Christmas

The snow is falling with whitely colored light
that brightens up the winter night.
So snuggle all up tight
there is nothing to fear when Santa comes near.
Then all the songs play quietly slow on the radio.
Christmas is a time for joy and cheer.
Christmas is a time of world and happiness.
Then it's Christmas

Charlie Fast Horse, Grade 6
St Michael School, IN

Thanksgiving's Specialties

People are joining together,
Forgetting about their pasts
Full of fusses and fights,
Just for this one special night.
The sun reflects off the snow,
Giving off a strange, eerie glow.
Sweetness and sourness,
And tastes all around.
Children are playing,
The sun is setting
Cooling down the fall air.
People are missing from their chairs.
Strange stories are being murmured around,
Covering up the rest of the different sounds.
The aroma of delicious food being smelled all around,
But less noticeable than all of the sounds.
All these great things being covered up,
By just chatter, chatter, chatter.

Bridget Sypniewski, Grade 5
EH Greene Intermediate School, OH

My Favorite Things About My Friends

They make me laugh
They are always there for me
They text me when I'm lonely
Comfort me when I'm sad
Help me with my homework when needed
Talk to me on Piczo
Fun to be around
Would do anything for me
Help me through hard times
Keep me happy
Trustworthy
Be fair to me
Don't leave me out
Help me up when I fall down
They are like family to me
Let me borrow their things
They make a bad situation a good one
They would never belittle me
They make me believe in myself
And finally, they are awesome.

Maddy Allen, Grade 5
Sanderson Elementary School, OH

Okha

The Okha and its pilot rest in a bomber,
approaching the drop point.
The pilot gears up
for his one-way trip.
The plane releases from the bomber,
soaring through endless flak,
and then…BOOM.

J.D. Rusher, Grade 6
Melrose Elementary School, OH

Cute Cat

Cute cat
Black, white, furry
Sleeping, jumping, playing
Silently creeping down the hall
My cat

Ashley Loose, Grade 4
Riverside Elementary School, MI

Ready, Waiting…Excited!

Ready now!
Waiting…

Costumes on!
Waiting…

Silent like mice…shhh
Waiting…

Music starts!
Smiles!
Cameras!
We sing…
Seven of us talking…
Singing again.

On stage.
In my very own costume.
My very own part!

Eva Bayliss, Grade 5
St Joseph Montessori School, OH

Outer Space

Earth is number one,
but she's not closest to the sun.
Outer Space has lots of stars,
it also has Mars.
Flying by the Milky Way,
we all have something nice to say.
Shooting through the galaxy,
with meteorites chasing me.
Home, home, home again,
back to Earth, my friend.

Victoria Martine, Grade 4
Stonegate Elementary School, IN

Archery

Amidst dark green trees,
my arrow strikes the target!
My shady cool place.

Madeline Fulton, Grade 6
Stanley Clark School, IN

Pumpkins

Pumpkins
Sweet pumpkin pie
Mmm! I eat pumpkin pie
I have a pumpkin for Halloween
Pumpkins

Joe Smolen, Grade 4
Bailly Elementary School, IN

Can You Imagine

A highway without cars,
A prison without bars.

A teacher without a brain,
A rain without a drain.

A mountain without a train,
A deer without a plain.

An airport without a plane,
A farm without grain.

A person without a heart,
A couple that parts.

Andrew Sebo, Grade 4
Stonegate Elementary School, IN

It's All the Same to Santa

It doesn't matter what cookie you leave
It's all the same to Santa.
Sugar cookies,
Peanut butter cookies,
it's all the same to Santa.
Chocolate chip,
or oatmeal raisin,
It's all the same to Santa.
It doesn't matter what cookie you leave
It's all the same to Santa.

Robin Calva, Grade 5
May V Peck Elementary School, MI

Chi-Chi

Chi-Chi
White and black, energetic
ball, stuffed toy, food
playful, leash, collar, Tennessee
pet dog

Steven Tanner, Grade 6
Union Local Middle School, OH

Basketball

B asket on the goal
A ccurate in the game
S hooting at the frame
K icking butts
E nergetic all around
T raveling around the court
B locking for other teammates
A ir ball, when I shoot
L osing games — hopefully not
L unging to get ready to shoot

Amber Willis, Grade 5
Perry Central Elementary School, IN

Sledding Fun

I love sledding
Down a hill!
What a thrill!
The tricks are fun
What a run!
I hit the ground
What a sound
It's the end
Of the run
That was fun!

Zachary Ulry, Grade 4
Licking Valley Intermediate School, OH

World of Agony

The summer days grow long.
The wind will sing its song.
Your destiny goes strong,
But soon falls to the wrong.
The sweet wind is gone.

The rain falls on spring nights.
The birds start taking their night flights.
The sun fights to show its light,
But the storm took all its might.
Sadness will reign all night.
Happiness has lost the fight.

The cry of pain crawls across the land.
Black falls upon the sand.
Darkness creeps up on man.
Evil will soon reign the land.
There's nothing man can do to stand.

Juliette Shaheen, Grade 4
St Lorenz Lutheran School, MI

Teacher

We love doing Math
Helping children is so fun
The kids are pretty.

Teryn Smith, Grade 4
Westview Elementary School, OH

Home Run?

The score was 0-0.
I twirled the bat in my hand.
The pitcher gave it his best.
Trembling and shaking I swing the bat.
Up, up, up.
Running,
Hoping,
The ball falls and hits the ground.
Rounding second,
The third base coach is telling me to go home
Running faster than ever
Thinking of what will happen
Going home,
I see the ball in the corner of my eye
Flying home.
The ump yells "You're out!"
A sad trip back to the dugout.

Charles Riddering, Grade 6
Assumption BVM School, MI

What a Hurricane

Hurricanes come big and strong,
like a giant smashing down stuff.
They crush everything they see, like a lion, plying down its prey.
They scream every time they make a total destruction
from a house, tower, or a fish market.
Then they walk away from their prey
and go slowly down the water.

Dustin Smith, Grade 5
Wooster Christian School, OH

November Is

Parades, feasts, it's Thanksgiving
friends, family come over for a fun holiday
orange, yellow and red leaves changing faster than the wind
On the coldest morning of the week
the school has donuts with dad
A's, B's, C's, D's, E's coming from the envelopes
It's report card day
hot, sweet, fresh cider that's as hot as a fire
tasty pumpkin coming from stores
like a bunch of maniacs coming to buy piles of pie.

Christina Atanasoska, Grade 5
Beck Centennial Elementary School, MI

It's All About Me!!

If I was in charge of the world I would…
make a holiday just for me.
have a day for the poor and helpless.
have a national money day for me
get a chocolate statue of me
I would get every lottery ticket until I found a winning one.
I would have a national bacon day
and that's what I would do.

Brittney Elliott, Grade 4
Churubusco Elementary School, IN

Yellow and Black

Yellow and black are the colors of the day
Like the yellow sun rays
And the black dark shadows that play all day
Yellow and black are the colors of night
Like the black dark night
And the yellow moon and stars that fill the night sky
Yellow and black are the colors of the sea
Because yellow and black equals olive green
For the green seaweed
And the rolling waves of the gentle sea
Yellow and black

Samantha Nalley, Grade 5
Henryville Elementary School, IN

Nature

So peaceful and so full of wonders
So full of love and gentleness,
Like raindrops sprinkling happily on a sidewalk,
Or trees dancing as the breeze goes by;
So fierce and mighty
Destroying and never forgiving.
Like a fire as it roars and consumes whole forests,
Or a hurricane spewing waves as high as buildings;
It is full of life
Summer, winter, spring, fall
Nature.

Michael Kalinowski, Grade 5
Assumption BVM School, MI

These Tears Were for My Country

Here I walk through Kabul's marketplace,
Though I must walk at this slow pace.
This heavy burqa is weighing me down;
The grill is blocking my vision, I can't see the ground.

I don't need a man to guide me, I just need to get out,
But I am waiting to hear an angry Taliban shout.
Here they come with a gun in their hand,
I can't stand this! What has happened to this land?

I remember them crashing through the door —
Afghanistan no longer is what we hoped for.
They banned flying kites, nail polish, even school,
And destroyed even more of our bombed out city Kabul.

They beat me and hit me and kept me on the ground.
I stayed there for a while and waited to be found,
But I got up to my feet and started walking away —
Away from this place, I just couldn't stay.

The sound of all the shopkeepers yelling faded from my ears,
So then I couldn't hold them in I let out all my tears.
These tears were for my country, and hope for my family,
The rest for all the women and that they could soon be free.

Elle Jansen, Grade 6
Ann Arbor Christian School, MI

If I Could Grant a Wish for You

If I could grant a wish for you
I'll get a thrill or two

May your life be filled with joy
May you get the perfect toy.

May you get candy
May you be so dandy.

May you get delicious cake
May you visit your favorite lake.

May you be the perfect sisters
May you never get blisters.

May you get the perfect gift
May you always get a lift.

May all your wishes come true
May I give the perfect wish to you.

If I could grant a wish for you
I'll get a thrill or two.

Alexus Flowers, Grade 5
Mark C Roose Elementary School, MI

Heroes

V ery brave
E leventh of November
T eam work
E very day heroes
R eally brave
A mericans
N avy

Michael Lloyd, Grade 4
Westview Elementary School, OH

What Is a Friend?

What is a friend?
Someone trustworthy
My safe person to be around
A leader
My hero
A comfort
That is what a friend is
Bethany Callahan, Grade 6
Tippecanoe Middle School, OH

Horse

If I were a horse
I'd hit flies with my tail and
I'd make hoof prints on your heart and
I'd run across the land.
I'd be black with white feet and face!
Casey Jay James, Grade 6
Perry Central Elementary School, IN

A Poem

A poem is a kitten that wants to be loved,
A treasure chest waiting to be found.
You can be a pirate on a pirate ship,
A scurrying chipmunk in a forest,
You can see the mountains white with snow,
A lizard in a dark and cold cave,
You can feel a soft, furry and fluffy rabbit,
A scaly, slimy, flappy fish also happy, sad, mad, and even silly,
In a poem as amazing as a wonderful, soft, chocolatey, chocolate chip cookie.
Maclaren Guthrie, Grade 4
University Elementary School, IN

Memories

I gaze upon the wilderness
Gnarled branches reaching toward the sky
Casting shadows on my life
Glaring at me with gaunt gestures
Finally I've found a serenity among memories
And I hold on tight

The scent of fermented apples
Mingles with the oaky wood
The access of autumn air fills me with these fragrances
Finally I've found a serenity among memories
And I hold on tight

Something snaps and startles me
Only to find a mere twig beneath my feet
High above songbirds sweetly sing while woodpeckers portentously peck
Finally I've found a serenity among memories
And I hold on tight

Apple orchards glow with memories of childhood
I try to let go but I can't seem to forget
For among the worst lies the best and this I cherish more than all else
Finally I've found a serenity among memories
And I hold on tight

Maggie Pizzo, Grade 6
Harding Middle School, OH

All About Me

Tommy
Athletic, talented, and aggressive
Brother of Dominic, Nicholas, and Mia
Lover of sports, Adidas, and Nike
Who feels nervous when the teacher yells at me
    and when I'm playing an extremely good soccer team
Who gets excited about a soccer and basketball game
Who needs to get more money and win a championship soccer game
Who gives kisses to my baby sister
Who fears a person breaking into my house and shooting me
Who would like to be a pro basketball player
Resident of Austintown, Ohio
Foley

Tommy Foley, Grade 5
Frank Ohl Intermediate School, OH

The Journey to Freedom

It was a warm summer night,
I was quite a sight.
My owner had caused me so much pain
I was almost insane.
Whips, and clips,
to putting family on ships.
That caused the final straw.
I was breaking the law.
Now I was on the lamb
from a guy named Sam.
From all the gunk and fog
I was sick as a dog.
All too soon you see
I was free as could be.

Samuel Harrison Milbauer, Grade 5
Central Academy Elementary School, OH

Playing

I like to jump and play
I do it all day
I get tired
I rest a while
Then I get up and play

Wyant Chester Held, Grade 6
North Knox East Elementary/Jr High School, IN

I Am

I am nice and sweet.
I wonder what my brother Thurman's doing.
I hear a bird barking.
I see a tree dancing.
I want a new softball bat.
I am nice and sweet.
I pretend to be a coach.
I feel surprised when I see a dog jumping rope.
I touch a talking softball.
I worry about my dog dying.
I cry when I see someone die.
I am nice and sweet.
I understand softball.
I say Gators Rule!
I dream of hitting a grand slam!
I try to be an outstanding first baseman.
I hope I get a Derek Jeter poster.
I am nice and sweet.

Alex McDaniel, Grade 6
Galesburg-Augusta Middle School, MI

Strawberry

Strawberry
soft, seedy
quenching, filling, thrilling
the juice never stops
Fruit

Evan Adinolfi, Grade 5
Washington Township Elementary School, IN

The Sleepy Little Timer

I am a friendly little timer,
Sleeping very soundly.
Abruptly, I wake up.
When the teacher requests my service
I quickly start the countdown,
Humbly waiting to be done.
As I eat my snack of minutes and seconds,
Time slowly dwindles down.
When no more numbers are left for me to eat,
I give a great big shout!
Then the teacher quiets me,
And I slowly drift asleep
Until the next time she needs me.
I am waiting for a job.

Tirzah Talampas, Grade 6
Wooster Christian School, OH

Too Sportsy!

Megan
Funny, athletic, smart
Sister of Matt
Lover of cats, Notre Dame, and swimming
Who feels nervous when I take a test
    and when I sing in a choir concert
Who gets excited about getting an A+ on a test
    and going on a roller coaster
Who needs to improve my grades
Who gives kisses to my cat and my mom and dad
Who fears snakes and the movie *Friday the 13th*
Who would like to go to Notre Dame University
Resident of Austintown, Ohio
Matasy

Megan Matasy, Grade 5
Frank Ohl Intermediate School, OH

I Am

I am smart and small.
I wonder why my mom smokes.
I hear the wall talking.
I see my eraser climbing the wall.
I want 10 million dollars.
I am smart and small.
I can pretend to care.
I feel happy when my dog climbs the wall.
I touch a robot.
I worry about smoking.
I cry about death.
I am smart and small.
I understand emotions.
I say death is bad.
I dream that I will have 20 million dollars.
I try at baseball.
I hope I can drive in NASCAR.
I am smart and small.

Bailey Wilson, Grade 6
Galesburg-Augusta Middle School, MI

Sports

I like to watch sports,
    And play them, too.
From the Cubs and the Bears,
    To the Spartans at MSU.

The stadium thrills me,
    With each man that's on base.
The crowd cheers in the stands,
    As we watch the race.

I love the Big Ten,
    Since I was quite small.
No matter the game
    Let the refs make the call.

The score can add up
    With each play of the game.
But a foul or an out,
    Can bring us to shame.

From tennis and golf,
    To soccer and bowling,
Sports make me happy,
    Whether playing or watching.
Brett Smith, Grade 6
St Gerard School, MI

The Halloween Scare

Halloween
Fun, happy
Jumping, trick-or-treating, laughing
Scaring, walking, jumping, exciting
Running, falling, throwing
Loud, screaming
Football
Sumaya Alkatib, Grade 5
Norwich Elementary School, OH

The Fall

The fall
Rakes are raking
Leaves floating in the breeze
Some people are hunting turkey
Dig in!
Christian Pizano, Grade 4
Bailly Elementary School, IN

Walmart

Walmart
Big, fun
Running, shopping, spending
A place to shop
Walmart
Jacob Kozma, Grade 5
Rootstown Elementary School, OH

I Am

I am the bright and the athletic child
I wonder if I will be rich
I hear music in my heart
I see lots and lots of money
I want to see the world
I am the bright and the athletic child

I pretend I am the best football player
I feel the best thing will happen
I touch the feeling of the world
I worry that I should not worry
I am the bright and the athletic child

I understand I can't have everything
I say everybody is equal
I dream of world peace
I try to do the best I can in school
I hope that my family gets better
I am the bright and the athletic child
Robert Allen, Grade 6
Helfrich Park Middle School, IN

Technology, Technology

Technology, technology
    You are the best
I wish there was a tech test.
    Technology, technology
    Now here's a quest
Go find me an iPod that stays in the west.
Now find me a Wii that will not break
    But do not get it from a great lake.
Go play a Gameboy and bake a cake.
    The quest is over so eat the cake.
Austin Breen, Grade 5
Kenowa Hills Intermediate School, MI

McCain

McCain
Is very awesome
That is why I voted
For him in the presidential
Voting.
Kohl Aufdencamp, Grade 5
Tremont Elementary School, OH

For a Friend

Austin Takacs was nice
He was a good friend and a good student
I loved to joke around with Austin
He had blonde hair
He was eleven
I will remember Austin
I hope no one will ever forget him.
Deven Schneider, Grade 6
Eisenhower Middle School, OH

Lightning

I am a bright streak of lightning
Feeling intensely charged up
Rocketing freely across the sky
When I arrive I strike fear
I'm electrified and dangerous!
Hey! Look out, Ben Franklin!
Elijah Woolum, Grade 5
Westview Elementary School, OH

What I Would Do

If I were in charge of the world…
I'd have one continent that I owned.
Have a whole track for ATV's and MX's
And invite all of my friends over to ride.
And have restaurants at my mansion.
I'd have a movie theater.
And that's what I'd do.
Riley Basinger, Grade 4
Churubusco Elementary School, IN

My Desk

Open the door
Down the hall
Past the library
To the 4th grade hall
Now going into the 5th grade hall
Into D4
Past Mrs. O'Connor
To my desk
Tristan Creech, Grade 5
Churubusco Elementary School, IN

Jumping Frogs

Frogs are jumpy, you can tell.
They are cute and cuddly,
And behave very well.
Some frogs can be blue,
Or some can be green.
Frogs can be dirty,
Frogs can be clean.
They eat insects and such,
But their favorite thing is a fly,
Which isn't hard to catch,
Even if they are in the sky.
A lot of frogs live in the lake.
That is called their home.
The reason why they live there,
Is for the water and the foam.
Frogs like to sit on rocks,
They sit on them all the time.
They also do other stuff,
Like jump and climb.
That's all in this poem that rhymes!
Carly Robb, Grade 4
Legend Elementary School, OH

I Am

I am cool and smart
I wonder what house I will live in
I hear the music on stage
I see my prom dress
I want to be a singer
I am cool and smart

I pretend to see my prom dress
I feel my microphone
I touch my pink sparkle dress
I worry if I can't sing anymore
I cry if people don't like my dance moves
I am cool and smart

I understand if I can't be a dancer
I say I love you
I dream to be a singer
I try to sing well
I hope to be a movie star
I am cool and smart

I am Cassidy Fitts

Cassidy Fitts, Grade 4
Floyd Ebeling Elementary School, MI

A Snowy Winter's Day

As I look outside, I see a perfect blanket of sparkling snow
Squirrels chase each other around trees
Light deer tracks are in the snow
The birds have headed south
I get on my snow gear and head outside
I decide to go sledding
I zoom down the hill
I feel like I'll never stop
Next I start to roll a snowball
I end up with a snowman
I finish it off with a carrot nose
I fall into the snow landing on my back
I move my arms and legs
The perfect snow angel
It's getting dark
I go inside and snuggle in tight
Nice and warm to go to sleep.

Morgan Benoit, Grade 5
Assumption BVM School, MI

A Better World

If I were in charge of the world…
I would use tax money to help the homeless.
They would have plenty of food and clothes.
I would also build hospitals in poor villages.
I'd make eating brussel sprouts go extinct.
The animals in zoos would have more room to move.
So if I was in charge people would live better.

Bridgette Foote, Grade 5
Churubusco Elementary School, IN

What Moves Me

My birthday moves me, my family, friends
Laughing, playing, having fun, singing
Happy birthday to me eating cake
Still laughing, having fun
I love my birthday
My family giving me presents!

Sierra Winding, Grade 4
Mayfield Elementary School, OH

Halloween

H appy but scared
A fraid every now and then
L aughing and crying
L ots of candy
O ptimistically falling all the time
W alking forever
E xciting scary houses
E xplore strange lands
N ervous all the time

Cole Schryner, Grade 5
Washington Township Elementary School, IN

An Ode to the United States Flag

The United States Flag is very important to me.
When I look at it I respect it.
It represents our country.
The flag brings to mind about the wars we won.
The colors red, white, and blue are important.
The flag has 50 stars like the states.
There's 7 red strips on the flag and 6 white stripes on the flag.
The United States Flag was made by threads.
Flag you are one of the unique flags.
You are like a friend to me.
It's great to be by you.
Flag thank you for being beside me every day.

Nicholas Tejeda, Grade 5
Allen J. Warren Elementary School, IN

Merry Christmas

M emories of holiday cheer
E veryone has fond memories
R eindeer fly Santa far
R unning presents is a hard job for Santa
Y early Santa watches you to see if you are naughty or nice.

C hristmas is a special holiday.
H is hobbies are to bring presents to boys and girls.
R eads over the naughty and nice list.
I s Christmas an important holiday to you?
S t. Nick is his real name.
T ogether we can celebrate.
M y mom and Dad get to stay home.
A n elf makes all the toys.
S anta is a worldly fellow.

Makenna McGlone, Grade 5
Spaulding Elementary School, OH

Forest/Desert

forest
cool, moist
hiking, hibernating, nesting
plants, animals, cacti, sand
cold blooded, poisoning, blowing
dry, hot
desert

Alysia Bansberg, Grade 6
Roosevelt Elementary School, OH

Powerful Playful Polar Bear

What does a polar bear know?
Meat!
Powerful swimmers
Found far out sea
Lives in cold, chilly region
Antarctica!
Named after
North Pole
As sneaky as a burglar
Find a seal to attack
Yum!
Cubs master hunting
Very rapid
Sharp, spiky claws
Thick fur to keep them
Warm
Make sounds to
Communicate
Feet guides them through the ice
And they are a true delight.

Rosemary Hanna, Grade 5
Riley Upper Elementary School, MI

Tennis Shoe

Oh, tennis shoe,
You filthy thing,
Now you're gone
And I can sing.

You stink so bad
That I want to yell.
But I don't care
'Cause it's in the well.

I miss you so much,
You dirty, old shoe.
But now since you're gone,
I'm feeling blue.

I can't cry now
Because you're gone.
I've got things to do
'Cause I've moved on.

Trey Pamer, Grade 6
Melrose Elementary School, OH

The Tuskegee Airmen, Fighting for Freedom

Whoosh! Planes fly through the sky in World War Two
Freedom: Bombs dropping, guns firing
Freedom: Four hundred and fifty black fighter pilots finally serving their country
Freedom: After years of training in Tuskegee, Alabama, earning their wings, they fought
Freedom: Wondering, wondering, when their chance would come
Freedom: Friends and partners being shot down, planes on fire, then boom, explosion
Freedom: Col. Benjamin O. Davis, Jr. leads them in North Africa and Europe
Freedom: Destroying land targets and wiping out German supplies
Freedom: Escorting bombers, shooting down German fighter pilots
Freedom: The heroic men flew 1,578 successful missions, never losing a bomber
Freedom: The red tails on the planes, a symbol of pride separates them from the rest
Freedom: They fought for us, for our country
Freedom: Struggling to earn their rights, at war and at home
Freedom: Fighting for equality in their very own country
Freedom: Overcoming obstacles, racism, fear
Freedom: The Tuskegee Airmen, fighting for what is right

Lauren Saxon, Grade 6
EH Greene Intermediate School, OH

The Ocean

In the abyss there was no light,
I wonder if any fish fight.
The higher I rise from the ocean I see,
Some floating seaweed that looks like a tree.

As I went back down to the ocean ground, I saw many fish,
Some were big, some were small, and some could talk I wish.
As I swam by a school of fish, they started to look like one big fish,
I want something to put the fish in, like a big dish.

When I turned around, I was surrounded by eels and sharks,
Suddenly, I saw strange things and the eels made sparks.
The strange things I saw were piranhas that were getting mad,
I left them, but something made me sad.

I realized I had enough air to stay longer,
From swimming so long, my legs got stronger.
I almost made it back to the beach,
I was close, but not within reach.

I was almost there, but something bit my hand,
It turns out I was just trapped in the sand.
When I got out of the water, it was night,
I saw that the lighthouse made the sky bright.

Adam Redlich, Grade 5
Akiva Academy, OH

Grandpa

My grandpa's wrinkles are like the ditches on the side of the road.
My grandpa's fingers are like gnarled twigs.
My grandpa's hair is as scarce as the oxygen in space.
My grandpa's eyes are as beady as a bunny's.
My grandpa's heart is full of sleep that is as black as the black of his eyelids.
My grandpa lives in a record player and eats up the tunes.

Jennifer Miner, Grade 6
St Maria Goretti School, IN

It's All About Me!

Taylor
Funny, active, talented
Sister of Dominic, Emily, and Ashleigh
Lover of my dog, football, and softball
Who feels nervous when I have a test
    and when I move to a new school
Who gets excited when getting As on tests
    and presents at Christmastime
Who needs to go shopping and clean my room
Who gives kisses to my grandparents and my dad
Who fears roller coasters and the dark
Who would like to have a puppy for Christmas
Resident of Austintown, Ohio
Warmouth

Taylor Warmouth, Grade 5
Frank Ohl Intermediate School, OH

A Golden Friend

My golden friend is my light of sunshine
My golden friend is the energy inside me
My golden friend is all mine
My golden friend is really sweet
My golden friend shines inside me
My golden friend is short and fluffy
My golden friend can be a pest but still…
My golden friend is the best!
My golden friend means everything to me
My golden friend is my golden puppy!

Ashley Moreman, Grade 6
Rocky River Middle School, OH

Basketball

Basketball is my favorite sport
There are a total of ten guys on the court.

We practiced all week long getting ready for this weeks game
I believe if we play we'll put them to shame.

The coach is preaching how we will do
At the same time giving us a play review

In the next poem I will tell you how the upcoming game goes
Or you could just ask my bros.

Bryce Kramer, Grade 6
Trilby Elementary School, OH

Bored Is Green

Bored is green
It tastes like eating peas,
It smells like cold chicken,
It reminds me of when I was home alone with
nothing to do and I didn't have sports that day,
It sounds like country music,
Bored makes me feel green.

Matthew Jeffers, Grade 5
Tremont Elementary School, OH

Basketball

From home and school to the basketball court
From responsibilities and demands to a stress-free zone
From the mental world to the physical world
Release the energy, work out the frustration
Nonstop action
Dribble, pass, shoot, rebound
Sensational outburst

Travis Bauer, Grade 6
Tri-West Middle School, IN

The Supreme Star

A bright red ball in the deep blue sky,
    rises and summons a new day.
It's warmth is like a thousand hugs
    casting a shadow as it sets,
yet leaving a promise of another new day.
Never getting tired of this routine,
    powerful and magnificent,
chasing darkness, guiding with light
    to you I lay my praise.

Sushanth Sunil, Grade 4
Red Cedar School, MI

Brody

My brother is as black and white like an old time picture.
My brother's hair is like a poodle's hair.
My brother is as wild as a monkey.
My brother's eyes are as big as the sun.
My brother's smile is as big as the moon.
My brother is as mean as a lion.
My brother can be as sweet as a lollipop.

Hannah White, Grade 5
Henryville Elementary School, IN

Granny

I hear her stories
They are so good.
I smell her cooking.
Biscuits and gravy.
I taste her cooking.
It is so good.
I can feel her hands.
They are so soft.
I can see her with me everywhere I go.
I can feel her touch me sometimes.
When I am nervous or scared.
I can see her sitting in her old chair.
Rocking in it.
I can see her opening presents on Christmas.
Like the pillow I made her
I lover her so much
I am sad that she is gone
but in my heart I know
she is with me everywhere I go.

Lauren Porter, Grade 4
Licking Valley Intermediate School, OH

Isaac Helterbridle

Isaac
Willing, long blond wavy hair.
Brown eyes.
Brother of Micaela.
Who loves rock music, God, my parents.
Who feels happy on warm days.
Who needs more faith.
Who gives joy to friends.
Who fears death.
Who would want to see Jesus.
Resident of Wooster, Ohio
Helterbridle

Isaac Helterbridle, Grade 5
Wooster Christian School, OH

Power in My Palm

It's yellow, thick, and round
And I can't help but leave it around
My pencil is like a knife
In which I carve my thoughts to life
It's my first hand friend at school
Even at other things, I use it as a tool
It's the power in my palm
Its presence always keeps me calm
My pencil, my pencil, my pencil
Oh, my favorite writing utensil!

Abhijeet Singh, Grade 6
Birchwood School, OH

Best of All, in Fall

In fall,
What is best of all?
Is it
Golden, ruby and auburn
Autumn leaves
Or
CREEPY, CRAZY COSTUMES
Maybe it's the
Clippity, clopping
Of hayride horses
In fall,
What is best of all?

Mikaela Padgen, Grade 5
Riley Upper Elementary School, MI

Mother

Mother, mother, mother,
Generous mother,
Forgiving mother,
Working, beautiful, caring mother,
Intelligent, helping, loving mother,
Last of all, best of all,
My mother

Aidan Mahern, Grade 5
St Jude Catholic School, IN

Sidewalk After Dark

Sidewalk after dark
Extreme sky so bright
Watch me as I run.

Molly Pierce, Grade 5
Westview Elementary School, OH

Ocean

Ocean
Sapphire, pleasant
Flowing, living, changing
Aqua-colored dream
Sea of life

Gabe Beugly, Grade 6
Melrose Elementary School, OH

Impressions of Fall

Rippling red fires roar
raging ring as rakes rangle
rustled leaves in rings rounding
in rippling roar.

Creepy crawlers come in colored
costumes cooking caramel corn
in cans of candy with clowns
counting crayons.

Hunting high hangin' low
having help heaving deer
hogging hagers. Hungry
happy hunting hugs.

Fluttering free fuchsia leaves
far from the tree.
Finally, falling freely
freezing flakes come.

Ashlee Yax, Grade 6
Holy Family Middle School, MI

A Day in Fall

Fall
Colorful, cool
Blowing, playing, laughing
My favorite time of year
Autumn

Shaynah Drohan, Grade 4
Floyd Ebeling Elementary School, MI

Apples

Apples
Big and crunchy.
Juicy and round and good.
Delicious treat you love to eat.
Yellow.

Andrew Gillen, Grade 4
Bailly Elementary School, IN

Trees

I am the tree on the bedrock ledge
overlooking the forest.
I see the lush green
filling the ground.
My brothers with me
protecting the forest.
Forever, I rest here,
forever.

Cameron Meadows, Grade 6
Northwood Elementary School, IN

Shooting Stars

Even if you shoot for the stars,
You might land on the moon
Even though you land on the moon,
You can always be a star
Even though you might miss,
You can gradually get there
If you miss, you might fall back
Don't worry, I will catch you
Even though you aren't a star,
You might become one.

Hunter Cassoday, Grade 4
John Simatovich Elementary School, IN

The High Dive

Freezing cold water —
I climb up stairs, cross cold board;
Want to jump off NOW!

Will Haines, Grade 6
Stanley Clark School, IN

I Am

I am pretty and athletic
I wonder if I will have a good future
I hear little whispers
I see beautiful things
I want the world to be a better place
I am pretty and athletic

I pretend I am a rock star
I feel as bright as the sun
I touch the fluffy clouds
I worry about my family
I cry when my sisters hits me
I am pretty and athletic

I understand that school is important
I say someday I will be famous
I dream about a wonderful life
I try to be a good role model
I hope for a good report card
I am Natalie Bielecki

Natalie Bielecki, Grade 4
Floyd Ebeling Elementary School, MI

Everything About You Is Something to Love

I love the moments close to you,
I love the secrets we share,
I love to have you in my thoughts,
Always everywhere,

I love the words you say to me,
I love all that you do,
I love to wish you happiness,
Because I'm in love with you.

Laurel Roelle, Grade 6
Harding Middle School, OH

One of Me

There is only one of me.
There is only one of you.
You should be proud of the things you can do
For if you are not, well that is just sad,
Because I know I am very glad!
But if there is one of me,
And there is one of you,
Then that means we're different,
And the same somehow too.

Julia Moroz, Grade 4
St Catherine of Siena School, IN

My Dad

My dad's eyes are as blue as the sky.
My dad's hair is as brown as a horse.
My dad's heart holds love as pink as a primrose.
My dad lives in a cafeteria and snacks on all the food.

Katelyn Duncan, Grade 5
Henryville Elementary School, IN

I Am

I am athletic and fast
I wonder if I will be a famous soccer player
I hear birds chirping, Africa animals
I see Bosnia
I want France
I am athletic

I pretend to be sad, happy, and good
I feel upset
I touch cars
I worry if I get a cool car
I cry for movies
I am cool

I understand life is good
I say you can be president
I dream I can be president
I try to dive good
I hope to be a good soccer player
I am Armin Crnolic

Armin Crnolic, Grade 4
Floyd Ebeling Elementary School, MI

Midnight Stars

The midnight stars are so beautiful and bright.
God made these for our twinkling light.
God made these stars in one whole day.
He can help in a marvelous way;
The gleaming stars way above me
Shine their beautiful light so I can see.

Doris Stillman, Grade 5
Rochester Hills Christian School, MI

All About Me, Myself, and I

Joe
Smart, fun, athletic
Brother of Nick
Lover of football, video games, and basketball
Who feels nervous when talking in front of a lot of people
    and going on a roller coaster
Who gets excited about going to a football game
    and getting a present
Who needs to get money to pay for a game system
    and clean my house
Who gives kisses to my mom and dog
Who fears black bears and wolf packs
Who would like to ride across a swamp on an alligator
Resident of Austintown, Ohio
McGuigan

Joe McGuigan, Grade 5
Frank Ohl Intermediate School, OH

When I'm Old Enough!

Car
Shiny, fast
Cleaning, driving, fixing
Exciting in my car
Ferrari

Christopher Verstreate, Grade 4
Eugene M Nikkari Elementary School, MI

So Now Here We Are

69 years ago in 1939,
Many men had life on the line,
As a letter was sent to many, not few,
and signaled the beginning of World War II
The many men then went to battle and train
Through snow, sun, sleet, or rain
On the move through the day or the night
Between camping on borders or stuck in a fight
Then six years later when all was thought lost
We had won; we had won! But at what a cost.
However, their work did not go in vain,
They stuck with it no matter the pain
So now here we are in 2008
Remembering all those who fought against hate
So basically what I'm trying to say
We thank you and have a nice Veterans Day.

Bailey McCarthy, Grade 6
EH Greene Intermediate School, OH

Christmas

Christmas reminds me of family.
Family reminds me of friends.
Friends remind me of games.
Games remind me of toys.
Toys remind me of toy stores.
Toy stores remind me of children.
Children remind me of school.
School reminds me of knowledge.
Knowledge reminds me of college.
College reminds me of teams.
Teams remind me of spirit.
Spirit reminds me of fun.
Fun reminds me of family.
Family reminds me of Christmas.

Sarah Kennedy, Grade 6
Waverly East Intermediate School, MI

My Hamster

My hamster's eyes are black as coal.
But they are shiny like lumps of gold.
My hamster's fur is soft as cotton.
Her claws as sharp as thorns.
I love my hamster very much.
All cuddly and warm.

Baylee Stewart, Grade 5
Henryville Elementary School, IN

A River Is Like a Toddler

A river is like a toddler
Searching and exploring
Gurgling on and on.

It stumbles and rushes,
Never wanting rest,
Gurgling on and on.

It is gentle,
Yet it is not,
Gurgling on and on.

It destroys and rebuilds,
Unselfish yet greedy,
Gurgling on and on.

It screams and continues,
Eventually slowing down,
Gurgling on no more.

Levi Lewis, Grade 6
Greencastle Middle School, IN

The Swarm

Sand under my feet,
Dusty air; I look above:
Hoards of vultures soar.

David Schena, Grade 6
Stanley Clark School, IN

Taj Mahal

The Taj Mahal sparkled in the distance,
From its solid white marble
with precious stones inlaid in it.
We approached a huge gate carved of sandstone.
Then we saw the Taj Mahal!
It sat on a platform littered with people.
It smelled of pollution and garbage because of all the people there.
Everything — Taj Mahal, statues and carvings —
Glowed of sandstone and marble.
In front of the tomb a huge pool of water reflected the pure white towers.
All around were green bushes and flowers of every color.
Dogs barked at each other and people yelled and chattered.
Hills stuck up on either side of the Taj —
On one hill rose a mosque,
On the other hill the ruins of the black Taj Mahal poked up.
At the back of the Taj Mahal, a huge green valley
dropped down hundreds of meters,
and at the narrow bottom flowed the ancient river, slithering like
a giant blue snake.

Rohit Das, Grade 5
Stanley Clark School, IN

A Great Day in Colorado

A huge hole lies in the middle of four surrounding mountains,
a beautiful lake filled with trout.
Just my relatives and I are having a glorious time.
Clever fish are taking the bait off of the angry fishermen's hooks,
and just then the cold weather becomes a warm soothing heat.
We sit down at the perfect destination
for a delicious lunch of peanut butter and jelly sandwiches
overlooking the beautiful
Crystal Lake.
After our lunch the feeling goes away,
so I said "good bye" to this great moment,
and I start back down the long trail,
away from this perfection.
I will remember it forever.

Augie Hartnagel, Grade 5
Stanley Clark School, IN

At the Airport

As I am getting off the plane.
I hear the roaring of planes taking off and touching down.
I smell the Pakistani smell, the spices and sweets.
While I wait for my mom,
who is giving the passports and getting the luggage,
I play around with the baggage racks.
We go to the meeting place for cars and people.
I am suddenly surrounded by my family who are hugging me.
I feel my grandpa squeezing me.
It is like I got a million dollars without even lifting a finger.
Now I hear the cars honking as
I climb in the car that will take me home to my grandpa's house.
I wave goodbye to my shining moment.

Ibrahim Haque, Grade 5
Stanley Clark School, IN

Our World Is Important

If I were in charge of the world…
I would stop the whaling industry
because we have so many other
sources of food, why do we need
to kill these beautiful giants?
I'd protect the last wild horses,
so we can have wild horses
roaming the plains once more.
I'd make the park patrol so strong
no one absolutely *no one*
would get away with poaching.
We need to protect our
endangered species.
I'd make more forest reserves
so we won't kill our animals.
I'd also make all the cars ecofriendly
so the world would not be polluted anymore.
If I were in charge of the world,
it would be the best place for everyone,
because our world is important.

Kate Cooper, Grade 5
Churubusco Elementary School, IN

Weather

The wind blew as soft as silk
Dripping rain came like a crashing wave onto shore
Blazing sun beat down like drums
Cold snow came like sheets on my bed
Clear blue sky as clear as glass
The leaves flew away like shed skin
Tornado ripped apart our town
But right inside my house
It's as quiet as a mouse
I feel like my world
Has totally zoned me out
All these crazy sounds
Are muted like my mom's TV
I missed out on all this weather
Don't know what has come and gone
Oh, please Mr. Roker
Show me what's going on!

Katherine Maher, Grade 6
Boulan Park Middle School, MI

Saver

Beep beep
The engine is roaring
red and white lights flashing
they're going to save the day.

The fire's blowing
they have to go in and take it out.
It's the firefighters.
THEY SAVED THE DAY!

Lindsay Lobodzinski, Grade 4
Midland Academy of Advanced and Creative Studies, MI

Autumn

the beautiful oak
its many branches waving
turning into gold

Shyam Raman, Grade 5
Washington Township Elementary School, IN

Football

Oh, how I like to play football with my friends
It is how we bond
Whether we win or lose
We all have fun on the field
Whether we have a good team or not
We all have fun
At the end of the game
We all shake hands and say good game

Nate Echterling, Grade 4
John Simatovich Elementary School, IN

Softball vs Basketball

Softball
Thrilling, nerve-racking
Diving, catching, sliding
Long socks, visor/knee pads, basketball shoes
Blocking, guarding, shooting
Fast, exciting
Basketball

Softball
Green, red
Lining, outlining, writing
Seams, split/dimple, pop
Dimpling, seaming, printing
Orange, black
Basketball

Field
Dirty, chalked
Thudding, cheering, yelling
Batting, throwing/blocking, shooting
Squeaking, chanting, encouraging
Wooden, typed
Court

Madison Gogel, Grade 6
Nancy Hanks Elementary School, IN

A Winter Wonderland

As snow falls it glistens in the wind
Reminding me of past Christmases

A white blanket has covered the ground
Hiding the green that once was around

Snowflakes fall from above
Revealing to me the beautiful winter's love

Allyson Fulton, Grade 6
Emmanuel-St Michael Lutheran School, IN

The Snowflakes

The snowflakes
Falling down,
Make the ground cold.
It makes the ground
icy.

There's no school,
But for a few,
Where teachers use salt
to make the ice melt.

Jacob Doneff, Grade 4
Legend Elementary School, OH

Me!

My hair is brown my eyes are green,
And I like eating ice-cream.

My room is squeaky clean,
My sister is sweet sixteen.

I like to bake, especially cake,
But right now I'm taking a break.

I like to hike on a bike,
As long as lightning doesn't strike.

I like apples and drinking Snapples,
And I like watching tadpoles.

Mendel Mangel, Grade 4
Cincinnati Hebrew Day School, OH

Untitled

Nine deer in the woods.
Snap! A twig breaks underfoot.
The deer run away.

Max Kirsch, Grade 6
Stanley Clark School, IN

$50 and Some Gum

I'm sorry
I hid your binder
I just wanted to borrow
$50

And your gum
I will not
Be paying you back.

p.s.
With $50 I got a new sweatshirt
It is really warm
You should
Have bought it.

Robyn Goettler, Grade 5
Tremont Elementary School, OH

Chipmunks

Furry, cute
running, climbing, burying
critter, acorns, tree, branch
falling, changing, blowing
crunchy, colorful
Leaves

Rachel Caviolo, Grade 5
Norwich Elementary School, OH

Freedom

From dawn till dusk
I work all day
We pick the cotton
If only I was free
I'd go to Canada
The Promised Land
For all the slaves
To live our lives
Freedom

Megan Boltz, Grade 5
Mayfield Elementary School, OH

Fangs

F rightened
A t
N ight I am full of
G reat big
S hivers

Gracie Joseph, Grade 4
Bailly Elementary School, IN

Cheerleading

Cheerleading is so fun.
Indiana Ultimate's my team.
Our colors
are
green and blue.
I can do a roundoff and a tuck.
Cheerleading rocks!!

Jenna A. Pittenger, Grade 4
Churubusco Elementary School, IN

Gymnastics

G reat for learning to jump.
Y ou have to keep trying.
M ore practice, you'll get it.
N o need to cry.
A ll the flips, all the twists.
S till something's not right.
T ry again, practice makes perfect.
I did it, fantastic!
C reative twists and twirls.
S tick it, land it, perfect!

Tori Stowe, Grade 5
Perry Central Elementary School, IN

Love...

Love is a mystery
Love is divine
Love can be patient
Love can be kind
Love can be fake
Love can be real
Love isn't something you can touch
Love is something you feel
Love means affection
Love means passion
Love is a feeling
Love means attraction
Love can be true
Love can be a lie
Love can be a girl
Love can be a guy
Love can be long lasting
Love can go by too fast
Love is in your future
Love is in your past

Josephine Brown, Grade 6
St Gerard School, MI

Colors

Colors, colors, colors,
They are never new,
Yellow, red, green, blue,
We use them every day
describing things in every way,
A yellow banana,
A big red barn,
Green grass,
A blue sky,
You don't say,
All colors are adjectives.
Adjectives describe everything,
In every way.
I use adjectives every day!

Hannah Rosenberger, Grade 6
St. Michael School, IN

The Cloud

A puffy, white, cold cloud,
Giggled quietly
When the wind blew on it.
It became happier than before.

Josiah Talampas, Grade 5
Wooster Christian School, OH

Fire Dream

Warm but dark and fierce,
A fire glows in the black night,
Calls me to come near.

Emily Beach, Grade 6
Stanley Clark School, IN

My Fun Fall

As fall dances into the season
strong winds whistle in between every branch.
I watch as every color on the leaves are
different like a flaming candle.

"Crunch!" goes the leaves beneath the kids' feet
as they dive into the colorful pile of leaves
like fish dive into water.
Kids laugh loudly for joy.

As the sun goes down,
fall dances its way into winter.
As the chill comes, the snow does too.
We all say, "Bye!" to fall and "Hello!" to winter.

Sydney Wells, Grade 6
Holy Family Middle School, MI

Basketball

B all. What you shoot in the hoop
A ggressive. How you act in the game
S ad. How you feel when you lose
K ool! What you say when you make a basket
E xciting. How it feels when you win
T all. A person who you guard
B asket. What you make when you shoot (sometimes)
A ngry. How you feel when you don't win
L ose. What you do when you don't win
L ove. How I feel about basketball

Emma Genson, Grade 6
Trilby Elementary School, OH

NFL

If I could score 20 touchdowns in one game
I would probably get in the world record book.
I'd do stunts like a front flip just because I can
I hope I don't break my leg
I would never be quarterback because I'm not a leader
I'd start a program for young football players just to be nice
And I would love to throw farther than my dad
But I wouldn't be mean about it if I could,
If only I could be in an NFL team
But I'm only 10 so I can't,
Can you catch my dream.

Nick Murphy, Grade 4
Churubusco Elementary School, IN

Grandpa

He always brought us candy
He was also very handy
He showed us love and care
And was always right there
But God decided to take him home
We might be very sad and miss him very much
But we will never forget what Grandpa taught us

Elizabeth Hoy, Grade 5
Northfield Baptist Christian School, OH

Leaves

Leaves, crunching, scrunching.
Red, brown, hard to believe they used to be green,
They fell from a tree, gosh they're up to my knee,
Left for me to…
Rake,
Rake,
Rake
Mom! Dad! I'm done!

Nyna Hess, Grade 4
Norwich Elementary School, OH

Veteran's Day

We remember the veterans who defended our country,
through exploding bombs and gunshots.
They risked their lives to save our freedom.
Some have survived
and some have not
in battle and in war,
but keeping peace is important to all of us.
We thank them for their bravery and courage.
That is why we remember the veterans.

Zachary Davis, Grade 5
Beck Centennial Elementary School, MI

Camping/Mall

Camping
fun, peaceful,
mesmerizing, fishing, tubing,
friendly, exciting, busy, crowded,
shopping, parking, walking
hectic, expensive
Mall

Kayla Sullivan, Grade 5
Washington Township Elementary School, IN

I Am

I am funny and kind.
I wonder, why did my cat run away?
I hear my dog saying, "Don't touch me."
I see my dog in jail.
I want a cat.
I am funny and kind.
I pretend to climb a mountain.
I feel upset that my dog gets treated better than me.
I touch a blue tiger.
I worry my dog has eye problems.
I cry when my dog gets sick.
I am funny and kind.
I understand that my cat is gone.
I say "hi" to everyone.
I dream that I have my lost dog back.
I try to be funny.
I hope to be nice to everyone.
I am funny and kind.

Kirstin Cox, Grade 6
Galesburg-Augusta Middle School, MI

Kwanzaa

Kwanzaa is the best of all holidays, families come together for just 7 days.
There is one thing about Kwanzaa that's the corn, represents all the children that have ever been born.
Kwanzaa, Kwanzaa just 7 days,
I think it's the best of all holidays.
Kwanzaa, Kwanzaa just 7 days,
I think it's the best out of all holidays.
It's time for the feast everybody get up, say prayers and blessings pass the unity cup.
The feast started; there is a lot of communication, put stuff on the mat to represent our foundation.
Red represents the blood, black represents my color, green represents the land,
And I think grass should be a part of Kwanzaa because it represents the trail we ran.
Kwanzaa, Kwanzaa just 7 days,
I think it's the best of all holidays.
Kwanzaa, Kwanzaa just 7 days,
I think it's the best of all holidays.

Latif Muhammad, Grade 4
Granville T Woods Community School, OH

Neptune

N eptune has an internal heat source that radiates more than twice as much energy as it receives from the sun.
E very study scientists find something new. Since
P luto's orbit is so eccentric, it sometimes crosses the orbit of Neptune making it the farthest. Neptune is a
T ypical gas planet. Like
U ranus, but unlike Jupiter and Saturn, it may not have distinct layering for the rings.
N eptune also has rings.
E arth's base observations showed only faint arcs instead of the complete rings.

Hannah Lyon, Grade 6
Pinewood Elementary School, IN

My Friend

My friend
Autumn
Athletic, wild, funny, daring
Daughter of Jerry and Gretchen Lain, sister of Bryce Lain
Lover of dogs, softball, and her family, Tray M.
Who felt happy, excited, and hopeful
Who needed love, boys, and friends
Who fears of losing, not being competitive, and her dad
Who gives love, hope, and understanding
Who would like to see herself graduate, meet her life time goal, and go to college at Indiana University
Resident of Gatchel
Lain,
Is a Best Friend to me,
And a Best Friend to others!

Blayre Underhill, Grade 5
Perry Central Elementary School, IN

Freedom

F ireworks shooting into the night sky while celebrating Veteran's Day
R ecognizing our past soldiers by stories and memories
E stablishing many changes in the Untied States government
E nabling people across the world to realize we have presidents and not tyrants
D ying devotion to our soldiers shown by wearing red poppies and donating time and money
O n Veteran's Day we honor troops by wearing red, white, and blue
M emorizing the Pledge of Allegiance and reciting it with our flag

Mallory Schmelzer, Grade 5
Sanderson Elementary School, OH

Apple Cider

Apple cider
Sugar, cinnamon
Golden brown, bronze
Served warm and cold
Beverage

Ruth Kurowski, Grade 4
Frank H Hammond Elementary School, IN

Pancakes and Waffles

Pancakes and waffles.
Waffles or pancakes
Pancakes are just like waffles.
We use butter and syrup for both.
For pancakes I use strawberries and whipped cream.
You may think there is no difference, but you are sadly wrong.
Pancakes have a different shape, color, and texture.
Waffles have many ways to be cooked.
You can buy a waffle iron; it will be easy as pie.

Calistia Meyer, Grade 5
Perry Central Elementary School, IN

I Am

I am polite and caring.
I wonder what student council does.
I hear eggs crying.
I see books walking.
I want a fairy tale wedding.
I am polite and caring.
I pretend I am a famous singer.
I feel jealous when I see my friends flying.
I touch pillows made by angels.
I worry that I will not get in a good college.
I cry when I get in trouble.
I am polite and caring.
I understand that I have great friends.
I say I am sorry.
I dream about failing school.
I try to get good grades.
I hope to have a great family.
I am polite and caring.

Sarah Millen, Grade 6
Galesburg-Augusta Middle School, MI

Freedom

Jump free
Laugh with glee
Nothing holds me back.
Like a butterfly, fluttering so free
Nothing holds me back.
Scream! Screech! Bark! Blast!
Nothing holds me back.
Run! Scamper! Dash! Charge!
Nothing holds me back.
Nothing holds me back!

Sydney Mullen, Grade 5
Wooster Christian School, OH

Autumn

A utumn comes and goes as it gets cold
U nder the moonlit sky temperatures drop
T he leaves start to change
U nder the sun leaves begin to blow
M orning leaves fall to the ground
N ow the trees are empty

Seth Gaghen, Grade 6
Eisenhower Middle School, OH

Brenden Gillespie

He loves girls and horror films
He has a romantic soul
He loves cars and wrestling
He loves the color pink
He loves to shop for shoes and bling-bling
He would love to have a red 1970 Chevelle super sport.

He loves romantic and action films
He loves to cook anything
He has to have a girlfriend or go bonkers
He plays video games all the time
He loves to write and lift weights
He also loves football and hockey.

And that he, is me!

Brenden Michael Gillespie, Grade 6
Trilby Elementary School, OH

Love

Love is to love, love is to give, love is to be taken care of
Love is for everyone, love is to be captured in your soul
Love is to kiss, love is to hug, love is to shake hands
And love is to be loved!

Dominique Brown, Grade 5
May V Peck Elementary School, MI

I Am

I am smart and funny.
I wonder why there are starving children.
I hear my pencil screaming.
I see my pencil dancing as I write.
I want to meet the Jonas Brothers.
I am smart and funny.
I pretend to drive.
I feel happy about going to Fairyland.
I touch the air as I walk.
I worry about when I might die.
I cry when I think about my Bumpa.
I am smart and funny.
I understand I'm alive.
I say I believe in God.
I dream that someday nobody dies.
I hope to live forever.
I am smart and funny.

Hali Steppenwolf, Grade 6
Galesburg-Augusta Middle School, MI

Rushing Waters

Leaping over rocks
Roaring, clear and cool, smoothly
Rushing vast and free
Taylor Fortune, Grade 6
Roosevelt Elementary School, OH

Two

Two people can start a relationship.
Two bricks can start a house.
Two boards can start a dock.
Two arms can give a hug.
Two friends can start a group.
Two fish can start a school.
Two lips can give a kiss.
Two feet can run a race.
Two flowers can start a bouquet.
Two seeds can start a garden.
Two hands can give a handshake.
Two streets can make an intersection.
Two ears can hold up a pair of glasses.
Two wheels can make a bike.
Two lines can make a cross.
Two halves make a whole.
Two shoes make a pair.
Two musicians can start a band.
Two singers can sing a duet.
Two people can start a conversation.
Two sticks can start a fire.
Kyle Malacina, Grade 6
St Gerard School, MI

Hot Cocoa

hot cocoa is so hot
just like a boiling pot
it tastes so good on a winter's day
watching the white snowflakes lay
Kaitlyn Klingle, Grade 4
Veale Elementary School, IN

Lovely Shatera

S tylish
H appy
A mazing
T alented
E xcellent
R eally amazing
A wesome

T olerance
A ctive
Y ellow
L ovely
h **O** nesty
R ed
Shatera Taylor, Grade 6
Eastmoor Middle School, OH

Friends

Friends are always there for you.
They never let you down no matter what.
You can hang out and talk and just be yourself.
Friends are loyal and you can trust them with anything.
With friends life is easier.
Without friends, the world is a lonely place and it doesn't have to be.
All we need is friends.
Murrah Sabouni, Grade 6
Abbott Middle School, MI

Life from a Flower's View

I love my home,
With trees as big and fluffy as clouds in the sky.
A big and beautiful butterfly,
Who comes and lands on me as gently as a feather.

When fall comes around, leaves lay on the ground as yellow as the morning bright sun.
The winter and spring once more come.
I rebloom just as red as a rose.
Then comes summer again,
And the kids frolic through the grass as green as a tree frog.

Then come the caterpillars who nibble on my stem,
And tickles me like a light windy breeze.
I look to the left and then to the right,
And see my brothers and sisters as colorful as a rainbow.

Then I start to wilt and die of thirst,
But the rain saves me, falling from the sky like a river,
It quenches my thirst.
Then a bug sneaks by like a lion on his prey.
Once more fall and winter pass, and once more I go to sleep.
Bridget Mary Jackson, Grade 6
Cloverdale Middle School, IN

October Is…

Picking the perfect patient from the bunch
Cut a hole in his head
And in go your hands taking out the unneeded guck from the inside of his head
He will smile and shine when you are done operating on him
His name is Jack
His face is now clear for everyone to see
The eyes, nose, and mouth, glow with a light
Just like a lantern
He is a jack-o'-lantern

Kids come to your doorstep, fearing that you will trick them
Instead of giving them treats
They do a "ding dong" at your door
And the one super scared kid says "Trick-or-Treat"

You see the moon smiling down at you
He laughs in the crystal clear night sky and says
"Happy Halloween."
Caroline Zacharias, Grade 5
Beck Centennial Elementary School, MI

I Am

I am friendly and kind.
I wonder if I will like volleyball.
I hear a creak when I erase with my eraser.
I see my eraser disappear into thin air.
I want to be a science teacher.
I am friendly and kind.
I pretend I am a pro soccer player.
I feel happy when I reach for the stars in the sky.
I touch the rainbow in the sky.
I worry about my grades in school.
I cry when I lose a family member.
I am friendly and kind.
I understand when I don't get to do something.
I say I wish you good luck today.
I dream good and bad dreams.
I try to get to school on time.
I hope to have a good future.
I am friendly and kind.

Ashley Whitman, Grade 6
Galesburg-Augusta Middle School, MI

My Favorite Time of Year

I wake up early to start the day,
And find my brothers to see if they'll play.

Our tree is lit up with colored lights;
We see the presents and now we are bright!

We wake up Mom and Dad to open up gifts,
And look out the window and see the snow drifts.

Later that day we'll build a snowman,
And throw snowballs as fast as we can.

Relatives are here, it's my favorite time of year.
Thank you God for all I hold dear!

Jacob Allard, Grade 5
St Jude Catholic School, IN

Thanksgiving/Thankful

Thanksgiving
Mashed potatoes
Excited and cheerful
Spending time with family
Thankful

Kristin Osborne, Grade 4
Frank H Hammond Elementary School, IN

The Giant Squid

There once was a giant squid,
Who could not open a lid.
He tried with all his might,
All through the night,
But it was child-proof and he was a kid.

Logan Swanson, Grade 5
Washington Township Elementary School, IN

November

People celebrate to give thanks and also for the fact
that I am two years beyond eight
Gusting winds, changing temperatures, colder and colder
as temperatures are about to freeze
Obama and McCain both sit and wait as fate takes first place
to see who will be the next great 08
Veteran's Day to Thanksgiving to Christmas Day;
time flies by in the blink of an eye
Frost blankets the ground as mornings roll around,
like a marshmallow exploded on the ground.

Luc Fluent, Grade 5
Beck Centennial Elementary School, MI

Veterans

They are there for us;
Constant.
Around to protect the promise of freedom;
Unbroken.
Until the assurance of our country's safety is at hand.
Determined.
Veterans
Our salvation in a dark world.

Abigail Tompkins, Grade 6
Monroe Elementary School, OH

Halloween

H alloween is a special day where you dress up
A s anything you want.
L iking Halloween is the best.
L oving it might be kind of creepy.
O n Halloween the adults hand out candy.
W hen you see a scary costume you scream or hide.
E specially Michael Meyers. That's what I'm scared of.
E ven when I do see Michael Meyers I'm not totally scared.
N o matter what I will always like this day.

Dustin Payne, Grade 5
Washington Township Elementary School, IN

Remember Them

Thy parents work under skies so blue
As you emerge from the womb
To care for you from the start
With gentle eyes and tender hearts

You lingered at your mother's breast
For comfort, food, and for rest
Your father's hand for fun and play
His voice for songs at end of day

Thank them always, thank them well
For wonderful words to tell
To be passed down for generations
To give gloominess a vacation
From which it shall never return.

Victoria Schemenauer, Grade 5
Michiana Christian Montessori School, IN

Roaring Rhino

Rhino rhino
So much like a
Freight train.
Bold
Strong
Front horn so long.
Not the smartest
People see
Trample anything
People flee.
Eyes not keen
But rhino so mean.
Trample all
That's in your path
Make the Earth
Shake and thrash!

Rhino rhino
Stampede pound
A trampled path
On broken ground.

Sam Ciancutti, Grade 6
Harding Middle School, OH

Together, Tonight

The moon shines so bright tonight.
But I sit here
    sad and alone
        because you're on the other side
            of the world.

I wish I could be that moon tonight.
So I can guide you
    to me
        and we will be together.

We will be on one side of the world
    looking
        at the bright moon
            together…tonight.

Alice Piatkowski, Grade 6
Schuchard Elementary School, MI

The Arena

I'm the arena after
The bull fight
I'm ripped, I'm shredded.
I'm hated by the bull.
It's fun to watch me,
Stomped to shreds.
My owner has to be quick
And repair me
After the damage is done.

Aden Triona, Grade 5
Westview Elementary School, OH

The Sun

I am the sun
I'm bright and happy…
But up in the sky, I'm lonely.
With nothing to do.
But watch over Earth
From high above.
I wish I had someone to talk to.

Darian Croson, Grade 5
Westview Elementary School, OH

Music

Music is everywhere,
    It's at your home,
        Your school,
            Your car,
    Even your neighborhood.

    Music is graceful.
    It can calm you down,
    It can even tell you things
    You didn't realize or know.

    Music is everywhere.
    I love it, music.

Keiara Gibson, Grade 6
Rocky River Middle School, OH

School

School
    Awesome, fun
Learning, playing, listening
    Get smarter.
Ebeling Elementary

Crystal Brunett, Grade 4
Floyd Ebeling Elementary School, MI

Colors

Blue is the color of the skies.
Green is the color of my mother's eyes.

White is the clouds in the sky.
Brown makes me want to eat pie.

Gray makes me feel sad.
Black makes me want to be bad.

Purple is the color of a flower.
Yellow apples are sometimes sour.

Red reminds me of fire.
Gold is the color of desire.

This is what colors are to me.

Nathan Murray, Grade 6
Roosevelt Elementary School, OH

Trail Riding

Trail riding is fun.
I feel leaves
Swooping from the trees.
I hear my horse's hooves
clicking on the ground as I trot him.
I taste the dirt
coming from the ground.
I smell apples
near us.
I see wild animals
running from me.
I feel so happy
trail riding.

Payton Brownlee, Grade 4
Licking Valley Intermediate School, OH

Baby Jesus

Christmas day
Jesus lay
On a pile of hay
He did not make a sound
As the cattle was lowering.

Nikita Highman, Grade 5
St Joseph Parish School, OH

My Name Means

N ice as I can be
I like to swim in the sea
C omfortable to be me
O pportunity to be free
L ove my family and Landon my dog
E xcited for snow but not fog

J oyful and jolly when I sing and play
E specially on Christmas Day
S chool can sometimes be fun
S pecially when we're done
I ce cream is my favorite thing to eat
C andy hurts my teeth
A lways like to do my dance

S omeday I will visit France
H ope to be a famous actor
E ven though shyness is a factor
R oad to goodness I desire
B ut I will get there by reaching higher

Nicole Jessica Sherb, Grade 5
Frank Ohl Intermediate School, OH

Snow Fairies

The snowflakes falling,
Are like small dancing fairies,
From the clouds above.

Jonathan Hang, Grade 6
Harmon Middle School, OH

October Days...

October,
Hoxey Acres haunted hay rides,
hear the hay crackle when scary people walk through,
the corn stalk whoosh through the wind,
all the leaves are crunching and I'm with fear,
Cider mill time I scream and cheer,
I crunch and munch my caramel apple,
gulp my cold sweet cider,
so sad I'm mad it's time to go,
all of a sudden I hear the crows calling through the air.

Sabrina Persichetti, Grade 5
Beck Centennial Elementary School, MI

Envy

Envy is dark green
Like the sky on a misty day in a cemetery
Or like nails screeching across a chalkboard
It creeps into my mind
Like a part of me I can't control
It reminds me of someone who can run faster than me
And can beat me to the finish line
It makes me feel like I need to get something better
Or something nicer than them
It makes me want to throw something

Maria Avellana, Grade 6
St Maria Goretti School, IN

Fun in Fall

Time for fun in fall
Hay rides and picking apples
Collecting leaves too

Ani Arzumanian, Grade 4
Frank H Hammond Elementary School, IN

If I Was in Charge of the World

People would never die
Grow more plants
Make gas lower
Everyone would have pets
Schools would have more time with kids
Have parties at school a lot
Play on the playground more than class
Have no more hatred
World peace
Everything is free
Make the world greener
Christmas every month
No more sickness
Have favorite meal every week
No more hunger
Everyone would have lots of family members
Dreams would come true
Schools would be on an ocean cruise line
More holidays for family members to be together

Hannah Chappelear, Grade 5
Sanderson Elementary School, OH

My Pencil Pouch

My pencil pouch
It doesn't slouch
It's full of pencils and pens
Every time I try to count, the number never ends
The brightest colors you'll ever see
They are all so sparkly
My pencil pouch is like a treasure chest
Come to me if you want the best
I might not get the best grades
But I always have the best ink shades

Kaleigh Robbins, Grade 6
North Knox East Elementary/Jr High School, IN

Money

Money can't buy everything,
It just makes people all stressed,
Especially when their lousy paycheck is not at its best.

Lindsey Corsaro, Grade 5
St Jude Catholic School, IN

Cloud of Destiny

A darkened room,
A deepened voice,
A saddened face,
An aching soul.

Stare at these, then look back.
Choose your destiny,
A cold heart, disheartened faith, angry life.
Fulfill your destiny.

An enlightened touch,
An optimistic spirit,
A happy pace,
An accomplished task.

Stare at these, then look back.
Choose your destiny,
A light heart, hopeful faith, a joyful life.
Fulfill your destiny.

Whitney Hoving, Grade 5
Assumption BVM School, MI

Spring

Green grass sprouts up through the cool ground.
Flowers, fresh air, and flowing rivers are all around.
Green plants are in sight,
The squirrels are here to stay.
Birds sing and dance every day.
Living, breathing...look!
There's dew on the grass.
The sun's shining, chocolate milk in my glass,
The babies aren't whining.
It's spring!

Desiree Fey, Grade 5
Northern Heights Elementary School, IN

Presents

P eople love them
R eceiving them is easy
E xcitement goes around the room
S assieness is not allowed
E xchanging happy looks
N ever forgetting them
T reating everyone nicely
S creaming for joy

Jennifer Hayton, Grade 5
May V Peck Elementary School, MI

Fish

There once was a fish on a dish
He was a fine looking fish
He jumped off the tray
Feeling gay
And ran away with Trish!

Marissa McGurk, Grade 5
Rootstown Elementary School, OH

Buzzing

B ees going
U p and down,
Z ipping and
Z ooming all around,
I n and out,
N ever stopping, always
G oing BUZZ, BUZZ.

Mitch Fink, Grade 6
Melrose Elementary School, OH

Snowflake

Snowflakes falling down
On the ground or in my hair
Snowflakes floating down.

Olivia Knight, Grade 5
Churubusco Elementary School, IN

Imagination

If you close your eyes
And think really hard
You may see a sparkle
But when you close them really tight
It seems you are in the dark
Then when you think it is all over
You see something up ahead
Is it the end of the tunnel
Or is it heaven
When I get a little closer
I think I know what it is
It isn't heaven
And I'm not in a tunnel
I actually find out
I am in a whole new world

Kasia Wanner, Grade 4
John Simatovich Elementary School, IN

My Guardian Angel

I hope that you are in a wonderful place right now.
I am not.
I am scared without you by my side, guiding me through my life.

I wonder each day what would happen if you were still alive.
I miss you so much.
Sometimes it feels like you are right next to me giving me your big hugs.

Every day I cry and cry wishing you were beside me.
I finish crying.
I think to myself, "Why did I just cry my lungs out?"

Crying doesn't make a difference.
You are not alive.
That kills me, Great Grandpa.

Rhonda Benjamin, Grade 6
Schuchard Elementary School, MI

One Child's Imagination

A child's imagination can make a dark room glow
A child's imagination can explore the unexplored
They can adventure beyond the limits
They can make a blue bird sing

A child's imagination is
When tea parties are for the big and small
A child's imagination is when fairy tales come to life
When they can change the story when all you have to do is listen

A child's imagination is when they can
Explore every corner, the simple floors become seas
A child's imagination is elephants, sailing ships, astronauts, and dinosaurs
Dancing on the moon

A child's imagination is rhinos playing dress up
A child's imagination
Is their ability to think anything is possible
A child's imagination is the way they smile with joy
That the elephants are sailing and they have explored the unexplored
A child's imagination is when they think inside
One child's imagination

Ann Marie Elaban, Grade 6
Harding Middle School, OH

Pookie

My dog his name is Pookie. He likes to jump and play.
We are together day after day.
Now it is 5 years later my new baby sister's on her way!
I am so excited but I'll have to give my poor Pookie away.
I will miss him terribly but I will visit him every other day.
(Every day in between is for homework so I can keep my grades ok.)
Now my sister is 6 and we can take my wonderful pug back today!
Now my sister loves him dearly, but my baby brother is on the way…
My mom said we could keep him as long as we keep him away from the baby, Jay.

Gracie Marble, Grade 4
Stonegate Elementary School, IN

I Am

I am unique and curious.
I wonder how old I will live to be.
I hear shoes talk as they slap the cold hard ground.
I see a pink and green girl.
I want to live in Hawaii.
I am unique and curious.
I pretend to be nice to my sister.
I feel excited about being in a movie.
I touch a unicorn's soft hair.
I worry about my life.
I cry when I fall.
I am unique and curious.
I understand what life is all about.
I say everyone is a winner, even if you lose.
I dream I can fly.
I try to stay as happy as I can.
I hope my family and friends will always be there.
I am unique and curious.

Caitlin Starkweather, Grade 6
Galesburg-Augusta Middle School, MI

Autumn

A lways windy on October mornings
U nusual colors in my maple tree
T he leaves are rustling on the ground
U ntouched pumpkins ready to be carved
M y favorite season of the year
N ice kinds of costumes on Halloween night.

Lynley Murray, Grade 6
Eisenhower Middle School, OH

Five Little Dogs

Five little dogs
Waiting for the bus
They wanted to go
To Toys-R-Us.

One wanted a dolly,
Another one wanted a bear,
The twins wanted matching make-up kits,
The last one wanted Hannah hair.

They were soon very excited,
They got on the bus with glee,
They were in the bus for an hour,
When one said, "I have to go wee!"

Arica Martinez, Grade 6
Eisenhower Middle School, OH

Stage Fright

I'm back stage right now, and I don't know what to do.
All I can hear is my heart thumping too.
I'm so frightened, I don't know how to react.
All I want to do is get out of this act!

Mason Van Houten, Grade 4
Northern Heights Elementary School, IN

My Journey Home in Wintertime

The school bell tolls
And children pinball to their lockers
Grab their coats and venture outside
This is the story of my journey back home
Through the extreme cold.

I brace myself before I open the school doors
Preparing myself for the cold, blasting wind
And for the piling snow
I go outside and trudge slowly through the eight foot snow
Headwinds pushing rigorously against me
Slowing me down even more
And after 45 seemingly endless minutes,
I make it home,
Nearly frostbitten,
And right there,
Sitting on the desk in my room
I see a steaming fresh cup of cocoa
Just waiting for me to drink it
And that's when I decide that winter won't be so impossible.

Devon Chodzin, Grade 6
Harding Middle School, OH

Amanda Lynn Paynter

A cause I work for is helping the poor
M y friends sometimes have helped more
A nd I hope world hunger will end
N ow that people have less money to spend
D ancing is a hobby of mine
A long with dancing all of the time

L ittle brothers, two I have
Y es, two I have, they make me glad
N icholas in 1st grade is one of them
N ow Zachariah has preschool fun again

P ainting, I like to do in art
A nd I think it's a really fun part
Y ellow is a great color I think
N ow I also love the color pink
T o be my friend you must surely know
E ither don't do drugs or leave and go
R unning I also love to do

Amanda Lynn Paynter, Proud and True

Amanda Lynn Paynter, Grade 5
Frank Ohl Intermediate School, OH

Car

Car
Boxy, black
Sleek, array of colors, trendy
Every kid wants one for their 16th birthday
Cadillac Escalade

Joey Skelton, Grade 6
Holy Angels School, OH

Friends

Friends, friends, friends
Thoughtful friends
Funny friends
Caring, lovable, respectful friends
Intelligent, athletic, energetic friends
Last of all,
Best of all,
My friends
Abby Povinelli, Grade 5
St Jude Catholic School, IN

Mystical Cloud

People wonder about me.
They can't figure me out.
To some people I'm strange.
I want to float away.
And be a normal cloud.
Kelley Woollet, Grade 5
Westview Elementary School, OH

Enjoyable Snacks

Candy
Chocolaty, tasty
Chewing, licking, rotting teeth
Gooey, sticky, juicy, tart
Biting, sucking, spitting seeds
Sweet, healthy
Fruit
Kathryn Berkemeyer, Grade 4
Norwich Elementary School, OH

The Circus

Feels like excitement all around
Looks like flexible acrobats
Sounds like people cheering
Smells like buttered popcorn
Tastes like cotton candy and hotdogs
Cetia Dawson, Grade 5
Northfield Baptist Christian School, OH

Football

Getting hit,
Getting back up,
Pure determination.
Being intimidated,
Blocking until the whistle blows,
Raw courage.
Practicing every night,
Taking harsh criticism,
Tough discipline.
Rising to the quest,
Accomplishing the goal,
True satisfaction!
Jude Diagostino, Grade 6
Tri-West Middle School, IN

Cocoa Beach

Wonderful, calm
Summers first day
Afternoon
Waves, children playing
Swimming, people, animals
Swimming, playing, eating
Not sure when I'm coming back
Relaxed, happy
Cocoa Beach.
Brooke Maez, Grade 6
Tippecanoe Middle School, OH

Christmas

C aroling at houses
H elping to make dinner
R ed and green Christmas
I just can't wait till we open presents
S omething smells good
T aste till it's just right
M erry Christmas
A ll people hanging lights
S pring and summer are coming!
Alexis Trenda, Grade 5
May V Peck Elementary School, MI

Secrets

Passing notes
All throughout class
This class is boring
Let the time pass

All the secrets
On this note
Must be kept
In my tote

This guy who sits across
Always tries to peep
But luckily he never sees
The secrets that I keep
Tiffany Jo Prephan, Grade 6
Trilby Elementary School, OH

Knights and Weapons

A knight with armor
Is the best in the world
Chain mail is good, but plate is better
I know a sword is the best
But I prefer a good dagger and an ax
An enchanted weapon hits lightning
A rapier is good for lunging and swiping
I know it's not a long poem
But it's time to say so long!
Harrison Phillips, Grade 4
Stonegate Elementary School, IN

Mrs. Byrn

Mrs. Byrn is very kind,
But she is not hard to find.

She is very cool,
But does not act like a fool.

She also rules,
But does not drool.

She does not know how to use tools,
But she has to put up with fools.
Mary Isho, Grade 5
Mark C Roose Elementary School, MI

My Saxophone

Breathing in
Blowing out
Reading notes
While I count
Music to my ears
Sweating fingertips
Nothing else in my mind
Feeling the reed touch my lips
Only my saxophone and I
Logan Hadley, Grade 6
Tri-West Middle School, IN

At the Beach

Sitting in the sand,
Hearing waves crash against shore,
Now I'm all alone.
Sam Sturtevant, Grade 6
Stanley Clark School, IN

Soft, Shy Sheep

What does a sheep know?
Warm, woolly winter coats
Farms with
Fields and barns
Bleating, baaing, beautiful flocks
Shearing time
10 pounds of wool?!
Black and white,
Brown and gray
Spun into blankets and sweaters
Male rams
Mother ewes
Baby lambs
Born in the spring
Grazing in grass
Roses, dandelions, leaves
Led by a sheepdog
The sweet sheep.
Hannah Meloche, Grade 5
Riley Upper Elementary School, MI

It's Our Choice

As people know,
The world spins, yet we can't feel it,
But what happens when…
The last tree is cut
The last river has dried
The last spec of oxygen has been polluted
The last oil rig pumped the last gallon of oil
And the last animal has been killed
Well…
The world will spin,
But we still won't feel it,
Because no one will be there to witness it.

To the people of the past:
What has happened can't be undone,
But don't look back,
Save what you can
So that we can live.
Make peace so children don't fight
And most of all, recycle, reduce, and reuse,
So that one day we can breathe the fresh air of yesterday.
So choose
What will you do today?

Kunal Garg, Grade 6
Boulan Park Middle School, MI

Brother Brian

Brother Brian broke a bone by the bay in Bybanks.
Brother Brian was bicycling when bumble bee's were buzzing.
Brother Brian pulled the brakes and blew right off and
Brother Brian broke his back bone.

Brooke Terrell, Grade 6
Tippecanoe Middle School, OH

The Season of Excitement

As the leaves begin to miraculously change
to brilliant colors, and sculpture the landscape

The temperature begins to plummet, and the
cool crisp wind begins to blow and rips the
leaves one by one from the branches, peppering
the ground with crunching fall colors.

Raking, playing, and enjoying the leafy frenzy,
till the short days come and long cool nights begin.

The turkey sits on the table, sizzling to perfection,
waiting to be devoured by family and friends.

Pie for dessert, football on TV, conversations
around the table — reminiscing the good fortunes
and all the things to be thankful for throughout the year.

Only one season away from winter…fall!

Jack Gluth, Grade 6
Allen J. Warren Elementary School, IN

Mars

M ars is the fourth planet from the sun, with an
A tmosphere of carbon dioxide. There are many
R ocks on Mars. The
S urface of Mars is mostly red dust with a few volcanoes.

Amanda Dibley, Grade 6
Pinewood Elementary School, IN

Christmas Reminds Me Of…

Christmas reminds me of joy.
Joy reminds me of sweet.
Sweet reminds me of almonds.
Almonds remind me of nutty.
Nutty reminds me of my brother-in-law.
My brother-in-law reminds me of my sister.
My sister reminds me of my mom.
My mom reminds me of my dad.
My dad reminds me of jolly.
Jolly reminds me of santa.
Santa reminds me of big.
Big reminds me of pine trees.
Pine trees remind me of angels.
Angels reminds me of ornaments.
Ornaments remind me of christmas.

Cameron Spees, Grade 6
Waverly East Intermediate School, MI

I Am

I am fun and cool.
I wonder if I am sleeping.
I hear "Barney."
I see Barney.
I want a Play Station 3.
I am fun and cool.
I pretend I'm a millionaire.
I feel happy for Barney because he eats ice cream.
I touch Barney's face.
I worry about my grandma.
I cry because of my grandma.
I am fun and cool.
I understand my grandpa loves me.
I say I'm cool.
I try to be good at basketball.
I hope to be rich.
I dream I am a millionaire.
I am fun and cool.

Miles Richards, Grade 6
Galesburg-Augusta Middle School, MI

Night's Burning Soul

Day sizzles to night.
One part of my soul is burning.
Night's burning light is
Burning inside me as if I were a paper,
And its luminous light is a lighter.

Jack Cowan, Grade 5
Washington Township Elementary School, IN

Brendan Davenport

B aseball rocks
R ocks at baseball
E ducated kid
N ice to people
D eclaration of Independence
　　is important to me
A ction figures (WWE)
N ever gives up

D oesn't boss people
A lmost perfect
V ideo games rock
E njoys ice cream
N osey most of the time
P lays board games
O strich speed
R are baseball talent
T elevision is something to do

Brendan Davenport, Grade 4
Keystone Academy, MI

A Better World

If I were in charge of the world…
I would change gas prices.
I would make smoking illegal.
I would stop slavery in Canada.
I would give money to a charity.
I would make chocolate a fruit.
The world would be a better place
If I were in charge!

Emily Murphy, Grade 5
Churubusco Elementary School, IN

Falling in the Season

Leaves tumble from the sky.
Pumpkins sitting on doorsteps
patiently waiting to spook others.

Brisk air brushes through bushes
as parents politely pass out yummy candy
to little spooks that trick or treat.

During fall, leaves change
and air gets chilly
slowly preparing for winter.

Before you know it,
snow is on the ground
trees slowly lose their leaves
and they go bare.

After about two months
fall is gone and winter is here
tumbling in with a white blanket.

Emilee Green, Grade 6
Holy Family Middle School, MI

Christmas

How do I love Christmas so much you ask?
Well I won't lie, I love the presents, but that's not the true meaning of Christmas.
The true meaning of Christmas is Jesus being born.
Most people don't think about that on Christmas morning, but as Christians we should.
Sometimes we are caught up in all the decorations, lists, and presents.
In this world today, not a lot of people stop to think about how lucky we are
to be able to give and receive presents.
Think about how lucky we are to have such a loving, merciful Savior
So, this Christmas let's stop and thank the Lord
Thank Him for all He has done for us!
Don't forget to have a Merry Christmas.

Elizabeth MacPherson, Grade 6
Crown Point Christian School, IN

The NIHL Championship

When I made it to the Northern Illinois Hockey League championship,
I saw the opening light show of almost every color in the world.
My stomach trembled.
The crowd roared as the rays shot around the ice.
Then they announced the dreaded names of the other team,
the Winnetka Warriors.
Their colors were green, yellow, and white,
like some kind of bacteria from Mars.
The game started, and five players on each team
skated out for the starting face-off.
The kids were puny but they had superchargers in them.
I knew it was going to be a challenge to win.
They could skate so fast, I thought it was a NASCAR event.
But they hadn't scored yet.
When they shot the puck, it just danced wildly over the ice.
Coach gave us encouraging words.
He told us we have to believe and trust each other.
We started passing as a team and scored.
The buzzer hit 0.00; we went crazy.
It was an amazing experience,
to stand on the ice as the champions!

Max Lerman, Grade 5
Stanley Clark School, IN

July 4th

I'm watching an exceptional fireworks display on the beach.
Sitting on the lush green fairway of a golf course,
watching the best show on Earth.
Sunlight dimming, reflecting on the shimmering water,
the lighthouse light beaming.
I hear merry people laughing and playing,
silence before the night of lights, and some expressive ooh-aahs.
How many people are enjoying this day as much as I am?
How many fireworks are there?
The show's as dazzling as the sun,
and sounds like an enormous bomb drop.
Ooh-aah,
Ooh-aah,
Ooh-aah.

Bennett Smith, Grade 5
EH Greene Intermediate School, OH

The Colors in Me

Part of me is devilish red…
    mad and angry,
    annoyed with the world
    yelling and shouting at everyone

But deep inside there's another part…
    ocean blue, like heaven above
    sweet and gentle,
    cheerful and happy
    loving the world.

Yes they're both real…and they're both me!!!

Mahalia Thomas, Grade 6
Abbott Middle School, MI

I Am

I am an athlete and nice
I wonder how my school year is going to be
I hear my classmates
I see Mrs. Barker
I want to be a teacher
I am an athlete and nice

I pretend to be a singer
I feel proud
I touch the sun
I worry that I am going to get sick
I cry when my heart is broken
I am an athlete and nice

I understand that I have to do homework
I say that I rock
I dream about having a pool
I try to do my homework
I hope to have a great life
I am Kayla Yonkos

Kayla Yonkos, Grade 4
Floyd Ebeling Elementary School, MI

The Pie

One time I was going to do a cheat,
Then I decided I was going to eat.
I took a dessert, which I call some pie
But it was for mom, not you or I
Then mom said "Did you take my pie?
Tell me the truth and please don't lie!"
I said, "It was aliens, they took it away,
But they might return it the very next day."
But she had known that I made a lie,
And I did take her apple cinnamon pie
So she said "You are going to pay,
So please rake the porch, clean it all away."
When I was done, I put away the rake
And then I went inside to take dad's chocolate cake.

Brendan Coffman, Grade 6
Ohio Virtual Academy, OH

Jaguar

Soaring on the road like a plane in the sky,
You glide smoothly and stealthily through the cold night air.
Your four wheels of fury make silent turns.
This is why you're mine!

You have two personalities,
One unlike the other.
You run through the jungle,
You glide across the road.
You run through bushes hunting your prey,
You fly over bumps day after day.
Your bite tears flesh,
But your seats heal wounds.
This is why you're mine
JAGUAR!

Sean Kwiatkowski, Grade 6
Harding Middle School, OH

If I Were a Pumpkin

If I were a pumpkin
I would taste pumpkin pie
I would be full of seeds
I would like to be picked from my patch
I would want to be stronger and bigger

If I were a pumpkin
I would make great pumpkin pie
I would wish fall stayed forever
I would love trick or treaters
I would listen for kids screaming
I would make great friends with scarecrows

Zachary Yohman, Grade 5
Reed Middle School, OH

I Am a Cranky Old Cat

I am a cranky old cat.
I'm so ugly I look like a rat.
Today, I was up in the house
When I saw a fat, juicy mouse.
I jumped at the mouse and it started to go.
I tried to chase it but I was too slow.
The mouse escaped through a crack in the floor.
That fat, juicy mouse was seen no more.
I fell asleep and loudly I snored.
Soon I was woken by a fat, juicy bird,
Singing the craziest song I'd ever heard.
Luckily the window was open a crack.
I thought I would finally get my snack.
As it sang the bird bounced,
Until finally I pounced.
Suddenly, I froze
As the window banged closed.
I caught a bird! Even better than trout!
But while catching that bird, I got locked out!

Alyssa Harvey, Grade 6
Crown Point Christian School, IN

Fall

Fall is here!
Let's give a cheer!
It's time to play,
Play every day!
Pull up your sleeves,
Jump into leaves,
Have a good time!
Let's all have a big time!
I love when fall is here
But I hate when winter is near!

Jordan Kemp, Grade 4
Chrisney Elementary School, IN

Christmas

Christmas
Joy to the world
Jesus was born today
Day to get a lot of presents
Thankful

Karsyn Zenor, Grade 4
Warren Central Elementary School, IN

Colors

Black is the color of the night.
Orange is very bright.

Brown is the color of my eyes.
Blue is the color of the skies.

Yellow is the color of the sun.
Pink is very fun.

Red is the color of jello.
Purple makes me mellow.

Green is like a frog.
Gray is the color of my dog.

What are colors to you?

Brittany Palowitz, Grade 6
Roosevelt Elementary School, OH

Silver Canoe

A silver canoe,
Floating down the gleaming lake,
Comes from the island.

Emilee Hernandez, Grade 6
Stanley Clark School, IN

Free Fall

Gripping metal rails,
Leaping into midair,
I plunge into water.

Leigh Van Ryn, Grade 6
Stanley Clark School, IN

Uncle Sam

Hat with a star
Very tall
Red, white, and blue
Standing on stilts
Wearing striped pants
Tall, thin, goatee
On posters for the army.
Fought in the Revolutionary War
Before he was Uncle Sam.
Sam Wilson.
Meat packer.
Lived in New York.
Starred in a cartoon.
Represents those who serve.
A hero.

Cailey Barnhart, Grade 4
Dobbins Elementary School, OH

Football

Locking on and never missing a tackle,
Interceptions and sacks all day long,
Defensive domination.
Throwing touchdowns,
No dropped passes and no interceptions,
Offensive domination.
Whether it's just passing with friends,
Or playing to be the champions,
I love playing football.

Avery White, Grade 6
Tri-West Middle School, IN

Chinese New Year

It's a new year in China,
And I get many treats.
I feel as happy as a graduate,
From my sugary eats.
I am indoors,
Outside is bright.
I feel as big as a tree,
In warm sunlight.
I hear some talk,
It's happy conversation.
My family is chatting,
They are full of jubilation.
I have some questions,
That I haven't answered.
Here are a few of them,
If you wondered.
Will the next year be a good one?
How is my family feeling?
These are some questions,
That I am asking.
I'm happy, happy, happy.

Jacob Wang, Grade 5
EH Greene Intermediate School, OH

Brisk Winter Day

Brisk cold nips my paws,
wind stings my face.
Damp fur doesn't help
me keep warm.

As I stare out into the white,
snow glistens under the moon.
Flakes fall in blankets
covering the world, my world.

The evergreens strain
to hold up the snow.
Flowers hide away
to wait out the cold.

Then I hear a distant laugh,
And a closer dog bark.
I scamper into my den
and sleep out the cold.

Brisk cold no longer nips,
wind no longer stings.
I no longer stare into the white,
but it will always come again.

Noah Aulicino, Grade 5
Central Grade School, MI

Things I Do to Be Responsible

Helping my grandparents
Looking, fixing, cooking
Helping my sisters clean
Taking care of my schoolwork
Studying without being told
Loving to read
Doing what my parents tell me
Without arguing
I'm responsible!

Zachary Jacobson, Grade 4
Dobbins Elementary School, OH

Sandy

S andy brown coat
A Golden Retriever
N ot a good listener
D isobedient dog
Y ear round she is loved on

Robin Flood, Grade 6
Sashabaw Middle School, MI

Nature

Nature is awesome
You can hunt animals there
You have lots of fun

Codey Roseberry, Grade 4
Westview Elementary School, OH

Christmas
Christmas will be here soon
Parents are working night shifts
To give their children gifts
Going to sleep happy to say
They're opening presents on Christmas day
Have a merry Christmas!
Ho ho ho!

Adrienne Hoar, Grade 5
West Washington Elementary School, IN

Spring
Birds sing and build nests!
Spring is fun for everyone!
Pretty flowers, too!

Sarah Olen, Grade 4
Eugene M Nikkari Elementary School, MI

I Have Won
I have won the race,
And it was very fun.
I have won trophies and more,
But everything is such a bore,
Because I've wanted more,
Than just score.
I have won so many times,
It's getting old like some sour limes.
It's not at all bad winning lots of races,
I get to visit lots of places,
And see lots of new faces.
It is fun to go there and there,
But because I might never lose and that won't be fair.

Luke Nachtegall, Grade 5
Auburn Hills Christian School, MI

How to Make a Perfect Cupcake
How to make a perfect cupcake,
there are many ways,
but the recipe that I like
is the one that I made up.

2 cups of flour
2 eggs
1 cup of sugar
2 tablespoons of vanilla
1 cup of milk
A stick of butter
A cup of love
2 pinches of fun
2 tablespoons of laughs
3 dashes of sweet
2 cups of hugs and
3 teaspoons of kisses
Mix it all up and you have
the perfect cupcake.

Aubrey Housand, Grade 4
Michiana Christian Montessori School, IN

Tornado
Tornado comes in rumbling
Like the enormous growl of a tiger.
It forms a spiral in the darkened sky
By the clouds somewhere dark and miserable.
Then it leaves, when not one person sees,
With only the evidence of the whispering wind.

Taryne Wenger, Grade 5
Wooster Christian School, OH

For the World
For all the trees
And the honeybees
For the birds that fly high in the sky
For the flowers that bloom for everyone to see
And for the fish that swim in the deep blue sea
For everyone to be happy
For the world, we shall be free

Carly Kwiecien, Grade 6
Kesling Middle School, IN

I Am
I am athletic and pretty
I wonder if I will be a professional soccer player
I hear me getting a goal to win the championship game
I see me going to New York medical school
I want to be a professional softball player
I am athletic and pretty

I pretend that I'm a professional soccer player
I feel that I'm competitive when I'm on the soccer field
I touch my future
I worry about getting bad grades
I cry when I get hurt
I am athletic and pretty

I understand why it is good to be nice
I say soccer is the best sport
I dream I get a good job
I try to do my best
I hope I get good grades
I am athletic and pretty

I am Princess Wells

Princess Wells, Grade 4
Floyd Ebeling Elementary School, MI

Roller Coaster
Burst into a hazy dark sky
Shatters the silence of the midnight atmosphere
Bright streaks of bright red flies past the stars
Always leaving something behind
Pops all nerves like a bag of popcorn
Causes an adrenaline rush
Finally there is a calm of nerves

Slaton Brummett, Grade 6
St Clement Elementary School, OH

Emma Ann I Miss

We all still cry, mostly her sister. Emma has passed away today. I still can't believe that she is gone. She was so cute, beautiful, and very young, just three months of life. And she was such a little hair ball. When she was born, she had a head full of it.
My baby cousin Emma was born December 29th. One year and a day after her brother. He loved her so much.
He would bend over and kiss her on the head. Emma would say "Ahh" or "Hee." Her sister called her "My Baby," and she was.
She was a baby to all of us.
Seeing her in that coffin the size of a cooler, a little cooler. It was heartbreaking. She looked like a baby porcelain doll.
She died of Sudden Crib Death.
Emma would always laugh and smile. She was such a happy little girl. I loved holding her in my arms.
Holding Emma was like hugging a pillow.
Emma Ann I miss you so.

Lucais Gutierrez, Grade 6
Winchell School, MI

Uranus

U ranus has an iron core that can get hotter than 4,000 degrees celsius.
R emember that Uranus also has a very icy and gassy surface. The surface made Uranus
A bsolutely impossible to live on. Scientists have seen Uranus very few times. The reason for this is that
N o Spacecraft or Voyager has been to it except for one which was the Voyager 2.
U ranus also lays on its side.
S ome people believe that Uranus lays like this because a meteor supposedly hit it and made it turn out that way.

Skye Montgomery, Grade 6
Pinewood Elementary School, IN

Virgo the Great

V irgo is a story of two women.
I n Greek mythology, Astraea or Astrea was a daughter of Zeus. That
R osey red bear that you see in the sky is one myth of Virgo. My
G reat opinion is that
O nce that bear was the shape of Virgo. Now she is a mother of a little cub that is the sky too.

Hannah Williams, Grade 6
Pinewood Elementary School, IN

The Forest Way of Life

Age is like the trees that just grow on for many years while getting bigger. Time is like a breezy wind because all it does is pass on by and sometimes, we don't even know it. Destiny is like a tiny seed that wanders across the land until finally, it gets buried in the ground and grows up with a very special purpose. Life is like everything in the forest because living or not, it has a special purpose and that is, to help everything else to have a purpose or to help it survive.

Cory Bishop, Grade 4
St Charles School, OH

Fall

My fingers touch a red gold leaf
The bark is like a foaming frothing sea
The trees are in a 5 neat row — they are strong, the steadfast sycamore
A golden-yellow tree like me
The neat-cut grass which we walk upon — the brown gold leaf litter the ground

The faded copper sundial which tells a story of the sun sits on a marble pedestal for all to see
The red brick building full of windows from which the longing faces stare outside the glory of mother sun

The tennis courts stand resolute from many matches won
A yellow-golden-brown leaf with green veins running through

This stands to be admired by all who do

August Bonacci, Grade 6
University Liggett School, MI

My Dream Place

After I fall asleep in bed.
Inside my head I dream that I'm in my dream place.
Outside my house I go over the mountains,
Between the trees, along the dirt road.
Near I see a pond I gather water
To bring it to the place I'm going.
Beneath the gravity.
Above the sky I know I'll have no trouble.
In heaven I'm home.

Samantha J. Lyons, Grade 5
Churubusco Elementary School, IN

Chocolate

Chocolate is so smooth and fine,
It's very sweet and so divine.

To the mouth a work of art,
It's so delicious from end to start.

In luscious flavors rich and light,
Like milk and dark and, of course, white.

But chocolate in all dismay,
When close to gone, just melts away.

So next time chocolate comes to pass,
Be sure you really make it last!

Serena Van Orman, Grade 5
Heritage Intermediate School, IN

Hunting Season

Winter is guaranteed the greatest season for me,
It's because of hunting day.
They call me big D,
Because I hunt every single way.

Deniro Faranso, Grade 5
Floyd Ebeling Elementary School, MI

Veteran's Day

Thank you for serving and defending our country.
You fought for our freedom,
and for that we will always be grateful.
Veteran's Day is a day we can honor and appreciate
all the men and women who served in the armed forces.
Some gave their lives for freedom,
others risked their lives to protect us.
Americans are very proud and thankful, and so am I
for all you have done to help our great country.
Even though our country is going through tough times,
I know you really love America as much as I do.
Your courage, strength, and patriotism has made this country
a better place for you, me, and millions of people.
I just wanted to say thank you for all your help
in making a difference in our great country and my life.

Samantha Ross, Grade 5
Beck Centennial Elementary School, MI

Halloween

Halloween is laughs and fun,
all night long we stop and run.
We run up the steps and jump on our feet
and ring the doorbell and say "trick or treat"
We get home and compare our booty,
and eat our lollipops, which taste quite fruity
We watch all the costumes that come to our door
and watch for candy that hits the floor
Sadly, we have to go to bed,
and look at all the candy that I will be fed.

Lucas Mata, Grade 6
West Middle School, MI

My Fun Crazy Life

Erica
Sporty, loving, and smart
Lover of hockey, shopping, and Aeropostale
Who feels nervous when I have to give a speech
    and at my hockey games
Who gets excited about going on vacation
    and getting to go on a shopping spree
Who needs to talk less and pay more attention in school
Who kisses my dog Riley
Who fears long snakes and big spiders
Who would like to live in New York City across from City Field,
    the home of the New York Mets.
Resident of Austintown, Ohio
Lehn

Erica Lehn, Grade 5
Frank Ohl Intermediate School, OH

Love

Love is a beautiful journey of the heart,
Love is unexplainable,
Love somehow completes you,
Love goes on every day, and never ends,
Love is an amazing and special feeling and emotion.

Love is perfect.

Helina Solomon, Grade 6
Woodward Park Middle School, OH

Winter Outside

I love when my mom makes hot chocolate.
It smells so good!
I like to shovel snow with my dad.
It is hard work!
Snow that sparkles like a crystal
Max is my dog
I love playing with him.
I like to play outside with my brother and sister
I also like to build stuff in the snow with my friends
I love sled riding with my family

Heidie Hall, Grade 4
Licking Valley Intermediate School, OH

Can You Imagine

Cars without wheels
bags without seals

letters without words
a sky without birds

a sea without sharks
a town without a park

a cup without a drink
money without a bank

a book without a title
a saddle without a bridle

a sky without a dove
a mom without love

Caroline Peters, Grade 4
Stonegate Elementary School, IN

Anger

Anger is not good
It is like a roaring fire
It's hot and burning
Kevin Krznar, Grade 6
Harmon Middle School, OH

Autumn

A utumn wind blowing hard.
U nusual dressing up.
T he leaves change colors
U ntil night comes.
M ore candy from trick-or-treat.
N o more hot weather.
Kaitlin Murray, Grade 6
Eisenhower Middle School, OH

Puppy Love

Sitting on their tails,
Hearing their whines and wails,
Barking, growling,
Panting, howling,
But begging never fails;
Chewing on chopping logs,
Chasing away first place hogs
Buying a beautiful brand-new cat,
Good riddance to all those dogs!
Hannah Novack, Grade 5
St Joseph Parish School, OH

Tether Ball at Camp

Hot sand in my toes
I see the ball fly at me
With intensity
Casey Crowley, Grade 6
Stanley Clark School, IN

The Skateboard Ramp

I rest on the top of the ramp —

I feel the hot rail against my hand.
H   H   H
O   O   O
T   T   T

I'm seven feet from the ground!
The ramp has white, black, and green skid marks.
So many eyes rest on me from the two ramps beside me.
I can feel the ramp's guide rail below, holding me in place.
I push down suddenly; I feel a burst of air, but nothing below me
only air.
BOOM!
My board hits the ground;
It feels like an earthquake below me.
I've done it: I've dropped in!

Joe Miller, Grade 5
Stanley Clark School, IN

Alien

Aliens are green like endoplasmic slime.
Aliens are hot like boiling water.
Aliens have a whooooosh sound like slow moving slime in a science lab.
Aliens taste fantastic like a caramel apple sucker.
Aliens smell bad like toxic waste.
Aliens are an unknown changing shape like an amoeba.
Aliens are slimy like half melted butter.

Robert Birkle, Grade 6
St Maria Goretti School, IN

Summertime

Day by day I walk along feeling the sun pound on me
like I was a magnet.

Walking along, I hear a roar as loud as an elephant getting shot.
I feel scared.

As I'm running along, I hear the rocks crackling beneath my feet.
I stop to hear if the monstrous beast was gone, it was.

Weaving through the trees as slow as a turtle I see all the magnificent bugs.
Some as small as an ant, some as dazzling blue as the ocean.

I've never seen a bug fly as fast as I did today.

That night I hear the crickets chirping so gracefully.
I fall asleep as fast as the average cheetah racing.

I awake to the morning birds chirping to the Blues Brothers.
Chirppity, chirp, chirrrp.

When I reach my house the sun is sparkling upon it
like a happily ever after fairy tale.

Christa Asbury, Grade 6
Cloverdale Middle School, IN

The Rainbow

The magnificent rainbow awakes the day
Bringing joy to the whole Earth
brings silence in the end.
Its enchanting colors of bright red, glowing green,
baby blue, orange, light purple.
Plays with thy clouds after a rainy afternoon.
Lightens the world and its surroundings.
Sits in the sky while the birds creep around it.
At the end everyone and everything is calm
like when flowers blossom and quiet
like when babies fall asleep.

Cassaundra Mierke, Grade 6
St Clement Elementary School, OH

Summer and Fall

Summer is a time to cheer,
For summer is coming early this year.
Summer is like the sun setting in the west,
Instead of playing in summer, in fall you have to take tests.
In fall you rake leaves and try new things,
But in summer you don't because you might sneeze.
Fall is the best time of year to ride your bike,
Or take short nature hikes.
In fall or summer you can catch some bait,
And maybe go fishing in the lake,
But just remember fall and summer are both great!

Ellen Kolb, Grade 6
St Michael School, IN

Halloween Night

It's finally Halloween night!
My costume is really quite tight.

I can see bats swarming out of caverns.
Don't forget your jack-o'-lanterns!

Werewolves howl in delight.
Aren't you glad it's finally the night?

Bones rattle from the midnight breeze.
Witches glide above the trees.

Winds moan through the graves.
Angry bears storm out of caves.

Clouds block the moon's shining light.
Ravens and hawks begin to take flight.

Children swarm across the neighborhood.
Someone's dressed as Little Red Riding Hood!

Look, is that the sun rising from the east?
Oh no, we have to end our Halloween feast!

Daniel Mathew, Grade 5
Browning Elementary School, MI

The Month of December

The nice frosty air in my face chilly but fine
Snowflakes falling from the dark night sky
Christmas lights light up like a star
The Christmas tree is decorated nice
White jolly snow on the ground
Snowflakes swirling around me
So icy and chilly I'm going to be frozen like a popsicle
So cozy drinking hot cocoa in the living room
Snowy and white so cold and delight
Pretty ornaments on the lovely tree
Time to open the presents from jolly old Saint Nick
Had so much fun celebrating the holidays

Bailey Bellish, Grade 5
Browning Elementary School, MI

Makayla Louise Shea

M aking crafts is my favorite hobby
A Great Dane/Boxer is my favorite type of dog
K ind is what I like to be to others
A sking questions is scary to me
Y ou would like me as a friend
L abeling my assignment book is confusing to me
A pples are my favorite fruit

L ol is my favorite abbreviation
O range is my fourth favorite color
U pside down is a funny word to me
I love to read
S inging is fun to me
E veryone tells me I am nice

S kating is what I do on Saturdays
H elping others is what I like to do
E veryone is usually nice to me
A good friend is what people describe me as.

Makayla Louise Shea, Grade 5
Frank Ohl Intermediate School, OH

Me, Myself, and I

Kelsie
Athletic, organized, smart
Sister of Isabella and Anthony
Lover of dancing, chocolate, and dogs
Who feels nervous when I get my grades back
and listening to sirens
Who gets excited about when I wake up on Christmas morning
and dance routines
Who needs to do my chores and practice my dance routines
Who gives kisses to my family and pets
Who fears clowns and spiders
Who would like to be a professional dancer
Resident of Austintown, Ohio
Diefenderfer

Kelsie Diefenderfer, Grade 5
Frank Ohl Intermediate School, OH

Monsters

Things are always watching.
Just out of sight.
Waiting!
Hiding!
Ready to take a bite!
Dean Evan Monnett, Grade 5
Cloverdale Middle School, IN

Football

The crack of two helmets
The slam of some pads
Your hands on the ball
You won't fall
Plow through the guy
With all your might
Don't go down without a fight
Score a touchdown
The crowd will cheer
So bring a win for all to hear
Jake Webb, Grade 6
St Michael School, IN

Perfect Little Island

What is Puerto Rico?
One of my favorite places
My first mission trip
A warm breezy beach
A rolling ocean with lots of waves
Tall palm trees with huge branches
A perfect little island
That's what Puerto Rico is!
Erica Hartman, Grade 6
Tippecanoe Middle School, OH

Alexis

A ffection
L ighthearted
E xtraordinary
X citing
I nsightful
S trong
Alexis Brown, Grade 4
Veale Elementary School, IN

Snowy Warmth

Outside in the snow
Around the fire
With my friends
Near New York
Beneath the night stars
In the park
Along the row of trees
Over the cities
Upon the lights
Chance Gallmeier, Grade 5
Churubusco Elementary School, IN

October Is:

When ghosts and ghouls roam the streets of my neighborhood,
demanding candy or else dry eggs stuck to your car in the morning,
paintballs on the wood siding of your house,
or your doorbell rang when there is no one there,

Teenagers and families sitting and waiting,
some eyes closed, some open,
bumping and rumbling up, down, up, down,

Creatures hiding in the corn,
waiting and watching your every move,

Vivid, sunset orange, golden, shimmering yellow,
crisp, crunchy brown, beneath towering, bald maples,

Radiant, orange sherbet, glowing, grinning faces
made gleamingly by a single slit of flame.
Adam Sieracki, Grade 5
Beck Centennial Elementary School, MI

The Fall Season

Fall is when the leaves fall freely from the tree.
Fall is when pumpkins are like orange basketballs in the summer.
The leaves are as colorful as bright, shining rainbows in the sky.
The rainbow leaves sparkle from the trees
Sparkle, sparkle, sparkle
The leaves tumble down from the branches
Down, down, down
The leaves sadly embark on their journey to death,
Awaiting new life in the spring.
I love the fall season.
Joshua Dorion, Grade 6
Holy Family Middle School, MI

Horses and the Wind

The wind is a horse.
The wind gallops through the sky on bare hooves, risking the stings upon his face.
It chases and dashes swiftly with you upon it,
Taking people on an ecstatic, and bumpy ride.
They both hold their heads high with
Greatness
And
Pride
The wind is very powerful; its force strong and might.
It whispers to the trees as it passes by.
It needs its rest in a stable after a hard day.
Both roll into the grass as the wind blows a big breath onto it.
It can pick you up and bring you to wonderful, different places.
Both are speedy whooshing past you so invisible so unlifelike,
They stand alone, mighty and strong.
Both live free in the wild,
Both have no fear of anything.
The wind swishes its mane over the world stating
I am the king.
June Wilson, Grade 6
Harding Middle School, OH

My Perfect Morning

I'm walking on the muddy ground, as brown as the brown hair on the old mare.
In front of me, a red barn towers over *everything*, dripping rain on my forehead.
I turn my face up into the rain, so white, so pure, so see-through.
To the right of me, I see my pig, Gabby, and my sister's horse, Bella, which means beautiful.
Her mane is a glossy brown, a result of my sister's brushing every day.
A scowl takes my face hostage:
Bella is stamping her feet on the ground, spraying me with mud. Gross!
I'm not sure I want a horse anymore.
In the far left of the barn, my redheaded friend, giggling, scribbles in her journal.
Adrianna, my friend, what are you doing here? I say silently in my mind.
She was *supposed* to leave after our sleepover. Anyway…
I take a breath. The air is sweet, like it always is after it rains.
I look up to the sky and see a beautiful double rainbow.
As I head to do my chores, I braid my hair and pin it up.
I hate the feel of my hair on my neck while I work.
Something brushes my ankle, and I jump.
I look down, and my cat Emma is brushing against my legs, marking me with her love.
Another simple, perfect morning.
I turn to face the rising sun and smile.

Sydney Matthys, Grade 5
Stanley Clark School, IN

My Friend the Spider

He started as a sack worm that looked just like his mom.
He turned into a big brown bug. He was as happy as the sun.
His favorite foods to eat were old corn nuts and berries
So he would grow big and tall like the tree in the sun.
He would sleep in a dead tree that has fallen in the weeds.
The wind moved it back and forth so it looked like a boat in the sea.
He covered himself with leaves that he found under an old pine tree.
It was covered with moss all over the trunk that makes him think of his old friendly pop.
His favorite thing to do was loop through the thorns just like the maypole at the fair.
He loved to jump up and down on the spider web. It was just like a trampoline in the air.
But his favorite thing to do when he got home was to shut his eyes and wait for that morning dew.

Miranda Williams, Grade 6
Cloverdale Middle School, IN

I Am Not Just Some Girl

I am not just some girl. I have a heart, and I dream, and like everyone I can cry out a stream.
I love arts, especially dance…where I can be myself without needing a second chance.
Where I can give it all I got, without being on the spot.
I go to school, where my friends are my life.
What it means to share happy memories well you'd have to know how much they care.
How much they really, really try, to keep my eyes not wet but dry.
How much everyone loves me, is too high to rate.
I can't wait to see my family who have passed through that heaven gate.
I know when I die, I will surely be missed, I am loved that much is kind of obvious.
My mom is my best friend. I can tell her everything, and she makes sure I am happy and safe.
She makes me laugh in the weirdest ways.
Whether it is trying to or not, it works, and I think of those happy memories for days.
People who know me know that I love to make people laugh.
They know that I see their inside before their outside and their personality before popularity.
I love everyone that makes me smile…It makes living kind of worthwhile…
I AM NOT JUST SOME GIRL!

Erin Gries, Grade 6
Abbott Middle School, MI

I Am a Mountain

I am a huge mountain.
Mountain lions step on me.
It hurts so badly I wish I could crumble.
But mountains must stand.
Strong and tall.

Jarett Saunders, Grade 5
Westview Elementary School, OH

Baseball

I am a ball
I get hit by a bat
I'm white and red sometimes
I am a sport
What am I?
Baseball!

Zach Stirn, Grade 5
St Michael School, IN

Chief

I have a dog named Chief.
He's a little thief.
He takes my stuff.
He says "Ruff."
Sometimes he can be a pain.
We even put him on a chain.
I love him to death,
But sometimes he has bad breath.
We play catch.
He can fetch.
Sometimes we fight,
The whole night.
Although he can be a brat,
I love him and that is that.

Samantha Cialdella, Grade 6
St John the Evangelist School, IN

Flowers

Flowers can be big
Flowers can be small
Flowers can be skinny
Flowers can be tall
Flowers can be ugly
Flowers can be pretty
Flowers can come in bundles
Flowers can come single
Flowers can come in
A billion different colors
Flowers can be plain
Flowers can be amazing
A flower could be
A daffodil or a flower
Could be a rose
But nobody knows

Stephanie Ovreset, Grade 6
St Gerard School, MI

Strider

S illy
T ense
R acing
I nstinct
D awning
E nergetic
R emarkable!

Harlee Fuetter, Grade 5
Cloverdale Middle School, IN

Barrel Racing

A galloping horse.
Barrel racing in an arena.
Can hardly wait to see her time.
Dancing around like a ballerina.
Her time is 13.7 seconds!

Bethany Fritts, Grade 5
Wooster Christian School, OH

Dancing

Dancing is like floating like clouds
Like wings on a butterfly
Hop, kick, skip, and wiggle
Make it up as you go

Dance is free you see
Dance is your emotions
Dance your heart
Just dance…

Leanna Campos, Grade 4
Red Cedar School, MI

Snow Days

S now
N ever not fun
O ff days are best
W ill be fun

D one working
A wesome
Y eah no school
S now will be high

Conner Novak, Grade 4
Northfield Elementary School, OH

I Love Puppies

P layful
U nhurtful
P etable
P atient (sometimes)
I ndulged
E nthusiastic
S o cool!

Carly Zunt, Grade 4
Sts Joseph and John School, OH

Band/Strings

Band
noisy, big
playing, performing, practicing
instruments, audience, bows, notes
plucking, bowing, tuning
fun, advanced
Strings

Davawnna Clark, Grade 5
Norwich Elementary School, OH

Writing a Poem

So many good ideas,
All flowing out of your mind.
Now it's time to pick one,
You're running out of time!
Should it flow nicely and rhyme?
Or should I write quickly,
There's not much time!
Finally, I got one,
That was easy.
I hope it impresses Mrs. Bertolini!

Alex Plantus, Grade 6
Abbott Middle School, MI

Sister

P retty
A ngel
I ntelligent
G enerous
E xcellent

S ensitive
I mportant
S weet
T errific
E nergy
R espectful

Paige Johnson, Grade 5
Becker Elementary School, OH

Rain

Rain comes falling down
he just lays there on the ground
wishing the rain will stop.

Zona Allen, Grade 6
Harmon Middle School, OH

The Bridge

All the scattered leaves,
Colors — anything but green.
Finally fall's here!
Warm weather's cooling down now,
Autumn, the bridge to winter.

Natalie Fowler, Grade 5
Westview Elementary School, OH

I Am

I am talented and fun.
I wonder what fish are going to look like in the future.
I see chickens playing poker.
I see a gangster chimpanzee.
I want to fix our four wheeler because my dad broke it.
I am talented and fun.
I pretend I'm a photographer.
I feel sad about my poker chicken losing his chips!
I touch the imaginary fat sumo wrestler monkey squirrel.
I worry about global warming.
I cry about my uncle Joe.
I am talented and fun.
I understand politics a little bit.
I say that we'll continue to stay free.
I dream about photography.
I am talented and fun.

Justin Goodwell, Grade 6
Galesburg-Augusta Middle School, MI

The Marker

I am an erasable marker.
I work on a very big board
I can make words, numbers and even a sword.
My tracks get taken off with an eraser or wipe,
I can fall down a sink, or even a pipe.
I can record games, grades, and even sports
I can make cats, dogs and other sorts.
My tip can get pushed way down
I can write verbs, adjectives, and even a noun.
I come in red, blue, and even green
I can write stuff that's cool, nice, and even mean.
I can work on any kind of board,
Unless it's made of wood, paper or even one with a cord.
I know all kinds of stencils
My friends are crayons, markers and most of all pencils.

Quin Van Proyen, Grade 6
Crown Point Christian School, IN

What if the World…

What if the world was upside down?
What if the world was ruled by crowns?

What if the world was all the way flat?
What if the world was made out of bats?

What if the world was made with no gravity?
What if the world had no infinity?

What if the world was dyed hot pink and green?
What if the world had no people that were lean?

What if the world had money on trees?
Would there be such a thing as poetry?

Kavya Ravichandran, Grade 5
Birchwood School, OH

What Moves Me

W ind passing through
H ow people smile
A baby animal just born
T he world moves me

M illions of sites to see
O r maybe millions of places to go
V oting for someone to lead the USA
E ven someone to lead the city
S erious it moves me

M illions of people being born every minute
E veryone has something that moves them

Clifton Snow III, Grade 4
Highview Elementary School, OH

For the Veterans

To all the soldiers that gave their lives,
For fighting in a war with no one by their sides.
For showing courage, bravery and strength,
For going without food for enormous lengths,
We are ever grateful.

To all the families that lost a member,
Due to a battle you will always remember.
For going through pain we will never know of,
For losing someone you so desperately loved.
We are not forgetful.

To all the children left alone,
Their parents may not be returning home.
The children's thoughts are taunted with nightmares of worry,
For letting their parents go, they are sorry.
They are still regretful.

To all the veterans living or dead,
Your hearts are full of pride or dread.
For fighting so bravely with so little to gain,
In wind, snow, hail and rain.
We are ever thankful.

Clara Chuey, Grade 6
EH Greene Intermediate School, OH

Waterfall

W ater pours off a cliff
A mazingly beautiful when the sun shines on the water
T here are big waterfalls and little waterfalls
E xtremely dangerous
R aging waters
F antastic to watch
A ll water pouring down hard
L ocks are made to get boats on the other side of a waterfall
L oud splishes and splashes can be heard

Jacob Roza, Grade 4
Keystone Academy, MI

I Am

I am funny and smart.
I wonder, what's in the galaxy?
I hear the world screaming with war.
I see the world not fighting.
I want $100,000,000.
I am funny and smart.
I pretend to be in the NFL.
I feel happy when I win the lottery.
I touch a green dog.
I worry when I don't hear from family.
I cry when a relative dies.
I am funny and smart.
I understand where Asia is.
I say the world is small.
I dream to be in the NFL.
I try to do my best.
I hope for my family to be healthy.
I am funny and smart.

Dale Torrey, Grade 6
Galesburg-Augusta Middle School, MI

Happiness Is...

Happiness is...

Happiness is pink
It smells like cake baking
It looks like a rainbow
It tastes like chocolate ice cream
Happiness feels like seeing your
    best friend that you haven't seen
    for three years.

Lauren Santus, Grade 6
Eisenhower Middle School, OH

I Am

I am cute and helpful
I wonder if I will be a famous dancer
I hear big crashing waves
I see seashells
I want to catch up on my work
I am cute and helpful

I pretend to be a mom and a teacher
I feel the wind in my hair
I touch my heart
I worry about my family
I cry when someone in my family dies
I am cute and helpful

I say there is a God
I dream about my family
I try to do my best in school
I hope for all my wishes to come true
I am Sydney Ann Bacic

Sydney Ann Bacic, Grade 4
Floyd Ebeling Elementary School, MI

Fall

Fall's leaves resemble the bright, blaze orange on a hunter's vest.
Fall's cold wind rips through the thin and frail branches of the dying trees.
Fall's animals walk along the hard, barren ground
searching for any leftover food that hasn't died or been eaten.
Fall's clouds are dark and gray
they usually send sprinkles of rain plummeting to the earth.
Fall's trees droop down at the ground
like they're looking at their fallen leaves that were on their branches not too long ago.

Jonathan Cochran, Grade 6
St Maria Goretti School, IN

A Letter to Mom

Dear Mom,
    Don't bother coming in my room to wake me up for school
because I can't write, so what would be the point of going?
I also can't speak, hear, or read. I think this might be the outcome
of a contagious disease. Wait! Today is pizza day! Never mind!

Signed,
Fred

Carly Stults, Grade 5
Michiana Christian Montessori School, IN

Seneca Native Americans

Seneca natives had three sisters: corn, squash, and beans.
They are part of the 5 nations.
Nearly 10,000 Seneca natives live on the reservation in western New York
They live in Salamanca, New York
Occupied territory from the Genesee River to the Ganandaigua Lake
The most important leader was Red Jacket (a man)

Felicia Densmore, Grade 6
Erie Elementary School, OH

Berry Picking

In Princeton, Pennsylvania, last year,
I went with my cousin Timmy to an orchard.
I stopped in one of the columns of trees that looked like soldiers,
as we walked to the strawberry fields.
We bent low to pick some strawberries,
I looked sideways, past strangers picking and laughing:
everything came together,
Everything depended on the warmed fruits and the trees in the orchard.
That was the best day of my life.

Matt Rush, Grade 5
Stanley Clark School, IN

A Poem

A jumble of words
Meaningless sentences
A project from someone's soul
But in those meaningless sentences a beautiful meaning is born
Nothing just nothing can overcome the beauty of those jumbled words
Meaningless sentences that projects from someone's soul
A poem is something special, something sweet to make people melt at their knees

Katie Paull, Grade 6
Rocky River Middle School, OH

Chocolate

Chocolate.	Chocolate
	I hate it!
I love it!	
	Too sweet.
Very yummy.	Makes you fat.
Kind of healthy.	
	Cavities
We got dentists.	
Chocolate.	Chocolate.
Get some more.	
	Throw it away.
Good.	Gross.
Tempting.	
	Revolting
Chocolate.	Chocolate

Kelly Chian and Tina Hohman, Grade 5
Tremont Elementary School, OH

Basketball Star

This morning I played a game of basketball
I liked it until I hit the wall;
I shot and shot until I scored,
And then noticed a point on the board!
Then I became a super star
Time to buy a brand new car
Now it's time to try a different sport
Maybe something on a different court.

Sophie Carson, Grade 5
St Joseph Parish School, OH

A Garden of Mystery

My eyes look left to right,
In search of the mystery
That lies in the garden.
My ears are shaken up
By the sound of a babbling brook,
Hitting a piece of wood that is hardened by nature's look.
The leaves fall from their trees.
The air is filled with the sound of honey bees.
Oh! Where are my car keys?
Oh! There they are right next to the water fountain,
Running into my garden's maple tree
Filled with bees.
A garden of mystery.

Nikola Ilic, Grade 6
St John the Baptist Elementary School, IN

Horses

Horses are so soft.
They are helpful too.
If you ever ride they are there for you.
Through rain through snow they will be on your side.
They love to be brushed and love to eat grain.
When they trot it sounds like rain to me.
I love my horses.

Taylor Shepler, Grade 4
Licking Valley Intermediate School, OH

Summer

S wimming all day.
U mbrellas you may need to block the sun
M elting ice cream on your face
M ay drink a lot of ice cold lemonade and
E veryone would love it to be cooler.
R eally fun days

Skylar Parker, Grade 5
Perry Central Elementary School, IN

The Cat

There once was a very dumb cat.
Who was sitting on a mat
A mouse ran in the door.
Chased it down the floor.
And caught it with his very large mat.

Jacob Burress, Grade 5
North Knox East Elementary/Jr High School, IN

The Spectacular Super Chihuahua

I got a new Chihuahua for my birthday.
My dog scratches my back when it's really itchy
"Oww," too hard
"No," don't eat my food
When are you going to bed? Go now
Let's take you a bath! Where are you hiding?
If you come I will give you a treat
A doggy treat! Bacon
It's really fun to have you here
Don't tell her! Not!

Nancy Zarazua, Grade 4
Churubusco Elementary School, IN

2008 Saleen

I hear the 500 horsepower engine
Smooth leather seats are warm,
Bright red paint job stands out
Glass roof sun shining through.
I feel the solid cold stick shift
The sweet 302 burble shaker revving up…
ZOOOOOOOM!!!!
130 mph down the highway
2008 #15 Saleen.

Logan Dore, Grade 4
Midland Academy of Advanced and Creative Studies, MI

Winter

W inter is my favorite season
I always go snow mobiling
N ever have I gotten hurt
T ara and I love snow mobiling
E very time, I go the fastest
R arely do I tip

Trista Finch, Grade 5
Rootstown Elementary School, OH

My New Volleyball

I got a new volleyball
When I went to the mall
I practice a lot
When it is hot
I have a bad serve
It gets on my coach's last nerve.

Danielle Seward, Grade 6
Immanuel Christian School, MI

November...

is the season for picking ice shards
as cold as the cruel witch's heart,
but the hot chocolate
as hot as the fire within your soul
will warm her up,
a time for picking apples
from the skeleton that used to be a tree,
a time for eating turkey, gravy, and jell-o
a time when ghosts, ghouls, and witches
return to their resting place
until next year when they'll haunt again.

Jack Tanner, Grade 5
Beck Centennial Elementary School, MI

Sunset on an Autumn Afternoon

the wind blows around
it ruffles my short dark hair
I heave a long sigh

Chloe Fellmeth, Grade 5
St Jude Catholic School, IN

Marsh Roamers

What does a moose know?
Bit soft brown noses,
Long wide velvety antlers,
Delicate slender hoofed legs,
Powerful kicks!
What is the softest bark to eat,
How to not be hunted for their meat,
The edge of conifer forests,
The biggest and the soggiest marshes,
The harshest storms,
People in swarms.

Veronica Nehasil, Grade 5
Riley Upper Elementary School, MI

God Is Good

God is always here,
When I'm not near.
He always gives me cheer,
When I sometimes fear.
Sometimes in the silence,
I wonder why there is violence.
God makes me feel good,
Like I always should.
I feel His presence everywhere,
I feel Him in the air.
I love Him in my heart,
I do not want to part.
God is good and kind,
He is always on my mind.

Corey Matthews, Grade 5
St Jude Catholic School, IN

Playground

I can picture myself at age four
playing outside on a hot summer day:
behind me I can see a playground —
the slide yellowish orange —
and I can hear those running kids
screaming like crows in the air.
I can still smell the spices
of the juicy hot dogs and hamburgers
over the grill.
I can still taste the hamburger.

Connor VanDeventer, Grade 5
Stanley Clark School, IN

If You Want to Be Me

If you want to be me
You have to be strong
You have to be wrong
You have to be smart
And love with your heart
You have to be wise
Keep friends on your side
And if you feel sorrow
Remember it's today not tomorrow
You have to have faith
You have to have hope
To live a life full of jokes
You have to have happiness
You have to believe
In your highest aspirations and dreams
You have to wear a smile
If only for a while
You have to have friends
That are there till the end
You have to live free
If you want to be me.

Allison Alexander, Grade 6
Miller City-New Cleveland School, OH

Deer, Deer

Deer, deer everywhere.
Bucks here, bucks there.

Get your gun case key.
Spray on some doe pee.

Shoot your buck Bam! Bam! Bam!
Down he goes Slam! Slam! Slam!

Isn't that neat?
Free fresh meat.

Gaige Schaefer, Grade 5
Perry Central Elementary School, IN

Spirit Bear

Bear so white, bear so white,
You seem to disappear from sight.
Bear so white, bear so white,
Your fur always shines in light.
Bear so white, bear so white,
I dream about you every night.
Bear so white, bear so white,
When I see you I take off in flight.
Bear so white, bear so white,
When you're here my face glows bright.

Becca Seeds, Grade 6
Harmon Middle School, OH

Minnows

Darting circles,
Creek dwellers,
Tiny fish,
Prey to snakes.
Predators to water striders,
Swimming over rocks,
Over and under,
Side to side,
Everywhere,
Swimming in unison!

Oscar Istas, Grade 4
Normandy Elementary School, OH

Conquer Fears

I used to be afraid of heights,
And dark and really scary nights.
Old ladies that mumble,
Lions and tigers in the jungle,
Mosquitoes that bite, bees that sting.
It seems I was afraid of everything.
But then on a dark and scary night,
I knew I had to conquer my frights.
So I closed my eyes, like I didn't care,
And then, guess what! I wasn't scared.

Justice Hiser, Grade 5
Spaulding Elementary School, OH

Volcano

The volcano awoke form its long deep sleep,
As quietly as a mouse,
It yawned drowsily,
A black puff of ash and smoke came from its mouth,
The volcano found something missing,
It roared with anger,
It exploded with rage and fury,
Showering numerous objects,
The volcano became sleepy,
And it went into another long slumber.

Lawrence Wu, Grade 6
Boulan Park Middle School, MI

Things That Are Quiet

A deer that is resting
A mouse that is running
Rain that is falling
A silent cemetery in the moonlight
A clock that is ticking
Midnight on the beach
The flow of water on a stream
A beach at sunset
The ocean waves going back and forth
Snow falling at Christmas time
Jack-o'-lanterns glowing in the Halloween night
Summer days in the sun
Leaves falling in autumn
Eyes that are staring
Little kids sleeping on Christmas night
Early morning winter
A boat rocking on the waves
People typing on a computer
Grass blowing in the wind

Anna Whitaker, Grade 6
Sanderson Elementary School, OH

Friendship

Friendship is understanding.
Friendship is having someone on your side.
Friendship is never being lonely.
Friendship is fun times.
Friendship is having someone to play a game.
Friendship is never the same.
Friendship is someone who understands you.
Friendship is someone who likes you for who you are.
Friendship is having someone wait for you.
Friendship is having someone to help you.
Friendship is trusting someone.
Friendship is caring for each other.
Friendship is spending time with each other.
Friendship is having someone to talk to.
Friendship is having someone to share with.
Friendship is understanding.

Carter Gadola, Grade 6
St Gerard School, MI

Goldie My Beautiful Fish

My fish Goldie was orange.
She swam in her little round bowl all day long, happy as ever.
Goldie felt free in her little round bowl.
Goldie shined as bright as the sun.
She glimmered like the stars in the sky.
I will never forget my Goldie girl.

Grace Wielhouwer, Grade 5
Kenowa Hills Intermediate School, MI

Cold/Hot

Cold
Frigid, icy
Snowing, freezing, shoveling
Snowball fights, winter, summer, sun tanning
Burning, sizzling, roasting
Muggy, steamy
Hot

Austin Mohler, Grade 6
Pike Delta York Middle School, OH

Four Little Girls

Can you imagine one of your kin,
Being killed because of colored skin.
But the worst would be yet to come,
The police let it go as if no harm had been done!

What would you do, what would you do?
If that sadness was given to you
Do you say, "I'm glad that's not me?"
Because it happened in Birmingham, 1963

The 15th of September, 4 little girls died
After the church bombing, their families cried
Alas, four who ran were not fast enough
Then they fell, and to get out was tough

The police knew who'd done it
But they didn't care a bit
Then the FBI came in
And didn't do a thing

They took 14 years to find a single person
By this time the families were shouting and cursin'
So take some time to think about these precious lives
As you go home to your families and your wives.

Divya Goel, Grade 6
Detroit Country Day Middle School, MI

Smile

A beautiful gift upon your face,
From a giggle or remark or a sign of joy.
Upon every day a discovered laugh or a bit of a grin,
Just above your chin.

Haley Wirth, Grade 5
Washington Township Elementary School, IN

Sparkly Night

perfectly still snow web
engulfing many a moon

perfectly still snow web
it will be gone by noon

perfectly still snow web
landing in a glen

perfectly still snow web
soon it may be spun again

Noah Razzone, Grade 5
Central Grade School, MI

Thanksgiving

T hanksgiving Day is coming
H arvesting turkeys
A ll kinds of them
N ear home while I hunt
K ind of hiding while I'm hunting
S o I can find food
G oing back home
I n the warm house because it's
V ery cold outside
I t's getting nearer to the holiday
N earer to a big feast
G et ready!

Cynthia Fraze, Grade 5
Perry Central Elementary School, IN

Jump

Jump up high
Jump down low
Jump real quick
Jump really slow.

Jump during recess
Jump in your dreams
Jump while you whisper
Jump while you scream.

Jump all night
Jump all day
Jump tomorrow
And jump today!

Hajira Afreen, Grade 5
Birchwood School, OH

I'm Finished

I have been beaten for the last time
They treat me like I am worth a dime
This has been the last day
Tonight I run away
They will act like I have done a crime

Morgan VonHolle, Grade 6
Mayfield Elementary School, OH

Veteran's Day

A holiday serving those who served in our armed forces,
Those who served way back then when they rode on horses,
Or these days when they drive in tanks
To these people, we give our thanks,
Those of the living, and those of the dead,
This experience will forever stay in their heads,
Those who served in peace, and served in war,
Parades and speeches, and ceremonies celebrate these people too,
Ones that you don't know and ones that you loved, and they loved you.
Those of the dead, who served in our military,
Will be visited in their cemeteries,
They went through years of seeing people fall to their death,
Every minute they wonder if this is their last breath,
And for years they were protecting us,
To survive courage is a must,
During this time they suffered pain
They even fought when it was pouring rain,
 They couldn't experience any fun,
But their job was to keep our country one,
So we shall give our thanks to all of thee,
For risking their lives to protect you and me.

Philip Silverman, Grade 6
EH Greene Intermediate School, OH

Christmas Morning

Outside snow is falling gently,
on the already white ground.
Inside the dark house,
only the evergreen twinkles with lights
and gleams with colorful ornaments.
Darkness begins to give way to dawn,
as Christmas morning arrives.
The sky turns from black to gray to pink as the sun rises.
A slight breeze blows, rustling frosty branches.
Birds begin to chirp, singing their own carols.
Blue jays seem to ask, "Was Santa here?"
Squirrels chatter to everyone they can,
"When will the children come out to play in all this snow?"
"When will everybody wake up?" the deer wonder silently to each other.
The green arms of the tree beckon the children of the house
to find the rainbow of presents arranged underneath it.
Everyone in the house is sleeping as soundly as a rock,
but suspense hangs in the air as they rise.
Their thoughts turn from sleepiness to growing excitement as they realize
Christmas morning is here! Christmas morning is here! Christmas morning is here!

Maya Sheth, Grade 5
EH Greene Intermediate School, OH

Green

Green is the sound of a meadow lark singing in the park.
Green is the taste of a sour green apple.
Green is the scent of mint in the evening.
Green is the color of life and peace.
Green is the feeling of victory when you have just finished a poem.

Mariah Tiano, Grade 6
Wooster Christian School, OH

Moon

M ercury is a hot planet
O n Earth they have become heroes
O ne astronaut, Michael Collins, stayed on the Columbia
N eil Armstrong was the first man to step on the moon.

Tristan Morris, Grade 4
Westview Elementary School, OH

My Grandma Joan

You died when I was only young
You used to make me cereal and a honey bun.

I roamed the house naked, wow! What a sight
I wouldn't change my diaper, without a fight.

I really did love you Grandma Joan
Whenever you baby-sat you would never moan.

When you passed away
It was a very bad day.

Chelsey, Devin, and I were very sad.
The room was quiet. No one was glad.

That's Grandma Joan, and I love you
I wish she could come back for you to know her too.

Anthony D. Aiken, Grade 6
Trilby Elementary School, OH

Pain

Pain is red like blood gushing from a wound.
It is like the fire of the blazing sun.
Pain reminds me of the time I plunged through a glass table.
It makes me feel achy.
Pain bolts through the body.
It makes me want to vomit.

Ryan O'Hara, Grade 6
St Maria Goretti School, IN

Kids Christmas

Sleigh bells ring on Christmas night,
while children are tucked away in their beds.
They stay so warm on this joyful night,
while Santa is flying around.

Laying presents under the tree,
Santa is filled with joy.

The next morning he flies off saying,
Ho! Ho! Ho! Merry Christmas.

The children are filled with happiness,
when they see what they have got,
and thank Mr. Santa very, very much.

Dane Craker, Grade 5
Central Grade School, MI

Me, Myself, and I

Mikayla
Smart, caring, organized
Sister of Molly and Megan
Lover of dogs, chocolate and cats
Who feels nervous when I talk in front of the class
    and when I hear about a tornado.
Who gets excited about when I wake up on Christmas morning
    and when I see my cousins
Who needs to do homework and chores
Who gives kisses to Mom, Dad and dog
Who fears tornadoes and clowns
Who would like to be a veterinarian
Resident of Canfield, Ohio
MacLochlan

Mikayla MacLochlan, Grade 5
Frank Ohl Intermediate School, OH

God's Beautiful Creation

When you hear the birds outside,
You hear the wind whistling
And you don't know what's going through your mind.
Listen to the soothing music of grass,
Don't want to hear anything else,
Not even the chimes of glass,
So when you hear the birds outside,
You hear the wind whistling,
And you don't know what's going through your mind.
Let it be,
And listen to God's beautiful creation.

Shannon Ferrier, Grade 5
St Ignatius School, OH

Penguins

I'm black
I'm white
I sometimes bite
But I'm a friendly flightless bird
I fly through the water
To catch some squid
With speed you've never seen
I perform a high dive
With grace you've never seen
I earn a perfect ten
I much enjoy being a penguin.

Nathan White, Grade 6
North Knox East Elementary/Jr High School, IN

Chloe

She is from **C** hina.
She is **H** appy and full of energy.
She **L** ikes to play.
O ver all she loves us a lot.
E ventually she will grow tall.

Austin Cowen, Grade 5
St Michael School, IN

The Bike

Daddy! Daddy!
Look at this bike;
It's just like Cousin Mike's.
I need it.
It's blue.
I'm sure, and it really is true
Look! My shoes would match it, too.
Oh, please do get it for me.
Do! Do! Do!

Rebekah Page, Grade 5
Rochester Hills Christian School, MI

In the Woods

As I am walking,
The animals pass by me,
And I am happy.

David Popoola, Grade 6
Stanley Clark School, IN

Happiness

Happiness is red
It smells like apple blossoms
It looks like fall colors
It sounds like the wind
Happiness feels like it's the
Happiest day of your life.

Jarod Jacobs, Grade 6
Eisenhower Middle School, OH

I'm Sorry

I'm really sorry Jarret
for eating your cake.
It smelled *sooo* good.
I couldn't resist.

If only it wasn't cheesecake,
with icing on top.

So next time you buy cake
make it chocolate.

P.S. I like chocolate cake too!

Yang Yang Ye, Grade 5
Tremont Elementary School, OH

Blue

Blue looks like the sky.
Blue sounds like a little blue bird.
Blue smells like flowers in a meadow.
Blue tastes like a blueberry pie.
Blue feels like soft silk.
Blue is like a huge ocean.
And blue is sad or happy.

Eric Buehler, Grade 6
Wooster Christian School, OH

Cookies

Chocolate chip cookies
Peanut butter cookies
And Snickerdoodle cookies

Cookies…Cookies…Cookies

So many to choose from
I'll take them all
Leave not even a crumb

Travis Miller, Grade 5
Heritage Intermediate School, IN

Fall All Over Again

Freezing frost fills the air
trembling kids everywhere
whistling wind
shimmering chimes
scary signs, ghosts arrive
feel the gooey
pumpkin seeds
carved pumpkins, here and there
"BOO"
goes a scare
twisting and turning branches swaying
leaves disintegrating down
brimstone, brunet, crimson
even lilac
creamy pumpkin pie
scrumptious cinnamon donuts
caramel apples on a stick
and finish it off with
a sip of apple cider YUM!

Alexis Van Horn, Grade 5
Riley Upper Elementary School, MI

Boo!

candy
houses
booing, scaring
trick-or-treating
fun stuff
scary stuff
booing stuff
Boo!

Connor Karman, Grade 4
Norwich Elementary School, OH

Puppy

Puppy
Cute, lovable
Running, sleeping, whining
A cute lovable dog
Boxer

Aly Suida, Grade 4
Floyd Ebeling Elementary School, MI

The Snowflake Dances

As the snowflake falls
It drifts slowly
Smiling, having a ball
As they look down
They see it's very snowy

All kinds of dances
Dancing all around
Dancing, dancing, dancing
Until they hit the ground

Getting near the ground
Saying bye to all their friends
Missing everybody all around
Finally there to an end

Allexis Weaver, Grade 6
Woodward Park Middle School, OH

Skating

Onto the swift ice,
Along the boards,
Among the other skaters,
Across the center line,
Around the corner,
Past the penalty box,
With graceful moves,
Between the other skaters,
From one side to the other,
I skate.

Jay Gramlich, Grade 6
Harmon Middle School, OH

Christmas

C is for the things we cherish
H is for home and family
R is for the respect we have
I is for the irreplaceable love we have
S is for sisterhood
T is for the time we share
M is for my mother and our love
A is for all the time we spent together
S is for the sister and motherhood

Edaja Johnson, Grade 6
Eastmoor Middle School, OH

Grandmas

Helping grandmas
Working grandmas
Kind grandmas
Pretty, smart, loving grandmas
Cuddly, skinny, baking grandmas
Last of all, best of all
Grandmas

Hannah Denney, Grade 5
St Jude Catholic School, IN

Tyler Howell

T yler is my genius name
Y oung professional basketball fan
L oves Indiana University basketball
E leven years old and loves it
R unning on water is my dream

H orrific is my "middle name"
O ranges make me wild
W ords like "wimp" make me angry
E very summer day is an adventure to me
L ucky as an Irish man
L oves to see a Pacers game

Tyler Howell, Grade 5
Perry Central Elementary School, IN

I Am

I am smart and sweet.
I wonder who the first author was.
I hear kids playing when there's no kids playing at all.
I see ghosts.
I want a microphone to practice singing.
I am smart and sweet.
I pretend I'm actually listening to someone.
I feel surprised even though I already knew
because someone already told me.
I touch a fish with fur.
I worry about my dog dying because she's fifteen years old.
I cried when my Nana's cat had to be put to sleep.
I am smart and sweet.
I understand what I am supposed to do when I am told so.
I say I can do anything I put my mind to.
I dream about becoming a singer.
I try to do my best on whatever I'm doing.
I hope my family will live longer than is possible.
I am smart and sweet.

Haley Cushing, Grade 6
Galesburg-Augusta Middle School, MI

Friends

I have many friends.
We like to set trends.
We like to do each other's hair.
There isn't anything we don't share.
We like to wear
Many different clothes
When we feel beautiful
We like to pose.
We like to put make-up on our face
And feel as pretty as a flower in its vase.
My favorite thing to do is to go shopping
Once I start there is no stopping.
I never want the time with my friends to be over.
I wish every night was a sleep over.

Morgan Thomas, Grade 4
Licking Valley Intermediate School, OH

Goodbye

Here I go,
Far, far away,
I wish I didn't have to,
But there is nothing I can say.

Getting on an airplane,
And going off tomorrow,
All I can do,
Is feel my deep, heavy sorrow.

I have no idea what my parents are thinking,
Or what's happening to them inside,
There are many things that they can do for me,
But how I will keep myself safe is what I have to decide.

Some people say to just go fight for your country,
Others say, "Don't worry about it. You'll be fine."
But they don't know what I'm going through,
Because I have no choice — rain, snow, cloud, or shine.

So here I go,
Far, far away,
This is to my family,
"Goodbye" I say.

Sneha Rajagopal, Grade 6
EH Greene Intermediate School, OH

Spring Is Here

The air is nice,
Flowers bloom,
Water flows through the river.

I can hear hummingbirds hum
Cause I know spring is here.

Can feel the air blow by me
Sun beams down, the snow melts
Now I know spring is here.

The air is fresh
Flowers grow
Fish swim smoothly in the flow
Butterflies fly in the air
As the season comes and goes.

Hannah Martin, Grade 4
Midland Academy of Advanced and Creative Studies, MI

Gifts

G ifts
I s it breakable?
F erret?
T oys are gifts.
S anta brings gifts.

Bailey Sullivan, Grade 5
West Washington Elementary School, IN

Red Is Enraged

Red is enraged,
It tastes like hot sauce.
It smells like hot sweat,
It reminds me of my little brother,
It sounds like a roaring tornado,
Enraged makes me feel red.

Christian Bastian, Grade 5
Tremont Elementary School, OH

It's a Dog's World

Dogs
Black, furry
Playing, running, jumping
Getting excited over people
Shih Tzu

Carissa Kloeker, Grade 6
Holy Angels School, OH

Winter

Deer tracks in the snow,
Ice crystals pelting my face,
Wind knocking at my jacket,
Exploring the creek,
Ice under my feet,
Listening to nature speak!

Jake Hussey, Grade 6
Tri-West Middle School, IN

McCain

McCain
Republican
Commercials, posters, facts
Voters are in long lines at polls
Winner?

Caroline Sarno, Grade 5
Tremont Elementary School, OH

Bowling

In a noisy building
With a sweaty hand
Across from some pins
Past the door
Near a trophy
In special shoes
Beneath the ceiling
On the floor
Throwing a bowling ball

Danielle N. Rollins, Grade 5
Churubusco Elementary School, IN

Archery Range

Looking at target:
The bow is strung, and ready
I let it go — Boing!

Jeremy Dorrell, Grade 6
Stanley Clark School, IN

Freedom

F lag flying high in the deep, blue sky
R espect shown to the veterans by having a parade
E agles flying high in the sky
E very veteran fought for our freedom
D eath is so sad because our veterans have fallen
O ur eyes looking at the veterans and thanking them for our freedom
M emories of our veterans

Nash Wilson, Grade 5
Sanderson Elementary School, OH

Wisconsin Dells

I remember the giant water park inside the hotel.
I froze at the top of a big water slide.
I grabbed a single tube and jumped down the dark, black tunnel.
I circled through as my stomach lashed turn after turn.
I was so scared: then there was a crack of light ahead. Boom!
I shot out and felt safe again. I kept my "Wow!" scream in my head!
I will never forget that moment.

Andy Scheel, Grade 5
Stanley Clark School, IN

Come and Look Around

Welcome to Wildwood Drive!
Grab that scooter and I'll give you the grand tour.
Look at all the trees winding into the five streets that surround us.
Do you see squirrels climbing up the tall maple trees?
There are leaves changing and falling off the tall maple trees.
Do you hear the honking of cars because of traffic?
There are seniors raking leaves.
Look at the kids playing baseball.
There are parties with screaming and yelling, hurting my ears.
There's the memory of me breaking my arm.
Now I've shown you Wildwood Drive, maybe now you can go on your own.

Anthony Kowalkowski, Grade 5
Allen J. Warren Elementary School, IN

Little Lives

The brown sides of the hatchery bag came up at me,
as I peered down. Peeps came up.

Then I smelled the brown bark shreds in the hatchery bag;
they smelled like a fresh pine forest.

Two little black and yellow mallard ducklings snuggled in my lap,
their down as soft as a fuzzy blanket.

I was so happy. I was going to have a
different year with the new little mallard ducklings.

I needed to name them;
their names had to rhyme.

Soon we would be home, and
our bond would begin.

Damaris Smith, Grade 5
Stanley Clark School, IN

If I Ruled the World

No school
Everything was free
Kids could drive
Kids could vote
No more wars
No cutting down trees
A bridge across the ocean
No homeless people
Everyone in Africa had food, water, and shelter
Every animal had their own area
No terrorists
Listen to the 3 R's
No home animals harmed
Cows would not be killed
Wolves would not be killed
Lower gas prices
Less candy
The White House would be moved to Lancaster, Ohio
No making fun of disordered kids
Flying cars.

Cody Taylor, Grade 6
Sanderson Elementary School, OH

Am I Like a Pie?

Am I like a pie? People come and take a piece of me
without saying "please" or "thank you."
I guess I am a pie. I feel like a rug,
always being stepped on and never cared about.
Until one day, my friend as an angel says,
"Please, I want a piece of pie. Thank you."
My life is now a very happy pie!

Sarah Heichel, Grade 6
Kesling Middle School, IN

I Am

I am funny and kind.
I wonder, why is my brother so weird?
I hear my book saying, "Read me, read me."
I see an orange dinosaur.
I want my dad to stay home.
I am funny and kind.
I pretend I can dance.
I feel happy that my books talk.
I touch my orange dinosaur.
I worry my dad will have to leave again for another month.
I cry when my dad has to leave again.
I am funny and kind.
I understand that life is tough and it won't always go my way.
I say my dad will be home soon.
I dream my life will be full of happiness.
I try to climb higher in my tree.
I hope I get all A's like last year.
I am funny and kind.

Paige Little, Grade 6
Galesburg-Augusta Middle School, MI

Fall

Red, green, and yellow leaves,
falling as free as falcons…
Fall
Leaves are falling left and right,
Just sit there and watch them what a wonderful sight…
Fall
Kids are running round and round
jumping into piles of leaves…
Fall
Halloween, the night where all the
creepy crawly creatures come out…
Fall
Halloween is the best part of fall,
There are lots of fun things so get on the ball.
Fall
Candy, candy dozens and more,
Gum, chocolate, and caramel galore.
Fall
Crazy kooky costumes are fun,
We'll all be sad when it's all done!
Autumn

Grant Miller, Grade 6
Holy Family Middle School, MI

I Am a Hungry Dog

I am a dog
I wonder if my owners will ever feed me
I hear people talking in the kitchen
I see them coming toward me
I want food
I am starving
I pretend there's food in my dish
I feel sick
I touch my mouth to the bottom of the dish
I worry that I will starve to death
I cry, "Feed me, feed me!"
I am sad
I understand that they don't know I am starving
I say I am starving to them but they didn't pay attention
I dream of a long strip of bacon
I try to bark to get my owner's attention
I hope they heard me
I am a starving dog

Nicole Stephan, Grade 5
Tremont Elementary School, OH

Snow

Snow falling,
Trees sway.
Feel the wind blowing on my back,
Snowflakes landing on my head.
Getting cold,
Goin' in.

Abbey Cook, Grade 4
Midland Academy of Advanced and Creative Studies, MI

Wonders of Fall

Leaves dangling
Chirping crickets
Cold air closing in
Eating apple crisp
Cawing crows
Green blades of grass
Moving with the wind
Leaves!
Crimson
Golden
Swoosh!
Fat squirrels gathering nuts
Chocolaty cocoa
Shorter days
Longer nights
Picking ripe apples!
Crackling glowing fire
Natalee Dagher, Grade 5
Riley Upper Elementary School, MI

What's Pumpkins Without Pie

Pumpkins
Round orange,
Scaring, sitting, lighting,
Seeds, slimy, delicious, tasty,
Making, slicing, eating,
Delightful, amazing,
Pie
Kyle Richardson, Grade 5
Norwich Elementary School, OH

Snowboarding

Floating through powder
It feels like you are flying
Just me and my board.
Clayton Kowalewski, Grade 6
Abbott Middle School, MI

Creek

Spiders crawling,
Snakes slithering,
Minnows dashing,
Rocks everywhere.
The creek,
A wonderful
Place to be!
Maggie Curtis, Grade 4
Normandy Elementary School, OH

My Outdoors

My pretty backyard
I hear the turkey gobble
I love my outdoors
Emily Current, Grade 4
Warren Central Elementary School, IN

At the Lake

Water
I crash up on shore.
You can see rhythm all day.
Again and again.

Butterfly
As I flap my wings,
I go flower to flower,
basking in the sun.

Deer
I see the flowers.
I race to them in delight.
Then I take a bite.
Katie Hubregsen, Grade 6
Sashabaw Middle School, MI

Beach

At the beach was the sun
I put sunscreen on so I wouldn't burn
Now time for fun!
Jade Karnosh, Grade 5
Rootstown Elementary School, OH

Kevin Charles Yacucci

K ind as can be
E mbraces the differences in people
V ery good listener
I ntelligent and friendly
N ever said a bad word

C harming and handsome
H appy and free
A friend to all
R eady to help others
L ends a hand
E nthusiastic for life
S incere and softhearted

Y oung and energetic
A lways helpful
C ourageous and strong
U nderstanding and patient
C reative and crafty
C onsiderate and caring
I nspiring to others
Kevin Charles Yacucci, Grade 5
Frank Ohl Intermediate School, OH

Horses

Horses running fast,
I like to see them running,
Such a pretty sight.
Angel Cahoon, Grade 4
Warren Central Elementary School, IN

Shining Rainbow

A rainbow shining
Like a bright star in the sky
At night by the fire.
Ben Stamets, Grade 6
Harmon Middle School, OH

Cocoa

Cocoa
Marshmallows, hot chocolate
Whirly, swirly, very good cocoa
So very good
Delicious
Madeline Hamady, Grade 4
Bailly Elementary School, IN

Scooby

S mart
C ute
O utrageous
O utgoing
B egging for food
Y elping for attention
Pamela D. Volheim, Grade 5
Cloverdale Middle School, IN

Thrashing the World

Blowing the winds come first.
Dancing in the treetops.
Howling the winds are getting harder.
Knocking down a tree in its path.
Bashing a house in its way.
Screaming the winds are even faster.
Destroying everything in its footway.
Silent the storm is now done.
Morgan Williams, Grade 6
Harmon Middle School, OH

Skate Rinks

I like to go to skating rinks
When I was there I got some drinks
It was very fun
I like to go run
My mom turned on all of the sinks
Bryce Adkins, Grade 4
Mayfield Elementary School, OH

The Snow Is Falling

The snow is falling,
I'm playing in the snow,
Then my friend is saying,
Ho-ho-ho,
She is pretending she is Santa,
And I laugh and say, Hello!
Alyssa Flores, Grade 5
May V Peck Elementary School, MI

My Place

What is my favorite place,
I wonder where it is?
Aruba, Bermuda, maybe even France,
Italy, Spain, all of Europe,
Australia, Africa, Florida,
New York, Dallas, Indy,
What could beat out all of those…
A place I call my house!

Dylan Reed, Grade 5
Northern Heights Elementary School, IN

Warmth

Inside and out I feel warm.
It's not from a fire and it's not man-made.
But when I'm warm it's my friends making me smile.
It's my mom greeting me in the morning.
It's my dog excited to see me.
You see, it's the love and happiness I'm given
That warms me inside and out.

Hannah Hasseler, Grade 5
St Joseph Montessori School, OH

Life

Life is sometimes boring.
Life is always fun.
Life sometimes stinks.
Life can be joyful.
Life can give you the blues.
Life can make you happy.
Life can be upsetting.
Life is always wonderful.
Life can be a pain.
Life is like a gem.
Life is like a rollercoaster.
Life has its ups and downs.
Life is full of disappointments.
Life is full of surprises.
Life is like a box of chocolates.
You never know which one you're going to get!

Jace McCloy, Grade 6
St Gerard School, MI

Tornado

Tornados are scary, awesome and exciting.
First moving dangerously full of hail and excitement.
Chasing down houses; trees and cars.
Exciting and cool to see from faraway.
Whirling winds, and it eating anything nearby.
Then spitting it out and sending it flying.
My mind and eyes cannot wrap around
how it gets its strength and the damage it causes.
Pictures in books and in movies on TV.
I hope it never happens to me.

Gerrit Reynhout, Grade 6
Crown Point Christian School, IN

I Am

I am sporty and funny.
I wonder what my mom does at work.
I hear my feet yelling.
I see a blue and yellow elephant.
I want to be a professional soccer goalkeeper.
I am sporty and funny.
I pretend to drive a car.
I feel sad when mom doesn't let the purple duck come over.
I touch a half-monkey, half-human.
I worry if mom got to work safely.
I cry when we go to Nana and Papa's grave.
I am sporty and funny.
I understand that my dad left me.
I say my dad will come back to see me.
I dream about owning a new car.
I try to play my hardest at soccer.
I hope I will have a lot of money.
I am sporty and funny.

Tyler Dunithan, Grade 6
Galesburg-Augusta Middle School, MI

Veterans

Our veterans stand, brave and proud,
they come to their family,
from the battle ground.
They wait and wait for their loved ones to come,
some families so scared,
wondering if they're gone.

Cries fill the air,
with sadness and happiness,
they cry from their heart,
like they're hopeless in life,
like they're overjoyed with love.

Our veterans stand, brave and proud,
soon just stand crying, not to look strong,
just as normal as they could ever since they left.

Our veterans stand, brave and proud,
worked for our nation,
and kept us proud.
Thank you, veterans.

Rachel Joo, Grade 5
Beck Centennial Elementary School, MI

Tears

Tears are dreams with wings to fly.
As a curious fellow, I wonder why such a thing
Would fall from your eye.
Do they come out when you're sad, mad, or happy?
Are tears just a watery thing to others,
Or is it I that love them so much?

Katelyn McBride, Grade 5
May V Peck Elementary School, MI

Ice Skating

Beautiful ice skates,
Wonderful ice skating blades
Glide across the ice.

Lan Nguyen, Grade 5
Central College Christian Academy, OH

Night

After the sunset awakens
the night darkness begins.
The twinkling of stars twist
into magnificent constellations,
while at times shooting stars
bounce across the night sky.
A giant silver dot lightens the sky,
from the moon's reflection.
For a long period of time
the only color known is
the dark colors of gray and black.
The last step of night
is the golden colors of dawn.

Amberly Leigh, Grade 6
St Clement Elementary School, OH

Dogs

Dogs fill your life with joy;
They're much better than any type of toy.
They are as sweet as candy,
Believe it or not they're also very handy.

Dogs will always stay by your side.
And always love to play outside.
Dogs were made to be mans best friend,
And will be to the very end!

Tanner Judd, Grade 5
Northfield Baptist Christian School, OH

Sad Is Purple

Sad is purple,
It tastes like sour grapes,
It smells like raw chicken,
It reminds me of my brother,
It sounds like death of my grandpa,
Sad makes me feel purple.

Sam Leonard, Grade 5
Tremont Elementary School, OH

Popcorn

POPCORN
Popping, snapping
Butter, salt, sugar, triangle
White, orange, yellow
Eating, chewing
Colorful, sweet
Candycorn

India Johnson, Grade 4
Norwich Elementary School, OH

October

It's time for apple abundance through
the orchard
ready to be picked
one by one.

There is pumpkin abundance too
all of the field of pumpkins
ready to be scary
Jack-
O-
Lanterns.

The sun dozing off
earlier
and
earlier
each and every night.

Spiders coming out
boogie down their skinny legs at nightfall.
Halloween is finally here going around the air
monster going around your neighborhoods the midnight hollows.
Sorry but now October has ended
November starts again.

Jacob Behounek, Grade 5
Beck Centennial Elementary School, MI

Tions

If you go to school, that's education.
If you move, that's a motion.
If you read lots of data, that's information.
If you add five plus five, that's addition.
If you go and ride a train, that's called going to a station.
If you make something capital, that's capitalization.
If you watch something very close, that's called an observation.
If you make something nice, that's a creation.
If something dries really fast, that's evaporation.
If you subtract four minus four, that's subtraction.
(And if you wonder what these words mean, is that an investigation?)

Ciarra Capito, Grade 5
Frank Ohl Intermediate School, OH

My Mom

My mom cooks breakfast and dinner for me so that I won't go hungry.
My mom works hard every day to pay for the cable.
My mom pays for me to go to school instead of going out every day.
And for that I say thank you.

My mom buys toys for me to entertain myself with.
She buys games for me to play with.
She washes my clothes so I won't have to.
And for that I say thank you.

I love you mom!

Marques White, Grade 6
University Liggett School, MI

Snow

Snow is so white and fluffy,
it's like a pillow on the ground.
It falls and falls till the ground is covered.
It goes on trees and makes them white and pretty.
You can make lots of things
like snowmen, snow angels, and other things.
Snow forts are fun to build
at anytime like at snow fights.
See how snow is fun?
Well, you better
because it's the end!

Abby Hochstetler, Grade 4
Michiana Christian Montessori School, IN

Tions

If you get hurt bad, you need something,
That's called hospitalization.
If you are hurt too bad, you need something,
That's called an operation.
If you start to cry and shout,
That's an emotion.
If you don't want to get diseases,
That's vaccination.
If you get a cough or a sniffle, you need something,
That's called medication.
If you put a band on your arm,
That ruins your circulation.
If you lay peacefully
That's called meditation.
If you sit quietly in a chair,
That's called relaxation.

Jennifer Franken, Grade 5
Frank Ohl Intermediate School, OH

I Am

I am imaginative yet curious.
I wonder if there is a God.
I hear a cow go, "Oink-oink-squeek!"
I see ghosts coming.
I want death to never happen.
I am imaginative yet curious.
I pretend to be funny.
I feel surprised when my puppy talks to me.
I touch a witch.
I worry about my parents dying.
I cry when I get hurt.
I am imaginative yet curious.
I understand people are destructive.
I say God is real.
I dream my dad will live forever.
I try to satisfy my friends and family.
I hope my dad lives forever.
I am imaginative yet curious.

Maggie Noel, Grade 6
Galesburg-Augusta Middle School, MI

Basketball

Looks like people dribbling the ball to the hoop
Sounds like the referee calling a foul shot
Tastes like chips, donuts and water going down my throat
Smells like sweat and a big rubber court
Feels like a sweaty jersey and a rough ball

Connor Louis, Grade 5
Northfield Baptist Christian School, OH

Season of Change

Colorful leaves falling down,
down,
down,
down,
Trees dancing in the wind
Like there is no tomorrow.
The wild wind whispering in my ears.

Trees shaking themselves silly.
The different colors of leaves
in red, orange, purple, and brown.
Leaves crinkling everywhere you go.

The pumpkins being sold
and then carved for all the children
on Halloween night; all of the pumpkins
glowing in the dark.

Kelsey Courier, Grade 6
Holy Family Middle School, MI

Foliage/Leaves

Foliage
Rainbow-like colors
Slowly swirl down
Gracefully sway in wind
Leaves

Kayla Williams, Grade 4
Frank H Hammond Elementary School, IN

Friends

Friends stand with you forever
Friends laugh together
Friends hold each other up
Friends never give up with each other
Friends will be with you until the end
Friends can be funny with each other
Friends are smart
Friends are always there when you have a broken heart
Friends are support
Friends make you laugh
Friends are kind
Friends give you faith and hope
Friends love to share
Friends stand with you forever

Lauren Pokrykfi, Grade 6
St Gerard School, MI

The Eagle

E agle is a constellation that is in Greek mythology, and is know as Aquila.
A quila was always at the side of Zeus holding his thunder bolts whenever needed.
G ods of all kinds envied Zeus for not just his power, but for his eagle that was trustable to be there always.
L ight and power from the thunderbolts was powerful enough to destroy almost anything.
E veryone who believed in the gods were proud of Zeus and the eagle.

Conner Flora, Grade 6
Pinewood Elementary School, IN

Christmas Time

The presents surrounding the tree, the sight of my stocking filled with goodies, the shocked eyes from the presents everyone has been waiting for. Then, it catches my eye, the bright sparkle of the star on the top of the tree, something I have wanted to see for a very long time. The illumination of the ornaments is also visible, giving them a nice sparkle and assortment.
As I open the presents, I hear the laughter, awe, and joy of the gifts we have received this year. Is there snow? Are there any more gifts we missed? Are my friends enjoying Christmas, as much as I am? This day is just about as good as my b-day, Thanksgiving, and Easter rolled together. Who wouldn't enjoy it? Who wouldn't enjoy it? Who wouldn't enjoy it?

Liam Stojanovic, Grade 5
EH Greene Intermediate School, OH

Perseus the Hero

P erseus is a Greek hero that became a constellation.
E very day the gods would guide him to his destiny.
R oughly he found his destiny. His destiny was to kill Medusa and to save Andromeda from the giant
S ea monster. He had to cut off her head and take it to the sea monster so it would die before it could kill Andromeda.
E ventually, the sea monster turned to stone when it saw the head of Medusa.
U ltimately Medusa's head was locked in a box and never seen again.
S o then Perseus got married to Andromeda and they both became constellations.

Amanda Bilancio, Grade 6
Pinewood Elementary School, IN

Inside This Picture…

Inside this picture is all the great joy at the one moment.
It's the only thing that will remember all the laughs, tears, smiles, frowns, and thoughts at this moment.
This picture holds everything everyone was feeling at a moment.
This tiny picture holds large things like all the words in one dictionary.
Whenever people are sad they look at this picture and see great joy.
Inside this picture…

Kaylee Russell, Grade 6
St Maria Goretti School, IN

Mercury

M ercury, the closest planet to the sun, derived its name from the Roman god Mercurius. According to mythology, Mercurius was the swiftest of the gods. Likewise, Mercury's orbit is the fastest in the solar system.
E xtreme ranges in temperature make Mercury inhabitable. Temperature's on Mercury's surface can range from as high as 430 degrees Celsius (800 degrees Fahrenheit) to as low as -170 degrees Celsius (-280 degrees Fahrenheit). Mercury lacks a substantial atmosphere to retain heat, consequently causing the drastic drop in temperature.
R ay craters cover much of Mercury's terrain. They are features generally found on moons. They are created when a large object, such as a meteor or comet, collides with the surface, flinging debris all around.
C ontaining an iron core, Mercury is one of the densest planets. Surprisingly, its also the smallest planet, with exception to Pluto (considered a dwarf planet, in the solar system.
U nlike many planets, color is not a predominant characteristic of Mercury, it has a dull gray appearance.
R otation on Mercury's axis is slow. A day on Mercury is equivalent to 59 Earth days. On the other hand, Mercury's orbit is quite fast. It takes approximately 88 Earth days to complete one year on Mercury.
Y ou can see Mercury near the sun at sunset and sunrise. A pair of binoculars may be needed, but at times its also visible by the naked eye.

Valeria Robles, Grade 6
Pinewood Elementary School, IN

My Fall Favorites

The fall morning expresses me.
I love the color of the leaves on the trees.
The red means love and the orange means kindness.
I love to jump in the leaves and make a mess.

The fall night is very cold and the moon is bright.
During Halloween, we like to scare little kiddies at night.
I like to dress up in my costume and go trick-or-treating.
I can't wait to get candy and start eating!

Fall means FOOTBALL!
On Saturday mornings, it's time for game day.
My dad, brother and I grab the seed and head out to play.
I juke out my brother and score first downs.
My dad throws me good passes and I score touchdowns.

Fall means cooking for me and Mommy.
We like to cook apple pie and chocolate chip cookies.
Fall is my favorite time of the year.

Connor Rucinski, Grade 6
St Gerard School, MI

Frost

O frost! O frost!
Early in the day
God paints the grass white, by His own way.
O frost! O frost!
Coming in as quiet as the breeze.
When I look out my window,
The frost is what I see.
O frost! O frost!
Leaving just as quiet as before.
It creeps away just once more.
O frost! O frost!

Alexis Webber, Grade 6
Wooster Christian School, OH

Grandma

Grandma,
I was there to watch you go.
I was there to see you die.
I was there by your side to watch you cry.

Grandma,
I miss your touch.
I miss your voice.
I miss your face.

Grandma,
Every night it's not the same without you.
Every night I sit on my bed and pray for you
To come back one day.
Every night I miss you very much.

Amber Schoedel, Grade 6
Trilby Elementary School, OH

War

Bombs exploding in the air!
Boom! Fire everywhere!
I hear a rumbling tank nearby!
Why are they attacking? Why?
People screaming here and there,
the noise — I can't help but despair!
Sky is shining like the sun,
this is definitely not fun!
Look! Look!
Wait there's more!
Our troops are coming, we've won the war!

Matthew Gordon, Grade 4
Midland Academy of Advanced and Creative Studies, MI

Bubbles

B lowing bubbles is so much fun.
U p   everywhere!
    down
B ubbles in the yard,
B ubbles by the water.
L et's go catch them as they float by.
E very time we get close, they float gracefully away.
S lowly, gracefully, floating away.

Isabella R. Bocija, Grade 5
St Joseph Montessori School, OH

Fall

Fall is here, time to cheer.
Time to dance about the leaves until the streetlights go off
That's when you will have to leave for home.
But you will come back the next day,
For it will be Thanksgiving day!
You will make the turkey and mac and cheese.
Don't forget the mashed potatoes, please!
We will have fun in the sun
All day long
And give thanks for what we have today.
Although it comes only once a year,
Don't forget to cheer!

Camille Nicole McKinney, Grade 4
Matthew Duvall Elementary School, OH

October Breeze

I walk through a neat row of trees
Like soldiers at attention
As golden brown leaves litter the ground
And fly in the sky
A light October breeze tells the trees to laugh and wave
As birds sing in a chorus of high tweets
For fall is here but in a welcome way
And feeling free is natural
As all troubles seem to be hung away on a rack
October can bring all these things

Griffin Wray, Grade 6
University Liggett School, MI

The Cat and the Brat

I had a cat who disliked a brat.
The brat's name was Pat.

I don't like it when they fight.
It just doesn't seem right.

I'll pretend to run away to Rome.
But first, I'd better go home.

Cassandra Ubelhor, Grade 5
Perry Central Elementary School, IN

What Makes Me Happy

What makes me happy…
Is being with my friends
Seeing all my relatives
And just having fun.

What makes me happy…
Is playing with my cats
Being by myself
And doing what I love.

What makes me happy…
Is being with my family
Meeting new people
And just being by myself.

Anna Ahee-Gillen, Grade 6
Trilby Elementary School, OH

Tweety

Tweety
Wonderful flying bird
She is beautiful and yellow too!
Flying high
Fun
Shiny coat
Sparkling yellow
Lovely

Abigail R. Stanford, Grade 4
Churubusco Elementary School, IN

My Dad

I hold my dad so dear to me
He doesn't know how nice he can be
I don't think even he can see
How much I love him.

Lars Hornburg, Grade 5
Central Grade School, MI

Water

Water so tasty
It glimmers like a big sun
Better drink some more

Jacob Braun, Grade 5
Perry Central Elementary School, IN

Autumn Pumpkin

I am an autumn pumpkin,
Orange and beautiful,
Big and plump,
Growing in a wondrous field,
Ready to be picked and enjoyed,
I am an autumn pumpkin.

Hannah McDonald, Grade 5
Westview Elementary School, OH

What Makes Me Move

S peed past everyone
O pen teammates to pass it
C ourage
C hampions
E nergized
R eady for anything

Jade Paris, Grade 5
Miller Ridge Elementary School, OH

What Moves Me

Classical music moves me
It's so smooth!
Animals move me
They're so cool!
Reading moves me
I love to read!
I like to sink into a book.
Magic Tree House is my favorite.
GATE moves me.
It's so fun!
And GATE is why I did this poem.

Bailey Steele, Grade 4
Mayfield Elementary School, OH

Glad

I am so glad.
Why are you mad?
I can see you're not happy
While I am very peppy.
You and I should be friends
Happiness will never end.

Sean Imholt, Grade 5
Spaulding Elementary School, OH

Apples

teachers love 'em
red
some sour
some sweet
fruit
all different
tasty treats
apples

Kristen Drippon, Grade 4
Northfield Elementary School, OH

My Chocolate Dog

I love my dog
her name is Jeddah.
I couldn't find a dog
that's any betta
I love my dog
she hops around like a frog.
She likes to play all day
but I love her anyway.
I love my dog
her name is Jeddah
I couldn't find a dog
that's any betta!

Dru Gibson, Grade 4
Licking Valley Intermediate School, OH

Four Seasons

F all
O ut hunting
U nlikeable cold
R ainy

S ummer
E at more ice cream on
A very hot day
S pring's beautiful weather
O ut we go to play
N o leaves in winter and
S uper freezing days

Lance Baize, Grade 5
Perry Central Elementary School, IN

Brothers and Sisters

Brothers and sisters are all around us,
They might not always be seen,
But they are always on your side,
They are the best thing God created,
They are with you in the good times,
And your bad times,
They help you in so many ways,
They make you laugh,
They make you smile,
But most important
You have someone that loves you.

Kassandra Cruz-Olmos, Grade 6
Abbott Middle School, MI

Autumn

A mazing, watching nature change with
U nique, different colors,
T o watch leaves fall
U pon the ground,
M ajestically in their own
N oble way.

Sydney Sleek, Grade 6
Melrose Elementary School, OH

Autumn

Fall is when the leaves change color.
The leaves fall slowly to the children below.

The children laugh and play.
Soon the autumn will be gone.

More leaves fall as the weather gets colder.
More children disappear into their houses.

As the last leaf of fall tumbled to the ground,
The snow started to fall gracefully.

Catherine Hall, Grade 6
Holy Family Middle School, MI

Friends

When I cry and feel upset,
you make me laugh and cheer me up.

When I say something I didn't mean,
you forgive me anyway.

The first time I saw you,
we became best friends,

Our friendship will never end.

Angel Sovia, Grade 4
Midland Academy of Advanced and Creative Studies, MI

Can Hope Survive the Bleak Panorama?

A lonely apartment building, bombed nearly to rubble,
Looking over the dreadfully desolate scene in Kabul.
Sighting the small ancient school complex next door,
Completely leveled, turned to dust and nothing more.

Contemplating the deserted field, once a bustling farm,
Filled with many craters, come to much terrible harm.
The land mines planted there harvested infuriated fear,
The crops sowed there, reaped no produce, only tears.

The Taliban strictly enforced many awful, appalling rules,
They destroyed many things, and the makeshift schools.
They forced women to wear heavy, depressive clothing,
All types of technology are outlawed, illiterates are cloning.

The Soviets came before, with the first terrible war,
After land mines and explosives, Afghanistan got sore.
In the great, joyous, and reliving December of 2001,
The Taliban's technophobia torture was finally done.

Relief workers quickly began to flood Afghanistan,
Rebuilding Afghanistan after the malicious Taliban.
New buildings and schools are beginning construction,
Land mine clearing operations are assisting everyone.

Ethan Curtis, Grade 6
Ann Arbor Christian School, MI

The Unfortunate Catastrophe

When the sky had started weeping,
The wisest were fleeing as quiet as a corpse.
They still remember like a book that once,
Their families in town died because of the sky storming.

Sadly the fools didn't realize this
And just thought the others were as mad as hens.
Abruptly a massive storm began to rage and roughen
The very ground the people would miss.

Fortunately the refugees were as safe as a house
Even though the lot was as dead as a doornail.
But because of a strong gale,
In the end everyone was as poor as a church mouse.

Sung Hyup Lee, Grade 6
Boulan Park Middle School, MI

Santa Claus

It is Christmas Eve and everyone is asleep.
There isn't a sound in the house, not even a peep.
But then, there is a jolly Ho, HO, HO!
And the sound of bells, jingling in a peaceful flow.
Then down the chimney comes a man in red.
He is quiet so he doesn't wake anyone in bed.
Then he places beautiful wrapped presents under the tree.
So when the kids wake up, they can all see.
As he walks away, he smells cookies ready for him to take.
They were so good, he knew it took a while to make.
With a cookie in his hand, he decided it was time to go.
So he walked to the chimney, and bent down real low.
He went up the chimney standing next to his reindeer.
Don't count on him coming to your house again, till next year.
When the kids hear his name, they will all pause.
I'm sure you know him, it's Santa Claus!

Kaley Mrozinski, Grade 6
Corpus Christi Elementary School, IN

Devil's Night

Toilet paper in trees doorbells ringing,
Shadows sneaking around laughter in the night,
Disintegrated remain of pumpkins,
Eggs splattered everywhere,
Paintballs stuck everywhere,
People spying out windows,
Lots of practical jokes,
Jack-o'-lanterns lit,
Glowing faces in the night,
Spooky, scary faces,
Some scary some silly,
Shadows of jack-o'-lanterns,
Lots of decorations,
Some houses spooky,
Spiders, ghosts and goblins.

Jacob Sandusky, Grade 5
Beck Centennial Elementary School, MI

Rain

There's a thunderstorm
The rain falls, the young boy cries
He hopes it will end

Claudia Butcher, Grade 6
Harmon Middle School, OH

The Diving Board

I stare down: I'm scared.
The wind rips across the lake.
My toes grip; I freeze.

Grace Landry, Grade 6
Stanley Clark School, IN

White

Relaxed is white,
It tastes like butter,
It smells like soft perfume,
It reminds me of water,
It sounds like a silent whistle,
Relaxed makes me feel white.

Santiago Barros, Grade 5
Tremont Elementary School, OH

I Am

I am nice and forgiving.
I wonder when school is out.
I hear SpongeBob laughing.
I see cool skeletons.
I want a new skateboard.
I am nice and forgiving.
I pretend to be an alien fighter.
I touch a robot.
I feel surprised when Bob talks.
I worry about homework.
I cry when I hurt myself.
I am nice and forgiving.
I understand I am smart.
I say volleyball is boring.
I dream of my sisters and brothers.
I hope to be a football player.
I am nice and forgiving.

Deoneis Riddle, Grade 6
Galesburg-Augusta Middle School, MI

Christmas

C are
H aving a good time
R eaching out for one another
I n holiday spirit
S mile
T reating each other with love
M ore time to have with family
A ngel
S nowflakes

Victoria Gonzalez, Grade 6
Erie Elementary School, OH

An Ode to Ken Griffey Jr.

Oh great Ken Griffey Jr. your 500 home runs excite me with great power.
Coming to the Chicago White Sox from the Cincinnati Reds filled me with hope.
Even though you are old you are still a decent runner,
An excellent 5 star batter, and a great fielder.
Oh, Ken Griffey Jr. you're still the best player in present-day baseball.
You are still skinny and hit lots of singles, doubles, and triples.
Your rare, soft, brown glove is so awesome.
You are so very important to me because
You are my favorite player on my favorite team.
Oh great son of Ken Griffey, good luck next season!!

Your biggest fan, Jimmy Hamilton!

Jimmy Hamilton, Grade 5
Allen J. Warren Elementary School, IN

I Am

I am athletic and willing.
I wonder, will the world ever end?
I hear books speak to me.
I see pictures move when I look at them.
I want a blue iPod that has a screen on it.
I am athletic and willing.
I pretend I am a leader.
I feel happy when my parents buy me a pet soccer ball.
I touch a silver monkey.
I worry about getting cancer.
I cry when people wish they could do something that they can't do.
I am athletic and willing.
I understand you shouldn't let anything or anyone
stop you from making a dream come true.
I say if you tried your best it is the best that you can do.
I dream that I have a dinosaur chasing me.
I try to do well in school.
I hope to be a professional basketball player.
I am athletic and willing.

Rachel Blood, Grade 6
Galesburg-Augusta Middle School, MI

A Louisiana Morning

In Louisiana every morning,
I would get up and go outside into the cool,
crisp morning air.
I would go out to get my dog Sam from the barn out back.
She is a big brown and black German shepherd
with brown sparkling eyes and a sweet personality.
She would jump on the gate and try to get out to see me.
The dew drops on the grass felt cold on my feet like little ice beads.
Every morning we went for a walk.
The morning bird would sing as Sam and I walked along.
Sam would bark at skittering squirrels and swooping crows.
As we walked along, the spring peepers
would sing us a song
like a sweet lullaby.

Emma Brewer, Grade 5
Stanley Clark School, IN

Books

Pages and pages
So much to do
What to read first,
I haven't a clue!
A variety of things you can read about,
Horses, pirates there's no doubt
So you think that I'm done?
Oh no, I have just begun.
So come on over, check me out
There's so much to learn and explore,
When you open a book, you open a door.
It's like magic, fiction, adventure,
Mystery, suspense, you never know what you might get,
Libraries are full of surprise and wonder,
You never know what you might stumble over,
So walk on over to the library of wonders,
And open a book, there's much to discover.

Courtney Gronewold, Grade 6
Pennfield Middle School, MI

Ten Mice

Ten mice went to climb a vine,
One fell off. Then there were nine.
Nine mice went on a date,
One got dumped. Then there were eight.
Eight mice went to see Kevin,
One fell in love. Then there were seven.
Seven mice went to eat Pixie sticks,
One ate too much. Then there were six.
Six mice went to a beehive,
One got stung. Then there were five.
Five mice went through a door,
One got stuck. Then there were four.
Four mice skied on the sea,
One drowned. Then there were three.
Three mice went to say moo,
One turned into a cow. Then there were two.
Two mice went to have fun,
One got hurt. Then there was one.
One mouse went to the bend,
He got hit by a car, and that was the end.

Kylie Bonnema, Grade 6
Crown Point Christian School, IN

Green

green the leaves in the spring
a witches face on Halloween
green the color of the grass
the color of pine trees
green like the emerald that sparkles
the color of a colored pencil
green the color of my Halloween costume
the color of palm trees.

Maggie Cook, Grade 6
Tippecanoe Middle School, OH

The Firework's Story

The fireworks sat on a boat and worried and scared
About the near future

Then the fireworks sprung toward its stage
Of summer's cool, dark, night sky

Unveiling a dance of
Shimmering, glittery, and sparkling lights

Yet, as they continued dancing,
The fireworks sizzled, faded, and fell

As they fell to the lake the fireworks
Held their breath through their final seconds of life

Yasmeen Pihlgren, Grade 6
Boulan Park Middle School, MI

Opposite Day

Opposite day is coming soon
On the day of a full moon
Listen here and be aware
Be careful what you say
On opposite day
And here is one more tip to give,
Whatever you say don't say I'm glad I live!

Bethany DeLoof, Grade 4
Sts Joseph and John School, OH

November Is Here

November is when
hot, creamy, rich hot chocolate pours into icy mugs
cider comes into a cup as if cider was going out of business
cake comes to the
amazing
super
fabulous Meghan
for her birthday

November is when
kids bundle up in jeans and colorful jackets
as if someone pressed the cold button
warm air comes into freezing houses
Mom bakes such hot cookies
that burn our mouths

November is when
Thanksgiving comes
adults talk like a baseball crowd cheering
Thanksgiving parties up and down stairs

Finally November is at winter's gate
the month ended
and coldness has begun even colder.

Alexia Miller, Grade 5
Beck Centennial Elementary School, MI

Outdoors

Hunting
Adrenaline rushing
Shooting, tracking, towing
The smell of gunpowder
Stalking

Fishing
Setting lines
Casting, reeling, catching
Landing the big one
Hooking

Camping
Exhausting play
Biking, hiking, roasting
Around the crackling campfire
Tenting

Four-wheeler
Fast excitement
Jumping, looking, exploring
Ramping through the ditches
Mudding
Aaron Mullis, Grade 6
Nancy Hanks Elementary School, IN

Summer

The flowers giggle hysterically,
As the sun shines off them a ray of light.

Popsicles begin to cry,
As they simply melt away.

Beads of grass plead in despair,
To get a drop of water.

Niagara Falls begins to pose,
For all his wonderful visitors.

The wind begins to huff and puff,
Because he can no longer stay.
Sunny Chiang, Grade 6
Boulan Park Middle School, MI

Football

A football is brown
with strings
McNabb our
quarterback
throws many
completions
Eagles will win the
Super Bowl
Hunter Adams, Grade 4
Northfield Elementary School, OH

Autumn's Colors

Colors
red or yellow
swaying, changing, falling
forming blankets on the green ground
Autumn
Scott Little, Grade 6
Roosevelt Elementary School, OH

Karate

Sweeps, throws, kicks, and punches
Self-defense, basics, and sparring
Discipline, memory, and stamina
Accomplishing my first kata
Twenty-two moves of power
Onward to gold and yellow!
Corbin Cox, Grade 6
Tri-West Middle School, IN

What If

What if
My bird
Could talk
And taught me how to fly
And gave me a good set of wings!
Wouldn't that be nice?

What if
My roller blades
Showed me how to skate
And spin and even flip in them!
Wouldn't that be great?
Clive Chan, Grade 5
Birchwood School, OH

I Am

I am funny and fun.
I wonder what the moon tastes like.
I hear mole people yelling.
I see a dragon's scale.
I want a new life.
I am funny and fun.
I pretend to die.
I feel sad for my blue cow.
I touch a dragon.
I worry about school.
I cry at happy things.
I am funny and fun.
I understand life.
I say life is a road.
I dream of blue cows.
I try to get a good job.
I hope for world peace.
I am funny and fun.
Aaron Daniel, Grade 6
Galesburg-Augusta Middle School, MI

Dreams

Come here.
Bring me your dreams.
Give me your feelings.
I will make you feel better.
I will wrap them in my heart.
I will never let them out,
For they are mine to keep
Forever to be held in my heart.
Haley Sue Begle, Grade 5
Nancy Hanks Elementary School, IN

Halloween

H orror
A ttack
L antern
L ighted pumpkin
O ctober
W itches
E erie
E vil
N ightmare
Brooke Whitaker, Grade 5
St Jude Catholic School, IN

Sad Is Purple

Sad is purple,
It tastes like my last grape,
It smells like onions,
It reminds me of salty tears,
It sounds like whining babies,
Sad makes me feel purple.
Will Sorrell, Grade 5
Tremont Elementary School, OH

What If?

A world without dreaming,
A girl without screaming,
A fruit with no seed,
A world with no greed,
A couplet with no rhyme,
A world with no time,
A name with no letters,
Oh! It's no use this poem's no better!
Sawyer Scheitler, Grade 4
Stonegate Elementary School, IN

USA Flag

American stars
American stripes
Our flag rocks all night
We stayed and fought and now we'll fight
The American flag
No need to brag
Alec Hickman, Grade 6
Kesling Middle School, IN

Mask

And the raccoons are the bandits of the night,
Slier than sly and ready for a fight.
Stealthier than a fox,
They use their smarts to sneak into your trash.
Then they feast on last night's tofu box.

The key to their success is their black mask.
With it they can complete any task.
Don't underestimate their nastiness,
And they have a tale of horrible sorrow.

What I say is true.
If you don't believe,
Just wait till they visit you tomorrow.
To get rid of them is a challenging assignment.
But the trick to finding them,
Is to find the mask.

Eron Henderson, Grade 6
Harding Middle School, OH

Walk Off Home Run

The wind blowing hard as I stepped up to the plate,
my jersey, says Yankees, the back says eight,
there's two outs and we are down by one,
as soon as I know it, the umpire screams STRIKE ONE!
It's the bottom of the ninth, I twist my shoe,
next thing I know, I'm down 0 and 2.
I point to the sky, I'm calling my shot,
I'm pointing to left field, that's my hot spot.
The next pitch came quick past my eyes,
I fouled it off with a big surprise.
The next pitch comes as hard as can be,
and I hit it so hard, the ball screams at me.
I look at the ball with a smile of joy,
then I hear the crowd scream run boy!
I look at the crowd, and their faces.
Now the game is over and done,
all because of my walk off home run.

Gary Miller, Grade 6
Woodward Park Middle School, OH

Casey

With hair as soft as a polar bear, the color of honey
With eyes as bright as the sun
Your voice can make anyone cry
And your cry can make them worry

You can break through walls
And make flowers bloom
You have good theories, but are to small to care

This is to the little girl that can do anything at all
My baby sister, the one I love the most

Caitlyn Viger, Grade 4
Red Cedar School, MI

Pine Trail

Pine trail is the place for me,
With sights smells and wonders!
It seems as if you are never more than
Five feet away from a tree!
It smells as if it had rained for hours.
As we sit on the dock
Splashing each other with sparkling water of the lake,
The sun beats down on us.
I think how lucky I really am!!!

Madisen Mrotek, Grade 5
Washington Township Elementary School, IN

Empty

The world is empty you know.
Full of life, but nowhere to go.
And whatever you're trying to find,
You're not going to find it nearby.

When I look around I don't see much.
All I see is a bunch of dust.
And when I think I see you,
I know that it can't be true.

As I look up into the sky,
I can't see up that high;
Because the clouds are blocking the view,
Of the sun that smiles to you.

Even though I am alone,
I start to feel this is my home.
I have a feeling you are there,
Floating out in the air.

Emily Patton, Grade 6
Harmon Middle School, OH

Autumn Images

My class goes for an autumn walk.
The clouds as puffy as cotton candy.
Red stars line the branches
As the trees are stripping in the wind

The leaves dance and twirl
Through the air.
Crunching leather pieces
Cover the ground.

The wind sounds like fresh mountain air
While below it blows grass of emeralds dotted with rubies.
As a nest floats through the air
You will see the trees start to go bare.

Autumn's treasure line the streets.
Once and for all you now know Autumn is here.

Paris L. Burton, Grade 6
University Liggett School, MI

Cookie Fun

To make a great cookie,
it helps not to be a rookie.
Use a little sugar, oil and flour,
the whole process takes about an hour!

Turn the mixer up high,
but don't let the dough fly.
If you make a mess,
clean it up; don't stress.

If you choose to sneak a bite,
it's all right!
It might be deceiving,
but the best part is eating!

Emma Alexander, Grade 6
Sashabaw Middle School, MI

All About Me

K itties are my favorite pet
A lways wanted to be a vet
R eally loves gymnastics
A nimals are very fantastic

N ever ending fun
I like to tan in the sun
C arebear is my nickname
O peration is my favorite game
L ove to shop 'til I drop
E njoys lemon lollipops

L avender is my favorite color
E veryone should like each other
A mber is my cousin's name
R eally loves the same
N o one is very lame

Kara Nicole Learn, Grade 5
Frank Ohl Intermediate School, OH

The Newborn Child

Sunlight heats up my body
and my excited spirit as it
blazes through the
apartment windows
like scissors through
paper. Doors open up
to the living room, where the
New one plays. The bed of blues
is on the left.
Toys jiggling and
laughter are in
my ears. I peek around
the door frame to see Mother and
my new brother. My tired spirits
revive like a plant absorbing water.

Christopher Yun, Grade 5
Stanley Clark School, IN

The Mountain

Mountain peaks are
As pointed as a freshly sharpened pencil

Goats on a mountainside cry
As noisily as a newborn baby in the middle of the night

The ascent of a snow mountain
Is as risky as walking on thin ice

Birds circle a mountain searching for prey
Like a child would seek a lost toy

Trees on the mountain were felled like a tornado hitting a city
A tremendous amount of damage was done

Creatures were examining the remnants of the mountain for a place to abide
As desperately as a destitute person would search for money

Restored was the area that was lost
Animals found homes like rain falls from the sky

Katie Schlafhauser, Grade 6
Boulan Park Middle School, MI

Saturn Planet

S aturn has rings made of ice and rock
A tlas is one of Saturn's moons
T itan (one of Saturn's moons) has a substantial atmosphere
U ranus is Saturn's neighbor
R hea is the moon just before Titan
N eighbors to Saturn are Jupiter on the left and Uranus on the right

Madison Germann, Grade 6
Pinewood Elementary School, IN

Fall

The fall leaves drop from the tall trees.
The leaves fall to their death on the forest floor.
The crunchy, dried-up leaves are crushed by the hooves of the deer.
Now the leaves will come again next year.

Halloween is most likely the most fun time of the year.
All the kids going door to door getting all kinds of candy.
The costumes, the houses, and the candy are really cool.
I love Halloween and I can't wait!

Football is the best sport in fall.
Not just pro and college but high school and middle school too!
I watch football every Sunday with my grandpa.
I love football because I can watch my favorite teams.

Fall is really cool.
It is my second favorite season of the year.
I love football and Halloween.
I can't wait for fall!

Jacob Lesniak, Grade 6
Holy Family Middle School, MI

Lindsie

L adybugs are my favorite bugs
I like to play soccer, it is my favorite game
N orway is a place I would like to go
D olphins are my favorite animal
S ummer is my favorite season
I really do not like the snow
E iffel Tower is something I like to see

L icorice is my favorite food
Y ellow is one of my favorite colors
N ancy Drew is my favorite movie
N estle Crunch bars are one of my favorite chocolates

S piders are gross they freak me out
H olly the Christmas Fairy is my favorite book
O hio is the state I live in
O hio State is my favorite college football team
D oing baton is something I like

Lindsie Lynn Shood, Grade 5
Frank Ohl Intermediate School, OH

A Man's Life

Once a boy comes out it all starts.
For instance, his little toothy falls out.
His first day of school.
His driver's license.
His last day of school.
College.
Work.
He has kids.
Then he becomes old and retires.
Then comes the sad part, he dies.
Another boy comes and history repeats itself again.

Allan York, Grade 6
Northwood Elementary School, IN

About the Wilderness

The leaves are green,
The birds are singing,
The frogs are croaking,
And the creek water is flowing.
The bugs are buzzin',
And the butterflies are drinkin'.
So come on, and tell me what you hear.
I told you.
So come on listen up,
'Cause all around you were talkin' to you.
Now come on and tell me what you hear.
"I hear it, the world is singing,"
So let's have some fun.
Come, and listen with us.
Yeah, please have fun,
And listen with us.

Lydia Clay, Grade 4
Legend Elementary School, OH

Faith

Faith is needed to live.
Faith is required to give.
Faith and hope are what you need.
Faith and hope can overcome greed.
Faith can make others glad.
Faith can help those who are sad.
Faith can also calm those who are mad.
Faith helps self esteem.
Faith helps show your gleam.
Faith will help you as it may.
Faith will guide you on its way.
Faith decides what's right and what's wrong.
Faith will be with you, no matter how short or long.
Faith in others benefits you.
Faith in others isn't that much to chew.
Faith allows you to banish the sorrow.
Faith now will change the world of tomorrow.
Faith is always going to help you live.
Faith will always let you give.

Alex Dolehanty, Grade 6
St Gerard School, MI

A Scrumptious Sundae

Building a sundae can be so fun,
Let's get to it, and get the job done!

I'm searching the kitchen for a bowl.
Yes, I found it — I achieved my goal!

Got the huge, pink bowl and got the scoop,
Open the freezer and take a snoop.

There's the French Vanilla that's sweet,
Now that's the beginning to a sundae treat.

Get the chocolate and drizzle it on top,
My mouth is watering, so I better stop.

Squirt the fluffy whipped cream,
It's so yummy, I could scream.

We're almost done, just one more thing,
A cherry on top and…cha ching!!!

Kaitlin Johnstone, Grade 5
Academy of the Sacred Heart, MI

Peaceful Green

Peaceful is green,
It tastes like a nice, juicy lime,
It smells like the beautiful flora in nature,
It reminds me of many juicy green fruits,
It sounds like the beautiful music from nature,
Peaceful makes me feel green.

Monika Satoskar, Grade 5
Tremont Elementary School, OH

Cats

Tabby cats, Tiger cats
I really like cats
Cats are fun
I have six cats
Lillie is my cat
She is really, really fun
Cats

Bethany Parish, Grade 4
Churubusco Elementary School, IN

Mars

Oh, Mars, purple and red,
I gaze at you from my bed.
I ask if you have seen
A little man of blue or green.

Roger Gehring, Grade 6
Melrose Elementary School, OH

Wintertime

Wintertime, wintertime
Nothing like the summertime
Wintertime, wintertime
Like I said the first time
Wintertime, wintertime
It is almost December 1st
Wintertime, wintertime
Winter is at its worst
Wintertime, wintertime
Winter is drawing to a close
Wintertime, wintertime
As I say, while I blow my nose
Wintertime, wintertime
Now it's time for summertime!

William Ten Eick, Grade 6
Abbott Middle School, MI

Elephant

Elephant
Enormous, gray
Sleeping, drinking, eating
Mud, zoo, meat, trees,
Stretching, fattening, walking,
Thick, tall
Elephant

Sam Krider, Grade 5
St Michael School, IN

Dogs

Dogs
Small, big
Barking, howling, growling
Loving, friendly, happy, excited
Puppies

Rebekah Hoffmann, Grade 4
Bailly Elementary School, IN

Peregrine Falcon

Beak
Feathers
Swift
Powerful
Large
The fastest bird in the world
Peregrine Falcon

Mitch Slater, Grade 6
Holy Angels School, OH

Life and Death

Life is a story,
Waiting to be told.
Death is a valley,
For things that get old.
Life is like summer,
Beautiful and fun.
Death is like winter,
Cold, with less sun.
Life can be exhilarating,
Surprising and rad.
Death can be dreary,
Hard and sad.
Whichever happens, we earn no less
And we lose no more
We have to push forward for
Things that are in store.

Gussy Crooks, Grade 5
Spaulding Elementary School, OH

Beach

Beach, cozy and nice,
Sandcastles big, short, and tall
Great place to have fun

Samantha Dawson, Grade 6
Roosevelt Elementary School, OH

Camp Cook Out

Meat smoke overhead,
Listening to birds chirping a song,
A relaxing song.

Malik Oudghiri, Grade 6
Stanley Clark School, IN

Winter

Winter is cold and snowy
You can make snowballs
And snowmen
And snow forts
And you can slide on the ice
And you can collect icicles
And make footprints.
Winter

Conrad Beyl, Grade 5
Henryville Elementary School, IN

Tions

If you put a period,
That's a punctuation.
If you throw a party,
That's a celebration.
If you move around,
That's motion.
If you get in trouble,
That's detention.
If you tell somebody something,
That's information.
If you go somewhere,
That's transportation.
If you play shortstop,
That's a position.
If you vote for somebody,
That's an election.

Nicole Backer, Grade 5
Frank Ohl Intermediate School, OH

Fruit/Candy

Fruit
Juicy, delicious
Eating, munching, enjoying
Lunches, dinner, snacks, dessert
Chewing, sucking, smiling
Yummy, sweet
Candy

Casey M. Bauchmoyer, Grade 5
Norwich Elementary School, OH

Riddle

Look at me
What do you see?
Nothing at all — just a fall cool breeze.
I got to admit I love to scare
But when they stare I cannot dare.

Can you guess what I am?
Come on let's hear it
I'll give you this I am a spirit.

Amber Deming, Grade 5
Reed Middle School, OH

Chocolate

Chocolate is sweet.
It tastes like heaven.
My taste buds go nuts.
I hear hallelujah when I eat it.

Chocolate can help you when you're sad.
It is sweet and delicious.
Chocolate helps your heart.
So you can live a happy life.

Hussein Ali Abouahmed, Grade 6
Trilby Elementary School, OH

Cheetah

Lightning is a cheetah
Faster than fast
They roam the Earth day by day
Waiting to strike their prey
Like a flash they can strike and make the kill

Dayon Meadows, Grade 6
Harding Middle School, OH

The Haunted Forest

I can hear the ghost screaming in the forest.
I can see the monsters creeping around.
I can feel the air around me.
It feels like something is breathing down my neck.
I can smell the four-eyed monster's breath.
Boo!
The ghosts are screaming to scare me.

Johnathan Binckley, Grade 4
Licking Valley Intermediate School, OH

The Golden Rules

Cities of gold, cities of silver
Sun is full and moon is a sliver.

Poor are rich, rich are poor
In love, integrity, and so much more.

Sapphire's blue, ruby's red
Don't let bad things go to your head.

Life's the beginning, death's the end
In the middle it doesn't matter who you befriend.

Stories new, stories old
Stories of friendship waiting to be told.

Remember these Rules of Gold if you can
They will be a silver command.

Freya Mohr, Grade 4 and Ana Mohr, Grade 5
Central Grade School, MI

Monster Under My Bed

I think there is a monster under my bed.
I don't know why it is there.
It's the strange sounds
And the glowing red eyes.
I think it is going to eat me alive.
I do I do.
As it has vicious teeth.
And it growled like a lion.
It then came out of its hiding spot.
I had recognized that face immediately.
It had a big slurpy tongue.
Then I came to know it was my dog, Rex.

Sacheth Chandramouli, Grade 6
Boulan Park Middle School, MI

I Am

I am fast and small
I wonder who will win the change wars
I hear everyone talking
I see darkness when I close my eyes
I want a billion dollars
I am fast and small

I pretend to do nothing
I feel weird
I touch my desk when I go to school
I worry about how good I get on a test
I cry when my dog dies
I am fast and small

I understand when I get in trouble
I say sleepovers are fun
I dream about nothing
I try beating *Guitar Hero Three* on medium
I hope to get *Rock Band*
I am Joey Aesy

Joseph Aesy, Grade 4
Floyd Ebeling Elementary School, MI

School, I Wish You Were Cool

School, school, I wish you were cool.
No math, science, or history!
It's no mystery, you're boring.
I wish you had a golf course, a waterslide, a pool!
School, school, I wish you were cool.
The teachers can certainly change a bit,
No homework! No homework!
No language or reading!
No sitting in hard maroon chairs, just sitting!
Alas, it's all in my imagination,
But the whole nation,
(At least the kids!)
Agree with me.

Taryn Cook, Grade 5
Northern Heights Elementary School, IN

The Death of Bob Fiber

It was October when Bob died.
He had a sickness which made us cry.
His funeral was on a Friday.
That is the day he went away.
He was very nice and very smart.
He will always be in my heart.

To Heaven I know my Bob went.
Until I see him again, my heart will have a dent.
God only knows why people must go.
I miss him a lot.
This is what I know.

McKenzie Fletcher, Grade 5
Spaulding Elementary School, OH

Sunburst 2008

Hearts pounding,
feet thumping,
minds racing,
crowds jumping,
the smell of popcorn fills the air.
I see the finish flags big and clear.
Like a victorious king,
I surge with pride
as I cross the finish line.

Alicia Porile, Grade 5
Stanley Clark School, IN

Deer

In the fresh, green woods,
Six caramel-colored deer stand.
Flash! They disappear.

Nicole Gorman, Grade 6
Stanley Clark School, IN

The Cold Winter Night

One cold winter night
stars bring bright light.
There might be a little breeze,
to make you freeze.
You smell the fragrance of cocoa,
might bring some warmth.
You're warm on the inside,
but you're cold on the outside
Christmas is on the way
for Santa to say...
Ho Ho Ho!
Come have some cocoa!
When it snows,
you will blow.
That's how I know
it's a cold winter night.

Adalay Yearby, Grade 6
Eastmoor Middle School, OH

My Dog

Bandit
She is great
She can catch lots of rats
Loving Dog
Cute
She is a good dog I love her
My dog is deaf

Griffin Young, Grade 5
Churubusco Elementary School, IN

Night Watcher

Trees with spiders.
Cicadas humming.
Everywhere at night.

Tavion Lane, Grade 4
Normandy Elementary School, OH

Navy

N ever forgetting their families back home.
A lways remembering the people that fought for our and their freedom earlier.
V ery good at helping kids in need where they're fighting.
Y ou should respect those who risk their life now and before.

Lindsay Dyer, Grade 6
DeKalb Middle School, IN

Lakeside

My friend, my friend, what do you see?
What kind of place can this be?

This place is big and shining down on Lakeside nice and bright.
The trains and cars are annoying speeding down the street and railroads.
My cat, Sasha, is eating in her bowl, some Meow Mix.
My sister, Ava, is crying in her bouncer noisily.
Children running in the yard happily.
Bikes are rusting in garages that are cold.
Always so chilly and blue, reading is the right thing to do.
My friends and I, running down Kennedy Avenue.

Although chilly, rusty and loud,
My neighborhood and I
Are always proud.

Serena Middleborn, Grade 5
Allen J. Warren Elementary School, IN

Looking Behind Me

Looking behind me, a creature I see.
Looking behind me, it's coming to get me.
Looking behind me, I am scared.
Looking behind me, I run away.
Looking behind me, I trip and fall.
Looking behind me, the creature is catching up.
Looking behind me, a pile of leaves are up ahead.
Looking behind me, I jump into them.
Looking behind me, the creature keeps running.
Looking behind me, I jump up and scare the creature and it falls down.
Looking behind me, I run away faster.
Looking behind me, I stop to take a rest.
Looking behind me, the creature has found me.
Looking behind me, I see the creature's face.
Looking behind me, I laugh and see that the creature was only my brother.

Victoria Guerrazzi, Grade 6
St Gerard School, MI

I Will Be by Your Side

You don't have to cry because I will be by your side,
No matter where you are at school, at work, at home, or outside.
You don't have to worry, I want you to not worry,
Because I will be by your side.
So don't cry,
Don't cry,
Because I will never leave your side.

Alonzo Williams, Grade 5
Auburn Hills Christian School, MI

Me and Only Me

Isabella
Silly, fun, smart
Sister of Anna and Elan
Lover of school spirit, dogs, and snowmen
Who feels nervous when at an amusement park
    and when the tornado siren goes off
Who gets excited about public speaking and singing
Who needs to get over fear of roller coasters
Who gives kisses to my dog
Who fears clowns and airplanes
Who would like to be a public speaker
Resident of Austintown, Ohio
Caruso

Isabella Caruso, Grade 5
Frank Ohl Intermediate School, OH

Bloodhound

Bloodhound
Soft, floppy-eared
Are you tracking down a fox?
Yes! You found a whole den full of them.
Tracker

Hayden Hilgenhold, Grade 5
Perry Central Elementary School, IN

Merry Christmas

M any reasons to be merry
E vergreen fills the house
R ed fuzzy stockings hang from the mantle
R eading good books under a blanket
Y ule logs crackle and snap by the fireplace

C risp snow falls to the ground
H o! Ho! Ho! Shouts Santa
R eindeer on the roof
I cicles shine in the night
S weet taste of hot chocolate
T he time of giving
M y family — the best part of Christmas
A nd…
S now, snow, snow

Emily Waller, Grade 5
Browning Elementary School, MI

He Creates

The leaves form in their own way,
they are the colors of June, July, and May.
They fly so gracefully into the wind,
they can be round, pointy, fat, or thin.
God created such perfect things,
lots of pleasure they will bring.
He still stands at heaven's gate,
and He still creates.

Mary Hall, Grade 6
Emanuel Redeemer Lutheran School, MI

Fall All Around

Fall, fall everywhere
Fall is even in my hair
Fall is in here, fall is out there
Fall is most-definitely everywhere
Fall is yellow, brown, orange, and red
Fall flew into my room and landed on my bed
Fall makes music underneath my feet
Fall is great for hopping and jumping
Fall is fun and fall is loose
Fall is sitting on my roof
Fall is every, every where

Maddie Kelley, Grade 6
Rocky River Middle School, OH

Guitar

I strum and hear
that wonderful noise,
the noise that makes me
grin from ear to ear.

It's hard to play,
but a gift to hear.
It makes me jump
from here to there.

As I jump for joy
I give Jesus back
that wonderful noise.

The noise that I hope to hear
as I play for Jesus,
my Father in heaven, one day.

Erin Kuker, Grade 6
Emmanuel-St Michael Lutheran School, IN

Winter Fun

Our sled falls down the hill
    while we grin with glee

Snowflakes fall on my face
    they won't stop hitting me

Snowballs fall from nowhere
    while we run about

The hot chocolate that falls in my mouth is so delicious
    it makes me want to shout

Another log falls on the fire
    to chase away the cold

If I've learned one thing
    It's winter will never get old!

Abbie Crick, Grade 5
Central Grade School, MI

Solar System

S paceship
O rbit around the Earth
L ayers of ice
A rmstrong
R ound

S aturn
Y ellow ice cubes
S paceship
T ells us there is
    a problem in space
E arth
M ars

Lyndsey Rivera, Grade 4
Westview Elementary School, OH

Falling Leaves

Falling, falling,
Falling!

The leaves tumble
To the ground.

Falling, falling,
Falling!

Temperatures dropping
Down.

Falling, falling,
Falling!

Like a raindrop
From the sky.

Falling, falling,
Falling!

Warm weather
Says goodbye.

Kevin Schilling, Grade 6
Wooster Christian School, OH

Morning Falls

When I wake up from bed,
The sun is in the sky,
The birds sing.
Time flies like a bird
When I'm having fun.
The sun starts to fall,
Then the moon comes up.
I go to bed
For the next morning.

Connor Carpenter, Grade 4
Legend Elementary School, OH

Summer Softball

I was number eight.
I played left field.
I played catcher,
and third base.
It was my turn to bat.
I hit it to the outfield.
I ran through first base,
Second base and third base.
I had to stay.
Everybody cheered.
I got runners in.
One of my teammates
Hit a home run.
She got me in.
We win the game.
Awesome!
We made it to the tournaments.
We cheered each other on.
We got 1st place!
Hooray!

Brin Fulton, Grade 4
Legend Elementary School, OH

World Colors

Red is a rocket glare.
Gold is the most valuable money.
Silver is the coins colors.
Blue is a never ending sea.
Orange is a Halloween pumpkin.
Black is the color of the night sky.
Green is a Christmas evergreen.
How do you see colors?

Anthony Galla, Grade 4
Northfield Elementary School, OH

My Dog

The big, brown eyes that look up at
Me when I'm sad and lonely.
The short little fluffy tail that
Wags 'til the sun goes down.
The highlight of my day and the joy
In my soul

She makes me feel nice and safe when
She lies next to me.
She can't stay with me forever and one
Day she will leave.
She will go to the gates of heaven and
Wait patiently for me

The dog I hold dearest to me just
Happens to be my precious dog
Hailey.

Nicole Richardson, Grade 6
Trilby Elementary School, OH

Disappear

As the world disappears,
and voices fade,
the voices;
once strong,
now weak;
we find ourselves,
locked in darkness,
never to be let out;
never to be heard,
now,
in our time of need;
who can save us?

Alexis Montpas, Grade 6
Hamady Middle/High School, MI

Winter/Spring

Arctic, brisk
Playing, sledding, skiing
Snowman, Christmas, shorts, pool
Melting, shining, blooming
Spring

Sean David Quinn, Grade 5
Floyd Ebeling Elementary School, MI

Team-Building Class

Stumps, boards, many kids,
But how can we get across?
Teamwork builds the bridge.

Claire Migliore, Grade 6
Stanley Clark School, IN

Monkey/A Chimp

Monkey
Soft, weird, hairy
Climbs, fast, swings, slow, crazy
Scary, bothers people, happy
A chimp

Hana Greene, Grade 4
Riverside Elementary School, MI

Fall

Fall
Thanksgiving day
Pretty birds flying south
Low sun sinking fast, night falls too
Light snow

Jonathan Jones, Grade 4
Bailly Elementary School, IN

Fall

Running through the leaves
Feeling a strong gust of wind
Fall is the greatest!

Mikey Durham, Grade 4
Westview Elementary School, OH

Fall

Windy weather whistles wildly through the trees.
Leaves changing colors and leaving the trees for death,
Going down down down to the ground.
The tree limbs look like arms reaching for the sky.

Pumpkin seeds roasting in the oven for kids to eat.
Pumpkins carved for people to see.
Pretty powerful colors falling from the trees;
what a treat.

Knock, knock, knock
Trick-or-treat.
Ghost and goblins here to greet.
Funny, scary faces we meet.

Caitlin Thomas, Grade 6
Holy Family Middle School, MI

Beneath and Above the Ocean

The ocean is calm at sunset and wild in the daytime.
Seagulls roam the air and whales breathe air above the waters.
I look at the dolphins that splash around,
And watch the crab on land make no sound.
The squid and octopus catch their prey,
While jellyfish swim away.
Fish and krill swim side by side,
While waves ride the tide.
When the day ends the sea and its animals rest so sweet.
The sea still is, so deep.

Austin Pister, Grade 5
Immanuel Scholars Home School Academy, IN

Halloween

Halloween is near
Come and play at the house of fear.
I'll scare your pants off and we'll have a dance-off.
The dance-off will be exciting,
We will be laughing all night,
In a spooky haunted house!

Jordan Hogue, Grade 5
Reed Middle School, OH

If I Were President

Thank you for voting for me.
I want to lower taxes for hard working Americans.
We need to lower gasoline prices.
We need to drill our own oil in Texas and Alaska.

I plan to have intelligent people as my advisors.
These people will make up my cabinet.
We will keep extremely dangerous criminals in prison for life.
There are too many poor children in the United States too.

I hope to be a president you can be proud of!

David Stebelton, Grade 4
Dobbins Elementary School, OH

An Afghan's Ups and Downs

Afghanistan is a mountainous landlocked,
Country in central Asia that's been mocked.

Flag — symbols — red, black, and green in thirds,
It has an emblem with wheat, a building, and words.

Government has been overthrown and disrupted.
Many times the Soviets and Taliban have erupted.

History of Afghans without many pleasant times.
Afghanistan has war, death, drought, and crimes.

Academics — poorly organized, girls can't go to schools.
Usually nobody gets educated, and learns any rules.

Icons from Afghanistan are Blue Mosque, the Taliban,
And Sharbat Gula's picture at a refugee camp in Pakistan.

Soviets — Russian soldiers who came to be great.
They tried to rule Afghanistan from 1978-1988.

Taliban — a group of people who have strict laws,
And try to take advantage of Afghanistan's flaws.

Art is made of beautiful tiles and paints by Afghans,
But the cruel Taliban will not allow any images of man.

Natural resources are mostly oil, dyes, gems,
And poppies that should definitely be condemned!

Tim Armbruster, Grade 6
Ann Arbor Christian School, MI

White Winter Wonderland

Snow spiraling down
Great cold drifts of cotton
Snowballs flying through the air
Icicles on every porch roof
The unmistakable beauty
Of the winter world
Snow glittering like a thousand diamonds
Nose red with cold
Easily cured
With a steaming cup of hot cocoa
Rich, creamy and chocolatey
Prepared especially for me
Cookies, milk and gingerbread men
Majestically marching to their death
In Santa Claus's mouth
Mr. Kris Kringle
Giver of gifts
To good girls and boys
Filling stockings high
Murdering the cookies

Kathryn Urban, Grade 6
Harding Middle School, OH

An Ode to Lily

Lily my favorite dog.
You are crazy and energetic
But so lovable and kind.
Your body is so furry
And your face is so cute.
You love walks mostly long ones.
When I heard that you were
Having puppies I was overjoyed!
When the day is done
Your heavy body lays on me
As we fall asleep on the couch.
Lily o Lily I love you so much
Especially your golden retriever
touch!!!

Sara Gordon, Grade 5
Allen J. Warren Elementary School, IN

Fall Leaves

red leaves, yellow leaves,
brown leaves, green leaves,
dark yellow, orange leaves,
all different colors falling to the ground,
the ground is now a colorful ground
making a rainbow blanket

Tyler Cross, Grade 4
Norwich Elementary School, OH

Fall

Fall, when the days are very long
When the leaves change colors
Fall, fall…when the air is crisp

Maddie Jones, Grade 4
Keystone Academy, MI

Stars, Stripes, and Colors

When little children raise the flag
On the 4th of July
The beauty of the red, white, and blue
I can tell it is no lie
When freedom rang the bells of liberty,
The British took a sigh
All the Americans jumped up and down
To show their joy and glee

Alexis Valles, Grade 6
Kesling Middle School, IN

Fall and Spring Gifts

Fall leaves
colorful, bright
falling, crunching, crackling
yellow, orange, red, purple
blooming, shooting, budding
beautiful, fragrant
Spring flowers

Mitch Vetter, Grade 5
Norwich Elementary School, OH

Christmas Morning

I see my tree covered with ornaments as I watch them dangle from the branches
Presents have colorful wrapping paper

I see the sun blasting in through the open windows,
Making the ornaments shimmer and shine
They look like little twinkling stars

My family laughs as we hear my dog bark, as he sniffs out his present
We enjoy the Christmas music playing quietly in the background

Why do I think Christmas is so awesome?
Maybe it's because it's so relaxing to be with my family and have fun

The cookies my mom and I baked yesterday are heaven
My stocking as fat as a cow

I LOVE CHRISTMAS!
I LOVE CHRISTMAS!
I LOVE CHRISTMAS!

Mary Fry, Grade 5
EH Greene Intermediate School, OH

Even Though My Life Is Hard It's Not That Bad

I am from chopped down corn stalks and houses that need cleaning.
I am from soccer geeks and non-apologetic sisters.
I am from yelling teachers to M&M eating teachers.
I am from kids that don't want to do their job at night
and parents don't want to eat pancakes.
I am from apple eating worms and redheaded girl books.
I am from smelly dry-erase markers
and two crazy, lazy, checker playing brothers.

Madalyn O'Malley, Grade 6
St Maria Goretti School, IN

I Am

I am hyper and jolly.
I wonder if I'll ever become a chef.
I hear Pokemon speaking.
I see my imaginary friends Joe, Jon, Puff, and Draco.
I want the games "Spores Creatures" and "Spectrobes Beyond the Portals."
I am hyper and jolly.
I pretend to be a fox.
I feel happy when my imaginary friends come to school with me.
I touch my imaginary friends.
I worry about my chickens.
I cry after I'm angry.
I am hyper and jolly.
I understand the truth.
I say my emblem (respect the truth).
I dream I have super powers.
I try to make my family happy.
I hope to get married.
I am hyper and jolly.

Jacob Booth, Grade 6
Galesburg-Augusta Middle School, MI

United States of America

U nder pressure you save us.
N ever backing down from challenges you're given.
I n our country's toughest situations you stay strong
T o the end of the world and back for us
E agles fly just for you
D edication to the U.S.A.

S tanding tall all night and day
T hanks for all you've done for us
A fter the work's done you come home with pride
T rainings hard but you don't care
E normously we have you outnumbered
S oldiers leaving the bad guy thinking what hit them

O verseas you fight for us
F orever your love will shine on us

A merica the great
M aking the world more peaceful
E ternal love you'll get too
R eminder why you're there
I njuries you've overcome to be there
C loudy days not going to stop you
A merica we'll sit you down

Sam Duncan, Grade 4
Stonegate Elementary School, IN

Weather

Chilly and cloudy
Rain slowly drizzles from clouds
Wind gusts leaves from trees

Caia Trykall, Grade 4
Frank H Hammond Elementary School, IN

Waterfall

My feet are cold as I poke them into the water.
They hurt from walking forever,
but the warm sun shines down on me.
I feel so alive:
water rushing past my feet,
little blue and black rocks pressing against my soles,
a small, cool breeze brushing past my face,
blue birds chirping above,
cubs eating berries in the distance.
My family is talking
and laughing around me
and having a good time hiking to the falls.

Here at a gorgeous waterfall
the rocks are painted black
and some feel as smooth as marbles,
so big that they are bigger than my dad.
So much fun here at the Smokey Mountains in Tennessee

Abbey Kaser, Grade 5
Stanley Clark School, IN

Baseball

My favorite sport is baseball.
I wish I could play during study hall.
I wish I could play every day.
That's how much I love to play.

I have been playing since I was two.
Even though the pros like to chew,
I know it is something I will never do.
Because it is bad and causes cancer too.

I now play on a travel team with some really cool friends.
I know we will always be together until the end.
We work well together like a team should.
And help each other whenever we could.

Tommy De Cero, Grade 6
St John the Baptist Elementary School, IN

Indiana Beach

A tall roller coaster soars ahead into the sunny blue sky,
and a giant Ferris wheel circles slowly
just past the entrance to the amusement park behind me.
On the right there is a lake,
I am watching a strange pirate show on the water.
Now to my left, another roller coaster whips around the track.
The screaming sounds like people falling off a cliff,
and the click-clack of many roller coasters makes me scared.
The hot sunshine beats down on me.

Dustin Kerckhove, Grade 5
Stanley Clark School, IN

Autumn

A wesome colors this time of year
U nharvested fields of corn
T remendous and amazing pumpkin carvings
U nbelievable weather night and day
M any people love the colors
N oises and spooks throughout the night.

Tristan Wilbur, Grade 6
Eisenhower Middle School, OH

The Dangerous Wolf

What does a wolf know?
Great hunters
Hunt for food
5 hours a day
Live in cold arctic regions
Wolves with slender legs
Run up to 45 miles for 20 minutes
Hunt for deer, cattle, sheep and other livestock
Farmers have fought back wolves
Live all over
Montana and Wyoming
And other states

Robert Maisonville, Grade 5
Riley Upper Elementary School, MI

Independence Day

Red, white, and blue are the colors that are shown on the flag for today is Independence Day
We jump up and down and say hurray for today is Independence Day
Family gathers around the streets to see the parade for today is Independence Day
People celebrate by wearing red, white, and blue for today is Independence Day
Candy is thrown, marching bands blow for today is Independence Day
Friends say hello, children's whistles blow for it is Independence Day
People have smiles on their faces as they have picnics in many different places for today is Independence Day
The parade is almost over but the baseball games have just begin for today is Independence Day
Children stop running the bases as their parents put their cameras in their cases for today is Independence Day
The fireworks start as our hearts get caught in the moment for today is Independence Day
Parents turn off the light as children say goodnight at the end of Independence Day!

Haley Kleimola, Grade 6
Abbott Middle School, MI

An Ode to Our Armed Forces

From the American Revolution to the War on Terrorism, you have fought for us.
During war, you have lived under the shadow of a great flag.
You carried it into battle on your smart uniforms fit for only the best.
If it tore, you would fight for it much more than you did before.
It has, as you have too, seen much more than a few mere fits.
To those who left the nest and never got to be Vets, we hope the best.
To light a battlefield with gunfire must have been a horrible sight, but you went through.
To put a stop to Hitler or Hussein's evil leer must have felt wonderful!
If you sought to be a decorated general, bravery, pride, and much, much more are better than stars and medals.
You were sent to wars large and small, and for protecting us, and the world, we thank you!
Even if you got covered in soot, you kept on fighting.
You're all amazing, right down to the core.
You might be short, but your spirit is tall and strong!
You stayed put, even if you were afraid to fight.
You may have been or be sore, but thanks for fighting, it's worth so much more!
On this Veteran's Day, please know how much we care and how much we're thankful!
Thank you!

Christian Fernandez, Grade 6
EH Greene Intermediate School, OH

Snow

Snow, snow everywhere, snow, snow in my hair.
I hear the kids laugh and play, although I'm cold I'll play anyway.
Enjoying the snow I freeze so much, as the snow picks up I feel its touch.
Knowing that later I'll be at home, that is why I'm writing this poem.
Snow is cold and makes your body freeze, as the wind grows I feel a breeze.
When I look at the snow it is as white as can be, I look outside and see the kids flee.
After I come in I have a rosy red face, then I drink my hot cocoa by the fireplace.
Winter weather freezes you, everyone is cold, I am too!
When you see the snow coming down, you are sure to never have a frown.
Waiting for a while until it is white, then I can go outside and have snowball fights.
Warming up after you play outdoors, you want to go back out for more.
Building up snow forts, playing on icy basketball courts.
Throwing snowballs everywhere, going in wild directions you play with no care.
I listen as I lay in bed at night, to the soft roar of the wind that gives me a fright.
When I wake up and see snow on the ground, I go outside, and it is still, not a sound.
Don't forget to put on your boots gloves and hat, before you come in be sure to wipe your shoes on the mat.
Soon the snow will be coming down more and more, I can't wait to see all the snow we have in store.
Yelling, shouting, and having fun, snow is great for anyone.

Sarah Norton, Grade 6
Corpus Christi Elementary School, IN

Birthday Parties

B is for balloons that you pop
I is for ice cream that you eat non stop
R is for the raindrops that spoil the fun
T is for teeth with chocolate. Oh fun!
H is for Holly playing with her friends all day
D is for dad who brought home cake today
A is for Ali blowing out the candles hooray!
Y is for yelling and shouting, yeah! Yeah!

P is for people all gathered around
A is for apples all over the ground
R is for Richard who gives out a treat
T is for table all decorated and neat
I is for impatient people waiting for the cake
E is for everyone drinking a milkshake
S is for summer birthday parties are the best!

Morgan Haynes, Grade 6
Trilby Elementary School, OH

Cancer

C ancer was put in the sky after Hera
A sked the crab to help Hydra kill Hercules, who was in
N eed of aid. Hercules accidentally stepped on the
C rab and killed him, therefore Hera gave him an
E qual place in the sky where the constellation
R emains to this day.

Jenny Rodriguez, Grade 6
Pinewood Elementary School, IN

A Scary Spooky Halloween

Ghosts are a scream,
Halloween is a dream.

When it hits midnight,
all the ghosts and goblins appear tonight.

There was a haunted house down the street,
there were monsters in it and they were eating meat.

There was a black rat,
under my yellow hat.

Under my bed,
I saw a creepy head.

Walking up the stair,
I saw a big creepy bear.

Trick-or-treating is so much fun,
I saw a big skeleton and I began to run.

The ghosts and goblins, witches too,
are going to sleep so I will have to wait to say boo!

Emily Williams, Grade 5
Browning Elementary School, MI

Spring

Spring is a beautiful time of year
Spring can get you into gear
Spring cleaning is not fun
Spring is when you can finally feel the sun
Spring into action by helping others
Spring to hug your sisters and brothers
Spring is when baseball starts
Spring is when you can go out and get exercise for your heart
Spring is sadly when some allergies come
Spring is when you go out and blow bubbles with bubble gum
Spring brings gorgeous blossoms and flowers
Spring also starts to give us longer hours
Spring is when we're still in school
Spring is when we fill up our pools
Spring means no more coats
Spring is time to put in the boats
Spring is a lot of things
Spring helps us spread our wings to all that summer brings

Michelle Hart, Grade 6
St Gerard School, MI

Fall

Fall is when people dress up to be someone they're not,
    trick-or-treating to get candy.
Fall is also where the leaves begin to change color,
    starting to go away from the trees
    like birds as if they were heading south
    but the trees stay north.
Fall is also when pumpkins pop out,
    Jack-o'-lanterns lit up on the porch.
Looking at them closely faces take shape,
    kind of creepy but you get used to it.
    If you look at the trees
    their branches like arms,
looking really closely you can see they look very sad indeed.
    Most of their leaves are gone away
    and they won't grow new ones till next spring.
    In Mexico they think of this season as
    "The Day of the Dead"
    celebrating in the streets
    and in their houses.
    Rising into their spirit's,
    celebrating that they can see life again.

Enrique Araujo, Grade 6
Holy Family Middle School, MI

Saturn

S aturn is a gaseous planet with an
A tmosphere composed of hydrogen and helium. It is
T erribly cold on Saturn. Saturn's gravity level is
U nder zero. This planet has many
R ings that can be seen during the
N ight with a telescope.

Nathan Munet, Grade 6
Pinewood Elementary School, IN

Candy Canes

Red and white
Oh, so bright
Lick lick lick
Oops it broke
Crunch crunch crunch
Oh, my teeth hurt
Lick lick lick
Oh no, it's all gone

Time for another one

Now don't break this one
or you're going to the dentist.
Mother said
NOT THE DENTIST!!!
Lick…lick…lick…
Very gentle now
This one might take a while
oh, now I'm done

Abbi Hawkins, Grade 5
Heritage Intermediate School, IN

Ghosts

G hosts on
H alloween in
O ctober are
S cary
T onight

Alexis Larson, Grade 4
Bailly Elementary School, IN

Fall

Fall
Wet, bare trees
Blustery wind, leaves falling, frost
Chili, dark holidays
Autumn

Sam Boland, Grade 4
Bailly Elementary School, IN

Missing You

Somebody asked if I missed you,
I didn't answer.
I closed my eyes and walked away
And whispered,
So much.
Later in the day, in the hallway
I was going to say,
But then I walked away.

You gave me your heart
But now it's gone
And it's still
Break of dawn.

Katrina Brann, Grade 6
Pennfield Middle School, MI

Freedom

F lags that represent our nation gallantly streaming in the sky
R ed, white, and blue are our nation's colors with no boundaries
E veryone has the same rights and
E veryone over the age of thirty-five can run for president
D ocuments such as the Declaration of Independence
   and the Constitution
O ne big independent nation
M any branches of government such as the U.S. Congress

Andrew Reliford, Grade 5
Sanderson Elementary School, OH

The Birthday Party

I see, one fine summer day, kids having fun;
At a birthday party with games galore, and heaps of presents too.
Surrounded by friends, the fun never ends;
Parties are the best in the world.
When sunlight, clear and bright, dances on the walls;
Leaping off the decorations, causing rainbows to dance around.
I hear everyone laughing, everyone singing;
Dancing, playing, talking;
Screams of sheer delight as well.
I think to those parties of long ago,
Who threw the first one? And where?
And in these parties nowadays,
What causes such fun that we share?
This extravaganza of merrymaking,
With colors shining like the morning sky.
The time to share and care,
To celebrate someone's birthday.
Now it's time for the luscious cake!
Now it's time for the luscious cake!
Now it's time for the luscious cake!

Lexy Rile, Grade 5
EH Greene Intermediate School, OH

Presents

Sneaking carefully down the stairs, to see if you have any presents.
Peeking outside, and seeing sparkling white snow.
Slowly, counting how many presents you got, hoping you have the most.

The bright sun is just coming up, early in the morning.
You can see your dark shadow creeping towards the tree.

You can hear nothing but dead silence.
You're not making a minute peep.

Is someone watching every step I take?
I'm desperate to see, when will I open my presents?

The ground is covered in a blanket of snow.
It is as silent as a graveyard.

Closer, closer, closer…

Serena Kaul, Grade 5
EH Greene Intermediate School, OH

Love Her

Laugh with her…
Play with her…
Watch her with pride…
Talk with her…
Learn with her…
Grow with her all your life through…
And she'll share a word full of gladness with you…

Emileigh Bechtolt, Grade 5
Birmingham Covington School, MI

Hockey

H ockey is a great game,
O sgood is a player's name.
C arrying a hockey stick,
K een to be the team's best pick.
E ven if your team hasn't won,
Y ou know that it is just for fun.

I like to play the game,
S omeday I'd like to be in the Hall of Fame.

F ighting hard to win a cup,
U ntil the season's up.
N HL!!!

Mordechai Zuroff, Grade 4
Cincinnati Hebrew Day School, OH

The Great Outdoors

The great outdoors
How adventurous and great
You smell springtime flowers
And autumn leaves
Birds are chirping
Snakes are lurking
In the great outdoors

Haley Nolan, Grade 5
Washington Township Elementary School, IN

An Ode to Lauren

My dear friend Lauren, you're sweet as candy.
The smile you have is oh, so dandy.
My face lights up whenever you're near.
Your kindness is what I love to hear.
You're as fit as a fiddle; one of a kind.
Nice and forgiving, never losing your mind.
You're my best friend right now, my best friend forever.
You're loyal, respectful, trustworthy, too!
These are just a few things that I like about you!
You're like a sister to me but we never fight!
Whether it's dark, light, day, or night.
We will never forget each other.
I know because you are my best friend right now,
My best friend forever!

Paige Renee Stange, Grade 5
Allen J. Warren Elementary School, IN

Courtney

C ool to be with
O utgoing
U ranus is her favorite planet
R andom sometimes
T alented in a lot of things
N eat in everything
E legant
Y oung and beautiful

Kayla Mollet, Grade 5
West Washington Elementary School, IN

Video Games

When I get a new video game
I can't wait to play it.
I get the new unlocked characters, from a new high score.
When I get on a new level
I cheer.
I love the controller
sticking to my hands with sweat.
That is why I love video games!

Fischer White, Grade 4
Licking Valley Intermediate School, OH

Eyes of a Soldier

It's my first time in Iraq.
The other guys say I'll be fine.
I've heard about it here.
What I heard wasn't pretty.
I came for my dad.
He was a Marine too.
My hands are shaking.
We're turning into the field.
It's on, I can't stop now.
It's over, I'm fine.
It went by fast.
I'm being sent home now.
I call everyone.
I'm old now because years passed too quick.
My son's going to war.
I'm scared but I tell him good luck.

Brandon Thiede, Grade 6
Northwood Elementary School, IN

Christmas

C hristmas is here once again!
H olly jolly time of year!
R udolph is leading the way.
I s there enough presents to go around?
S anta ate my cookies!
T ime to open presents!
M rs. Claus is baking cookies.
A way Santa Claus goes!
S anta is giving away presents to everybody!

Lindsey Russell, Grade 5
West Washington Elementary School, IN

Tornado

Oh, tornado with high winds,
Your cyclone will spin and spin.
As it tears down our homes,
We stare at what has been.

We wonder what to do next.
The wind has scattered things.
Our memories are lost —
Who knows what the future brings?

Austin Miko, Grade 6
Melrose Elementary School, OH

Dodge Ball

Dodge ball
Exciting, skillful
Throwing, hitting, paining
Violent sport
Bruise machine

Ped Paul, Grade 6
Melrose Elementary School, OH

An Ode to Oakley

Oh Oakley,
So playful and cute.
Whenever I hear you're coming over,
I always give a hoot.

Oh Oakley,
Always giving me those puppy dog eyes,
Just so you can get,
Whatever you decide.

Oh Oakley,
Waking me up with your wet kisses,
Pulling down my blanket and waiting
For your breakfast in the kitchen.

Oh Oakley,
You're my best friend of all.
Our friendship will last
Forever so long

Oh Oakley,
There's not any bit of doubt.
That you're my best friend.
I couldn't possibly live without.

Brittany Brzek, Grade 5
Allen J. Warren Elementary School, IN

Lightning

Lightning shocks!
No sound!
Quick as a bullet!

Chance Koogler, Grade 4
Normandy Elementary School, OH

Winter and Summer

Winter,
cold, snowy
skiing, sledding, snowboarding
hot chocolate, fire, warm, hot
swimming, running, jumping
pop, water
Summer

Mackenzie Cleary, Grade 6
Harmon Middle School, OH

Kick Me

I am a football
Thrown and kicked around
Rolled in the grass
Overfilled with joy.
Sometimes, I'd just like to be
Kicked out of the stadium.

Chase Spriggs, Grade 5
Westview Elementary School, OH

What Is Blue?

Blue is a sea,
A spacious sky
Blue is my jacket,
A color of independence
Blue is for a blue stripe on a rainbow,
The color of icicles on a snowy day
Blue is blueberries
And also bluebells
Blue is a blue jay,
Flying sky high
The lightest crayon
In the box
Blue is soft,
Blue is dreamy,
Blue is a rainy day.

Claire Kim, Grade 4
University Elementary School, IN

Fall

Oh, how I love the fall,
Leaves changing and trees so tall.

Playing in the leaves
As I am looking at the trees.
The multicolored shapes continue to fall.
The pillar of piles grow so tall.

Carving pumpkins with my friends,
It seems like the fun never ends.

Oh, how I love fall, fall, fall!
Having fun and that's about all.

Mary Grocholski, Grade 6
Holy Family Middle School, MI

The Water Snake

Eating
Minnows
Fast and swift,
Smooth and slithery,
In his wet home.
He waits,
For his next meal,
Wondering,
What's next
On the menu
Gulp!

Joseph Navarra, Grade 4
Normandy Elementary School, OH

The Farm

I've been working all day,
in the sun.
I've been resting on the hay,
I've been having fun
I've been in the water,
and having a blast,
and I see some otter
oh, how they swim so fast!

Alex Droste, Grade 5
Mark C Roose Elementary School, MI

Migration

Out of the nest
Above the trees
Through the leaves
Around a branch
Down below
In the sky
To the south

Dominic Testa, Grade 5
Rootstown Elementary School, OH

The Rose

The rose, it stands
So big and bright,
The color red,
For the blood
He shed.
In fact, He is called the
Rose of Sharon
What a beautiful
Name for the
Son of God.
The sharp bloody thorns
Are for that beloved crown.
For the blood that
Streamed from His brow.
How beautiful is the Rose.

Anna Pankiewicz, Grade 6
Crown Point Christian School, IN

Love is the Answer

A shot is heard,
A hand is held,
A life is lost.
Another pointless war has begun.
Death and violence are no way to solve things
We should all join hands,
Not fight for power or goods,
Loved ones are killed in pointless war
For no good reason,
Love is the answer,
Love can move mountains,
So why can't it stop a war?
Love is the answer to everything.

Blake McWatters, Grade 5
Assumption BVM School, MI

Payday

Mayday! Mayday!
There is no payday,
Not a check in the mail,
No money for me,
For things that I see,
Not even a penny or two,
I'll have to mortgage my house and my mill,
To play for my electricity bill,
Give me some money,
Oh please, please, please!
I'm starving,
I'm homeless,
I think I might even freeze!
I've worked too hard to let this down,
But I'll never ever frown.

Matthew Kennedy, Grade 4
Northern Heights Elementary School, IN

Halloween

Halloween is the best day ever.
It is so fun, it should go on forever.

Some people give out Almond Joys.
Other people give out toys.

Scary costumes sometimes bring fears.
And for children, even tears.

You might get a lot of treats.
That you want to go home and eat.

I wish 8 o'clock would never come.
That's the end of all the fun.

At 8 o'clock it's the end of Halloween cheer.
I can't wait to get dressed up next year.

Jonah Ian Summerford, Grade 6
Trilby Elementary School, OH

My Favorite Friend

Christmas is my favorite friend,
Like something you've never seen,
The smell of my cocoa,
The lights on my tree,
The lights that seem to twinkle for me.
Christmas is my favorite friend,
The Christmas joy that fills the air,
The carols I hear being sung over there,
The questions I seem to never forget,
What's in my present?
What will I get?
Christmas is my favorite friend,
An angel glowing upon my tree,
The happy kids yelling with glee,
The crackling fire that burns like the sun,
The music that's jolly for everyone,
The sound of paper getting torn and thrown,
The sight of the snow drifted and blown,
The jingle of my jingling bells,
My nose being tickled by wonderful smells,
Christmas is my favorite friend.

Sam Lareau, Grade 5
EH Greene Intermediate School, OH

Second

I hear the whistle blow
I see the swimmers go;
to the other side and back,
their time the judges have to track.

Finally it's my turn on the block,
the starting whistle gives us a shock.
Immediately we all dive in,
all we can think is win, win, win.

I get to the other side first,
I intend on not being the worst.
Finally we touch the wall.
We're tired and breathless, we feel like we'll fall.

Then I hear the judge call my name,
second place is where I came.

Rebecca Sosa, Grade 6
St John the Evangelist School, IN

Basketball/Football

Basketball
Orange leather b-balls, tan hard wooden floors,
Winning, scoring, fouling,
Pacers, Lakers, NBA finals, Giants, Colts, Super Bowl,
Tackling, passing, sacking,
Green manicured fields, brown pigskin footballs,
Football

Verna Schwartz, Grade 5
Perry Central Elementary School, IN

Magic

She dropped her purse
He picked it up,
They watched us
We looked into each other's eyes,
It was beautiful.

Jayna Binkiewicz, Grade 6
Harmon Middle School, OH

Mother

Mother
Radiant, faithful
Loving, caring, forgiving
Warm like a summer's day
Angel

Emily Clevidence, Grade 6
Melrose Elementary School, OH

My Brother

C ollects cards
O bvious to me
D id you know he can be sweet
Y ou should get to know him

M ovies, he likes them
O h we have a really good time
O bvious he'll do anything for a dime
R eally cool, sometimes
E veryone should meet him

Maria Moore, Grade 5
St Michael School, IN

The Man from Guam

There once was a man from Guam,
Who always liked to chew gum,
One day he blew a bubble,
And he was in trouble,
After that he sucked his thumb.

Jake Miller, Grade 6
Roosevelt Elementary School, OH

Locker

You look so great
So neat and tidy
Yet you don't notice
The craziness you cause
I can't reach the top of you
I can't hang supplies up
You are so convenient
You hold all my work
You are the protection to it
You have to know the numbers
To reveal your secrets
What you hide behind your door
In that small dark orange room

Kelsey Kvasnicka, Grade 6
Harding Middle School, OH

Opening Presents

I am sitting on the floor with my family gathered around me.
I open the first present and a feeling of extreme delight fills my body.

The lights are focused right on me.
The sun is low, but we can see perfectly
Because the nine branched candle called a menorah, is lit.
The colors of the room sparkle around my body.
The air is serene except for the tearing of paper.

Then, everybody gasps.
I have gotten the present that I have always wanted.
Even though they can't hear me
I start thanking whoever sent me the presents.

Can I play with this present?
What will the next present be?

Opening presents is like winning a first place trophy!
Thank you. Thank you! Thank you!!!

Rachel Cogen, Grade 5
EH Greene Intermediate School, OH

Fall Evenings

Tiny golden paintings spiral down from tired trees;
The ones that still remain are ruffled by the chilling breeze.
Ready-to-harvest cornstalks bend and bow as I pass by,
The husky green so striking against an empty, cold blue sky.
The cricket-chirping soundtrack slowly fades away
As the owl's calls of autumn slowly slip in yet to stay.
Summer will always be my favorite, but when seasons decide to move on,
Those cozy fall evenings make it every bit better summer's gone.

Hanna Sullivan, Grade 5
Westfield Intermediate School, IN

I Am

I am athletic and cool.
I wonder when the world is going to end.
I hear my desk screaming.
I see my teacher playing *Rock Band* in the classroom.
I want an iPod Nano for Christmas.
I am athletic and cool.
I pretend that I live in Hollywood.
I feel excited about my trip to Mars.
I touch a lion's back.
I worry about my grades on my report card.
I cry when I don't get to see my mom.
I am athletic and cool.
I understand when I get yelled at because I did something wrong.
I say, "Treat other people how you want to be treated."
I dream about having 100 million dollars.
I try to do my best in school.
I hope I get an iPod Nano for Christmas.
I am athletic and cool.

Alyssa Whitney, Grade 6
Galesburg-Augusta Middle School, MI

I Am

I am athletic and sweet.
I wonder what my teachers think of me.
I hear my book telling me a story.
I see trees waving to me.
I want a chestnut horse.
I am athletic and sweet.
I pretend that I am a teacher.
I feel sad that my pencil has flown away.
I touch my imaginary horse.
I worry that I won't pass a test.
I cry when I think about my dog that was killed.
I am athletic and sweet.
I understand the game of volleyball.
I say that volleyball is fun!
I dream that I will go to WMU for volleyball.
I try hard in school.
I hope my mom and dad will get me a horse.
I am athletic and sweet.

Kealey O'Day, Grade 6
Galesburg-Augusta Middle School, MI

Seasons

There's summer, there's fall, there's winter, there's spring.
Oh, what joy these seasons can bring.

In the summer the heat blazes down from above,
'Tis a blessing given by God's own special love.

In the fall the leaves change color and drop to the ground.
It brings joy and love, plenty around.

Winter comes with a chill and some snow,
Along with the story of a baby born long, long ago.

Spring brings new life and a sense of peace to the mind.
With things so fragile and timid, we tend to be kind.

Seasons tell us if it should be warm or cold.
They also bring peace to the young and the old.

Jonathan Charles Adair, Grade 6
Emmanuel-St Michael Lutheran School, IN

Jesus Christ

He is the son of the one true God
He is the Savior of the land
He died for us to be forgiven of sin
He and his followers traveled to preach the Bible
He healed the sick
He gave sight to the blind
He is the one you pray to when in need
He is there, at the gateway to Heaven
He is there waiting for you
He wants you there, come to him

Christopher Graman, Grade 6
North Knox East Elementary/Jr High School, IN

Christmas Day

On Christmas Day it is so joyful.
We take turns opening presents,
Eat good foods and friends come over.

Outside the sun is so bright and
It falls through the windows filling it with light.
Inside the house there is a sparkling tree.

Happy voices can be heard
And the sound of opening presents.
Laughing fills the air making the household pleasant.

Questions ring throughout the day:
Will it be snowing?
What is for dinner?
Who thought of Santa?

Christmas makes me feel happy and joyful;
It is like a dog with a bone.
A time for families to get together.

Merry Christmas.
Merry Christmas.
Merry Christmas.

Wessel Bleesing, Grade 5
EH Greene Intermediate School, OH

Kaitlyn

My hair is like sand blowing in the wind.
My eyes are like beautiful green leaves.
My ears are like fox ears.
My smile is like shining stars going through the sky.
My heart holds happiness that is blue as the sky.
I live in a southern Indiana town.
I eat away the words in a book.

Kaitlyn Goss, Grade 5
Henryville Elementary School, IN

Sports

I like sports because it's filled with fun,
When I'm on the field I really get it done.
It's not because of Gatorade,
It's my physical play when I play my game.
I put on my shorts or pants when I'm ready to play,
I get on the field or court, then I blow 'em away.
Now you know how I spend the rest of my week,
Because I wanna hear 'em say Go Maalik!
Barnett Park is where I play,
When they reach for the ball, I will make them pay!
When I shoot the ball, I scorch the net,
When I make my move, I'll make you fret.
You'll get worried and even scared,
When I'm in the zone, I go on a tear!

Maalik Muhammad, Grade 6
Granville T Woods Community School, OH

Soccer

Soccer, soccer
You get to
Kick the ball and
Have some fun.
You get to hit the ball with your head.
You can't hit it with your hand.
Walid Abuhashim, Grade 4
Northfield Elementary School, OH

Day to Remember

V ery brave
E very day things
T hank you
E leventh day of November
R ed, white, and blue
A rmy
N ever quit!

Ethan Kallner, Grade 4
Westview Elementary School, OH

Winter

Winter blows in with
sleds coming down mountains
and snowballs in the air
on a bitter, cold day
with children all bundled up
and Mom making hot chocolate.
Samir Samuel, Grade 4
Floyd Ebeling Elementary School, MI

Christmas

Christmas
Joyful, peaceful
Loving, giving, sharing
The most wonderful time of the year
Xmas
Samantha Kosmalski, Grade 4
Floyd Ebeling Elementary School, MI

Jets

J ets are fast jets are high
A beautiful sight in the big blue sky
C ool and awesome yes they are
O utrageous things
B ecause of all those nice wings
Jacob Foster, Grade 4
Veale Elementary School, IN

Turkey

Brown and yummy
Gobbling, flapping, pecking
Tasty treat that melts in your mouth
Golden fowl.
Trent Franzman, Grade 5
Perry Central Elementary School, IN

All About Me

A cceptable to many people
L iar, not me
E ntertainer to others
X -mas, my favorite holiday

E arns love and care
D oes what he is told
W ants a happy
A nd healthy life
R emains all right for now
D ad is my best buddy

A nd everyone too
N ever does anything wrong
Z ero friends, no way because
E veryone cares for me
L ike my family
M y family I love
O r my family loves me
Alex Edward Anzelmo, Grade 5
Frank Ohl Intermediate School, OH

Soccer/Hockey

Soccer
Fast, accurate
Cleats, goals, fouls, refs
Skating, checking, icing
Tough, physical
Hockey
Matthew Seeds, Grade 4
Norwich Elementary School, OH

I Am

I am cute and athletic
I wonder what I will be for Halloween
I hear the waves at the beach
I see the sun shine in my hands
I want to be an engineer when I grow up
I am cute and athletic

I pretend I am famous
I feel the power in my face
I touch the flowers in the sky
I worry about my family
I cry when something bad happens
I am cute and athletic

I understand that school is important
I say I get A's in school
I dream about happy things
I try to be a good person
I hope to get A's on my papers
I am cute and athletic
Lauren Dimitrievski, Grade 4
Floyd Ebeling Elementary School, MI

My Black Rug

My black rug is furry and big
My black rug eats like a pig
She waits outside my bath tub
Waiting for me to give her a rub
She laps up the water that trickles out
I use my towel to wipe her snout
I don't know what I'd do without
My black rug that's outside my tub
My black dog is furry and big
My black dog eats like a pig
My black dog is my black rug
Anna Spoto, Grade 6
Abbott Middle School, MI

Softball

Softball is awesome, softball is great,
let's just hope I get on base.
Swing the bat, hit the ball,
just don't trip and fall.
But just stay calm,
and hit the ball!
Madeline Irmer, Grade 5
St Jude Catholic School, IN

Rivers

a river rushing
thundering down a steep cliff
spraying cold water
Caleb Dimery, Grade 6
Roosevelt Elementary School, OH

Best Ever

Leaves, trees, pumpkins, gourds
Sweet smell of autumn lingers
Earth looks glorious
Smells are wonderful, like fall
I hope it's the best ever!
Bethany Elliott, Grade 5
Westview Elementary School, OH

Trouble Maker

I'm your little nuisance,
Bugging you every day,
Using your things without being told.
Irritating you, nonstop!
Every night and day,
I make a mess,
Causing you stress,
But when the sun falls and,
The moon rises,
I fall asleep.
Somehow I'm not the little nuisance
I once was.

Kyle McCloud, Grade 5
Westview Elementary School, OH

An Ode to Lorraine

My friend Lorraine
Is caring, smart, oh so kind
She thinks of others
And not just her
My parents love her oh yes they do
And I bet she loves them too
Every time I see her she reminds me of family
Who are always there for me
She helps me with everything
she always compliments me
We will be together forever and ever
You are always welcome to
Come home with me

Jade Wright, Grade 5
Allen J. Warren Elementary School, IN

One

One smile can make a friend.
One seed can make a tree.
One person can make a difference.
One bee can make a flower.
One book can make a new world.
One adventure can make a story.
One game can make a win or lose.
One hug can make a tear go away.
One picture can make a memory.
One memory can make someone laugh.
One hand can help someone.
One bird can make an egg.
One egg can make a new life.
One truth can set you free.
One friend can help you through anything.
One step forward can start a new beginning.
One inspiration can lighten your heart.

Angela Magbag, Grade 6
St Gerard School, MI

Curly My Bird

C asually pecks you
U rging to get out of her cage
R arely is let out of her cage
L oud and rambunctious
Y ells at me (actually tweeting) when I walk
　　near her cage while she's eating

M aking a mess with her seeds
Y ellow sun gleaming on her gray-white feathers

B etter at singing than talking
I llness is the one thing she never has
R eally loud when she sings
D own when she falls, then she gets back up

McKenna Burke, Grade 4
Stonegate Elementary School, IN

My Birthday

My birthday is very special to me.
I get presents, cake, and birthday wishes.
I love to celebrate it with my friends and family
As long as I don't get a pinch to grow an inch.

My birthday is very special to me.
I love to open my presents and blow out my candles.
Then I have to say good-bye.
My birthday is over.
I can't wait until next year!

Ryanne Marie Stamper, Grade 6
Trilby Elementary School, OH

US Presidents

U ndoubtedly the most loved or hated man in the country
S tubborn personalities

P atriotic and peacekeepers
R eligious men
E mbraces many cultures
S peeches are a must
I ndelible footprints left on our nation
D ecisions affect the world
E motional decisions made
N egotiators
T hankless job
S trong relations formed

Trevor Lee, Grade 5
Central College Christian Academy, OH

Allisyn Mary Mahoney

A lways ready for something new
L ooking for fun things to do
L oads of laughter and smiles are things I got
I love my family and friends a lot
S ports take up a lot of time in my days
Y et I finish my schoolwork and bring home A's
N ever hurting others or telling a lie

M aking people laugh even though I'm shy
A lways trustworthy and caring
R eally fun and daring
Y oung and knowing

M aturing as I'm growing
A ctive, crazy, and a lot of fun
H onestly when I'm with my friends
　　I never want the day to be done
O utstanding and outgoing
N ever sad when it's snowing
E ager to play a new sport
Y es, some people say I'm short

Allisyn Mary Mahoney, Grade 5
Frank Ohl Intermediate School, OH

Snow

Snow snow blowing

Left
    And
        Right

Snow is very cold and very bright
Snow is falling to the ground
Making the world so nice
Snow is very little and keeps falling
To make the world so bright.

Matthew Hagood, Grade 5
St Joseph Montessori School, OH

Through My Mother's Eyes

Deeper, Deeper, Deeper
Into mommy's eyes
Love, of her children
Is all I see when I
Look through my mother's eyes

She might be stressed, she might be sad
But she doesn't show it when I
Look through my mother's eyes

She gives me strength,
She gives me faith when I
Look through my mother's eyes

She tells me how she really feels
In her deep down heart when I
Look through my mother's eyes

Hannah Tkacz, Grade 5
Leo Elementary School, IN

Veggies to Candy

Veggies
Earthly, snapping
Growing, eating, living
Slender, seeding, sweet, sticky
Chewing, wrapping, snacking
Fragrant, crunching
Candy

Madison Oakley, Grade 5
Norwich Elementary School, OH

Snowy Flower

I love the snow
But not on my petals.
I love to see it fall,
But I'm so cold.
I love the clean smell of snow,
But sometimes my petals freeze.
I'm a cold, snowy flower.

Tiffany Waulk, Grade 5
Westview Elementary School, OH

Sapphire Blue

Sapphire blue is a color of mystery.
It swirls around the ocean and glitters in the gem.
Sapphire blue splashes all around, filling you with sadness and peace.
It tastes like fresh blueberries.
It smells of an ocean breeze on a crisp summer day.
Sapphire blue swims like a mermaid and pierces the heart.
Sapphire blue is mystery.

Annie Thompson, Grade 6
Harding Middle School, OH

November Is…

Leaves falling off trees like graceful dancers dancing in the moonlight
Hunters driving like race car drivers, make their way up north
to their cabins to begin their hunt for deer
Animals getting chubby collecting and eating food for their long winter's nap
Juicy, hot turkey waiting on the table ready to be stuffed into your mouth
Roasting mashed potatoes with steaming hot gravy makes my mouth anxious.

Morgan Baron, Grade 5
Beck Centennial Elementary School, MI

Zipline in Costa Rica

Rare birds sing sweet, peaceful songs,
I stand on the gently swaying platform,
in the canopy of trees
humidity making me hotter.
I see emerald rolling hills of lush green tropical forests.
I hear Howler monkeys calling madly.
I latch to the wire and fly on the zip-line to the next platform.
A Macaw rises squawking, flapping,
its electrifying blue and red wings.

Philip Hostetler, Grade 5
Stanley Clark School, IN

The Horror Known as War

War
The word feels awful on one's tongue
Death and despair at every turn
All to keep our country free.

War
Watching your world go to wrack and ruin
The explosion of a shell and a cloud of toxic gas
A man's dying screams penetrate the fog.

War
People losing limbs and their sanity
Destruction beyond human comprehension
Horrors beyond belief day after awful day.

War
The least we can do is to honor those who survive
And honor them we do one day a year
Yet we do not know truly how awful the horror known as war is.

Zachary Susskind, Grade 6
EH Greene Intermediate School, OH

Bored

Bored is white
It tastes like butter popcorn.
It smells like my parents vacuuming around me,
It reminds me of sitting in front of the TV,
It sound like sister on the phone,
Bored makes me feel white.

Lauren McMillan, Grade 5
Tremont Elementary School, OH

My Family

My family is my joy.
I hold within me.
They are my love
I have with me wherever I go.
We may fight a little, but it will end.
They help me through my difficulties
And they guide me through my work.
They make me happy.
They make me sad.
But they love me no matter what.
I love them no matter what.
Because we are one and nothing can defeat our love.
I know that
There are things that may happen to part us.
I will love them even though we are apart.
Love in a family is stronger than anything.
It is the greatest power there is and will ever be.

Kelsey Bryant, Grade 5
Akiva Academy, OH

It's All About Me

If I were in charge of the world…
I'd eat big, juicy stakes for breakfast, lunch, dinner
I'd stay up until 11:30 every night
I'd put my siblings in a big room
I'd drive a Lamborghini
I'd have a pet Elephant
I'd have a Jacob Bear as my body guard
I'd make sugar a food group
I'd live in a castle
    That would be me

Trevor Kelley, Grade 4
Churubusco Elementary School, IN

Plane/Jet

Plane
loud, slow
flying, riding, landing gear
land, takeoff, turbo, slick
soaring, flooring, gliding
fantastic, futuristic
Jet

Craig Lundy, Grade 5
Washington Township Elementary School, IN

If I Were a Pumpkin

If I were a pumpkin
I would taste really sweet
I would be full of small seeds
I would like to be carved nicely
I'd want to be in your front window

If I were a pumpkin
I would say trick-or-treat
I would wish for fall to last all year
I would love to smile all the time
I would listen for kids saying trick-or-treat
I would shine all night so you could see me

Amanda Wylie, Grade 5
Reed Middle School, OH

Arapaho

If you were to live in an Arapaho tribe,
you would live in a teepee painted spiritually,
travel far on horseback, shoot buffalo for food,
and wonder why the white men are taking your land.
Why are these people here? Where did they come from?
And why are you now hiking to reservations so far away?

Sarah Dilz, Grade 6
Barrington Elementary School, OH

True Friends

My friends are my life, and that is true.
The past, the future, and the present too.
They are true because they are kind.
They are nice, funny, exciting, and they're mine.
Mine to help. Mine to care for.
And mine to be friends with.
I look at them and I see,
That they are a part of me.
We are true friends.

Emily Brandenburg, Grade 5
Spaulding Elementary School, OH

Sisters

Sisters 'til the end
a friend that never bends
ups and downs
a merry-go-round
the wonder sibs have been found
they can't stop us now
clothes shoes purses are what we share
and of course a mommy that's always there
sis I had a bad day
come talk and tell me about the pain
speaking is the best when trust is in the way
you tell me your secrets and I'll tell you mine
you wish you had a sister better than mine.

Erin Norris, Grade 6
Eastmoor Middle School, OH

Precious Moments
Baby
Cute, cuddly
Crying, eating, sleeping
Smile, giggle, laughter, fun
Playing, running, learning
Active, talkative
Child
Demi Kunkel, Grade 6
Harmon Middle School, OH

Friend
F un
R eally cool
I ntelligent
E xtremely goofy
N ice
D ominic
Jacob Dudley, Grade 5
Rootstown Elementary School, OH

The Sun
While playing in the sun,
Kids are having a lot of fun;

Sharing the energy with plants,
Then the energy goes to ants;

The energy is a great gift,
So things can grow and lift;

The sun helps the world shine,
I'm glad it is partly mine;

The sun is important, can't you see,
It also gives food to you and me!
Kenna Bowers, Grade 5
GATE Mayfield Elementary School, OH

Outside When It Is Hot
One day it was hot
and it made me want to trot
it was very fun
and I started to run.

I went into the pool
and it was very cool
I went to play basketball
but I did not do good at all.

I went inside to eat
and it was a good treat
and now today was fun
and now I am all done!
Logan Jacques, Grade 4
Floyd Ebeling Elementary School, MI

Trumpet
Beautiful sounding things
Beautiful music rings
Brass shines in the sun
Sweet sound has begun
Hold it in your hands
The rickety stand
Brass and gold
New and old
The beautiful sound
The trumpet found.
Colt Kelso, Grade 5
St Joseph Parish School, OH

I Am
I am curious and adventurous.
I wonder if I can learn to play the guitar.
I hear the stars talking to each other.
I see the dogs playing poker.
I want to play the guitar.
I am curious and adventurous.
I pretend I have magical powers.
I feel sad that the stars won't talk to me.
I touch a sprite.
I cry when animals are abused.
I am curious and adventurous.
I understand animals.
I say that magic is real.
I dream I'm a really great cook.
I try to save money.
I hope to be rich.
I am curious and adventurous.
Kennedy Mazza, Grade 6
Galesburg-Augusta Middle School, MI

Football
Down set hut
The ball is snapped
Shoulder pads hit
Fingers crack
Players shout and catch the football
The fans shout and scream
Off to the races!
Ref will say
TOUCHDOWN!!!
Syd Gieseking, Grade 5
Henryville Elementary School, IN

Fall
Fall
Leaves are falling
That thankful time of year
Gets chilly again
Autumn
Erin Grimes, Grade 4
Bailly Elementary School, IN

Autumn
Going to the Fairfield County Fair
Riding rides like Zero Gravity
Trying new foods like elephant ears
Seeing the animals in the barns
This makes autumn.

Raking leaves into piles
Then jumping in them
Watching the leaves fly up
Like little flower petals
This makes autumn.

Picking out the perfect pumpkin
Carving a face on it
Putting a candle in it
Watching the pumpkin's face glow
This makes autumn.

Seeing all the costumes
Like vampires and ninjas
Going door to door
And getting free candy
This makes autumn.
Jayda Wion, Grade 5
Sanderson Elementary School, OH

Music
It's my favorite thing to do
Listening to music, it's me, it's true
Listen when I'm happy
Listen when I'm sad
Every day a new song I will add
Love songs, sad songs, I love them too
Morning, noon, and night…
It's all I want to do
Ellie Sargent, Grade 6
Holy Angels School, OH

An Ode to Ice Cream
Oh, ice cream,
You're so cold and sweet.
You remind me of
Ice in a fridge.

Oh, ice cream,
You're so colorful.
Your colors
Remind me of a rainbow.

Oh, ice cream,
You're so good to eat.
You're the only cold treat that
I will always enjoy forever and ever.
MJ Dela Cruz, Grade 5
Allen J. Warren Elementary School, IN

The Trotting Star

C entaur is a constellation that has a story to it about a half-man half-horse.
E very night in the cold winter nights you can see Centaur trotting along the Milky Way.
N ights are when you see him up above the sky so high he really shines.
T ough is what he was alive or dead he had courage oh every day of his life.
A rrow is what killed him with poison at the tip oh what a sad day occurred.
U p above is where he lies cause when he died that is where Zeus put him.
R ight in the sky a wonderful constellation lays that is in the cold gleaming winter nights.

Tiffany Lemus, Grade 6
Pinewood Elementary School, IN

Father of the Forests

The days I live are as big as Earth.
The nights only to fly by like a dragonfly.
If not for the sunlight, I would be as weak as a twig.
But I stretch high and mighty in all my glory.
The green grass is my neighbor, building towers with the ants
As big as the dandelions that I watch in the morning.
Cardinals and robins hide in my branches, far away from the monster-like hawks.
To hear the creek trickle is like a Sunday spa day when the week has gone bad.
Vines of purple, yellow, and blue cut through the morning rays like a machete in a jungle.
Songs from the chikadees' homes in the small wooden boxes,
Comes the sweet echo of what sounds like a child on Christmas morning.
Daffodils and tulips with the rest of their flower friends grow tall
And powerful, never giving up to the un-God like insects.
In the fall, leaves from my enormous branches twist and blow in the virtually unbearable breeze.
In my hollow, squirrels build their homes, hoping for a winter as cold as ever.
I am an oak tree, tall and strong.
I will be as brutal as a bully when punched, and I won't give up!

Bailee Rayne Stevens, Grade 6
Cloverdale Middle School, IN

My Friend

Her house is small and yellow. Her room is full with stuffed elephants. The room smells like nothing I have smelled. There are high ceilings, wooden floors, and light blue paint around the room. One HUGE poster of *Jaws* and a big shell case that is full of sand dollars. Her name is Paige. She is always laughing. She has strawberry blonde hair with braces on her teeth.
She is my best friend.

Haylie Rupnow, Grade 5
Washington Township Elementary School, IN

A Secret Place

There I was, my hooves on the soft green grassy ground. My mane waving in the wind like dead leaves falling off a tree.
I don't have much time before fall is over, so I'll spend as much time as possible here at my secret place.
The water I drink from is as blue as the sky, and as sparkly as a diamond. This place is like no other place I've been to.
The birds chirp all day long.
My fur is as black as night, when I canter through the woods, the leaves crunch, like the sound of kids eating a bag of chips.
Leaves fall from a tree like rain falling from the sky. The wind blows only a little.
There is so much to do here, at my secret place, I jump the fallen down trees, like I'm flying with the birds.
The horse flies, fly around me like bees getting honey for their queen.
The big brown trees are standing as still as a house, and the green benches are as green as green grass.
The purple flowers are so pretty during the day, and all the thorn bushes are gone far away from here.
The yellow flowers are as yellow as the sun, and the big white rocks surround the pond but only one spot has no rocks;
A spot where there's enough room for the animals to get their water.

This place I shall never forget!!!!!!!

Kyleigh Roberts, Grade 6
Cloverdale Middle School, IN

Home

Home is where we rest our heads,
When our day is done.
Mom, Dad and my brother,
Together makes me glad.
Our home is filled,
With lots of love,
Because Jesus is in our hearts.
Salvation keeps us all together,
Even when on Earth we part.
When we are feeling down,
We need to pray to God to help us,
Because He makes everything right.

Caylee Sue Corlew, Grade 6
Immanuel Christian School, MI

Basketball!

There's only one minute left in the game.
The red team steals the ball.
The brown team pushes the red team.
They call foul.
Red gets two foul shots.
They miss one.
Ten seconds left in the game.
7…6…5…4…3…2…1…
Red shoots from the half way line.
0.00
Beep…they made it in.
The red team wins the game.
The crowd goes wild!

Marla Scott, Grade 4
Legend Elementary School, OH

What Moves Me

Golf is what moves me.
Grass as far as the eye can see.
The sound of a club hitting the ball.
All is silent as we wait for the ball to fall.

Regan DeLong, Grade 6
Mayfield Elementary School, OH

Marcus Thomas

M arvelous
A cademic
R owdy
C reative
U nselfish
S cientific

T remendous
H onorable
O pen-minded
M astermind
A dventurous
S loppy

Marcus Thomas, Grade 5
Perry Central Elementary School, IN

Mother Earth

The rivers are flowing, the wind is blowing
Butterflies in bright, blue skies
A light breeze always going through trees

The sparkling sun is shining while animals run
Shadows of animals running free, what more could there be?
The foaming seas of blue and green, the variety of colors, a bright sheen

You can hardly hear a sound, just a few leaves crumpling on the ground
Laughter can be heard throughout the town, waterfalls are gushing down
People chatting in parks, dogs communicating with barks

How many countries celebrate Earth Day?
In what country did Earth Day originate?
Is there any particular reason Earth Day is on April twenty-second?

The stars are twinkling like millions of bright diamonds glistening in the night sky
The wind is a ballerina as it gracefully waltzes across the skies
The moon is a shimmering lake of liquid silver

Take care of Mother Earth,
Take care of Mother Earth,
Take care of Mother Earth.

Nora Dukart, Grade 5
EH Greene Intermediate School, OH

Slavery

S lavery can beat you down and make you think there is no hope
L et the sun shine in they would sing, voices weak
A nd, when times were tough, they didn't stop looking for hope
V ery brutal scars on their backs, signs of strength
E very sparkle in their weary eyes show hope
R eaching out for the Lord to help them
"**Y** ou," the master says, weary eyes look over, "Get out of here,"
He says, "There is hope for you on the northern side."

Ellen Hart, Grade 6
Mayfield Elementary School, OH

Loneliness

Loneliness is a dark and deep hallway that you are walking alone in.
Loneliness is sorrow of having no one there.
Loneliness is a deep pain that sinks down deep when there is no one there.
Loneliness needs a friend to heal it.

Loneliness can be fixed by a simple friend.
Just a friend to help you out when you're down or when you're new.
Your friend could be a hound and your mom or dad or maybe even a clown.
Anyone to help the pain go away, just a friend.

When you have a friend the pain will go away and be filled with joy.
When you have a friend lend a hand to someone that doesn't.
Lend a hand for anything that you can do.
Help someone out with anything.

Noah Deems, Grade 6
Harmon Middle School, OH

Fall

School starts
Kids fill the hall.

Time to get ready for fall
Spiders with legs; eight in all.

The leaves are falling
Halloween's calling.

Scary costumes all around
Many cavities will be found.

Scary Jack-O-Lantern eyes
Some delicious Thanksgiving pumpkin pies.

Turkey is frying
Now we're all good-byeing.

Fall is over, sorry to say
Don't worry, winter is on its way!

Molly Coughlin, Grade 6
Rocky River Middle School, OH

My Mom

My mom, my mom
She is the bomb
She's a nurse
And carries her purse
My mom, my mom she's the best
That is why she is blessed

Cody Apple, Grade 5
North Knox East Elementary/Jr High School, IN

I Am

I am dependable and scientific.
I wonder if the rumors I hear are true.
I hear the sun rays scream as they sizzle the sidewalk.
I see the pumpkins in a pumpkin patch talk.
I want my day to be terrific.
I am dependable and scientific.
I pretend I don't really care.
I feel happy when I see my dog do the cha-cha with me.
I touch the leaves on the trees in the winter.
I worry that I won't get to class on time.
I cry when I think no one cares.
I am dependable and scientific.
I understand that coats keep you warm.
I say computers are helpful.
I dream about being stuck in a maze house.
I try to get straight A's.
I hope I am successful in all I do.
I am dependable and scientific.

Rachel Forrest, Grade 6
Galesburg-Augusta Middle School, MI

Volleyball with Rachel

I see people setting and bumping the ball
Me and Rachel bumping the ball
We spike the ball
Over the net
I can hear the ball hitting the ground
I can smell the stinky sweat
Pee U!
I can see people sliding
On their knee pads
It gets so hot under your knee pads
The refs blowing their whistles
Yeh!
We Won the Game!

Morgan White, Grade 4
Licking Valley Intermediate School, OH

The Things I Love the Most

The things I love the most are the people in my house,
They are fun, generous, and supporting.
The things I love the most are my friends
They cheer me up when I'm down.
The things I love the most are the pets I own,
They are cute, cuddly, and loving.
The things I love the most is school,
The teachers help me learn and become smart.
The things I love the most is my home, it keeps me warm
In the winter, and cool in the summer
It keeps me safe from intruders.
These are the special things I love the most!

Kaitlin James, Grade 6
Abbott Middle School, MI

Thank You Veterans

You march the dirt road waiting for destruction
You sacrifice your life for our loving country
So brave, such courage
The strength you had to fight,
The freedom to battle,
Honoring your life, we thank
Many of them died
Soldier from Soldier
The flag still up at the dreadful end,
Marching home so much freedom
All the emotion
Tears running cheek to cheek
Risking your life,
Keeping peace
Protecting us from harm,
We appreciate you so much
What braveness you had when the battle was over,
Protect us, you did
Thank you for our Freedom.

Noelle Bailey, Grade 5
Beck Centennial Elementary School, MI

School
It is spectacular
This is the best school I've ever been to
School is awesome
Eagles
It is gnarly
Sweet
It is full of teachers
Trey Michael Springer, Grade 4
Churubusco Elementary School, IN

The Election
McCain
And Obama
We need to stop the war
Obama won the election
Voting
Kiefer Pottschmidt, Grade 5
Tremont Elementary School, OH

I Am: Spider
I am poisonous
I am small
I am hungry
I am smart
I am fast
I am a spider
Caden Southard, Grade 4
Westview Elementary School, OH

Sisters
They love each other
Always spend time together
A very strong bond
Sharing hopes and dreams and fears
Late night talks and lots of laughs
Shelby Meyerrose, Grade 6
Harmon Middle School, OH

Fall
It's almost time for leaves to fall,
And time for grass to stop growing tall.
It's almost time for colder wind,
And time for flowers to now bend.
Fall is my favorite season,
Now here are the reasons.
Summer is steaming hot,
That's when I think I might rot.
Winter makes me really sick,
I want to give winter a kick.
Spring has too much rain,
It fills me with pain.
That is why Fall
Is the best season of all!
Trinity Thomas, Grade 4
Chrisney Elementary School, IN

Big Tornadoes
Tornadoes come very
Fast like a car.
They answer to the call
Of the wind.
They scream to the heavens
So loud that you shout.
They then realize
That it's
No use.
Hanna McClure, Grade 5
Wooster Christian School, OH

My Dragon
Ram horns
Neck like a giraffe
Huge eyes
Red apple body
With spots like little black flies.
Wings that stretch out
Tiny black toenails
Not too dangerous.
My dragon.
Mike Mastoris, Grade 4
Dobbins Elementary School, OH

Hockey
Hockey
Aggressive, exciting
Playing, shooting, skating
You take shots with your stick
Life!
Andrew Deeter, Grade 4
Floyd Ebeling Elementary School, MI

Fall
Fall is the season of colored leaves,
swirling and twirling in the breeze.
We fall, we trip, we splash, we play,
we go to a barn and relax on some hay.
So what is the season I love most of all?
Fall
Kalen J. Sipl, Grade 5
Norwich Elementary School, OH

Snowflake
A sparkling wonder
A gentle beauty
An ice cold thing
A fragile creation
It is small but neat to look at
As it shimmers floating down
If you see it you'll be amazed
That object is a snowflake
Emily Lalonde, Grade 5
May V Peck Elementary School, MI

Interception
Tied 7 to 7; 30 seconds left
I'm on defense playing corner.
The enemy approaches the ball,
The quarterback says "hit."
I watch the tight end.
He releases
I backpedal to guard him.
I see the quarterback drop back
And he throws.
Silence
Ball sailing closer,
I jump
The football is mine.
The crowd roars like a tiger.
I come down on my feet and run.
I run faster than ever.
The 50, the 40, the 30, the 20, the 10
Dive
Touchdown!
Travis Hoving, Grade 6
Assumption BVM School, MI

The Mirror
Minnows
Daring,
Snakes slithering,
Dragonflies gliding
Through the sky,
Showing reflections
Of wildlife.
If you notice,
You're included!
Marianne Kingrey, Grade 4
Normandy Elementary School, OH

Autumn
The weather is cold
Autumn's leaves fall to the ground
Like kites in the wind
Hunter Morgan, Grade 6
Harmon Middle School, OH

Halloween
H aunted House
A blaze
L ow creepy voice
L oud thunder
O ut back
W itch
E nemy
E normous ghost
N ightmare
Rachael Barnhorst, Grade 5
St Jude Catholic School, IN

Life Will Never Be the Same

As I waved goodbye, gave hugs and kisses,
I thought about what I was going to endure,
The pain, suffering, and sorrow,
I thought and thought,
Life will never be the same.

I boarded the ship,
It would take me to a dark, gloomy land,
A land where nobody wanted to arrive,
I thought and thought,
Life will never be the same.

As I boarded off the ship,
I heard guns, a sound nobody wanted to hear,
I fought and fought for freedom,
I thought and thought,
Life will never be the same.

Finally, it was time to come home,
Where I would be filled with happiness yet again,
I got off the ship, was greeted by family and friends,
I thought and thought,
Life will never be the same.

Ellen Martinson, Grade 6
EH Greene Intermediate School, OH

Sharks

Deadly fish, swift, gills
Dorsal fin, underwater,
Strong, surprise attack!

Christopher David Grupp II, Grade 4
Eugene M Nikkari Elementary School, MI

The Question on Election Day

The question on election day is McCain or Obama?
Republican or Democrat?
Don't forget Independent!
Everyone should vote on November 4th!
It doesn't matter what party, race, or who you're voting for!
Just get your vote out!
So, the question on election day is very simple.
Just pick one, McCain or Obama.

Morrisa Clayman, Grade 5
Akiva Academy, OH

Disgusted Green

Disgusted is as green color,
It tastes like burnt toast,
It smells like the cat box,
It reminds me of a dead squirrel on the road,
It sounds like people getting sick,
Disgusted makes me feel green.

Emily Shambrock, Grade 5
Tremont Elementary School, OH

White Winter Songs

W armth from inside
H uge Snowman's
I love you
T ender holy-songs
E verlasting snow

W inter blizzards
I nteraction with family
N ighttime sparkles
T ender voices
E verlasting love
R eal hot cocoa

S parkling snow
O val cookies
N ighttime wishes
G orgeous lights
S ites of Santa

Kathryn Newsom, Grade 5
Northern Heights Elementary School, IN

Things That Are Quiet

A small, cold, dark, empty room
Reading silently inside a dim, creepy tent
Bushy green trees blowing in the wind
Walking tiptoed on the soft squishy carpet
The newborn baby wrapped in a cozy blanket
The warm air blowing across the baby's soft face
White puffy clouds floating across the sky
The hungry tiger creeping up on an antelope
Fresh dew filling the grass in the foggy morning
A silver car stopped at a bright red stop sign
The baby deer eating the red, shiny berries off a tree
Rabbits hopping along a slippery stone path
The American flag blowing in the cold winter air
A tiny pumpkin seed sprouting in the brown soil
A class of children thinking hard on a test
Two children whispering in the peaceful meadow
Bright shining stars twinkling in the night time sky
The soft misty rain falling on the green grass
A family roasting marshmallows over a sparking crackling fire
Lavender flowers filling the sparkling glass jar.

McKenzie Bates, Grade 5
Sanderson Elementary School, OH

Gifts

G iving gifts to people is nice on Christmas.
I vy is decoration people put around the gifts.
F aces are happy when they open their gifts.
T ime is what the children watch
    as they wait for Santa Claus to bring the gifts.
S anta Claus brings gifts on Christmas Eve.

Andrew Sullivan, Grade 5
West Washington Elementary School, IN

An Ode to My Mother

I feel very happy around my mother. She helps me with homework and when I am sick. She makes me just feel proud.
I'm always excited to see her. She helps others like my brother, cousin and more. She has a good attitude. I love my mom.
She always says goodnight and always says that she loves me. She never says I love you to friends. But I think she is the nicest,
sweetest, kindest person, I've ever seen.

Ryan Fiegle, Grade 5
Allen J. Warren Elementary School, IN

Christmas Morning

Inside the house
It is about eight o'clock in the morning
The sky outside still gray
But the lights inside are bright and cheery
With many different colors everywhere

A green pine tree covered with ornaments from the past
With many gift-wrapped presents under it
The taste of morning breath still in my mouth
The smell of my sister and my mom baking cookies and cakes
Excited for the day coming to be

Joyful voices are heard throughout the house
As with strict instructions to not burn the cookies
My mom has put classical music on
And it rings in the background of everyone's excited minds
There is laughter and happiness
That adds to everyone's joy

Would everyone be there?
Would it be a good time for everyone?
But the joy and happiness in the room is as bright as the sun
And there is always the star that shines as bright as an angel on top of the tree
But the joy and happiness will always be there in the room as bright as the sun, sun, sun

Priscilla Wu, Grade 5
EH Greene Intermediate School, OH

Aries the Ram

A ries is a constellation named after a flying ram in Greek mythology, who saved a
     couple of sacrifices from being killed to rid famine.
R eaching the ocean, the woman fell off the magical ram's back and drowned in the deep
     salt water, but the man and the ram made it to shore safely
I n return, to thank Zeus, the man sacrificed the ram, to show his appreciation…to
     Zeus, rather than the ram.
E fforts have been made to track down more of the Greek story of the flying ram, but
     nothing has been discovered yet.
S cientists have discovered that the star on the edge of Aries has a planet, just
     slightly larger than Jupiter in its rotation.

Kaitlyn Ramsey, Grade 6
Pinewood Elementary School, IN

Night

Night called like a buffalo calling its stampede. Quickly, the wind runs as if it were being chased by the unknown. You could
feel it but it was no warmer nor colder than the air itself. So quiet that nothing could echo over the boisterous sound of the
wind. The darkness taking over the time of day. The more you went into it the less you could see it. For the last voice you ever
wanted to hear was the first to be heard.

Erin Thomas, Grade 6
Westfield Intermediate School, IN

I Am

I am fun and happy.
I wonder if I will meet Tony Hawk.
I hear the cracks of pencils.
I see a big turtle in the sky.
I want a million dollars
I am fun and happy.
I pretend I am in WW2.
I feel excited when my dad gets home from Iraq.
I touch a poison dollar.
I worry about my mom.
I cry if my feelings get hurt.
I am fun and happy.
I understand games.
I say hi.
I dream I am in a video game.
I try to help people.
I hope my dad gets home safely.
I am fun and happy.

Dakota Mazza, Grade 6
Galesburg-Augusta Middle School, MI

Air

I am clear
I am extremely light
I am out and inside.
I am sometimes windy.
I have trees clean me.
I have gas pollute me.
I can't be found in space.
I am breathed in by animals and people.
I am in tanks so scuba divers can breathe.
I am air.

Tyler Cunningham, Grade 5
St Michael School, IN

Christmas

Christmas, I love that season. Why, there is no reason
The snow is like a winter show
It's time to see family and friends
Hey it's Christmas the fun never ends.
I love the winter delays especially on Mondays
I love sledding and singing Christmas carols
And spreading love and joy all around
In this season Jesus was born
Then a couple of years later it was the crown of thorns
Jesus, God's only Son died on the cross for me and you.
Christmas is my favorite season
My favorite is the snow I love candy canes
And all of the presents all of the love and joy
It is a time to spend with all your friends
Hey, it's Christmas the fun never ends
Have a Merry Christmas

Jacqueline Parish, Grade 6
Crown Point Christian School, IN

Freedom

F lag of our country waving at the trees
R ed, white, and blue represents our nation
E agles show just how free we are
E very morning we respect the flag with the pledge
D o not have war in this country
O pen doors to peaceful lives
M any historic landmarks like the Liberty Bell
and the Statue of Liberty

Emily Johnson, Grade 5
Sanderson Elementary School, OH

Cobras

Slither, slither on the ground
Cobras go along without a sound
Tiny sacks of poison, made to kill its prey
Come too close or harm it, bite you it just may
They have special flaps on their neck
If you go near a snake, for the flaps you better check
It can bend and it can flex
So just be careful or you may be next!

Jacob Smith, Grade 5
May V Peck Elementary School, MI

Sad

Sad is Dylan,
It tastes like spicy wasabi
It smells like dead flowers,
It reminds me of salt water,
It sounds like uncooked mac and cheese,
Sad makes me feel Dylan.

Dylan Strahm, Grade 5
Tremont Elementary School, OH

Christmas

Christmas is a special time of the year,
When the time for Santa Claus is near
Little children can't wait for the day
When presents will find their way.
Under the tree so green and bright
Sitting there lonely till the time is right.
For little fingers to open each gift
That carries their name that they lift.
As the day goes on,
The dinner is placed upon
The table beautifully set
With enough food to begat.
A king or queen would not regret
The love and caring that it shares
To everyone in our tender care.
The day is done
The packages and all the fun
Are put away until the next Christmas Day!

Emily Best, Grade 6
Crown Point Christian School, IN

Twirling

T is for takes talent
W is for wrist twirls
I is for interesting music
R is for routines
L is for lots of practice
I is for in-step shoes
N is for nice costumes
G is for glow batons

Kaitlin Gillman, Grade 6
Holy Angels School, OH

Fall Feelings

Birds finding south
Gentle wind
Pumpkin pie
Apple picking
Popcorn popping
Leaves falling
Crimson
Old amber
Gold
CRUNCH!
Goes the leaves
Shivering teeth
Blazing fireplace
Burning chocolate
Doorbell ringing
Bats floating in the air
A breezy fall night.

Vinson Chen, Grade 5
Riley Upper Elementary School, MI

Baseball

Standing for my team
Dirt beneath my feet
Executing precise motions
Displaying perfect eye-hand coordination
Anticipating a grand slam
The ball is in the air
Fans are awestruck
Outfielders throwing down their hats
The game-winning run!

Sean Smith, Grade 6
Tri-West Middle School, IN

Finally Fall

Cool breezes and light jackets
Bare trees and leaves down
Birds disappearing
Deer blending with the brown
Round and round the yard
Sprinting with my pup
Finally, fall is here.
Leaves are piling up!

Haley Lawyer, Grade 6
Tri-West Middle School, IN

Like-A-Me

Like a poison ivy, I am sly and well hidden.
Like a fox, I am clever and devious.
Like the colors yellow and black, at times I am soft and gentle,
and at other times I am strong and mean.
Like a seaweed, I am skinny and agile.
Like a light bulb, I am bright with new ideas.
Like Mica, I am fragile and easily broken.
Like a Cadillac, I shine in the dark night.
Like a computer, I have new information stored inside me every day.

Jason Ji, Grade 6
Boulan Park Middle School, MI

Veteran's Day

An American holiday
Honors the veterans of World War I was called Armistice Day or Remembrance Day
November 11 is when it's celebrated
Their memories will not have faded
On November 11, 1919 an Armistice Day was first proclaimed by Woodrow Wilson
The allies will win
Is referred to as end to the war of all wars
Then changed to Veteran's Day on November 8, 1954
That's celebrated for all veterans, was a better way
It's celebrated by parades, public meetings, and a brief suspension to the work day
Is called lots of different things
Like Poppy Day, Remembrance Day, and even still Armistice Day!!
But really means the same thing
It doesn't make a difference what you call it
Only if you celebrate it
And that's Veteran's Day!!

Anna Garrett, Grade 6
EH Greene Intermediate School, OH

If You Are

If you are willing to fight for your freedom and put your life at stake,
You are a veteran.
If you change your way of living because you love your home.
You are a veteran.
If you have the courage to sacrifice your life to your nation,
You are a veteran.
If you have given years of your life to the armed forces,
You are a veteran.
If you can leave your friends and family to go to war.
You are a veteran.
If you can go to war, get shot, and want to go back,
You are a veteran.
If you can say "why couldn't it have been me."
You are a veteran.
If you can give up for your country,
You are a veteran.
If you can proudly return to war,
You are a veteran.
If you can leave all you desire,
You are a veteran.

Reed Bie, Grade 6
EH Greene Intermediate School, OH

My Dad

Sometimes my dad likes to play with me.
He likes to win!
I love my dad.
His name is Ed.
I like to play football with my dad.
Sometimes my dad takes me to a football game.
My dad bought me popcorn and a football.

Trey Hisle, Grade 5
Henryville Elementary School, IN

I Am

I am athletic and awesome
I wonder if I will make it to a college or pro football
I hear the crowd cheering
I see me playing football with the Patriots and Texas
I want to make millions of dollars
I am athletic and awesome

I pretend it is Christmas every day
I feel I can score a touchdown
I touch a football
I worry about tornados
I cry when I get hurt
I am athletic and awesome

I understand people die
I say Santa's real
I dream it's Christmas
I try my best
I hope I grow up to be a football player
I am athletic and awesome

I am Anthony Rizzo

Anthony Rizzo, Grade 4
Floyd Ebeling Elementary School, MI

A Story of Dianna

Dianna
Athletic, silly, loving
Sister of Amanda, Kristin, Joshua, David, Donald
Lover of roller coasters, animals, family
Who feels nervous when I get in trouble
 and when someone yells at me
Who gets excited about going on vacation
 and when it snows
Who needs to improve my grades
 and I need to study more
Who gives kisses to my mommy and my hamster
Who fears spiders and scary movies
Who would like to move into a big house
Resident of Austintown, Ohio
Yeager

Dianna Yeager, Grade 5
Frank Ohl Intermediate School, OH

Hanukkah Cheers

Friends, cousins, aunts, uncles, grandparents
Chatter all around
Present giving, chocolate eating, and playing dreidle all over
My dad lights the candles
They have a bright glow
It illuminates the darkness, as we all say hello
Laughing, talking, footsteps, mocking, and little cousins crying
Their parents just sighing
How long will the candles stay lit?
How long will the people stay?
Soon I had my answer
A while, hooray
The goodbyes are like the whistle at the end of every game
To signal the end of another Hanukkah
Goodbye
Goodbye
Goodbye

Max Weiss, Grade 5
EH Greene Intermediate School, OH

Dance

I'm in my dance outfit ready to start
It's evening on Thursday night
My teacher April is about to call us up
I have my shoes on and a bottle of water in my hand
Then my teacher calls my class to start our Pirouettes
We are halfway done just a minute away
I take a deep breath for a Chaine.

Andrea Aung, Grade 5
Churubusco Elementary School, IN

December 1st

Today's December 1st. What should I wear?
What about my shirt? What about my hair?

I looked around my room, then gasped in sudden shock.
I'm gonna be really late! It's almost nine o'clock!

I flew down the stairs, then threw my backpack on,
Grabbed a powerbar, and in a flash was gone.

I sped down the sidewalk, then, came a patch of ice,
And let me tell you what, it didn't turn out nice.

That happened again and again, almost ten more times,
I won't touch ice again, if I get paid 500 dimes.

I finally got to school, and I was so relieved you see,
That I threw my stuff in the air, and shouted out: "Yippee!"

I ran up to the door, then something blocked my way,
I read the sign and it said: School's out! Stay home! Snow day!

Sally Squires, Grade 5
St Joseph Montessori School, OH

November Is…

Changing leaves are as bright as Skittles,
The morning day is as soft as giggles.
Cool crisp air,
Anticipating the Thanksgiving fare.
Turkey, stuffing, mashed potatoes,
Everyone is saying no tomatoes.
Pumpkin pie looks too good to eat,
Dip in a finger it tastes so sweet.
Family fun with lots of snacks,
A football game with a quarterback sack.
Some games are won in a snap,
Then we snuggle for a little nap.
A lot of Laughter, a lot of fun,
November is time to run.

Brandon LaBonty, Grade 5
Beck Centennial Elementary School, MI

Live Life Large

Love leads to marriage.
Marriage produces children.
Children increase stress.
Stress builds up anger.
Anger becomes tension.
Tension cries for a massage.
Massage brings relaxation.
Relaxation becomes happiness.
Happiness falls in love.

Allison Pawlicki, Grade 6
Pike Delta York Middle School, OH

Fall and Spring

Fall
Colorful, leaves,
Jumping, running, climbing,
Chilly, nippy/warm, hot,
Sweating, playing, laughing,
Sunny, breeze,
Spring

Fall,
Football, harvest,
Walking, riding, talking,
Dead trees/flowers, pretty,
Happy, Birds,
Spring

Fall,
Labor day,
Picking, raking, exploring,
Cold, cloudy/nice, dark,
Holding, sharing, living,
Spring

Shyann Smith, Grade 6
Nancy Hanks Elementary School, IN

The Waterfall

Dangerous water,
That floats with the fish, gently,
Bubbling beautifully.

Jonah Klumb, Grade 4
Normandy Elementary School, OH

Playing Hockey

Welcome to the jungle
We're going to have fun and games!
Let's play some hockey!
Boom!!!
The puck is hit.
Errrrrrr!
Goal!!!!

Tyler Robinson, Grade 4
Churubusco Elementary School, IN

Fall

Fall
dull, breezy
shivering, dancing, throwing
scarecrows, crows, pumpkin pie, crops,
sledding, running, working
colorful, beautiful
December

Pete Jarrett, Grade 4
Norwich Elementary School, OH

If I Could Grant a Wish for You

If I could grant a wish for you
I would get a thrill or two.

A cool little mouse or an awesome house
a blue blouse or an evil joust.

A piece of candy
oh so fine and dandy.

All I want to do…
is grant a wish for you.

A special wish
or maybe two.

A perfect life
or a small knife.

But all I want to say and do
is grant a wish for you.

A special wish just for you
is LOVE from me to you.

Ireland O'Dell, Grade 5
Mark C Roose Elementary School, MI

Ants

Insect,
Tiny animals
Around my food,
Working hard as possible!
Ant.

Tyler McCafferty, Grade 6
Harmon Middle School, OH

Friends

Roses are red,
Violets are blue.
Remember this message
From me to you.

A best friend
Is always there for you,
Whether you're happy
Or just feeling blue.

So be good to your best friend
Whatever you do.
Remember this message
From me to you.

Haley M. Hamm, Grade 5
Cloverdale Middle School, IN

Embarrassment

Embarrassment is red
It smells like failure
It looks like a bad grade
It tastes like broccoli
It sounds like a rainstorm
Embarrassment feels like a school day
that never ends.

Megan Ulrich, Grade 6
Eisenhower Middle School, OH

My Name Is Zach

My name is Zach
I love the color red
My favorite sport is basketball
I have a dirty blonde head

My house is big
But not so pleasant
When Christmas comes
I'd like to get a present

I love to eat pizza
I eat it every day
Even though my mom doesn't like it
That's all I have to say

Zachary Jacobs, Grade 6
Trilby Elementary School, OH

I Am

I am a sweet and happy girl
I wonder what I will be when I grow up
I hear the sounds of babies crying
I see a huge pretty house
I want a new cell phone
I am a sweet and happy girl

I pretend I'm a teacher
I feel the wind blowing my hair
I touch my grandpa's hand up in heaven
I worry about my grandma
I cry when I think about my grandpa
I am a sweet and happy girl

I understand you can't always have what you want
I say you can't judge a book by its cover
I dream about me being a teacher
I try not to get in trouble
I hope I will be a teacher
I am a sweet and happy girl

Alexandra Bullington, Grade 6
Helfrich Park Middle School, IN

Fall

Fall is great, not to mention…
        Lots of pie,
    With fresh cream
        Bunches of colorful
Leaves!!
    Not to mention some unpleasant
        Screams. (Darn, now my ears hurt.)
    Lots of cute little
        Pieces of candy
    And more leaves colored
        Golden yellow,
            Purple,
        Brown!
    Falling all the way from the sky…
To the GROUND

Jacob Cornell Grosan, Grade 5
Riley Upper Elementary School, MI

Night

Night pours on the city.
Light twinkles like distant stars in the far universe.
The city takes up every crack,
Every crevice in the land.

The darkness of night is a stop sign.
All quiets down.
The city that was once a rapid, raging river,
Is now a quiet, gentle creek.

Brett Brown, Grade 6
Harding Middle School, OH

An Autumn Day

On an autumn day
My classmates and I
Went on a poetry walk.

We saw trees getting ready for prom.
They were stripping as the wind was howling.

Crunchy paper running in the streets.
Scarlet berries as red as the sun.
Fluffy marshmallows flying in the sky.

I felt that nature was dancing around me.
I felt I was dancing with them.
I felt peace.

Carina Ghafari, Grade 6
University Liggett School, MI

Dear Santa

You may not get this until Christmas Day.
But I had to thank you in some special way.
You give great, awesome presents to me —
The drop-off section is under the tree.
I know it's true and that you live —
The presents I get you really give.
I give you cookies and chocolate milk,
You give me slippers and a robe of silk.
No one does care much for clothes,
We want toys — that really shows!
Please fill our stockings up to the top —
With candies, goodies, and great pop.
Tell the elves (those who don't know)
The way the children think Christmas should go!
No go! The reindeer are excited and can't wait,
Just do me a favor — don't give me a slate!

Caroline Lukehart, Grade 5
Northfield Baptist Christian School, OH

Christmas Joy

Thanksgiving is over and done,
It's time for Christmas fun!
I begin to decorate the tree,
It's just Dad, Mom, and me.
My grandma starts to bake,
And I chow down on her homemade cake.
Red and green are all around,
Filling stores with joyful sound
The snow on the ground is shimmering brightly,
As all children add to their list nightly
I hear Santa's sleigh bells ring,
While my family and I sing
Christmas is finally here!
We all smile and cheer!

Katelyn Mellady, Grade 6
St John the Evangelist School, IN

Flowing

Under the layering rocks
Along the grassy banks
Among the trees so high
Across the glossy rocks
Down the cliff so great
By the tiny cottages
Beneath the damaged bridge
Outside of a big city
Past the boulders
Into a concrete tunnel
Of the countryside
Runs the flowing stream

Jessica Groves, Grade 6
Harmon Middle School, OH

The USA Flag

In the parking lot
Blowing in the wind
Above the kids
On a pole
By the Indiana flag
With stars
Below the moon
Outside in the storms
Above the ground
Our flag flies so high in the sky
Stands for the brave and liberty

Cody Thomas, Grade 5
Churubusco Elementary School, IN

The Butterfly

Nervous
Waiting on the block
Hearing the buzzer
Taking flight
Soaring through the water
Watching competitors out of
The corner of my eye
Landing on the touch pad
Relief

Madison Jones, Grade 6
Tri-West Middle School, IN

Snowflakes

S nowflakes are
N ever the same, they are
O rnaments of beauty —
W onderful gifts from above,
F alling down,
L anding,
A nywhere you can imagine.
K ids catch them on their tongues.
E verybody loves
S nowflakes.

Tess Caldwell, Grade 6
Melrose Elementary School, OH

Life

The real world teaches you to take a giant leap
To create yourself as an individual,
To test what you've learned,
To not keep quiet,
To scream out loud,
To go have an adventure and
To not stay in an area.

To not say, "Oh, yes, Ma'am,"
To have people say, "yes, Ma'am" to you,
Fill up on the fuel you need for the course of life to take you on its wild roller coaster.
Life can be cruel, but it's the way the Heavenly Father created it; UNEXPECTED.

Mary Najjar, Grade 6
Schuchard Elementary School, MI

Christmastime

Sipping sweet hot cocoa, from a warm, steaming mug.
Watching the soft, white snowflakes, float down toward the Earth.

Bright twinkling lights, illuminate the snow,
Red, green, and white, Christmas colors, we know.

Warm, crackling fire, music drifting through the room,
Bells jingling in the distance, as wrapping paper tears.

How many snowflakes fall in a year?
Is every snowflake truly unique?
How does Saint Nick's magical reindeer fly?
How does jolly old Santa get down our tiny chimney?

Gingerbread cookies, as sweet as a sugar cube.
Peppermint candies,
They melt in your mouth just as ice cream melts on a warm summer day.

Our house smells of evergreen trees,
With homemade cookies and wholesome milk, waiting to be devoured.
Stockings hanging over our mantle, waiting to be filled.
A thick blanket of snow, waiting to be played on.
Waiting, waiting, waiting.

Emma Burge, Grade 5
EH Greene Intermediate School, OH

Christmas Time

Oh it's Christmas where people are jolly and so folly we drink cocoa.
It's a time of cheer to spend time with our family.
It is the time of year when our Savior was born in a manger,
And people fall in love.
Kids get presents.
We sled or snowboard down a long hill with mom and dad.
The snow is so awesome.
Christmas is truly special.
We listen to Christmas songs and go caroling from house to house.
That is Christmas time.

Charles Howard, Grade 5
Auburn Hills Christian School, MI

Home Sweet Home

My home is sweet where my family meet.
Daddy and mommy are busy as bees, as we feel cozy and ease.
My home is like a symphony, which is filled with harmony.
Joy and happiness be with me.
Home is where my heart supposed to be!

Sophia Yang, Grade 4
Driscoll Elementary School, OH

Things That Are Quiet

The whispering wind
The darkness of the night
A fire with an unnatural flame
A tree swing
Soft snow in dawn's mist
My dog swift and cute
A fast tarantula quietly hunting
The small small woods
Water where the fish swim
The sky where the sparrow flies
The almighty light of God
Smoke I cannot grasp thee
A wonderful rose
Soft sand in my hand
DNA silent but important
Flag swaying in the wind against a stormy sky
Rain in the soft breeze
Nature quiet and delicate
A cloud as soft as cotton candy
Death a gentle thing where you slip into the dark

Mickayla Davis, Grade 5
Sanderson Elementary School, OH

Winter

I love winter. It is my favorite season.
I love it for so many reasons.
I love the feeling of snow blowing against my cheeks.
I love to watch the snow falling to my feets.
I enjoy the sight of snow falling to the ground.
I have fun making the snow into a large mound.
I love to go and cut down a Christmas tree.
It makes me happy and full of glee.
And those are some reasons.
Of why I love the winter season.

Kate O'Neill, Grade 6
Corpus Christi Elementary School, IN

My Dad

My dad is exciting,
Extremely extraordinary,
A spectacular man to be with.
He cares for my siblings and me like
We are rare jewels, silver, and gold.

Alejandra Ibarra, Grade 5
Washington Township Elementary School, IN

A Touchdown Pass

I said, "Hut hut!" and the center snapped the ball,
The wide receivers were so short
And the defenders were so tall,

I looked to my left,
I looked to my right,
I held the ball with a grip so tight,

I threw the ball and let it fly,
"Wow," I thought as it flew so high,
It went over the defender, into the wide receiver,

I got so nervous, that I think I caught a fever!
He caught the ball and ran as fast as he could,
He scored the touchdown, and I knew he would.

Hunter Buchanan, Grade 6
St John the Evangelist School, IN

At the Notre Dame Stadium

Six Air Force flyers
float down
from the sky in parachutes
with pink smoke
coming out of the chute.
People are cheering,
and I see Notre Dame
scoring on Michigan.
I see the sea of blue, yelling like a tsunami.
My friend Blake smiles,
and he gives me a high-five.
The wet, cold rain thumps on my feet.
I taste the soggy hot-dog
but it is the best hot-dog
because it is so salty and warm.
Notre Dame fans are waving their arms
for an interception of a Michigan pass and
returning it for a touchdown!

Josh Isaacson, Grade 5
Stanley Clark School, IN

Snow

I love the snow in the winter because it glistens like a jewel,
I'd even rather be in snow than swimming in a pool.

I love when we get a snowstorm since it is very cool,
Especially when we find out that the district closed the school!

It really makes my day seem great when it's thirty-two degrees,
Everyone really likes it when the icicles start to freeze.

The trees look really pretty from the snowflakes in the breeze
I just can't wait for Christmas and all the fun festivities!

Marissa Hansen, Grade 6
Abbott Middle School, MI

Jack-o'-Lanterns/Pumpkins
Jack-o'-lanterns,
Glow, Halloween,
Scaring, frowning, smiling,
Night, cool, orange, seeds,
Planting, roasting, cooking,
Picked, eaten,
Pumpkins
Spencer Lydon, Grade 4
Norwich Elementary School, OH

Seasons
Fall
Colorful, bold
Blessing, thanking, rejoicing
Beautiful sites and sounds
Season

Winter
Quiet, still
Chilling, freezing, breathtaking
Snow flakes falling all around
Cold

Spring
Bright, lively
Buzzing, storming, raining
Flowers blooming all around
Allergies

Summer
Hot, humid
Swimming, playing, tiring
Children out of school
Vacations
Kara Dilger, Grade 6
Nancy Hanks Elementary School, IN

Song
Listen carefully
and you will hear
a peaceful tune of a song.
Open your eyes and you will see
the notes in the air.
Younghyeon Ryu, Grade 6
Melrose Elementary School, OH

Autumn Pleasures
Rainbow-ruby leaves
Crisp fall air smells heavenly.
Halloween scary!
River water — clean and clear.
Hot chocolate, liquid gold.
Quinton Vance, Grade 5
Westview Elementary School, OH

The Ocean
Waters rushing
Waves crashing
Gulls calling
Balls flying

People swimming
Life guards blowing
Kids screaming
Parents relaxing

Sun setting
People packing
Cars rumbling
Waters rushing
Jarrett Bates, Grade 5
Tremont Elementary School, OH

The Wild Life
The squirrels are playful
The birds are singing
The trees are swaying
The bears are joyful

Baby cubs are with their mother
Crickets are chirping
The water is crashing
The dolphins are jumping

Coyotes are howling
The bees are stinging
Then they are dying
The sun is shining away

The wind is blowing
The snow is crunching
Bears are mauling
The moon is glistening
Ashley White, Grade 6
Harmon Middle School, OH

Covers
Snow covers the ground,
to make it a glossy white.

A blizzard covers the sky,
to cause a lengthy fright.

Sparkling ornaments cover the floor,
to create a pretty tree.

Company covers the room,
to form a festive jamboree.
Evan Cramer, Grade 5
Central Grade School, MI

Molly
Annoying at times
Lovable sometimes
Short blondie
Sweet as sugar
My playmate
A dog and horse lover
A 3rd grader and a spunky kid
A helper for surprises
Little prankster
A wild maniac
An 8 year old
That's my sister and
I love all 8 years of her!
Katie Spitzer, Grade 6
Tippecanoe Middle School, OH

The Great Outdoors
Nature
Green, wild
Changes, satisfies, pleases
Out my back door
Outdoors
Nick Rourke, Grade 6
Holy Angels School, OH

Christmas Presents
In the front room
Under the tree
Above the floor
On a nice rug
Beside some toys
From people in your family
With a bow on top
Near the tree stand
Sits a lovely present wrapped
In Christmas wrapping paper
Anna Bulmahn, Grade 5
Churubusco Elementary School, IN

Deer
The deer run wildly
In the woods during summer
Deer sleep in winter
Toby Ellis, Grade 4
Warren Central Elementary School, IN

Tree Snake
Tree snake
Tree snakes are green
Slither creeping striking
The tree snake likes bugs and hanging
Green snake
Adrian Long, Grade 4
Riverside Elementary School, MI

My Guitar

My guitar is loud
I have my own crowd
I also have my own band
We are called the Purple Sand
I am a pro
I even have my own show
I have a lot of cha ching
And I buy a lot of bling bling!
But then I woke up

Jake Elkins, Grade 4
Northern Heights Elementary School, IN

Summer of the Lioness

Summer is a lion with a glorious mane.
Summer stalks her prey quickly as striking;
radiant heat around the Earth.
She protects the Earth from winter,
as if she is a lioness protecting her cubs.
She finds food and water for us;
she gives us warmth —
and when she is hidden away in her den of clouds,
we hide too.
She lights our day with her inviting rays.
vehement
fiery
passionate
Summer is a lioness, roaring her way through spring,
Changing, all things green…

Chelsy Brewer, Grade 6
Harding Middle School, OH

I Am

I am flexible and sneaky
I wonder where I got my musical ability
I hear a patriotic song
I see the finale of fireworks
I want a gold medal from gymnastic Olympics
I am flexible and sneaky

I pretend I'm a professional dancer
I feel like I'm flying in a hot air balloon
I touch the shell of my turtle
I worry if I'm grounded
I cry if someone talks about my uncle
I am flexible and sneaky

I understand that music is a great invention
I say supercalifragilisticexpialidoucious
I dream about winning a gold medal from the Olympics
I try to do my best in school
I hope to be a gymnastic champion
I am flexible and sneaky

Brianna Daniels, Grade 5
Beck Centennial Elementary School, MI

Fall Is Here!

I see the new colors on the trees.
Leaves are dancing on their way down
making a cascade of colors.

The farmers build piles of pumpkins
ready to sell for the Halloween celebration.
The beginning of fall
always brings excitement among the children.

The carving of pumpkins,
the horror stories and the bags full of candies
are in every child's mind and memory.
Trick-or-treating is one of the sweet ingredients of fall.

The first bell of school and the chilly mornings,
with the yellow busses swarming around town
is a sign that fall is HERE.

Dylan Gligor, Grade 6
Holy Family Middle School, MI

Slavery

S o sad and frightened.
L ack of a good meal.
A ll hope is still here.
V ery tired.
E veryone is grouchy.
R un away for freedom.
Y ou are so lucky that you are not a slave.

Sarah Ann Chaney, Grade 4
Mayfield Elementary School, OH

Things That Are Gross

Ooey, gooey boogers
Stinky port a-potties at the park
Me when I wake up in the morning
Old green and blue mold
Ancient, shriveled, frostbitten pizza
Half-eaten, decomposed animals in the front yard
Red blood out of a cut
Fly eaten, rotten fruit squishing underneath your feet
Long tapeworms in specimen jars
Slippery, wet guts
Black, furry flies that land on your food
Ugly mosquitoes that suck your blood
Crusty scabs that are tempting to pick
Green barf on the floor
Sickening, multicolored bug juice and guts
Annoying, water filled blisters on your heel
Crystallized eye crust in the morning
Smelly, black toe jam underneath your toe
Dead, flaky skin that you scratch or peel off
The dirty floor of a city restroom

Noah Ball, Grade 5
Sanderson Elementary School, OH

Monkeys

Monkeys are cute
Monkeys are fine
Monkeys are so divine

They may eat bananas
And sit around all day
But in my mind they are…

Cute
Fine
And
So divine.

Emma Schroeder, Grade 6
Pennfield Middle School, MI

Colts vs Chargers

Chargers lose Colts win
Colts run dive gain catch touchdowns
Chargers lose get sacked tackle miss
Colts win
Chargers lose

Colin R. Mullins, Grade 4
Churubusco Elementary School, IN

School

School is like a big fun pool,
It is also very cool.
Sometimes it makes me want to drool,
I'm glad I don't go to Saturday school.
You can't overrule,
Just don't be a fool.
In the very cool school,
Just listen to every rule.
In all of the schools,
Teachers are the jewels.
You can even carpool
To go to school.

Logan Roberts, Grade 4
Chrisney Elementary School, IN

Stars

Up so high, big and bright
In the night sky, shining with light
Every star filled with gas
Every star has a past
Late at night, wished upon
Disappearing at the break of dawn

Shining bright with shades of yellow
Always feeling calm and mellow
Looking like a million miles away
Turning night into day
Stars bring both hope and joy
Giving faith to any girl or boy

Kelsey Gasso, Grade 6
Abbott Middle School, MI

Christmas Reminds Me Of…

Christmas reminds me of faith.
Faith reminds me of the creator, God.
God reminds me of life.
Life reminds me of love.
Love reminds me of warm fires.
Fires remind me of the North Star.
The North Star reminds me of the four wise men.
The four wise men remind me of gifts of frankincense and gold.
Gold reminds me of the rich smiles on the 25th day of December.
December reminds me of joyfulness.
Joyfulness reminds me of Christmas.

Justin Hatt, Grade 6
Waverly East Intermediate School, MI

Myself and I

DeAndre
Athletic, fun, and smart
Brother of Victor and Victoria
Lover of food, basketball, and swimming
Who feels nervous on the first day of school
    And when doing something wrong when
    People are in front of me
Who gets excited about seeing a famous person
    And getting to go to my friend's house
Who needs to do my best and stop watching TV
Who give kisses to my mom and my pets
Who fears my dad when he sneaks up on me and my friend's dog
Who would like to go to Las Vegas
Resident of Austintown, OH
Flowers

DeAndre Flowers, Grade 5
Frank Ohl Intermediate School, OH

The Best Football Game

The sky was gray.
The air stung, cold and brisk; I waited for the ball to be snapped.
The grass in my cleats was Kelly green with some brown.
I heard the birds and the neighbors down the street.
Someone was mowing their lawn.
My blue jersey
smelled like the outdoors;
the smell of wet grass and sweat filled the air.
The soggy football made my grip tricky.
I was nervous, happy, and excited as I waited.
The tall defender looked like a wall.
He would make the small ball fall to the ground.
"Hike!" I burst off the line.
The brown ball climbed the air and…Incomplete!
Second down. "Hike!"
I burst off the line again, and
I stretched out and caught tit!
TOUCH DOWN!
WE WON! I bumped Evan's chest, and we screamed like crazy!

Blake Harman, Grade 5
Stanley Clark School, IN

The Seed

It is dark, damp, and cold here in the ground
All of a sudden, crack my hard shell breaks
And part of me is now slowly moving to the surface
Oh how I long to see the surface
With its green grass, gargantuan trees, warm sunlight
But I know I have to be patient
It has been many days and many nights
But my stalk has finally grown
On the end of my sturdy green stalk are dainty pink petals
I have finally seen the surface
A tall women with a straw hat feeds me
The taste of the moist brown dirt satisfies me
I then see a strange creature
It has fur
It is called a dog
The surface is full of surprises
I love it

Auburn Walls, Grade 6
North Knox East Elementary/Jr High School, IN

Someday…

Someday I will graduate from high school.
Someday I will graduate from college.
Someday I will own a mansion.
Someday I will be an OB nurse.
Someday I will own a Ford F150.
Someday I will own an Escalade.
Someday I will get married and have kids.
Someday I will make a difference in my kids' lives.

Ashianna Chapple, Grade 5
Becker Elementary School, OH

Pizza

Pizza, Pizza, Pizza
It is the greatest food
It is not always the greatest food
With sardines, mushrooms and all that other stuff
But, it is always great with cheese or pepperoni
The greatest pizza is
Super Sized

Neil Thompson, Grade 4
John Simatovich Elementary School, IN

Leaves

Leaves falling through the air
Scratchy leaves falling in my hair
Here comes my brother
Now here is my mother
My brother asks, "What's going on?"
I yell, "Leaves, leaves falling on the lawn!"
Leaves falling from the sky
Oh, here's one in my eye!

Kaylene Summers, Grade 5
North Knox East Elementary/Jr High School, IN

Me and My Life

Toniann
Spunky, happy, and loving
Lover of vacations, the malls, and Italy
Who feels nervous when I go to school on the first day
  and when I swim with sharks
Who gets excited about going on vacation
  and when I see my family from New York
Who needs to get more clothes and shoes
Who gives kisses to my baby cousins, my cat, and my dog
Who fears my mom when she's mad and the basement at night
Who would like to be a famous horseback rider
Resident of Austintown, Ohio
Minardi

Toniann Minardi, Grade 5
Frank Ohl Intermediate School, OH

Cocoa

I'm walking up the driveway,
  With a snowball in my hand,
I throw it to the ground in the snow that looks like sand.
I walked into my house and much to my surprise,
  I see a cup of Cocoa,
  The normal kiddy size.
I sip the great delicious treat,
  The Cocoa delight,
This Cocoa is more than just the normal all right.
It's good, it's perfect, and it's great,
This is the Cocoa I don't dare to hate.

Jalen King, Grade 5
Auburn Hills Christian School, MI

The Season of Autumn

In the fall, I go back to school.
An exciting time!
Seeing old friends and meeting new ones is great.
New teachers and schedules, my next step in life.

In the fall, the leaves make a dramatic change.
From green to nature's own special colors.
Warm colors that match their unique shape.
Slowly they fall to the ground,
  dancing in the cool breeze.

In the fall, I go to the pumpkin farm
To pick out the perfect pumpkin.
It will make my jack o' lantern the funniest on the porch.
Hot apple cider is the best way to finish the day.

In the fall, Halloween comes.
Walking down the block, I trick-or-treat.
The smell of the cool night air is great.
Fall makes me want to have fun.

Julia Weller, Grade 6
Holy Family Middle School, MI

Mom

M oms you don't know
    what you can do without them.
O h
M oms are the best.

Randy Terry, Grade 4
Shoals Elementary School, IN

Family

Mom
Strict, cool
Caring, yelling, forgiving
Scrapbook, read, coach, news
Hardworking, laughing, love
Patient, nerd
Dad

Ashley
Loud, crazy
Loving, joking, cooking
Talk, golf, travel, trumpet
Caring, helping, cooking
Quiet, sensible
Alex

Tom
Young, silly
Bugging, skating, screaming
Soccer, DQ, football, truck
Running, laughing, smiling
Old, wise
Bob

Hope Park, Grade 6
Nancy Hanks Elementary School, IN

Awesome Autumn

Eye watering
Winds
Lovely leaves
Ruby red
Outstanding orange
Golden yellow
Zipping zippers
Warm cozy blankets
Fuzzy boots
Hot chocolate
With melting marshmallows
Carving pumpkins into
Creepy, crazy jack-o-lanterns
Whistling warm air roasting
You by the fire
Eating delicious doughnuts and
Cider

Olivia Rampersaud, Grade 5
Riley Upper Elementary School, MI

Christmas

In winter
outside of my house
it was almost Christmas Eve
Santa will be coming with his reindeer
red and green

Morgan Dease, Grade 5
Floyd Ebeling Elementary School, MI

My Dog Ruby

Ruby
Black, fun
Training, yawning, barking
Funny, crazy
I love my dog Ruby.

Payton Brackin, Grade 5
Cloverdale Middle School, IN

Charlie

Charlie, a little dog that walks on four,
That I adore,
He can jump and dance,
He'll even eat food off the floor,
He sneezes a lot,
Oh, yes it's true,
You will never forget his little ACHHOO!
He prances about,
With that furry little snout,
He's a mighty 'O fellow,
Oh, yes it is true,
Even when you are in the fog,
Charlie is a loyal dog.

Camden Grendow, Grade 6
Rocky River Middle School, OH

Lego

I like legos, yes I do
I like legos, how about you?
I like legos because they are fun.
You should try getting some
I like legos from the store
I think I should get more
I like legos because they are neat
I think they are a sweet treat

Makayla Munoz, Grade 4
John Simatovich Elementary School, IN

Snow

snow is great
snow is all around
snowball fights are so awesome
skiing and snowboarding are great too
snow is cool

Andrew Shields, Grade 5
Floyd Ebeling Elementary School, MI

Cooking Is My Thing

Take a look
I like to cook.

I like to bake
Seasoned steaks and frosted cakes.

I boil water in a pot
Because I like it steaming hot.

I like chocolate chip cookies,
Peanut butter too.
I also make a great beef stew.

Take a look
I like to cook.

Logan Cukierski, Grade 6
Trilby Elementary School, OH

Old Tired

I'm an old, tired dog
Always sad, never hugged
Grumpy all day long
My owner never lets me be free.
When someone comes over
They don't even notice me.
I'm just an old, tired dog.

Caleb Wolfe, Grade 5
Westview Elementary School, OH

Ocean Treasures

Marvelous creatures
Blue wonders of the ocean
Twinkling waters.

Sarah Stafford, Grade 5
Westview Elementary School, OH

Dreams

A dream is a whole world
A dream can be a friend
It can be an enemy
An enemy to your worst nightmare

You can run and run and run and run
But fast as a cheetah it will come
Dreams are frightening yes they are
They come from here or there
Near or far

Dreams dreams whoever you are
Dreams dreams I know where you are
Dreams dreams come out and play
Dreams dreams I'm never going away!!

Karina Varner, Grade 6
Woodward Park Middle School, OH

My Sister

C ora is very sweet
O h I love her
R unning is what she likes
A kindhearted person

W e like to play volleyball
E very time she sings it sounds like an angel
I can't live without her
S he can sing really good
E veryone I know likes her
N obody can be as nice as her
B ut sometimes she is mean
A loving girl
C an she get any nicer
H ugs and kisses are what she gives

Luke Weisenbach, Grade 5
St Michael School, IN

I Live in the Library

I live in the library, surrounded by books,
in the library I love to look and look,
to find my most favorite book.
I have so many to choose!

From wizards to owls,
shape shifters to water fowl,
cats to rats,
horses to bats.

History to mystery,
classics to fables,
mammals to camels,
wars to farm stables.

Books on books,
biographies,
encyclopedias!

In the library I love to look and look,
but why do I have to choose just *one* book?

Angeline Donahoe, Grade 5
Heritage Intermediate School, IN

The Silent Seconds

Deep in the fourth period
10 seconds on the clock
He dribbles up and down the court
5, 4, 3, 2, 1 the buzzer
The crowd is silent
As they watch the ball sail into the air
All you hear is swoosh!
The crowd goes wild!

Bradley Hurtig, Grade 6
St John the Baptist Elementary School, IN

Bears

B east of the plains and forest.
E arnest animals of the plains.
A rriving from hibernation
      to seek their territory for fish and berries.
R evising their dens for hibernation.
S ecuring their territory for intruders.

Treston Eblin, Grade 6
Harmon Middle School, OH

I Am

I am athletic and smart.
I wonder if I will get a scholarship for basketball.
I heard the basketball screaming as I shot it.
I saw the basketball smile.
I want to make it to the WNBA.
I am athletic and smart.
I pretend to fake someone out.
I feel happy when the basketball smiles.
I touch my basketball scholarship.
I worry that I won't make it on the A team for basketball.
I cry when my team loses.
I am athletic and smart.
I understand that it is hard to make it to the WNBA.
I say that everyone should be a good sport.
I dream that one day I will go to the state finals in high school.
I hope that I will meet Candice Parker.
I am athletic and smart.

Holly DeLeon, Grade 6
Galesburg-Augusta Middle School, MI

Gone in the Iraqi War

I sit on my bedroom floor,
I cry while I sit,
Because my dad is in the Iraqi war,
I try to settle down bit, by bit, by bit.

I tell myself he will be home soon,
But it doesn't help me.
Because right then I heard a knock,
I could hardly believe what I could see.

A Lieutenant standing there,
Right in my front door.
I knew I needed to hear more.

Then one year later Mom says let's go,
I don't know where,
So I try to walk slow,
Then when we get there…

It said "Welcome home from the Iraqi war"
I never cried on my bedroom floor, again.

Katherine Blocker, Grade 6
Pennfield Middle School, MI

Fairies

Fairies, tiny as can be,
flying up, up and away
like an airplane in the gleaming sunlight,
tickling our imaginations,
like nothing else can.
But when it turns noon,
they will disappear,
into nothing but dust.

Ally Szukaitis, Grade 6
Melrose Elementary School, OH

Carry

I carry the pine tree
home to create

I carry the tree lights
to decorate

I carry the ornaments
to lay along

I carry joy
in a very graceful song
Reid Bailey, Grade 5
Central Grade School, MI

The Talk About Tacos

I love tacos
The soft tacos
Yum!
The cheese
and the meat
Watching people bite
into the tacos
Oh!
Have you ever had
Taco Bell?
If not,
you're missing out
You don't even want me
to tell you about
Chipotle

Cade Torbert, Grade 4
Licking Valley Intermediate School, OH

White House

One hundred thirty-two rooms
Movie theater
Tennis court
Swimming pool
Twenty-eight fireplaces
Thirty-five bathrooms
One president and his family
Our White House!

Gina Cooper, Grade 4
Dobbins Elementary School, OH

The Pond

I paddled in my canoe —
Not a single disturbance in the water,
The smell of water like nature's perfume.
I could see the sun setting over the horizon,
Fish jumping in and out of the water.
Up ahead I could see a bright green moss bed just floating there,
A flock of geese flying overhead,
Trees full of color, orange, yellow, and blazing red,
A nearby island with grass as green as an emerald.
I could hear squirrels scampering up a tree as if they were being chased,
And the canoe just cutting through the water like a knife.

Elijah Yu, Grade 5
Stanley Clark School, IN

I Am

I am honest and funny!
I wonder, are my neighbors going to move to New York?
I hear the chalk screaming as it's being used on a chalkboard.
I see a book come alive and read what it says to the class!
I want my mom's family to get along again.
I am honest and funny!
I pretend to become a winning author!
I feel sad that my imaginary pet monkey died.
I touch a unicorn on the head.
I worry that my neighbor's dad is going to die because he has cancer.
I cry when I think about my great-great-aunt that sadly died last year.
I am honest and funny!
I understand how my friend feels about her parent's divorce.
I say you should always have something you love to do.
I dream that my parents will get back together.
I try to get good grades.
I hope my great-grandma is feeling better.
I am honest and funny!

Emily Midgett, Grade 6
Galesburg-Augusta Middle School, MI

School

As soon as I walk through those doors, the pressure has long been gone.
This time to forget about the past, a new day has begun.
Although sometimes it can be stressful,
most of the time we have to be careful.

A majority of people have failed to see…
just how fun school can be.
There's no better place to teach people who we are,
no matter how dark the sky, you will be a shining star!

So go on and study for that test.
You don't have to be like the rest.
Because school is cool, you've got to admit.
There, everyone could be perfect
if only we believe. If you want a place that you can always go to,
try your school — the place where you can truly be you…

Shayla Cabalan, Grade 5
St Jude Catholic School, IN

Waiting Flower

I am a flower waiting to bloom,
My stem is strong,
My petals are colorful, ready to explode,
My golden bursts blend with my surroundings,
I really want OUT!
Spring — here at last!
Bloom — boom!

Abby Van Allen, Grade 5
Westview Elementary School, OH

Hold Tight

I am holding on tight and never letting go
through the bad times and the good times
I will always love you, and you will always love me
We think the same thoughts, and love the same things
living here is hard enough, but letting go is the worst
and I know I have to remember…
LIVE life the way I want to live it
LOVE like I've never loved before
and LAUGH until it hurts
I will remember this moment for ever and ever
and you will always be watching over me, no matter what
please don't go away because I know I won't survive
without you by my side
and falling asleep on your smooth, black, skin
hugging you as tight as I can
thank you for all you've done for me, goodnight mamma

Emma Harper, Grade 6
Northwood Elementary School, IN

Baseball

I hear a loud banging noise,
It's the balls being hit by the boys,
The balls roll on the ground,
Where they can be found,
I step on the base,
In a very fast pace,
They throw me the ball,
While I wait for the call,
HE'S OUT! Calls the ump,
Boy am I pumped,
My teammates are rooting for me,
That's the third out, you see,
In the dugout we go,
Faster than lightning you know,
It's the bottom of the seventh inning,
And I'm just beginning
Slam goes the ball into a home run,
And that's the game, Hon.
1, 2, 3, 4, 5, 6, 7,
All our balls go up to heaven, when I get there I will repeat,
"HUSTON PLUMBING CAN'T GET BEAT!"

Dillon Athey, Grade 4
Licking Valley Intermediate School, OH

I Am

I am funny and happy.
I wonder how cool it would be to fly.
I hear a purple bear talking to me.
I see Fred, my friend, in the tree.
I want a monkey.
I am funny and happy.
I pretend to play with Fred, my imaginary friend.
I feel happy because my paper tells me the words.
I touch a bird's mohawk.
I worry about polar bears.
I cry when my pets die.
I am funny and happy.
I understand that my dog runs faster than me.
I say I love animals.
I dream about getting a horse.
I try hard to get great records in gym.
I hope I can get a new dirt bike.
I am funny and happy.

Nathan Belland, Grade 6
Galesburg-Augusta Middle School, MI

Baseball

The announcer calls your name and you're up to bat
The pitcher throws in a curve ball, then whack!
You hit the ball with eyes open wide,
You think to yourself, "That ball is now fried!"
The fans stand up, clap their hands and go wild
You wave to everyone and give coach a big smile

Kory Gilbert, Grade 5
Birmingham Covington School, MI

Christmas

C andy canes hanging on the Christmas tree.
H oliday season begins.
R eindeer pull Santa's sleigh.
I cicles hanging from the houses
S tockings get filled to the top.
T raditions are what we do every year.
M istletoe is hung in the doorways.
A ngels on top of the Christmas tree.
S anta visits every house.

Ryan Lowe, Grade 6
Pennfield Middle School, MI

When I Grow Up…

When I grow up I want to be a veterinarian,
or maybe a doctor.
I want to move to Laingsburg.
I want toy poodles and a Siamese cat!
I'll read fantastic books about animals.
I want a family.
I want a nice life!

Hailey Hug, Grade 4
Eugene M Nikkari Elementary School, MI

Thanksgiving 2008

There is so much to be thankful for
on this Thanksgiving day.
I am thankful to our soldiers
even more than I can say.

They risk their lives for America
and countries across the sea
so life will be safer
for you and for me.

Thank you to our President
who has served our country well.
Through the good times and the bad,
he has loved God without fail.

I am thankful for my country,
my family and my friends
and will remain thankful
until the very end.

Thank you Lord Jesus
for shedding your blood at Calvary
so that one day I will be with you
for all eternity.
Daniel Brandenburg, Grade 6
Immanuel Christian School, MI

trapeze artist

gliding through thin air
stretch to grab the next trapeze
land and hear applause
Lauren Gibbard, Grade 5
Calvin Christian Elementary School, MI

Fall and Halloween

apples, bats,
candy,
door-to-door,
eating, farming,
ghost, harvest,
impersonate,
jack-o'-lantern,
kites, leaves,
monsters, nutmeg,
October, pumpkin,
quilt, raking,
September,
turkey, unmask,
vampire,
witch, x-ray,
yellow squash,
zombie
Clayton Hara, Grade 5
Norwich Elementary School, OH

Thanksgiving

Families have a big feast
The turkey on the table with our family
So, so hungry,
Sharing the feast with each other
And for dessert, pumpkin pie!
Remembering
Native Americans and pilgrims shared
Thanksgiving
Gathering fruits and vegetables,
Thankful for all their blessings!
Yordi Vallecillo, Grade 4
Matthew Duvall Elementary School, OH

Farming

I like to farm.
Drive the tractor all day long
Feed the animals
Before you go
Man what a life!
Neal Hughes, Grade 5
Henryville Elementary School, IN

Frantic Freeze Forest Fox

What does an arctic fox know?
Snatching scraps from a
Sleepy polar bear
Blossomed berries best
In the summer
White sleek fur
Snuggling tail and nose
Bathing away in the
Last summer sun
Fading fairly for
Another fierce frozen winter
Kelsey Cunningham, Grade 5
Riley Upper Elementary School, MI

Nature

The woods were cold,
Nothing was in sight,
Then Spirit Bear appeared,
All fluffy and white.

I couldn't believe my eyes,
I didn't know what to do,
I had to do something,
But it had to be wise.

So I lifted my arm,
I lifted as slow as a sloth,
But that was a mistake,
Because the Spirit Bear was alarmed.
Kaylan Kerbler, Grade 6
Harmon Middle School, OH

The Game

The game is about how you play it
It's not about how good you are

The game is about being a team leader
It's not about bragging

The game is about being unselfish
It's not about the stardom or the fame

The game is about how hard you try
It's not about winning

The game is about having fun
It's about the love for the game
Mike Rickard, Grade 6
Trilby Elementary School, OH

Friday the 13th

Don't spill the salt
Don't walk under a ladder
Or something will be the matter.
Don't step on a crack
Or you'll break your mother's back
Just remember, Okay?
Today is a bad luck kind of day.
Joanah Larkin, Grade 5
Spaulding Elementary School, OH

Light Steps

Glowing all around
Without making a sound
Light steps
Light steps
Staring at them for a while
Making lots of people smile
Light steps
Light steps
Millions of them everywhere
Man it looks beautiful up there
Light steps
Light steps
Those light steps are stars
Positions are close to Mars
Those stars
Those stars
Victoria Monaghan, Grade 6
Pennfield Middle School, MI

Snakes

Slimy and scaly
Quick and slick and poisonous
Wrapping and binding
David Fuqua, Grade 4
Stonegate Elementary School, IN

Veteran's Day

Today is the day when we will give,
Honor to all 24.9 million military veterans who lived,
They saved our country at least one time,
When they come home the bells will chime,
We should always keep clear a place in our heart,
For each has a value beyond precious art,
You wear your uniform with pride,
And use your skills, so well applied,
One final day each faced their call,
Each gave their best enduring all,
We'll never let their special day,
Their time for honor slip away,
We stood for freedom just like you,
And loved and cherished the flag you cherish too.
President Dwight Eisenhower made this day true,
He did that to honor the veterans who always came through.

Gian Carlo Valli, Grade 6
EH Greene Intermediate School, OH

Death

Death is something that makes you cry.
Holding back the tears is hard to try.
Death brings memories,
Some good, some bad.
Not all memories of death are sad.
When the thought of death comes to your mind,
You know your loved ones are at peace.
Although you don't know when your time will come,
One thing you do know is that there's no place to run.
You will travel through many heartaches and pain,
Then one day you will see them again.
When your day finally comes,
Just think about the ones that you know and love.

Justin Bradley, Grade 5
Spaulding Elementary School, OH

Alaska

Along roads
Near cities
In bays, off ocean shores, everywhere
Nature follows you by your side.
It's freedom
In the silence of nature's sounds continuously changing
And nature's landscapes watching you

Grant Senger, Grade 6
Harding Middle School, OH

Black Jack

Black Jack, amazing canine with a sweet personality.
He looks like a cool night sky,
Is as fast as a bullet train,
With the most wonderful doggy face.

Trenton Rhodes, Grade 5
Washington Township Elementary School, IN

Freedom

F lags flying high in the sky
R espect that we give our veterans as thanks
E agles that fly high with no boundaries
E ducation to choose what we do in life
D emocracy that gives us our electoral system
O ur rights to vote for our president
M arines fought for our freedom

Dominick Draper, Grade 5
Sanderson Elementary School, OH

My Friend Pramod

As I look out the window
I see my friend
Pramod
As proud as a lion
Yet as timid as a koala
He is the perfect choice for a friend

As useful as a supercomputer
He is interesting
With a spicy tooth as big as the universe
Eating food that would make some tongues burn
And a love for drawing even bigger than that
He is one of my best companions
Thin
Yet strong
He is a wonderful person

His friendship spreading farther than the sun
And higher than Mount Everest
He will show you
What a true friend is.

Dhruv Medarametla, Grade 5
Indus Center for Academic Excellence, MI

What Is Over the Rainbow?

That beauty of sun and rain,
It shines with all of the colors
Red, blue, purple, green.
What's over this beauty?
What's over this rainbow?
Maybe it's a pot of gold,
Shining in the sun,
Glistening in the light.
Or, maybe it's a leprechaun
Dancing and singing the day away,
Ready to be my friend.
Maybe over this glory is a beautiful valley.
Full of flowers as pretty as this rainbow,
Full of bright green grass, ready to be played in.
I don't know if Ill ever find out what's over this rainbow.
Maybe it's just a sweet secret, not meant to know.

Jenna Deathe, Grade 5
Northern Heights Elementary School, IN

The Merriest Time of Year
Christmas is the holiday that makes my heart joyfully jump around,
The warm aroma of hot chocolate, coffee, and cookies surround me,
As I descend the curving stairs fresh in the morning.
The Christmas tree is smothered with presents underneath,
It's nearly as drenched with wonderful toys as a toy store!
Everybody is merrily discoursing to each other as they drink and eat Christmas treats.

The sun; just beginning to shine upon the Earth,
After all, I have a craving to come down early after that thrilling night of waiting for presents.
The entire house is overcrowded with lovely, joyful Christmas lights and decorations!
The house feels cozy with the reds, greens, and sparkly tinsel; floating and looking gorgeous.

Cheery, but muffled music is playing quietly in the background,
You don't want to disturb all of those jubilant giggles and conversations!
Dogs are barking and of course the oven timer is loudly ringing!!

It's as cheery as an amusement park.
Christmas is a fun and gentle reminder that everyone is capable of giving a little.

The entire house is overcrowded with lovely joyful Christmas lights and decorations,
The entire house is overcrowded with lovely joyful Christmas lights and decorations,
The entire house is overcrowded with lovely joyful Christmas lights and decorations!

Ambika Miglani, Grade 5
EH Greene Intermediate School, OH

Nature's Wonders
One Pink Rose that seems to outshine the rest with the morning dew still fresh on its petals. Its leaves are green as a lima bean. The water of the river flows gradually as it crashes to the bank leaving only a trace of where it has been. All the other flowers look dull today because this One Pink Rose shines like the sun on a cloudless day. As the sun shines like a spotlight squirrels are running around as if playing tag.

Sarah Neeley, Grade 6
Cloverdale Middle School, IN

Christmas
Christmas is my favorite holiday.
When we get up, it is 6:00 a.m., and the sun has not yet risen.
Christmas music plays softly in the background as my mom takes pictures of our happy faces.

As the kids unwrap their presents and see something that they wanted, they yell Hooray!
That is why Christmas is my favorite day.
The smell of ham cooking in the late afternoon makes my mouth water.
The cool winter air feels great when I walk outside to play in the snow.

Why does my mom always get a kitchen appliance?
That is what I ask myself while in a trance.

Christmas is as joyful as a little kid playing in the summer sun with his friends.
It is as great as the ripest strawberry in the batch.

Christmas is the sight of happiness.
It makes you feel warm and cozy inside.
It makes you feel warm and cozy inside.
It makes you feel warm and cozy inside.

Christopher Seger, Grade 5
EH Greene Intermediate School, OH

Joy

I am joy.
You know me for bringing laughter, smiles, and amusement.
I was born in the hearts of many people
Who truly know the meaning of me.
My best friend is the gleaming glee
Because we like to bring laughter to the young.
My enemy is sorrow
Because it does no good to the world.
I fear the terrifying tears
Because it means that I'm nowhere near.
I love to see a smile from ear to ear
Because that means I've fought the ferocious fear.
I wish I could be with everyone,
But don't worry because my journey has just begun.

Monica Harris, Grade 6
Harding Middle School, OH

Doubtful Feelings

Every day there is a doubter.
A doubter is a mean monster.
People say stuff to hurt you.
But believe in yourself.
Think about it.
They may say you're too short to play basketball.
Believe in yourself you can do it.
You may want to be a designer but can't draw.
Then work on your drawing and believe in yourself.
You can be whatever you want
Don't let anyone stop you.
Just like our first African American president Barack Obama.

Tersail Chapman, Grade 6
Woodward Park Middle School, OH

Flying Without Wings

I gallop my horse
Straight to the hurdle.
Everyone's watching me.
I rise in the saddle,
And for a moment, I'm flying —
Just Starlight and me.
Thud!
We land,
My moment is shattered.
I gallop her to the next hurdle,
We fly again.
When I'm done, the judge walks up to me.
She hands me a silver trophy.
As I raise it over my head,
I hear cheers from the crowd.
I whisper to myself,
"Starlight and I —
We flew."

Jacklyn Vander Zee, Grade 6
Crown Point Christian School, IN

Gifts

G ive thanks on Christmas.
I nside opening presents.
F un with my family.
T o the North Pole he goes.
S aves money to buy presents.

Angie Smith, Grade 5
West Washington Elementary School, IN

Who's at the Door?

Beep! Beep!
"Hey mom!"
Knock! Knock!
Meosha yells,
"I'll get it!"
A red car pulls in,
Music cranked up
My dad, up at 7:00 to start the food
Yum! That smells good!
Smells like pie!

Onalesa Sovia, Grade 4
Midland Academy of Advanced and Creative Studies, MI

Planet Mercury

M ercury is
E ven smaller than Earth.
R ecently we have been working on
C ollecting things from the planet.
U nderneath Mercury's
R ock hard core there is hot lava that would burn
Y ou in less than a second.

Vincent Schnell, Grade 6
Pinewood Elementary School, IN

I Am

I am fun and athletic.
I wonder what my cousin Airyka is doing.
I hear growling at night.
I see yellow people.
I want a four wheeler.
I am fun and athletic.
I pretend to listen.
I feel mad when I don't get my way.
I touch a ferry.
I worry about my family.
I cry for my cats Sunny and Billybob.
I am fun and athletic.
I understand I am going through a hard time.
I say don't give up, keep trying.
I dream about cats.
I try jumping on the trampoline.
I hope my brother is doing fine.
I am fun and athletic.

Liz Misner, Grade 6
Galesburg-Augusta Middle School, MI

Evergreen

Evergreen
Tall, pointy
Decorations! Family gatherings!
Beautiful, nice happiness, thankfulness.
Yuletide.

Dana Hightshoe, Grade 4
Bailly Elementary School, IN

Colors of the World

Green is the stem of a flower,
Red is a colorful rose.

Orange is the color of my door hinge,
Blue is the color of my nose.

Yellow is the steaming sun,
Purple is a pretty blooming flower.

Gray is like a pigeon,
Brown is like the Twin Towers.

We all love different colors,
But of course there's others.

Cameron Gamble, Grade 4
Northfield Elementary School, OH

Fall

Trick or treat trick or treat.
I hear from door to door.
As I'm walking down the street.
And with the kids all on the floor.

I smell pumpkins and cinnamon.
Oh wait! Candy too.
I hear kids screaming c'mon c'mon.
And people yelling BOO!

I see goblins and ghouls
And monsters too!
I also see covered pools.
How about you?

Valerie Jablonski, Grade 6
Holy Family Middle School, MI

I'm a Tree

I stand up stiff
All alone
My friends fly down
But not for very long.
They can leave
But not me.
I can only stay in place
And watch them go.
Maybe the wind will visit me today.

Evan Rumble, Grade 4
Dobbins Elementary School, OH

The Forest

As I walk into the forest, I see the trees sway like a cool breeze of air.
I hear the rumble of a car like an angry bull.
The leaves crumble under my feet like a devastating earthquake.
I walk across a bridge that is as rough as a corncob.
I sit on a table as if a long day is done.
I see a walnut on my path as still as a tree stump.
The oak tree's bark was as rough as leather from a bull hide.
I see a dam the beavers have built as it looks like brown chocolate.
I see chopped up logs, as they look as sad as a crescent moon.
As I walk home, I walk across the grass that is as green as the leaves.

Mark Sprinkle, Grade 6
Cloverdale Middle School, IN

Christmas

The sun is hiding behind the clouds,
But the crystal light snow brightens the morning sky and puts a sparkle in my eye.
It's Christmas morning!

I leap out of bed,
Dash down the stairs.
A Christmas tree as tall as a mountain is waiting for me.
It's Christmas morning!

What is in the stockings?
How many presents are there?
What is the best present of all?
It's Christmas morning!

Ornaments on the Christmas tree,
Presents all around me.
The Christmas tree lights brighten the colorful presents and ornaments within.
It's Christmas morning!

Christmas is the greatest time of the year,
We should all have a great cheer.
It's Christmas morning!
It's Christmas morning!
It's Christmas morning!

Daniel Mills, Grade 5
EH Greene Intermediate School, OH

I Am From

I am from the cold stormy nights on the lake where I spend my summer days
I am from the roar of the crowd from my first time on stage
I am from the tall tales about the little red barn on the hill
I am from a friendship that will never fail
I am from skipping rocks on the sandy shore of my lake
I am from the trees in my front yard who's leaves I always have to rake
I am from the dusty old books I've read a million times
I am from fairy tales and crazy little rhymes
I am from a family no one seems to understand
I am from a life where only I know who I am

Madison McGuire, Grade 6
Northwood Elementary School, IN

I Am
I am serious and scientific
I wonder if I'll be a scientist when I grow up
I hear my inventions rumbling
I see my inventions all over
I want to be an inventor
I am serious and scientific

I pretend to be a scientist
I feel test tubes
I touch my inventions
I worry about my family
I cry tears of joy when my inventions work
I am serious and scientific

I understand not all inventions will work
I say if you focus on what you do, you can do it
I dream to be a scientist
I try to get good grades in science
I hope to be a scientist when I grow up
I am serious and scientific

I am Derek Simmons

Derek Simmons, Grade 4
Floyd Ebeling Elementary School, MI

Life
Life is nice, oh yes it is
Sometimes it is horrible.
Maybe it will be with various surprises,
Both good and bad
You may want to run away
To a land with no stress
To feel like you have butterfly wings
To sprout and fly away.
Tear drops falling like rain
You just want to get out of here
But you feel God is holding you back.
Right now, you don't know why.
Soon, you will find out that it is for good
God has placed you here for a special reason
To help others just like you.

Ben Jasek, Grade 6
Crown Point Christian School, IN

Athlete
Athlete
Healthy, strong
Running, catching, throwing
Omar, Derek, kids, adults
Jogging, sprinting, walking
Tall, small
Runner

Casey Grant, Grade 6
Peaceful Children Montessori School, OH

September Bee
It was time to go
But I had a few
Last minute things
I had to do
Like share a pollen flower with another bug,
Say good bye to flowers as I drift away
And say one last goodbye to everything I love…
Until spring comes again.

Dylan Robinson, Grade 5
Riley Upper Elementary School, MI

Jack
Jack is an active boy you can enjoy.
He is running up and down the hall.
He can be cranky,
He can be cute, but he is my brother and I love him.
He is adorable,
And I can't live without him.

Thomas Setser, Grade 5
Washington Township Elementary School, IN

My Three Dogs
I have three dogs of mine
A Chihuahua, Spaniel, and Beagle.
The Beagle, Lucy, jumps so high
She seems to soar like an eagle.
The Spaniel, Rosie, acts so sweet
And also cute and loving.
I can hardly stop holding her
And it feels hard to stop the hugging.
Lucy and Sally, the Chihuahua, of course
Together they roughly play.
Chasing balls and bones and toys,
Sometimes they romp all day
When I feel lonely they can be my friends.
And when I feel as green as some frogs,
They lay with me and comfort me.
I love all three of my wonderful dogs!

Kristen Duryea, Grade 5
St Joseph Parish School, OH

Springtime
Springtime is here
but daylight is coming
the birds are singing
the animals are waking.
The cool breeze is swaying in the air,
the fawns were just born so the doe just cares,
about her little five fawns in the air.
So that is just all for next spring will come,
just one more year,
and spring will be here.

Selin Turan, Grade 5
Kenowa Hills Intermediate School, MI

Scuba Diver

I dive beneath the surface,
Of the great vast ocean waters.
To meet my eyes a beautiful sight,
Of the wonderful ocean floor.

There are colorful fish,
And bright rocky coral,
And creatures I can't describe.

There is dark green seaweed,
And soft white sand.
As I explore this underwater world,
Bubbles burst from my mouth.

It seems like a dream,
This great big mass of blue.
I check my air,
And I don't have much time,
But that's what makes it so special.

Gabrielle Hammarlund, Grade 6
Rocky River Middle School, OH

What Moves Me

My baby cousin, Lacy, moves me
Because she loves me
Deep down in my heart
My life, she is the start.

When she comes over,
My love just falls out,
I tell everybody I love her
And I do, no doubt.

Logan O'Leary, Grade 6
Mayfield Elementary School, OH

If I Were in Charge

If I were in charge I'd...
Have a mansion with 5 bathrooms
I'd make different state names
I'd tell gas companies to drill
I'd tell people they'd have to have
    two different names

Randy P. Johnson, Grade 4
Churubusco Elementary School, IN

Life

When you look at me
I just turn and look away.
Living life as a child,
Not always knowing what to say.
You may walk away thinking
you have the greatest life;
Not knowing that we live as ants,
And among us live giant mice.

Kaitlyn Sutton, Grade 5
Norton Elementary School, MI

Imagine That

Have you ever imagined that you were a rock star
Or have you ever imagined that you were a football or baseball player
If you did, you have a good imagination
If you didn't, that's okay
You still have a good imagination
Try to imagine you're a rock star, football or baseball player
Or anything else
You will have an awesome imagination

Lexia Darnell, Grade 4
John Simatovich Elementary School, IN

Gemini

G emini was two twins. They were boys. One boy's name was Pollux.
E verybody was scared that the people in the boat would die.
    The people in the boat were in a bad storm.
M any people loved them after that.
I n the parade they cherished them.
N obody was hurt.
I n the end they ended up in the sky.

John Robbins, Grade 6
Pinewood Elementary School, IN

Have You Ever Noticed?

I'm sitting on my driveway, just taking in it all.
I zip up my green jacket, it's feeling more like fall.

I see the purple sunset, and the moon starts to rise.
A little beetle scuttles, then takes off towards the skies.

I'm taking in the night air, it smells sweet like dew.
I've never taken all this time to do this, have you?

I lie down on the driveway, and look up at the sky.
I see stars shining oh so brightly, and so beautifully side by side.

I'm lying here so quietly, I feel like a mime.
Until my mom shouts out to me, "Dinner time!"

I guess I have to go now, as I look out at the moon.
I hope that I can come back, very, very soon.

Meredith Mackowicz, Grade 6
Saint Michael School, IN

Fearless

As I skate on the open ice
My feet glide like a shooting star
I feel no fear, as I take a check into the board
I lift myself up like a bear about to attack
Standing on its hind legs
Fearless, I glide again, taking the puck and shooting a winning goal.
As the game is over, I take pride, and thank the other team
Win or lose, we all will be teammates and fearless on the ice.

Richard Sklenar, Grade 6
Harmon Middle School, OH

I Am

I am athletic and fun.
I wonder what my job will be when I'm older.
I hear my dog talking.
I see a wall with colorful paintings on it.
I want a golf cart.
I am athletic and fun.
I pretend to write on the wall.
I feel surprised about my mom talking to a wolf.
I touch a pumpkin made out of fur.
I worry when I don't get my work done.
I cried when I sold my cow at the fair.
I am athletic and fun.
I understand what school's about.
I say that I have a lot of friends.
I dream about getting a cell phone.
I try to play softball as best as I can.
I hope I can get an iPod.
I am athletic and fun.

Estee Ostlund, Grade 6
Galesburg-Augusta Middle School, MI

When Fall Is Here

The world knows when fall is here,
When the summer birds no longer sing
And the autumn air begins to sting.
When the days get shorter and the air gets colder,
That's how the world knows.
I know when fall is here when I step outside and shiver,
And see the leaves quiver,
And the trees shake them off.
I can smell maple from a mile away,
I hope that fall is here to stay.
And that's how the world knows when fall is here.

Maeve Cook, Grade 6
Gesu Catholic School, OH

Fall

When the leaves change colors I shout out "Hurrah!"
When I get my coat on to go outside to play,
I know I'll have a good day!

I rake the colorful leaves into a great big pile,
Jumping in I'd thought I'd sit awhile.

I look above at the empty trees, the autumn colors fade
away
away
away
to come again another day.

The trees are sentinels watching, guarding nature
until it comes back to life in the spring.

Noah Szczypka, Grade 6
Holy Family Middle School, MI

Basketball

Swoosh!!!
The crowd goes wild!
I hit a three pointer!
The game is tied at fifty-seven,
And there are two minutes left.
I am so shaky, that my heart is beating fast.
Five seconds left, BOOM!!!
I hit a three pointer again!!!

Mason Becher, Grade 5
Nancy Hanks Elementary School, IN

Game Day

I awake in my bed feeling that dread
I don't want to get up; I'd rather be dead
I am too tired to move; I don't like Mondays
But then I remember, no school, it's Sunday!

I hop out of bed; this day is going to rock
I grab for my shirt and my NFL socks
My anticipation is great, it gives me a thrill
I jump on the couch; I am ready to chill!

My big bowl of chips is overflowing
I am more than excited, I must be glowing
Remote in my hand I am ready and set
I hope my team wins; all my friends I have bet!

When they announce the games that are going to air
I don't hear my team and I say that's not fair
But wait, if they are not playing on Sunday
That must mean my team is playing on Monday!

Did I say that Mondays fill me with dread?
That I don't want to get up I'd rather be dead?
I guess I was wrong, it's ok after all
Because what could be better than Monday Night Football!

Andrew M. Brown, Grade 6
Emmanuel-St Michael Lutheran School, IN

Football

My dad asked me if I wanted to play,
And I figured, "Why not, what the hey."
It started out with all kinds of fun,
And then the dad coaches told us we all had to run.
They made us do bear crawls and all kinds of drills,
I just wanted to scream and head for the hills.
Gassers, monkey rolls, and the gauntlet are hard to do,
But after it was over there were only a few.
Thank God there are helmets and pads,
Because there is no mercy from any of the dads.
Our record is great…we haven't lost yet,
I guess it was worth all of the hard work and sweat.

Cam Kysela, Grade 6
Rocky River Middle School, OH

The Winter Star
Winter is like a shooting star.
It comes and goes.
And as it passes,
It sparkles in the night.
Evan Filion, Grade 5
Birchwood School, OH

Veterans
V eterans are honored on a special day.
E very day they fight for our country.
T hey fight for us overseas.
E ntrusted in them was our country.
R emember them when you pray.
A soldier risked his or her life for us.
N ever giving up on us.
S ave our U.S. citizens.
Sydney Lambert, Grade 5
Spaulding Elementary School, OH

Christmas
Come, hear us
Rejoice because now
It's Christmas Eve.
We sing and laugh and play.
Today, we sled ride and run
Merrily through the snow, making
Army forts and waiting for
Santa Claus to come down the chimney.
Alexis Pittman, Grade 5
Perry Central Elementary School, IN

In the Water
Splashing and laughter —
Wicked waves licking my feet,
The cold, cold water.
Indiana Cote, Grade 6
Stanley Clark School, IN

The Grand Escape
Two little cats
Chased by river rats
Into the water they fell.
That was not swell
Two little cats
Wet as can be
(I would not like that if that was me)
Climbed onto a log,
Surrounded by fog,
Saved by an old man,
Set down on dry land,
Ran to Texas Jake,
They're saved for goodness sake.
Colton Reed, Grade 5
Wooster Christian School, OH

Chocolate
Chocolate is so creamy
so yummy and delicious
and when I take a bite of it
I fall into suspicions

Who made the chocolate bar?
Who made it taste so good?
The chocolaty, chocolate,
Chocolate bar…is absolutely
good!
Chloe Schmucker, Grade 5
Heritage Intermediate School, IN

United States of America
U nited Nations
N ebraska
I owa
T he Battle of Gettysburg
E nglish
D emocracy

S hining
T renton
A rkansas
T he War of 1812
E lected officials
S tars and stripes

O ceans
F ifty states

A wesome
M aryland
E xciting
R epublic
I nteresting
C olorado
A mericans
Jon Delaney, Grade 5
Central College Christian Academy, OH

Fall
Already Fall
The squirrel holes in the trees
All the leaves with hints of ruby red
I can smell the fresh Fall air
As the leaves fall down, down, down
When I walk back to the house
I can smell the pumpkin pies
Sitting still on the window sill
I can taste the wonderful whip cream
On my pumpkin pie.
Colin Burford, Grade 5
Riley Upper Elementary School, MI

Winter
See white fluffy snowflakes
Falling to the ground
Hear the laughter of children
Making snowmen, sledding, skiing
Smell hot cocoa with marshmallows
Waiting to warm you up
Taste the hot cocoa
Chocolate, warm, yummy
Feel the cold biting you
As the scarf falls off your face
Winter is an awesome season!
Bushra Varachia, Grade 6
Boulan Park Middle School, MI

Keys
KEYS
Up, down, up, down
My piano keys go
As my hands drift across
A song that is slow

Black, white, black, white
My piano keys go
As one hand plays the scale
And the other hand is low

Loud, soft, loud, soft
My piano keys go
As my hand presses harder
On the notes that flow

Low, high, low, high
My piano keys go
As my hands join together
And play to and fro
Swathi Iyer, Grade 6
West Middle School, MI

Thanksgiving
Thanksgiving is almost here
With turkey, yams and
Much, much more.
We play until it's time to eat
And then we eat the pie!

I love Thanksgiving!
That means meeting new family and
Getting together with family
We already know.

Thanksgiving is a cheerful
Time of year!
Destiny Barnes, Grade 4
Matthew Duvall Elementary School, OH

Fish

The fish swims up and down
The fish swims side to side
The fish swims in a circle
The fish likes to swim up to eat
It is nasty to clean the fish bowl
You have to use your hands
It is hard to take care of pets
You have to remember to feed it every day
It is also hard to take care of cats
Cats will claw your new furniture

Nathan Bauknecht, Grade 4
John Simatovich Elementary School, IN

Thanksgiving

Thanksgiving is the day in November
To remember your friends and family

Thanksgiving is the day to be with loved ones
That you might not see a lot

Thanksgiving is a time to talk with one another
To tell what's been going on in everyone's crazy
roller coaster lives

Thanksgiving is the day to EAT
To eat turkey and stuffing, dressing, potatoes,
and so much more!

But most of all Thanksgiving is the day to be thankful
for everyone and everything that has been helpful in our lives.

Karissa Miller, Grade 5
Heritage Intermediate School, IN

Halloween

Halloween is the time of year
When ghosts and goblins do appear.
Caramel apples and frosted cake
Sometimes make my stomach ache.
Decorating is so scary
All the bats and spiders are so hairy.
What to be is the question.
While searching through the great selection.
Will it be the Grim Reaper?
Or an ordinary zookeeper?
Frightening hay rides and haunted houses are so fun
When you scream, it has only just begun.
My favorite are the corn mazes,
Especially when they spell kooky phrases.
October 31st is just once a year
So you better have fun while it's here.
Trick-or-treat smell my feet
Give me something good to eat!

Jonathon Sparks, Grade 6
St Gerard School, MI

Math

Math is always around us.
It can always be seen.
Math is mainly numbers.
Numbers can be seen anywhere.
You can find them on bags.
On papers.
And on books.
A word with four letters,
And amazing possibilities.
God has given us a gift to help us with math.
Our brain.

Siddharth Tirumala, Grade 6
Abbott Middle School, MI

Florida

Having **F** un in the sun!
Fee **L** ing the sand beneath my toes!
L **O** ving vacation!
Wate **R** splashing in my face!
Palm trees swaying **I** n the wind!
D isappearing in the wave.
Warm be **A** utiful beaches!

Elizabeth Edwards, Grade 6
Holy Angels School, OH

Snake

I can see very slightly
I can see my prey my predator
I can smell the trail he leaves behind
I can smell where he is
I can taste the animal
I can taste the trail
I can feel the vibration of the person or animal
I can feel the animal
I can hiss for as long as I want to
I can rattle my tail
I can hear my predator
I'm a snake

Alyssa Summers, Grade 5
North Knox East Elementary/Jr High School, IN

Halloween

Creeping, crawling,
scary, spooky,
darkening, cool,
wind rustling
through the leaves,
door-to-door,
we do go,
along the way,
we meet a…
BOO!

Rachel Jakes, Grade 4
Norwich Elementary School, OH

Old Elf

Santa
Jolly, kind
Giving, caring, sharing
Knows when your awake
Saint Nick
Melinda McBride, Grade 6
Holy Angels School, OH

Toads

Toads
Hop like the wind
Flipping their tongues
Catching bugs
To eat
To survive!
Morgan Cline, Grade 4
Normandy Elementary School, OH

Bubbles

Bubbling, rushing world,
Down the streams and undisturbed,
Moss and waterfalls.
Erin Jackson, Grade 4
Normandy Elementary School, OH

Short Dog

Short dog
White, black, playful
Jumping, running, scratching
Noisily running down the hall
Cute dog
Kloe Pettit, Grade 4
Riverside Elementary School, MI

Roses

Roses are so red.
They are as soft as my cat.
Pretty blossoms too.
Every night I love them so.
Good night little soft flowers.
Julia Weiland, Grade 4
Mayfield Elementary School, OH

Our World

Crashing waves upon which saves
the world's most powerful glory.

The flowers swaying in the wind silently
as though you wouldn't know it
The clouds soaring in the sky
o, so enchanting.

The loyalty to keep our world
in the horizon's loom
Lily Chapman, Grade 4
Stonegate Elementary School, IN

Mom

Beth
Caring, loving, compassionate, almost perfect
Relative of many ancestors
Lover of Dad, Maria, and Allyson
Who feels loved, happy, and weight on her shoulders
Who needs caring, a house, and lots of love
Who fears our safety, my family, and growing old
Who gives food, friendship, and joy
Who would like to see the dishes done, supper made, and chores done
Resident of a warm caring home
Mom

Allyson Thompson, Grade 6
Helfrich Park Middle School, IN

November

In November it is the perfect month to have a Thanksgiving parade.
The parade has floats, streamers as long as shoe laces,
and don't forget the turkey.
When I watch the parade,
I love to snack on my favorite, beef jerky.
It is nice to sit on the couch,
sorry I can't help it, but I have to slouch.

For my dad's birthday,
we dined at Red Robin, Yum!
People in red uniforms carry ice cream and balloons
as big as the moon
then they sing "Happy Happy" when they come.

November also means to me,
my family goes to Disney.
Rides, shows, and warm weather will be great,
don't you wish you were me?

November is full of fun.
Now that November is done,
I can't wait to see the sun!
Morgan Sobkowicz, Grade 5
Beck Centennial Elementary School, MI

Voice

Everyone has a little voice inside of them it's true,
Your mom, dad and even you!

If you follow this voice it will lead you into the light.
Don't forget your voice is always right!

What I mean is when your friend Jan says something mean about Shawn,
You may want to say "yeah I know" back, but you know it would just be wrong.

That's your little voice inside of you.
It brings out the true you!

Natalie Nepa, Grade 6
Birmingham Covington School, MI

Baseball!!!

Baseball, baseball! It's the greatest show on Earth
I've been around the game since birth
It's the game I do my best and great
I won my first championship playing at 8

My jersey number's twenty one
Whenever I pitch they use the radar gun
I throw a fastball, and a curve
When you hit it, it takes nerve

I love to hit and run the bases
And look in the stands and see all the faces
There's not a word that can describe this game
Though it can get you in the Hall-of-Fame

Chandler Sedat, Grade 6
Abbott Middle School, MI

Autumn

Leaves leaving far away.
Falling, falling down.
Acorns falling all around.
Wind blowing everywhere.

Squirrels
running on the streets, on wires, on trees.
Eating acorns in their cheeks.
Being weird and scurrying back and forth.
Very very bushy tails.

Leaves very crunchy on the ground.
Many leaves spread all around.
Flaming red, vibrant orange, shiny yellow
Like a hot fire touching down.
Autumn.

Michelle Leppek, Grade 6
Holy Family Middle School, MI

Komodo Dragons

K iller
O utrageous
M onstrous and muscular
O ffspring by laying eggs
D aring
O bserves his prey

D angerous
R uns up to 35 mph
A ttacking and fierce
G ross the girls because they're messy eaters
O ut of sight
N ot extinct, but endangered
S wimmer

Zachary Schafer, Grade 4
Keystone Academy, MI

As I Walk Through Afghanistan…

Billions of land mines cling to the dirt,
Lurking, waiting, for children to hurt.
Land mines destroy young children's lives,
Disguised as toys to catch their tear-stained eyes.

Central Asia is where Afghanistan lies,
Afghanistan is full of deserts, wide in size.
Afghanistan's mountains are enormously tall,
Afghanistan rivers like glass, admired by all.

Men work long and hard to sell their wares,
The women bake nan, and sell it in their chairs.
People who work as farmers, have it tough,
Jobs of Afghanistan are difficult and rough.

People used to live in warm comfy places,
But their buildings were ruined in front of their faces.
Now the people survive in whatever they can find,
The people live in huts, in which they are confined.

People of Afghanistan live in poor health,
Many are ill and need help or some wealth.
Death is a word that is known by all…
No one knows when the next person will fall.

Jonathan Kanzelmeyer, Grade 6
Ann Arbor Christian School, MI

There Once Was a King

Once long long ago and far far away
Something happened on a very certain day
This is a story about a king who ruled a town
He was the only one who wore the golden crown

The king of the town was very very nice
But, the king did have a bad case of live
The sad part is the king had an accident
He choked on some gum, the brand it was spearmint

Since no one else wanted the king's lice
No one would look at the royal crown twice
There was only one person the crown would fit
To wear this crown he could not wait one bit

He was a clown with even worse lice
Problem was he wasn't that nice
The clown was now king no matter how mean
For it was too late he ruled with his queen

He turned the palace into one great big circus
And the changes he made caused quite a large ruckus
The clown disappeared but the circus still stays
It actually stays to these very same days

Danny Gilbert, Grade 6
St John the Evangelist School, IN

Webkinz

W ishing well is a game
E specially fun
B est animal toys
K ind toys online
I t totally ROCKS
N on living stuffed animals
Z any

Ashley Brooks, Grade 4
Northfield Elementary School, OH

Christmas Eve

Cookies, Santa, presents
has a big rosy nose and big cheeks
family
sleigh bells ring
I love my mom, dad, Santa
family loves presents
Santa Claus is friendly

Cheyenne Smith, Grade 4
Churubusco Elementary School, IN

The Mouse

There once was a girl,
Her name was Pearl,
She went to her house,
And found a mouse.
She grabbed it by the tail,
And named it Male.
She showed her mom
And her mom said, "Wow."
Pearl said it's a mouse
And her mom said, "I see."
She took it outside,
And her mom said, "bye,"
Pearl said, "Why?"

Salma Flores, Grade 5
Auburn Hills Christian School, MI

Sorry

I'm sorry I lost your kite.
I really wanted to fly it.

It's just that
I wanted to see how high it could go
So I cut the string
And it floated away.

It was very tiny, very soon
Because it was so high up.

P.S. You're not getting another from me!
P.P.S. It was very pretty!

Franny Wiggins, Grade 5
Tremont Elementary School, OH

Autumn Fun

Bright leaves are golden
Pumpkins are ripe and ready
Air's crisp and lovely
Breezy, cool and chilly nights
Jumping in leaves is such fun.

Audrey Haning, Grade 5
Westview Elementary School, OH

Snowboarding

S werving back and forth
gri **N** ding rails
O ut of control
going do **W** n so fast
having a **B** last
g **O** ing off ramps
going cr **A** zy
doing t **R** icks
down and **D** own again
go **I** ng up and down ski lifts
N ever giving up
G oing down like a pro

Rocco Catanzarite, Grade 6
Holy Angels School, OH

Gloomy

Why do I feel upset
I think I need a little rest.
I'm feeling really blue
I think I'll take a pill or two.
This space is not very roomy
I think I'm feeling gloomy.

Samuel Bloch, Grade 5
Meadowbrook Elementary School, MI

Piano

Playing the piano
In a variety show
Warming up my body
From head to toe
I knew I was nervous
And seen I was red
I said, "I need to go to bed"
My teacher Mrs. Schultz
Caught me and said,
"I know you'll do good"
So I played the piano
As good as I could
And after I was done
My teacher said,
"You did fine
And if I could rate your playing
It would be a nine!"

Victoria Keller, Grade 5
St Joseph Parish School, OH

Dogs

Dog
Troublemaker, destroyer
Chewing, slobbering, barking
K-9 teeth, chasing tail, hairy
Bulldog

Alex Iafrate, Grade 4
Floyd Ebeling Elementary School, MI

Winter Is Coming!

Here it comes.
The cold winds!
You better get ready!
Winter's coming!
The cold winds blow!
The trees move back and forth!
It starts to get cold, really cold!

Brianna Sikes, Grade 5
Kenowa Hills Intermediate School, MI

Christmas Morning

C heer
H appiness
R eindeer
I ce
S now
T oys
M usic
A ngels
S nowflakes

M erry
O utstanding
R inging bells
N aughty
I icicles
N ew clothes
G ames

Jewel White, Grade 6
Erie Elementary School, OH

Bad Weather

Today I think that it will snow,
Yes it will snow, I know, I know.

Today for sure the wind will blow,
The wind will blow and blow the snow.

Today I think a blizzard will come,
The blizzard will make the weather glum.

Today there will be a terrible storm,
I wish, I wish the weather was warm!

Joseph Maltinsky, Grade 4
Cincinnati Hebrew Day School, OH

A True Friend

I need a friend
Not a friend that will boss me
Not a friend that will toss me
But a friendship that will be close
Like an apple in a tree
Just like their close bond
I hope that will be you and me
And when I find you
I will make sure I remind you
To define friendship and make sure it's real
And it will make me feel
Good about our friendship
Good about me and you
Good that we are friends
And that it is really, really true

Aniyah Jones, Grade 6
Woodward Park Middle School, OH

Freedom

F ighting in wars to be free
R emembering the ones who died for us
E agles represent the United States
E lecting presidents who care about our country
D emocrats and Republicans voting
O pen our minds to freedom of speech
M aking memories of veterans
    who have fought for us

Meghann Ferguson, Grade 5
Sanderson Elementary School, OH

In Danger

This place.
This special place.
As still as the moon.
But then you hear talking.
Faint talking. Everything is moving.
Animals are moving in the other direction.
The wind is doing the same. I hide.
I see and hear feet crunching with every step.
They have guns, knives, traps. Poachers.
I run. I think they see me. Time.
It takes time for us to set a trap.
We see them. Anger is in everyone.
We all charged.
I threw the net at the poachers.
It was like they knew.
They dodged the net, then took us on.
We got slaughtered. I survived.
Some others did too.
They took us away.
Away from that place.
That special place.

Conrad Shreiner, Grade 6
Virgil I Grissom Middle School, IN

Moms

Moms, moms, moms
Awesome moms,
Intelligent moms,
Caring, loving, unique moms
Dependable, courageous, amazing moms,
Last of all, best of all,
My mom!

Abby Hines, Grade 5
St Jude Catholic School, IN

Things That Are Quiet

People looking over the harbor on the Statue of Liberty
Wind blowing through the leaves on a tree
Spiders spinning silky webs
Authors writing a book
Deer eating grass
Planets orbiting
Minnows speeding through the water
Crocodiles swimming in the water not making one ripple
A rabbit sleeping in its burrow
Cheetah running after his prey
Air as still as can be
Water smoothly going down the river
Drawing a tree on a snowy day
Mice munching on Swiss cheese
A caterpillar eating a nice green leaf
Thinking of something
Walking along a path

Dylan Destadio, Grade 5
Sanderson Elementary School, OH

All About Me

L ove to play football
O f course there's always inaccurate calls
G reat at school
A nd love to swim in the pool
N ever did anything really bad

P lus I do sometimes get mad
E xcellent breakfast cook
T ake time to read a good book
E njoy doing math
R eady to pick the right path
S uper at doing the right thing
O h but I don't really like to sing
N obody thinks I'm not nice

K ind of like to be precise
U nable to skate really well
S o when I tried, I fell
K ind is what people say of me
Y ou read this poem so you know more about me

Logan Peterson Kusky, Grade 5
Frank Ohl Intermediate School, OH

Sunset

As dark skies approach,
The sun dips into the lake;
Wind fills the night air.
Devin Murphy, Grade 6
Stanley Clark School, IN

An Ode to Haikus

This is a Haiku
The poems go five seven five
They are very fun

They are rather short
People from Japan make them
They are fun. Try one!
Nikola Dodig-Drahotusky, Grade 6
Birchwood School, OH

The Sun

A beaming
Light of wonder,
The Earth's heater,
A big miracle,
Floating,
In a pool of blue,
As cotton candy, clouds
Float by.
Lexy Harris, Grade 4
Normandy Elementary School, OH

True Friend

Friends that are there
Friends that help you
Whenever you are stuck they help you
Doesn't call you names
Supports you all the time
Will be your friend no matter what
Is nice and polite to you
If you call them they call you back
Treats you a certain way
Is like a pillow for your head
That's a true friend
Dacia Brooks, Grade 6
Abbott Middle School, MI

The Deer

After night,
Before the dawn,
In the woods,
In the snow,
Eating grass,
Crushing the snow,
Running fast,
Under the tree,
There stands a big big deer.
Landon Harris, Grade 5
Churubusco Elementary School, IN

Raccoons

Raccoons come in the dead of night coming and going like ghosts do.
They raid trash cans as if they were pirates raiding a small village.
They slip away as does heat from your body in the Antarctic.
But most of all…
They are hungry the way kinks of girls fight over new, cool and expensive outfits.
Raccoons are like thieves who have mastered the art of breaking and entering.
Steven Hokky, Grade 5
Harding Middle School, OH

October Is:

Strolling through the pumpkin path, we see orange and green everywhere
We trip over the long vines trying to find that perfect pumpkin
Small, large, round, oval, brightly orange,
so many pumpkins
which one do I choose?

My large, perfectly round pumpkin now sits at our table
waiting to be carved
Another Halloween here,
and what do we want to carve on the pumpkin?
Sad, happy, funny, scary,
which face will it be this year?

"Wait," my dad yells
It's the best part of carving the pumpkin
We need to scoop the goo
and save every
last
seed,

In our house there's no Halloween unless there's pumpkin seeds to eat.
Megan Maloney, Grade 5
Beck Centennial Elementary School, MI

August

August, the month in which my day of birth lay.
My favorite month.
The last month of summer break.
The month where the grass is velvety green and the tree bark is warm.
The hottest month, as hot as the big star itself.
The month where children play without a care in the world.
When the sidewalk is warm beneath your bare foot.
The time of warm rains and high clouds as proud as the sun.
No jackets or coats.
No homework or school.
No timed recess or lunch.
No bedtime.
Time for relaxing.
Beautiful, brilliant rainbows, birds, and flowers.
A sparkle in the eyes of every child.
Bright grins.
August, the happiest, most beautiful month.
Grace Auls, Grade 6
Granville T Woods Community School, OH

Mount Rushmore

Four presidents' faces carved in stone
Washington, Jefferson, T. Roosevelt, Lincoln
In South Dakota
Taking fourteen years to build
At a cost of $900,000
Sixty feet high
A work of art.

Seth Hammond, Grade 4
Dobbins Elementary School, OH

Jupiter

J upiter is a planet in our
U niverse. There is a red spot on the
P lanet called the Big Red Spot.
I nteresting enough,
T he Big Red Spot is a never ending storm. Almost
E very part of Jupiter's surface is smooth. Jupiter is a
R eally awesome planet!

Alex Ganshorn, Grade 6
Pinewood Elementary School, IN

I Am

I am artsy and athletic.
I wonder if there's a world where you never die.
I hear the twinkling of the rain.
I see a figure with 7 1/2 arms and 15 1/2 legs.
I want my own laptop.
I am artsy and athletic.
I pretend to be the tickle monster when I play
with my little sister and my 8 month old baby cousin.
I feel scared of the multi-colored monster.
I touch a 3-eyed white, green, and yellow monster.
I worry when I will score a point and not mess up
at a basketball game.
I cry when someone else cries.
I am artsy and athletic.
I understand that I am not that good at everything.
I say that you should never say you can't.
I dream that I can get 15 horses.
I try to do my best at everything.
I hope that I can be an artist.
I am artsy and athletic.

Ana Bonifas, Grade 6
Galesburg-Augusta Middle School, MI

Ocean

Sings a lullaby to the night shore
Crashing down like a shooting star
Filled with colorful and dark creatures
Going till the eye can see
Covering the Earth farther than man can swim
Turning wet soggy sand into beautiful pearls

Brett Gruenwald, Grade 6
St Clement Elementary School, OH

I Am

I am funny and unique.
I wonder what Mars is like.
I hear my horse talk.
I see my fish cry.
I want a pet monkey.
I am funny and unique.
I pretend I am a professional dirt bike rider.
I feel sad when people say I am as short as an ant.
I touch a green dog.
I worry about my cat.
I cry when my animals die.
I am funny and unique.
I understand no one will live forever.
I say I will be rich.
I dream of peace in the world.
I try to be the best I can be.
I hope I never go to jail.
I am funny and unique.

Hudson Blayden, Grade 6
Galesburg-Augusta Middle School, MI

Homework

H orrible
O ther stuff is fine but homework is too much!
M ore and more each day.
E xciting not!!!
W ay to much work
O verrated
R estrict this homework!
K iss this homework goodbye!

Jada Faith, Grade 4
Veale Elementary School, IN

Lights

Flicker on, flicker off
I illuminate the dark
Switch on, switch off
I am your eyes for your trail
On a midnight walk
Clap on, clap off
The clapper works just fine
Sunrise, sunset
I'm just so beautiful
Walk in, walk out
A sensor makes me light up
What am I...
I am a light
Sometimes I take batteries
Sometimes you plug me in
If you clap or walk in a room to turn me on
You can count on one thing,
I am there to help.   I light the dark.

Jason Moore, Grade 6
Abbott Middle School, MI

Sports Rivals
Red Sox
Defense, pitch
Stealing, running, pitching
Ortiz, Crisp/A-Rod, Jeter
Exciting, amazing, hitting
Score, home run,
Yankees

Colts
Level, clean
Passing, covering, comforting
Manning, Wayne/Welker, Moss
Passing, blitzing, annoying
Pass, dirty
Patriots

Lakers
Ball hog, signal
Losing, driving, missing
Bryant, Gasol/KG, Peirce
Winning, passing, scoring
Pass, team
Celtics
Davis Jochim, Grade 6
Nancy Hanks Elementary School, IN

Painted Parakeets
What does a parakeet know?
Pure water,
Seeds, canary, wheat, millet,
Fruits, apples, oranges,
Vegetables, carrots, lettuce,
How to
Imitate (copy)
A human's voice,
Colorful, fluffy feathers,
Their smooth short neck,
Large head,
Thick tongue,
And they know that they
Belong in the
Parrot family!
Sherlin Chacko, Grade 5
Riley Upper Elementary School, MI

Another
Another month…
Another year…
Another smile…
Another tear…
Another winter, a summer too…
But there can never be another you!
Hannah Daily, Grade 6
Kesling Middle School, IN

Fall Comes and Goes!
It's September and fall is coming,
It's October it's already here,
It's November and we are playing,
It's December presents here and there.
Fall is my favorite time of year,
It's always a time for fun,
But now it is January,
And winter has just begun.
Anna T. Schumacher, Grade 5
Norwich Elementary School, OH

Boom, Catch, Touchdown!
Tweet, the whistle blows.
The kicker running,
Me sweating,
Boom!
The ball is soaring right to me,
Catch,
Hesitation,
Crowd yelling,
Run,
    Run,
        Run,
Running for the end zone,
Still going,
Sprinting, juking,
The crowd roaring like a tiger in a cage,
The touchdown well in sight,
A deep breath,
I turn on like the jets of a plane,
The whistle blows,
The ref's hands shoot up like a rocket,
Touchdown!!!!!!!!!!!!!!!
Alexander Bolin, Grade 6
Assumption BVM School, MI

On Thanksgiving Day
Thanksgiving is in November,
On Thanksgiving you eat chicken,
Fruit and vegetables,
Plus pumpkin pie,
But most importantly
You eat turkey!

Now, that's when you start to feast!
And that is when family and friends
Get together.

The pilgrims first crossed the Atlantic
In the *Mayflower*
Now that's what we are thankful for,
And that's what Thanksgiving is all about.
Alexis Wilfong, Grade 4
Matthew Duvall Elementary School, OH

I'm Sorry
I'm sorry I pushed you
Into that well
I just wanted to see
How deep it was.
At least it was for science
You love science, right?
Jürgen Wilkes, Grade 5
Tremont Elementary School, OH

First Snowfall
I pull into my worn winter hat,
glide into my soft woolen gloves,
jump into my old snow pants
slip into my scraggly boots
and receive the transformation.

Jack Frost greets me with a gust of wind,
snowflakes fall upon my brow,
whirling, twirling, as they fall,
through the darkest of the nights,
into the lightest of the mornings.

When winter ends I am not forsaken,
for as long as I live in Michigan,
it will always come again.

So as I look out the window,
listening to the busy world,
know that I am waiting,
waiting, for next year's first snowfall.
Erin Kiessling, Grade 5
Central Grade School, MI

Day of Hope
V eterans we honor
E very day we should repay them
T hey protect us
E very day we should remember
R ememberance Day
A ir force
N ovember 11, 2008
Jay Kisor, Grade 4
Westview Elementary School, OH

Dull to Lively
Dull
Lame, unsuspenseful,
Tiring, boring, uninteresting,
Dumb, dreary — awesome, bright,
Shining, interesting, inspiring,
Suspenseful, energetic,
Lively.
Maddie Hubert, Grade 5
Perry Central Elementary School, IN

I Am

I am very athletic and funny.
I wonder if I could make my brother fly.
I hear my zit's cry as I pop them.
I see a dog flying.
I want to be a professional pitcher.
I am very athletic and funny.
I pretend I am a singer.
I feel crazy when I have a spaz attack.
I touch a googlewofernooner's fur.
I worry when I pitch bad.
I cry when I do not have any new clothes.
I am very athletic and funny.
I understand that money is tight.
I say, "Yo, sup?"
I dream to be a great basketball player.
I try so hard to pitch good and make b-ball hoops.
I hope for a good career.
I am very athletic and funny.

Secilie Lock, Grade 6
Galesburg-Augusta Middle School, MI

Clever Gift Ideas Under $10

Some clever gift ideas under ten dollars
A little toy truck, a doll, or even colorful collars.
These ideas will make children whoop and holler.
Buy some chocolate for your son or daughter,
Buy a book for some smart aleck scholar,
Purchase a model train that is a lot smaller,
Get a basketball hoop for someone as tall as a giraffe.
For this Christmas, make someone laugh.

Matthew Albring, Grade 6
Pike Delta York Middle School, OH

The Lion

Fearless,
A stone.

Sleeps as peaceful as a newborn,
And noble to his pack.
Hunts as a warrior,
As he ambushes, leaps, pounds to his prey.

Bows down to nothing,
As he's ruling the jungle kingdom.
Yawns with his tongue hanging proud and wide.
And roars its song beating in the wind.

Peeks around a tree,
Does whatever it has to,
Just to show who's king.
Darting, dashing, and dancing.
The lion.

Margaret Horn, Grade 6
Harding Middle School, OH

Not Alone with Nature's Snow

I just sat there myself, thinking life was a bore
but then I saw something I hadn't before!

When I blinked what I saw was too good to be true!
Snow smiling, trees waving,
no need to be blue!

I was not all alone! I had nature to play with
oh, what would I do if it was not here to be with.

Now here is the message that I must tell you,
if it weren't for nature
then I would be blue!

So please save my world oh! Don't hurt it please!
Save the water, the soil, the animals and trees.

You will be thanked, I guarantee!
Save it for nature; save it for me.

Anna Roth, Grade 5
Central Grade School, MI

The Busy Girl

Soriya
Athletic, caring, beautiful
Sister of Camran and Alex
Lover of singing, softball, and swimming
Who feels nervous when I get in front of people
    and when I get in trouble
Who gets excited about going on vacation
    and performing in front of people
Who needs to learn how to snowboard
Who gives kisses to my parents
    and my Jonas Brothers poster
Who fears poisonous snakes and robbers
Who would like to meet the Jonas Brothers
Resident of Austintown, Ohio
Rezapourian

Soriya Rezapourian, Grade 5
Frank Ohl Intermediate School, OH

Birthday

8 people around a table,
celebrating the birth of a girl 7 years ago,
that very little girl opened presents wrapped in colored paper,
squealing with joy at every newfound discovery,
while I sat hoping that mine would be last,
when she opened it the hug cam fast, as always.

Nina, little one,
I now wish that,
I hadn't cringed away when your open arms came near.

Shawn Sovie, Grade 6
Harding Middle School, OH

Summer

Running, yelling, and playing.
Sleeping in, no homework or school.
Having no worries.
Thinking about what game to play next.
Dashing, jumping, and staying up late.
Roasting s'mores by the fire.
Enjoying the still night.
Swimming, splashing, and diving.
Enjoying my time at the pool.
Spending time with friends.
Tasting sweets and relaxing,
Lying upon the grass,
Gazing at the clouds far above,
Saying to myself,
"I love summer."

Logan Martin, Grade 6
Tri-West Middle School, IN

Veterans Day

Veterans battling in Iraq
risking lives for our country,
sacrificing and having tons of courage,
honoring the brave one
that want to get freedom in America,
keeping peace
protecting our country
appreciating all of the soldiers
that risked their lives,
having a lot of strength
and defending our country.

Christian Rossol, Grade 5
Beck Centennial Elementary School, MI

I Am

I am excited
I am proud
I hear everything
I see my class
I want everybody to be proud
I am nice

I pretend I'm silly
I feel excited
I hug my brother
I worry if I brush my teeth
I cry when my family does
I am shy

I understand my classmates
I say I'm really excited
I dream about my family
I try to do my best
I hope I'm clean and special
I am proud of my class

Jacob Sajewski, Grade 4
Floyd Ebeling Elementary School, MI

Halloween

The spooky house across the way, is even scary during the day.
On this Halloween night it will give us a fright,
when the witches cast up a spell tonight.
Goblins,
Black cats,
And brooms,
Watch out for their smelly fumes.
The night is ending enough with the fear but it will return next year.

Abby Lewis, Grade 5
St Jude Catholic School, IN

Twilight

Twilight is a play
As the sun dims out
And the stars dance across the sky in a solar serenade
The moon rises to join the show of night
Maybe a comet, too
But only to see no crowd in sight
The wind whistles wildly
The thistles sway
But then the violet clouds role in
Closing that act
Just by having the glow of the breaking dawn greet us as we leave Twilight
Play of night

Sarah Smith, Grade 6
Harding Middle School, OH

The Joyful Peace of Christmas

Bright red stockings over the vivid orange fire
Faces light up as they open presents wrapped in green, red, silver, and gold.
Snowflakes fall softly onto the puffy white ground during the morning snowfall.

Twinkling lights and shiny ornaments dapple the tree, making it joyfully glow.
The orange fire in the fireplace lights up faces and casts shadows in corners.
Golden sunlight spreads over cold, cold snow, making the world alive.

Crackling flames, laughter, and music fill the room.
Distant carolers echo outside my bedroom window,
As I lay in soft quiet snow, just to escape it all,
I hear the silence of a snowflake falling on my pink frozen nose.

Why do you only come once a year?
Why can't this peace and joy last forever?
What will become of us until we see you again O Christmas?

The toasty warm flames in the fireplace lick cold faces like a happy puppy,
Everyone is as happy as angels winging swiftly, softly, through the sky.

Joy fills each room, and everywhere you look,
Peace on Earth,
Peace on Earth,
Peace on Earth.

Kathryn Burress, Grade 5
EH Greene Intermediate School, OH

From a Single Snowflake

Blizzards start from a single snowflake
Then roar in with powerful winds,
Making the world blind so no one can see.
They die down
Leaving nothing but frosty snow.

Valerie Harley, Grade 6
Wooster Christian School, OH

Seasons

Softly and swiftly, the sound of the wind blows.
Will there be a thunderstorm or a tornado?
Why am I this restless?
Why am I asking so many questions?

Snowflakes are falling from the sky.
Will there be hail or a few flurries?
Why am I so cold?
Why am I asking so many questions?

Spring is yet to come.
Will I pass the IOWA Test or will I fail?
Why am I this scared?
Why am I asking so many questions?

Summer has now approached.
How many days till schools close?
Why am I this happy?
Why am I asking so many questions?

Glenn Ayieko, Grade 4
Red Cedar School, MI

Sunday and Monday

I'd like to ride my bike on Sunday.
I'd rather ride my skateboard on Monday
And as for the rest
I'll sure do my best,
But I'd like a chocolate sundae.

Hunter Guthrie, Grade 5
Henryville Elementary School, IN

River Otter

Whoosh, I hear as though I go through the water like a torpedo
As I surface, I see bears flipping fish for breakfast
The smell of fresh-peeled pine from deer antlers
I hear the cascade of rushing water
I race under again to grasp a small smooth rock
I feel the gooey inside of breakfast
Water so cool as I drink
Life is good here in Colorado
Otters feel good here
This is a good home
Life is good for a river otter

Casey Moody, Grade 6
North Knox East Elementary/Jr High School, IN

The Firecracker

A sparkling rough red firecracker flies into the dark ivy,
Scaring my little brother.
He is screaming like a hooligan.
On the patio my grandpa and I are laughing, "Ha ha ha!"
My mom is being frantic like bees in a swarm.
My grandma is yelling, "No, no, no!"
The smell of sulfur is heavy in the air.
By the light of my flashlight I see birds fly in fright.
This is a memorable night.

Alex Searfoss, Grade 5
Stanley Clark School, IN

spiders

spiders are scary
they creep up on you in the night
they have legs as long as yours
they are mostly black some are white
they're more scared of us than we are of them
some are in danger of us squishing them
and there is still a lot of spiders to be afraid of
but there will never be more spiders than humans

Kayla Impellizzeri, Grade 5
Kenowa Hills Intermediate School, MI

Superman/Hero

Superman
awesome, wonderful
flying, serving, caring
helping people every day
hero

Matthew Wood, Grade 5
Washington Township Elementary School, IN

I Am

I am athletic and nice.
I wonder if ghosts are real.
I hear a phoenix screeching at me!!
I see a unicorn walking past my mom!
I want to live in a mansion.
I am athletic and nice.
I pretend to sing into my hairbrush.
I feel sad about Esperanza losing her dad.
I touch the evil garbage can every day.
I worry that my mom might have another heart-attack!
I cry that my great-grandma died.
I am athletic and nice.
I understand that everyone goes through adolescence.
I say that I believe in God.
I dream that I will grow up and be happy with my life.
I try to get straight A's in school.
I hope my mom and dad will be proud of me.
I am athletic and nice.

Amber Lucas, Grade 6
Galesburg-Augusta Middle School, MI

I Am

I am short and smart
I wonder what my family with a husband and kids will be like
I hear medals clanking that are wrapped around my neck, that I won from my dance competition
I see dancers dancing
I want for everybody in the world to be nice, great people
I am short and smart

I pretend that I own all the malls in the world
I feel great when I dance
I touch my dance shoes
I worry if I don't know all the steps to a dance I learned one week, before I leave class
I cry when I see a commercial about dogs that are sad-looking with a sad song too
I am short and smart

I understand not everything will go your way
I say I love to dance
I dream to dance my whole life
I try my best every day at dance and at school
I hope to be a professional dancer
I am short and smart
I am Alexandra Cooper

Alexandra Cooper, Grade 4
Floyd Ebeling Elementary School, MI

Dustin O'Hara

Dustin
An athletic person, a good listener, always tries to get my homework done on time, and has brown hair and eyes
Brother of Christopher and the son of Tamie
Lover of my family because they respect me, my dogs, Bean and Cassy,
    my cats, Oreo, Socks, and Tiger, and the television show, "Tom and Jerry," because they are funny
Who feels happy when my homework gets done, angry when I get in trouble, and sad when I get hurt
Who needs health so I won't get sick easily, friendship so I have people to play with, and my family to take care of me
Who gives love to my family because they are my family, friendship because I would hate to be without a friend,
    and my best at school so I can get good grades
Who fears the dark because I would hate to fall and break my arm,
    ghosts because they are scary, and being alone because no one would be around to help me if I needed it
Who would like to win the championship football game to be in first place for the season,
    to go to California to see Hollywood, and be on a cruise to see dolphins and all kinds of fish in the ocean
Resident of Lancaster
O'Hara

Dustin O'Hara, Grade 5
Sanderson Elementary School, OH

The First Christmas Day

Mary and Joseph traveled for so long, but the inn was full so they slept in the barn. Far away the shepherd see a bright light in the sky. It was a star they saw. An angel appeared and told them to follow it so they traveled all night long. Farther beyond three kings see it too. They were wise so they knew what to do. They also followed the star. They had brought gifts of gold, frankincense, and myrrh, but to their surprise they were stopped by King Harod. Once he had heard that there was going to be a baby born that they said was going to be a king, king Harod was roaring mad. The three kings were told that once they found him to come back and tell him where he is. They did not know that he wanted him to die. Once the shepherds and the kings got there they all said hi. That night while the kings rest in a dream an angel appeared and said that King Harod wanted Jesus dead. So the next day the kings and the shepherds went a different way as little baby Jesus slept on the hay and that became to be known as the first Christmas Day.

Carissa Gettelfinger, Grade 5
West Washington Elementary School, IN

Mouse in the House

When I opened the refrigerator
I thought I saw a mouse.
I was surprised that instead
It was my shadow in the house.

I was so hungry
that I could eat a horse.
But all we had was ham
So I ate it of course.

Later I went to play with my sister
And she screamed and jumped on the couch.
I asked her "what is wrong with you?"
And she said "I think I saw a mouse."

I told her it was her shadow
Then she started to calm down.
We both started laughing
Like we had seen a clown.

I was glad it was our imagination
Working at its best.
We thought we saw a mouse
But it was only an imagination test.

April Starks, Grade 4
Detroit Academy of Arts & Sciences - Jefferson Campus, MI

Bills!

When my mom sees a bill she gets ill.
She has to take pills when she gets ill from bills.
She thinks bills are big spills.
My mom likes to kill bills when she takes pills for bills.
When my mom kills bills she uses quills.
That's why my mom hates bills.
My mom would rather give up her will than pay a bill!
But when we lived on a hill near a mill,
We got more and more and MORE bills.
Then we moved away.

Hannah Pease, Grade 4
Northern Heights Elementary School, IN

Hank the Snowman

Oh, Hank the snowman,
You look so sad, why can't you look a little bit glad?
Why are you on the cold hard ice?
The kid who had made you must not have been nice.

Oh, Connor my friend,
If I look so sad, I am actually very, very glad.
I am on the hard ice, because to me it's very, very nice,
And the kid who had made me was you…
And you are very, very, very nice!

Connor Bohn, Grade 4
Floyd Ebeling Elementary School, MI

A Meadow's Grace

One bright spring morning,
I took a walk in the meadow.
The wind has a soft voice,
And my dress flutters in the air.
Once I get there,
I go to sit on the top of the hill.
My hair moves with the soft breeze,
I close my eyes and listen.
I hear blue birds singing their song.
The grass shaking,
And the newborn leaves saying hello to the world.
The delightful smell of daisies warms my heart.
The beautiful view from the top of the hill is,
The most beautiful of all.

Micah James, Grade 5
Auburn Hills Christian School, MI

I Am

I am funny and emotional.
I wonder if there are aliens in space.
I hear a horse croaking.
I see a pony/unicorn/turtle mixed together.
I want to start my own business.
I am funny and emotional.
I pretend to be an animal care taker.
I feel mad at the flying monkeys taking my clipboard.
I touch a unicorn's horn.
I worry about the extinction of animals.
I cry when I see sad movies.
I am funny and emotional.
I understand that some animals are endangered.
I say stop abortions.
I dream about buying every single animal in the world.
I try getting good grades.
I hope I get a D.S. one day.
I am funny and emotional.

Alex Weese, Grade 6
Galesburg-Augusta Middle School, MI

I Took My Dog for a Walk

My dog can talk?
I took my dog for a walk,
Then I learned that she could talk,
She finally had the nerve to say,
How are you doing today,
I took her home and told my dad,
He said he was very glad,
He went back to his football game,
And I said this is very lame

That's the story of the dog that talked
If you think that's weird wait till you hear her cawk!

Taylor Brooklier, Grade 5
Mark C Roose Elementary School, MI

Turkey Feast

Fall can have pumpkin pie
And Thanksgiving turkey
But the rest of fall
Doesn't matter now.

With leaves on the ground,
Let's make a leaf pile!
And laugh and bake the turkey.

But one thing we are missing —
The family and friends!
We are going to have a great
Turkey feast!
Talazia Gross, Grade 4
Matthew Duvall Elementary School, OH

Snow

Snow
Beautiful, white
Drifting, dazzling, floating
Soft, fluffy
I love the snow.
Ashley Minton, Grade 5
Cloverdale Middle School, IN

Reading

R eally fun
E xcellent way to learn
A dventure inside every story
D efinitely awesome
I nteresting stories
N ever boring
G reat

Maegan Powers, Grade 4
Sts Joseph and John School, OH

Mom

Nice, kind
Cleaning, mowing, washing,
Mean, mad
My mom works too much.
James Neier, Grade 5
Cloverdale Middle School, IN

Dinosaur Bones

Across the country
In the bad lands
Under the sun
Beyond sight
Except for paleontologists
Since the dawn of time
On the rocks
Below the ground
Lies dinosaur bones
Reed Geiger, Grade 5
Churubusco Elementary School, IN

Me, Myself, and I

Alexia
Artistic, athletic, smart
Sister of Gabriella
Lover of reading, animals, and basketball
Who feels nervous on the first day of school
 and when I read something in front of the class
Who gets excited when it's Christmas and when I go on vacation
Who needs to clean out my desk and earn money for a new radio
Who gives kisses to my dogs
Who fears snakes and big spiders
Who would like to play basketball in high school and college
Resident of Austintown, Ohio
Carcelli

Alexia Carcelli, Grade 5
Frank Ohl Intermediate School, OH

Twinkling Candles

Warm and crisp potato latkes
The candles in the golden menorah
The kids look at the clock and tisk
We still have minutes to spare before sundown
The children sit and give out joyful cheers
Watching the dreidle slowly…
PLOP down on the ground
Cheer and whine depending on what we got this time
When we finished our game I had a mound of chocolate gelt
It reached as high as the sun at noon
We hear, "It's time to light the candles!"
We run as fast as a lion trying to catch its prey
The candles are lit one by one
The bright candles twinkle in the dark
I take a big whiff of them as we say the blessing
The sound of our prayer fills my heart with glee
We exchange gifts to one another
I gently touch the colorful wrapping paper
When we open our gifts our joyful yells and screams were heard from down the block
I got sick from all of the chocolate gelt and potato latkes
But that was not even close to ruining my favorite holiday!!!
Becca Moskowitz, Grade 5
EH Greene Intermediate School, OH

My Daddy

My Daddy is happy he's never grim
that's why I want my unborn son to be like him.
He always makes a great teacher,
that's why God chose him to be a great leader.
He teaches me right from wrong
that's why I'll be moving on.
My Daddy, My Daddy is so sweet and kind,
but if you push his buttons, he'll check you and blow your mind.
My Daddy, My Daddy is such a great man to see
that's why he's my inspiration to me.
Mia Pearson, Grade 6
Cornerstone Schools – Grove Campus, MI

Gifts

G lide on the ice.
I s Santa on the roof?
F ood is on the table.
T is the season.
S now is falling.

Austin Cooper, Grade 5
West Washington Elementary School, IN

All About Taegen

Taegen
Caring, athletic, and strong
Sister of Jacob, Kaelee, Tristan, and unborn Baby Catlin
Lover of animals, chocolate and sports
Who feels nervous when she lies and gets in trouble
Who gets excited about karate and soccer
Who needs to do her chores and be good
Who give kisses to my family and pets
Who fears spiders and sinking at sea
Who would like to overcome her fears
Resident of Austintown, Ohio
Catlin

Taegen Catlin, Grade 5
Frank Ohl Intermediate School, OH

What Makes a Child Happy?

What makes a child happy is joy.
It shines above us in every way.
What makes a child happy is faith.
Patience is in the air.
What makes a child happy is beauty.
It should be by your side.
What makes a child happy is love.
Its warm welcome is hugging you!

Audrey Diane Cain, Grade 4
Northern Heights Elementary School, IN

The Bat

There was a bat
Who was really fat
The bat flew to Hollywood
Well, so far so good
He zoomed to the brook
To take a look
But he could not find his mother,
or his brother
The bat was lost
O yes he was
He tried Indiana
He tried Louisiana
But all he found was Tropicana
Suddenly there was a gleam
And he found out it was all a dream.

Benton Buskirk, Grade 5
North Knox East Elementary/Jr High School, IN

Me, Myself, and I

Tarin
Athletic, sly, and shy
Brother of Tryce
Lover of basketball, food, and toys
Who feels nervous when the first day of school comes
    and makes mistakes in front of a large group of people
Who gets excited about Christmas and my birthday
Who needs to do my chores and take out the recycling bin
Who gives kisses to girls
Who fears being buried alive and dying
Who would like to join the NBA
Resident of Austintown, Ohio
Lawrence

Tarin Lawrence, Grade 5
Frank Ohl Intermediate School, OH

Fall Sports

Fall is full of sports and games
Baseball, basketball, football, hockey,
The winning of the championship is what every team aims
Hockey
The beginning of the season
A goal is scored
Both teams have a reason
Football
Fridays, Saturdays, Sundays
T.O. waves his open arm
Romo throws it…
Touchdown with no harm
Basketball
Still hasn't started
Teams are working on plays
They want to perfect it for the important days
Baseball
The closing
The season is almost done
HOMERUN
A great feeling for fall

Will Summers, Grade 6
Rocky River Middle School, OH

Dreams

Dreams are the things that light up the world,
Dreams make our minds go wild day or night,
Dreams make us every emotion in the universe.
What is a dream, you might be thinking?
Well, I'll give you this hint,
    Never be without dreams.
How to dream?
Well, I can't answer that.
But this is how I started.
    JUST DREAM!!!

Bryssa Helton, Grade 4
Bright Elementary School, IN

Robin in the Tree

Robin, robin
in the tree
won't you sing
a song to me?
Oh sing so high
Oh sing so low
Oh sing so fast
Oh sing so slow
Robin, robin
in the tree
won't you sing
a song to me?

Sydney Kieleszewski, Grade 5
May V Peck Elementary School, MI

I'm Sorry

I'm sorry...
I have eaten
All of your
Halloween candy.

That you were probably
Saving to eat later.

Please forgive me.
They were delicious
So gummy, so sweet.

Aly Bond, Grade 5
Tremont Elementary School, OH

4-H

4-H
Head, heart, hands, health.
Long hours,
Take time,
Projects due,
Get judged,
Win ribbons,
Purple, lavender, blue
Red, white, green,
Great projects,
Rabbits, cats,
Farm scene, models,
For kids,
Food everywhere,
Smells everywhere,
People everywhere,
Kids having fun,
Games,
Clean up,
Take projects home,
Rest!

Holly Rose Gentry, Grade 6
Nancy Hanks Elementary School, IN

The Iguana

What does the iguana know
It is
Rough and scaly
Heavy and long
Has claws and
Spines yet
Likes leaves
And twigs
But also stay
Away when orange and pink
It's not very friendly
Then it can be
Thirty pounds!
And six feet long!
So look out!

Tyler Smith, Grade 5
Riley Upper Elementary School, MI

A Life in Me

There is a life in me
With surprises like
Birthdays
And things that are
Yet to come
It burns out
But keeps going
Like a clock on
Low batteries
It lives in my body
And makes my body run
I wish it would run forever

Stan Mattingly, Grade 6
St Maria Goretti School, IN

December

December
on my chilly street
we had a snowball fight, sweet!
we also built a snowman, frosty!
Christmas snow!

Taylor Jacques, Grade 5
Floyd Ebeling Elementary School, MI

The Creek

Minnows
In the water
Trying to find a meal.
No luck!
Soon they will hide
From birds swooping down
Hoping
They are not found.

Travis Grile, Grade 4
Normandy Elementary School, OH

October Freeze

I am having luck
On my sixth grade walk
I can see
Nine trees looking like giraffes
The way they bend and filed like an army
I see a tree bigger than the others
It looks like a shower of gold
But what is this a lonely leaf
Two naked trees
Getting ready for the breeze
Sticky green crab apples
Scattered the floor
Almost like the world had no more
I see spider webs worm the bushes
No more pushes
A gentle breeze
Hit the leaves
Making them dance in the air
Because winter is near
Here outside I feel so free
From the school that teaches me

Maxwell Yoshida, Grade 6
University Liggett School, MI

I'm a Dog

Hi my name is Willa,
I love to jump over poles,
My owners trained me,
Not to fall into holes.

I'm the best in my jumping class,
I'm always number one,
I do not gloat when I win,
I only jump for fun.

I'm going to the jumping tournament,
I bet I'll win it all,
Not that I'm gloating
But...I hope I do not fall!!!

Katie Emch, Grade 6
Eisenhower Middle School, OH

Football Is My Life

The helmets clashing
Nerves raging
Waiting for Sunday to come
Practicing Monday through Friday
Trying to become a champion
Thinking football when it's off-season
Always playing football
This is my life
How about you?

Andrew Daniel Shuherk, Grade 6
Trilby Elementary School, OH

My Sad Heart

Ridin' my go-cart
With a sad heart.

Tear up the field
Till the grasses yield.

Like to jump
Bump, bump, bump.

Hit my dad's tree
Want to flee

Muffler disconnected
So unexpected!

Want to know
Will it blow?

Bailey Pouliot, Grade 4
Midland Academy of Advanced and Creative Studies, MI

I Am

I am sweet and athletic
I wonder who is going to win the change war
I hear sadness
I see revolution
I want peace
I am sweet and athletic

I pretend I'm a professional soccer player
I feel awesome
I touch my pencil at school
I worry about my dog
I cry when I get hurt
I am sweet and athletic

I understand I'm turning 9 in October
I say Sawyer is a great friend
I dream of angels
I try to be a good person
I hope we win the change war
I am Salena Lumetta

Salena Lumetta, Grade 4
Floyd Ebeling Elementary School, MI

Halloween

Halloween might seem very fun,
unlike Christmas cheer,
ZOMBIES pop out of nowhere!
when you say trick-or-treat
spiders creep by your feet,
all those crazy things you'll probably get scared,
but the scariest is when you say…boo!

Ashley Worline, Grade 5
Norwich Elementary School, OH

What Kind of Presents Are There??

P olly Pockets
R ockets
E gg (No way!)
S ahara (The movie)
E lmo
N intendo DS
T alking Bird
S urfboard

Macenzie L. Lane, Grade 5
Northern Heights Elementary School, IN

Friends

Friends mean all the world to me,
Their personalities are just like mine,
We are just meant to be.
I love to hug them
We laugh *all* the time
We have sleep-overs,
And most of all we enjoy ourselves.
Whenever I'm sad, my friends make me glad
My friends are intelligent and funny
Let's thank God for friends!
We stick together like puzzle pieces.
So, if you ask me who my best friends are someday,
Jacqueline and Elizabeth I'd have to say.
Best friends forever those two and I
Friends are a gift from God,
So take the time to say "hi."

Kaitlynn De Young, Grade 6
Crown Point Christian School, IN

Christmas Joy

On Christmas Eve, as the snow fell down
Each child was excited but wore a frown
"But I want to open them today" they cried
"What will we get?" they thought as they pouted and whined
As the day went by, they sipped their drinks
Hot cocoa, as warm and as comforting
As a wool blanket being wrapped around them
The day passed and the night was near
The children had just one more peak
As daylight came, the children rushed to the tree
Wearing only smiles as happy as could be
Opening gifts, tearing the paper. Rip!
On and off went new jackets. Zip! Zip!
And the laughter and cheer carried on
Before they went to bed,
Thank you they'd say
As their parents lied down,
And called it a day
That night nobody wore a frown
As the snow fell down, down, down.

Marisa Koster, Grade 5
EH Greene Intermediate School, OH

One

One day can change your life
One wish can come true
One word can make you smile
One move can change the world
One helping hand can give you support
One laugh can make a friendship
One wave can start a hurricane
One tree can start a forest
One grain of sand can start a beach
One building can start a city
One strong wind can start a tornado
One star can form a constellation
One worm can feed a flock of birds
One strand of grass can form into a lawn
One angel can perform many miracles

Hannah Hutchinson, Grade 6
St Gerard School, MI

Flying with God

The feeling of no one
being able to touch you,
The sky is clear blue,
Soaring above all,
Only God can call,
Wings out wide,
Enjoying the ride,
Flying so free,
Nothing to hold me,
God by my side,
From Him I will never hide.

Katie Adams, Grade 6
Holy Angels School, OH

Snow

S parkly
N ot warm
O ften seen in winter
W et and cold

Halle Robinson, Grade 4
Northfield Elementary School, OH

A River

The river is very cold
When I step in the hard wet sand
I feel I am cold
My wet toes touch a crab
A big red crab
But still I feel cold
The river
Is flowing
I feel cold
I get out
I am
Warm

Baleigh Carithers, Grade 5
Heritage Intermediate School, IN

The Busy, But Beautiful Girl

Alison
Creative, optimistic, caring
Sister of Daniel and Katherine
Lover of animals, poetry, and the Steelers
Who feels nervous when I'm in a play at church
	and when I get my tests back
Who gets excited about going to amusement and water parks
	and when my teacher brings her grandson to class
Who needs to learn how to do CPR because I would like to baby sit
Who gives kisses to my dog
Who fears sharks and burglars
Who likes to swim with dolphins
Resident of Austintown, Ohio
Rein

Alison Rein, Grade 5
Frank Ohl Intermediate School, OH

Soccer Ball

Black, white, round
People shoving to get to you,
Kicking you as hard as they can,
Some dribbling you
Others throwing you into people
Defenders blocking you so you can't get in the goal.
Goalie picks you up and punts you.
At the end of the game one team is mad at you because you made them lose.
The other team is proud of you for helping them win.
You get put away and you're done until the next game.

Veronica Passkiewicz, Grade 6
Abbott Middle School, MI

The Poor and the Rich

There once was a man with a headband.
He could never understand why he was so poor.
But he had hope.
One day a rich man with rich clothes had a good tan.
Asked the poor man if he wanted a coin.
The poor man ignored him and snored off to sleep.
The rich left him the coin.
But the poor man didn't snore anymore. Instead he said,
"Why do you give me a coin?"
The rich man said, "You have no hope.
I am mad that you are sad.
So here is a coin to make you glad."
The rich man said,
"One day I will be rich and you will be poor.
So when I am rich I will give you food.
If you are nude I will give you clothing."
So one day the poor was rich and the rich was poor.
And the poor man said, "Here, come with me and I'll take care of you.
I have so much money I can afford 100 pens."
So the man took care of the other man until the very end.

Arsenia Georgopoulos, Grade 5
Akiva Academy, OH

Mercury

M ercury is the hottest planet in our solar system because it is the closest planet to the sun.

E ntering the atmosphere of Mercury the temperatures can get up to 800 degrees and down to -300 degrees.

R otating once around the sun on Mercury is only 88 Earth days.

C amera satellites in space have proven that Mercury's atmosphere is made up of sodium, potassium, oxygen, and a little bit of helium.

U nlike the other planets in our solar system Mercury has the shortest orbit around the sun which means that Mercury has the shortest year.

R eflecting telescopes allow us to get a closer look at Mercury and its surface.

Y ou wouldn't want to go to Mercury because no human being could withstand the extremely high and low temperatures. That is why no life has been found on Mercury's surface.

Hannah Quinn, Grade 6
Pinewood Elementary School, IN

The 2 Definitions of Cool

There are 2 definitions of *cool.*
One definition of cool is to be popular for the *wrong* reason.
Have a lot of friends for the *wrong* reason.
Get guys' attention for the *wrong* reason. And be the boss for the *wrong* reason.
The other definition of being cool is to have friends for the *right* reason, be your own person,
And be the boss of you and nobody else.
You wouldn't try so hard to be popular that you wouldn't have any friends at all.
You'd just be *you*. If you ask me, I'd be cool — for the *right* reason!

Rachael Thomas, Grade 6
Abbott Middle School, MI

My Favorite River

The river that runs through the mountains is as clear as a gleaming crystal.
As I walk the water tickles my toes as the rocks on the bottom massage my feet.
The birds whistle like my favorite tunes.
Squirrels swing like monkeys from hickory tree to hickory tree.
As the trees shake, leaves green as a tropical rainforest fall to the ground.
The sky is as blue as the sea.
This river will always be as clear as a crystal, and will always be the most gorgeous river ever seen.

Jacob Roach, Grade 6
Cloverdale Middle School, IN

The Raging Storm

The storm raged and the thunder sounded as if I were pounding a nail into the solid wood of a house. The wind whistled like a train. The rain echoed like millions of pennies dropping on a counter top. The lightning was like flashlights falling from the thunder. Afterwards, the clouds look like cotton candy, gray and puffy. The beautiful luminous rainbow looks like a freshly opened box of crayons. On the damp grass you can see a reflection of that rainbow.

Alex Williams, Grade 5
Washington Township Elementary School, IN

Scorpius

S corpius stands for everything we

C onsider evil. The Greek goddess Hera sent Scorpius to kill

O rion the hunter. Scorpius

R aised up from the ground and attacked Orion the hunter

P urposely. Orion and Scorpius are now opposite

I n the sky, fearing that the feud would continue. Being

U nder these circumstances made Scorpius one of the most popular constellations in the

S ky.

Lexi Jacobs, Grade 6
Pinewood Elementary School, IN

Just One

One spark can start a fire.
One droplet can make a cloud.
One seed can form a blossoming tree.
One shingle can fix the roof.
One person can make a stand.
One word can make a difference.
One question can make you think.
One shot can win the game.
One flame can light the room.
One day could be your last.
One sentence can finish a book.
One grade can be enough.
One enemy can start a war.
One friend can mean peace.
One meal can end your hunger.
One sip can end your thirst.
Just one is enough.

Matthew de La Fé, Grade 6
St Gerard School, MI

The Shot

The ball clips his hand
Penalty kick
Ball rests on the line
My hands roast from the goalie gloves
Fearsome opponents smash the ball
Going faster,
    Soaring through the air,
        The crowd on their feet,
            Wham!
I jumped like a kangaroo
And smacked the ball
No score!
The crowd responded
Our turn
Our hero flew past the players
Shot the ball like lightning
We all shouted
1-0
Game over.

James Doman, Grade 6
Assumption BVM School, MI

Crickets Song of Summer

Deep in the meadows crickets sing
Their beautiful song of summer
They chirp and roam
They hop they sing
And summer slowly fades
They say goodbye to the setting sun
As they hop into the night
While summer slips away

Kaitlyn Milano, Grade 6
Sashabaw Middle School, MI

Music

Many types of music,
So little time.
Some songs are rap,
Some even rhyme!
Most make my foot tap,
In a steady beat.
Life is music,
Music is soul.
You can even make a dance,
Or even a video!
All I know is that,
Music is spirit,
And I will never let it go!

Morgan Gallas, Grade 6
Saint Michael School, IN

The River

The water
    Is silent,
        Covering
The muddy ground,
    As it pushes,
    And swerves
        Around rocks.
    It encounters
        Obstacles
    With all sorts
    Of creatures,
    Rushing through
        Its silent
    Flowing stream,
    Producing threats
    Of rising water,
        After any
            Storm.

Jonathan Vicarel, Grade 4
Normandy Elementary School, OH

Football Pain

I'm a football
I'm stomped on all the time.
Sometimes I go sailing sky high
I am spun all the time
And I just want to go home!

Reagin Conley, Grade 5
Westview Elementary School, OH

All About a Dog

A dog was sitting on the ground
He was missing from the pound.
    When a girl took him in.
    And gave him lots of loving!

Brieanna Gordon, Grade 5
Rootstown Elementary School, OH

The Perfect Day Out

The wind in your hair
and the breeze in your face
    Is part of the perfect day,
and the perfect way.
    Going to the mall
and have a ball.
    Is part of the perfect day,
and the perfect way.
    Hanging with your friends
with a big old grin
    Is the Perfect Day!!

Montavia VanBuren, Grade 6
Eastmoor Middle School, OH

Whisper Game

A whisper game
Thoughts run wild
You can fly
Run
Swim
Different worlds
Galaxies
Universes
It's all in the mind
You can teleport
Time-travel
Do anything
And it's limited
Only
By your own imagination.

Evan Grossman-Lempert, Grade 6
Abbott Middle School, MI

What if It Were Spring?

What if it were spring?
That would be a wonderful thing.

If it were spring
I would shout and sing.

Then I could see all the deer
that live here.

Oh, spring
would be a wonderful thing!

Nathaniel Calabrese, Grade 5
Birchwood School, OH

Sky

Full of puffy white clouds
I could stare at them all day
While listening to the wind.

Austin Arthur, Grade 5
St Jude Catholic School, IN

Swimming

I swim…
"Swimmers step up!"
I jump on to the blocks.
"Thump, thump, thump"
This is my heart racing
And adrenaline running through my veins.
"Take your mark!"
I bend down, grab the blocks, waiting.
"BEEP"
The water glides past me
As I dive into the stillness.

The pool is my sanctuary.
It is where my heart races.
I feel like I am on fire.
My heart beats so fast like there's no tomorrow.
Swimming is my sport,
My place to be.
I swim…

Sydney Asselin, Grade 6
Corpus Christi Catholic School, MI

Gifts

G ifts are great
I f you get what's cool don't
F orget though what it's about
T he savior was born
S ome gifts are great

Shayla Walton, Grade 5
West Washington Elementary School, IN

I Am

I am flexible and athletic
I wonder what my cat does at home
I hear my cat's sweet meow
I see me and my cat playing in my backyard
I want a pony or a horse
I am flexible and athletic

I pretend that I am a professional gymnast
I feel like running and scoring a goal in soccer
I touch the soccer ball and me kicking it
I worry about if I play soccer or gymnastics I may get hurt
I cry when I get hurt badly
I am flexible and athletic

I understand that if you want to play sports you have to try
I say that not everyone is good at everything
I dream that I will be a professional soccer player and gymnast
I try to do my hard pages on homework
I hope that I will be a good soccer player and gymnast
I am flexible and athletic

Sabrina Pacitto, Grade 5
Beck Centennial Elementary School, MI

Fall

A cool breeze is in the air
As leaves fall here and there
Yet there are still leaves
Rustling up in the trees
A tree's branches bend and sway
As a gentle wind blows throughout the day
Pumpkins grow on a vine
As the sun continues to shine
A still cool air cloaks the night
As the dark overcomes the light
And when dawn comes the sun arises
Lighting the sky with its powerful ray
And with the dark diminished, it's the start of a new day

Sara Herman, Grade 5
Norwich Elementary School, OH

Bloody Nose

Nobody likes Jim Crutose
He always gets a bloody nose
When he does, he begins to yelp
Somebody please, "Help! Help!"
Then everyone says "Gees!
Jim, shut up and go home, please"
I sort of like Jim Crutose
He cannot help his bloody nose
Faster, faster the blood pours
Man, I bet his nose is sore
The teacher says, "Get Jim a tissue
Because his nose is a major issue!"
His nose will not stop
The blood hits the floor, plop!
"Please help," Jim cries
But nobody even tries
I take Jim to the nurse
But she went home to get her purse
Finally Jim's nose is done
It stopped just like it had begun

Kirsten Waggoner, Grade 5
North Knox East Elementary/Jr High School, IN

Snow Blanket

As the snow falls
It covers the Earth
It adds a layer to the first
It covers the humans
In or out.

It feels comforting,
Warm and snugly
You can leap around and have a pleasurable time.
I would like to have it all year long.
It's called a snow blanket.

Megan Hogya, Grade 6
Harding Middle School, OH

How to Be Sad

Make your eyes red
And your sad frown
And a sad sound.

Make your cheeks red
But first remember why
And then, cry cry cry.
Christine Bashour, Grade 5
Birchwood School, OH

School

School is fun I must admit.
But when do I get my permit?

I twist and turn in my chair,
Bugs are flying in the air.

Clocks are ticking very slow.
Seven hours in the day, woah!

Reading, writing, science, math,
Why go home and take a bath.

Teachers giving piles of homework.
One more reason for parents to lurk!

You just get home to take a break,
When mom says it's time to bake!

Nighttime comes and you fall asleep.
Morning dawns and you hear a peep.

School is fun I must admit.
But then again, when do I get my permit!
Hailey White, Grade 5
Calvin Christian Elementary School, MI

Winter/Summer

Winter
freezing, pearly
caroling, sledding, snow blowing
Santa, Christmas, pools, vacation
swimming, tanning, heating up
Summer
Hannah Heide, Grade 5
Floyd Ebeling Elementary School, MI

Reindeer

Reindeer on your roof,
Flying the sleigh,
Jingling bells,
Up, up and away!
With flying magic,
Guided by Santa's reins.
Olyvia Myers, Grade 5
St Joseph Montessori School, OH

Winter Snow

Winter snow is white, fluffy, cold, and wet.
Everybody is waiting, wanting, and wishing for the snow to fall.
But what people don't know is that you can't be anxious
For the snow to fall, but to be patient is the true key.
Hannah Ehmen, Grade 5
Cloverdale Middle School, IN

The Teacher's Rules

Don't doze of…
Don't get a parent's signature when you forget to do your homework
You can't study in class
Stop reading that book!
Don't eat the goldfish in class
Don't drop the pencils in the middle of the test
Memorize the entire Oxford Dictionary tonight
Stop sticking erasers up your nose
Throw that gum away and come for detention!
Stop talking to your classmates
You can't go to the restroom until school's out,
You should have gone at the beginning of school
Don't talk back
And
Whatever it is,
YOU CAN'T WRITE
POEMS ABOUT THE
TEACHERS RULES
Hassan Sayed, Grade 6
Birchwood School, OH

Halloween Treat

Little kids dressed as fairies, witches, and more.
They sing "Trick or treat!!" with galore.
Candy rustling in their bags
Shaped as princesses, ghosts, and some just a gag.
They laugh and sing
As if they were birds just chattering.

The leaves on the trees are bright,
Reds, oranges, and yellows, what a sight!
Swaying in the wind
As the tree starts to swing
On the ground they fall.
Making a pattern to be seen by all.

There is quite a chill
Stopping the evening from being still.
The sun is setting
Children are regretting
Staying out so late even though they knew it would not be great.

What is so special about this day?
The leaves swaying with no dismay.
The kids and candy meet
Just because they say "Trick or treat, trick or treat, trick or treat!!!"
Mira Prabhakar, Grade 5
EH Greene Intermediate School, OH

Fall

Breezy, calm, quiet
colors changing before our eyes.
From green to yellow,
red to orange,
then suddenly brown floating to the ground.
The trees now bare,
the ground now colorless,
bare like the world is empty.

Lia Ferguson, Grade 4
Norwich Elementary School, OH

If I Could Grant a Wish

If I could grant a wish for you
I would get a thrill or two

Whatever you please I will do
Because you know I really love you

Even though you have the illness of the flu
I hope you will be better soon

If there is a frown inside of you
I'll stop that frown and make a smile or two

I hope you have a good job in your life
May you never be a wife

Oh, if I could grant a wish for you
I would get a thrill or two

Regina Dominick, Grade 5
Mark C Roose Elementary School, MI

One

I was born on the 30th of May.
Now that is my favorite day.
I have a twin sister who was born first.
She thinks it makes her better, but I think it makes her worst.

I have a dog that's bigger than I.
When I wear a dress shirt, I have to wear a tie.
Chocolate milk is my favorite drink.
I like math because it makes me think.

I keep three turtles as pets.
I like to fish with rods and nets.
Chocolate chip cookies are my favorite food.
I am almost always in a good mood.

I'm writing this poem for English class.
I'd like to get an A, so I hope I pass.
Here's the fourth stanza, and here's the fourth line:
When I go golfing I shout "fore" all the time.

Bennet Sakelaris, Grade 6
University Liggett School, MI

Soldiers

It's not the reporters who gave us freedom of the press
It was the soldiers who fought for us
It's not the hunters who gave us the right to bear arms
It was the soldiers who fought for us
It's not the priests who gave us freedom of religion
It was the soldiers who fought for us
So why not take a moment or two
To honor these great soldiers
Who were fighting for us
Through and through
Fighting for the rights
That we all have today.
These great soldiers
Shall always be remembered
For the times that they fought
For the things that we take for granted.
And so let us say
"Let Freedom Ring!"

Andrea Goldstein, Grade 6
EH Greene Intermediate School, OH

Brian Beany

Brian
Athletic, funny, sporty
Brother of Dylan and Emily
Lover of Steelers, Yankees, and Ohio State Buckeyes
Feels nervous when pitching in the bottom of the 6th inning
    and when Steelers are losing in the fourth quarter
Gets excited when Steelers are in the Super Bowl
    and on the last day of school
Needs to study more for tests
    and practice at being a quarterback
Gives kisses to grandma's cat
Fears tornadoes and earthquakes
Would like to own a Lambourghini
Resident of Austintown, Ohio USA
Beany

Brian Beany, Grade 5
Frank Ohl Intermediate School, OH

Baby Sister

When she was finally born, I was excited.
I walked past many doors down the shiny hallway —
I was going to see her for the first time!
Dad held my hand as we went in.
She was as small as a doll,
wrapped in a pink blanket
that was very soft like a kitten's fur.
I sat next to her as she slept in Mom's arms.
Her name was Sabrina.
I was so excited to see her!
Soon we would go home!

Hannah Isaacson, Grade 5
Stanley Clark School, IN

Pizza

Pizza is good and cheesy,
it smells so nice and crispy.

You can make it however you like,
just as long as you think it's pleasy.

Pepperoni, mushrooms, peppers,
are all ingredients it's true.
You could even make your pizza blue.

Now that you know what pizza is like,
come on and let's make some,
tomorrow night.
Isabella Staltari, Grade 5
Heritage Intermediate School, IN

Autumn

The autumn season is finally here
It's my favorite time of year
The night air is crisp and cool
All the children are back in school

The leaves will turn a brilliant hue
Of yellow, red and orange too
Soon the beautiful leaves will die
And with the next big wind, fall and fly
Elizabeth A. Weger, Grade 6
Rocky River Middle School, OH

Fall

I love fall, it's my favorite season of all.
Fall is the best time to play ball.

The leaves fall off the trees,
they go with the breeze.

Fall is cool, fall is sweet
at the end of fall we get a big treat…

Halloween!
Riley Spearing, Grade 5
St Jude Catholic School, IN

Samantha

S weet at times
A lways fun to be around
M ean sometimes
A lways easy to make fun of
N ice sometimes
T iny
H appy all the time
A lways going to be my friend
Kelsey Fain, Grade 5
St Michael School, IN

Snow

Blizzards
Freezing
Wet
Slippery
Icy
Cold
Ray Guy, Grade 5
May V Peck Elementary School, MI

The Night Hike

Night falls on these woods.
I look up high in the sky:
What a starry scene!
Quin Matthys, Grade 6
Stanley Clark School, IN

Horse/A Colt

Horse
Brown and black mane,
Grazing in grassy field.
Stallions watch over their babies
A colt
Mikki Wise, Grade 4
Riverside Elementary School, MI

Summer

Green grass is growing
Graceful summer leaves are here
Summer is here!
Alli Leach, Grade 4
Westview Elementary School, OH

Lunch

Don't let your belly roar
Go to lunch and ask for more
Talk to friends, have some fun
Your belly will say, "YUM!"
You could have lunch under a tree
But that's not where you'll find me
I'll be in the school's lunch room
But soon…
I'll be back in class.
Trent Szczepaniak, Grade 5
May V Peck Elementary School, MI

Autumn

A pple pies baking
U nknown mysteries to uncover
T rees changing colors
U ncarved pumpkins on the porch
M olasses beans with biscuits
N ut collecting squirrels running around
Lydia Reichow, Grade 6
Eisenhower Middle School, OH

Ode to My Pencil

It waits hidden in some desk
a cylinder of lead
protruding from the hole
from the time I pushed
the little clicker
on the top
now I sit in class
and weep for my pencil
only to suddenly find it
in the opening of my desk
Prithvi Pendekanti, Grade 6
Birchwood School, OH

The Sky

The sky is blue
The birds are too.
The clouds are white
And hide the light.
The night is dark
With the moon in the sky
It's always there, I don't know why.
When morning comes
The moon is gone
Its replace is the sun.
Jake Kratkiewicz, Grade 6
Abbott Middle School, MI

Pencil

Pencil
click and clack
pull it back
tapping sounds
as it goes around
as it makes a track.
Daniel Leyburn, Grade 5
Henryville Elementary School, IN

Pumpkin Pie

I
love pumpkin pie
for Thanksgiving
at Grandma's house
because she always makes it
for just me, myself, and I.
Hannah Edwards, Grade 6
Perry Central Elementary School, IN

Friends

Funny, playful
Playing, dancing, hanging out
Having friends is awesome!
Buddies
Casey Luce, Grade 4
Northfield Elementary School, OH

I Am

I am athletic and boyish
I wonder if Mr. Ledbetter used to play any sports
I hear a bouncing basketball
I see the gym
I want to try out for basketball
I am athletic and boyish

I pretend to be a pro basketball player
I feel like an athlete
I touch a basketball or a football
I worry about getting hurt in sports
I cry when I get hurt in sports

I am athletic and boyish
I understand the rules of some sports
I say that anyone can play sports
I dream of weird stuff that has to do with Mr. Ledbetter
and him cracking clipboards
I try to understand the rules of basketball
I hope I can accomplish some things
I am athletic and boyish

Kayla Chambers, Grade 5
Beck Centennial Elementary School, MI

Bored

Bored is white,
It tastes like plain pasta,
It smells like stale air,
It reminds me of sitting at home in the winter,
It sounds like positively nothing,
Bored makes me feel white.

Annie Kuehn-Everson, Grade 5
Tremont Elementary School, OH

Holiday Spirit

It's the holidays again and everyone is merry
My little sister even thinks there is a holiday fairy!
But before I think of presents, trees, or lights,
I think of all the people
Alone on holiday nights.
It makes me sad to see
People without a wreath
Who survive on little or no pay
Who don't eat on holidays
Who don't eat during the week
Mostly humble and mostly meek.
I want to help ease their pain
When they get caught in the rain
Even though their times are hard
Even though they can't afford a car
I see their hearts always lit
With a bit of holiday spirit!

Christina Ciofani, Grade 6
Gesu Catholic School, OH

I Have a Friend

I have a friend named Fred
His favorite color is red
But for some strange reason, he always stays in bed.

I have a friend named Mellow
Her favorite color is yellow
But for some strange reason, she always eats Jell-O.

I have a friend named Jean
Her favorite color is green
But for some strange reason, she always looks so mean.

I have a friend named Hue
His favorite color is blue
But for some strange reason, he can't tie his shoe.

I have weird friends.

Katilynn Renee Crowley, Grade 6
Trilby Elementary School, OH

Veteran's Day

When I hear artillery I think of the Fourth of July,
Shooting off fireworks as a kid,
Seeing clusters of light fly.

Then I realize I'm in a war,
People die all around me,
Seeing them cry out makes my heart sore.

When we're fighting here in 'Nam,
Defending our country,
With guns and with bombs.

All of us want to leave,
We all want to see our families,
And the killing makes us grieve.

I can't wait to get back,
Just hoping to see your face,
To get so far from this place,
And the thing I most lack,
Is your adorable smile.

Stephen Mills, Grade 6
EH Greene Intermediate School, OH

The Beach

The seagulls flying peacefully above your head.
The sand mashed beneath your feet,
Squeezing between your toes.
The waves crashing upon the sea shore
In the distance, a group of dolphins playing tag
This is the sign of freedom.

Reily Victoria Atchison, Grade 5
Nancy Hanks Elementary School, IN

My Families and Me

I am from a skateboarding, phone talking, funny dancing, noisy family,
and a sports loving, food making family.
I am from a three foot front yard, a cement backyard and dead flowers family,
and a family with a two and a half acre yard.
I am from a Wabash, Cathedral loving family,
and a Zionsville loving family.
I am from a gigantic brother
and a yelling sister kind of family.
I am from a family with a dad, a step-mom, and a brother,
and also a family with a mom and a sister.
I am from a family living in the woods with a couple neighbors
and also from a family living in a neighborhood with a gigantic amount of neighbors.
I am from a family that sells tic-tacs and make crafts,
and also from a family that sells medicine to people.
I am from a family that loves golf and football,
and a family that loves football and golf.
I am from two families that seem different,
but they are the same in many ways.

Blake Matthews, Grade 6
St Maria Goretti School, IN

The Diverse Planet Neptune

N eptune is a planet in our solar system: eighth planet from the Sun.
E ighteen forty-six, on September 23rd, is when Neptune was discovered.
P lateau rings make up part of Neptune.
T his gaseous planet has many rapid winds that are equivalent to storms or vortices, reaching up to 2,000 km. per hour.
U nfortunately, this planet is colder than the summit of Mount Everest.
N ineteen eighty-nine, on August 25th, Voyager 2 was the one, and so far, the only spacecraft that has visited Neptune.
E nergy radiates from Neptune creating an internal heat source.

Christine Cunningham, Grade 6
Pinewood Elementary School, IN

Summer Sunrise

Every morning, I wake up, put on my shoes and run out to my woods.
Running through the wet grass with dew on my shoes as if running on the beach next to the seashore.
I see a sunrise pop out of nowhere, like a light bulb shining on my face.
Running through the woods with water dripping on my face, as if it was raining.
It is a little cold, but dark in the woods.
Little spots of a glare are coming from the sun into the woods, as if I were waking up on a bright morning.
I hear many birds chirping, like church bells ringing, and choirs singing.
When I walk into the woods, the air makes me feel as light as a feather.
While the breeze is a glistening, light sound like the ocean waves tumbling down on top of each other.
I run over to the creek, and in front of my face I see this,
The most beautiful, old bridge across the woods.
I run over to it and as I stand on it, I feel, when I close my eyes, with a soft breeze on my face,
Like I am a ship, sailing across the sea.
I look down, and see my shadow just lying there, on the ground, while the sun comes up.
It feels like I have a close friend, always on my side.
There are flowers all over the ground, and many mums, with dew all over them.
It looks like the mums had got out of the shower this morning, and are drying off.
I feel the soil on my feet, as if I were sinking in the ground, and the path in front of my eyes,
I walk and follow my woods.

Jessica Winders, Grade 6
Cloverdale Middle School, IN

My Grandpa

His name is Sparky, so funny and brave
He saw my sister's birth, oh what a glorious day
Longing to see my birth
Fighting the cancer
Month after month
Waiting in pain for me
So strong and brave
Trying to hold on
He got called by God
Mixed emotions around the room
So sad he died
Happy he's in a better place
I wish I could see him today.

Andrew Kohn, Grade 6
Trilby Elementary School, OH

I Am

I am funny and sneaky.
I wonder, why don't people believe in God?
I hear my dog talking to me!
I see a zombie sleeping in my bed!
I want everyone to be saved.
I am funny and sneaky.
I pretend to go into the past.
I feel afraid when monsters talk to my mom.
I touch my paper's hand.
I worry about my grades.
I cry when I get yelled at.
I am funny and sneaky.
I understand why my mom wants me to get good grades.
I say God is real!
I dream that everyone was a Jesus freak.
I try to get good grades.
I hope someday everyone is happy.
I am funny and sneaky.

Bessie Shade, Grade 6
Galesburg-Augusta Middle School, MI

Summer Fun

No more snow and winters glow
'Cause now the seasons start to flow
No more hats and winter coats
It's time for swimming and fishing boats
Now that winter's finally done
Let's talk about some summer fun

Summer, summer is finally here
Let's all give a great big cheer
C'mon let's go swim in the pool
Let's say up late before the start of school
Every day with my best friend
I hope the summer will never end.

Emily Shearer, Grade 6
Harmon Middle School, OH

BFFL

We take each other's weaknesses
play them to the best so we don't cry
You're my BFFL forever, for life.
If I lost you I'd have nowhere to go
You make me happy the doors never closed

My BFFL does everything with me
She stands by my side fills my every need
I cry with her, I'd die for her
BFFL's forever for life.

Emily Whiteley, Grade 6
Union Local Middle School, OH

The Animal Kingdom

The animal kingdom, the animal kingdom
oh so many teeth and bristles
also lots of tweets and whistles
all kinds of feats and roars
soon you'll be wanting more
so many animals it may seem hectic
but they are all so graceful and majestic
The animal kingdom, the animal kingdom

Myles Ginter, Grade 5
Kenowa Hills Intermediate School, MI

Winter Is White

Winter is white
like a pine tree dressed in snow
like a snowball being thrown
like a snowman greeting
ME

Cameron Stewart, Grade 5
Birchwood School, OH

Football

Football, football you are tough!
Football, football you are rough!
Football, football you have such good grip!
Football, football 100 yards is quite a trip!

Ryan Smith, Grade 4
Northfield Elementary School, OH

Index